The Craft
of Qualitative
Research

The Craft
of Qualitative
Research

A HANDBOOK

EDITED BY

Steven W. Kleinknecht,
Lisa-Jo K. van den Scott,
and Carrie B. Sanders

CANADIAN
SCHOLARS

Toronto | Vancouver

The Craft of Qualitative Research: A Handbook
Edited by Steven W. Kleinknecht, Lisa-Jo K. van den Scott, and Carrie B. Sanders

First published in 2018 by
Canadian Scholars, an imprint of CSP Books Inc.
425 Adelaide Street West, Suite 200
Toronto, Ontario
M5V 3C1

www.canadianscholars.ca

Library and Archives Canada Cataloguing in Publication

> The craft of qualitative research : a handbook / edited by Steven W. Kleinknecht, Lisa-Jo K. van den Scott, and Carrie B. Sanders.

Includes bibliographical references and index.
Issued in print and electronic formats.
ISBN 978-1-77338-097-1 (softcover).--ISBN 978-1-77338-098-8 (PDF).--
ISBN 978-1-77338-099-5 (EPUB)

> 1. Qualitative research--Methodology. 2. Qualitative research--Textbooks. 3. Textbooks. I. Kleinknecht, Steven W. (Steven William), editor II. Scott, Lisa-Jo K. van den, 1977-, editor III. Sanders, Carrie B., 1978-, editor

H62.C693 2018   001.4'2   C2018-905037-3
                                                            C2018-905038-1

Text and cover design by Elisabeth Springate
Typesetting by Brad Horning
Cover image: Inside Out Project, New York City, May 2013, by JR

Printed and bound in Ontario, Canada

Canadä

To Billy, who taught me not to settle for McIntosh when there is Honeycrisp.
   —Steve

To Jeff, my most beautiful beloved, who stands by my side always.
   —Lisa-Jo

To Fischer and Kinleigh, who inspire me every day with their never-ending curiosity and innovation.
   —Carrie

CONTENTS

SECTION III. MANAGING INSIDER/OUTSIDER STATUS WHILE GAINING ACCESS

SECTION IV. EXPERIENCING EMOTIONS WHILE ESTABLISHING TRUST AND RAPPORT

SECTION V. DOING OBSERVATION

SECTION VI. DOING INTERVIEWS

SECTION VII. COLLECTING OTHER FORMS OF DATA

SECTION VIII. ANALYZING YOUR DATA

SECTION IX. LEAVING THE FIELD

SECTION X. DISSEMINATING YOUR FINDINGS TO SCHOLARS AND OTHER AUDIENCES

PREFACE

The Craft of Qualitative Research is a handbook. As a handbook, you will find it a useful reference in navigating the different stages of your own qualitative research projects. Our approach stresses that qualitative research is best learned in practice. It is in the *doing*—the active accomplishment of qualitative research—that you will learn the craft. The title of the book, section headings and introductions, practical exercises, and chapters reinforce this point. You will formulate, discard, and reformulate research plans. You will confront and respond to ethical issues. You will negotiate access to participants and field settings. You will experience the emotional highs and lows involved in doing qualitative research. You will meet with participants, examine their cultural artifacts, observe their everyday lives, and discuss their experiences. You will analyze data, develop and stumble upon insights, build and rebuild theories. You will, in time, exit and maybe even re-enter your research settings. You will establish connections to your research, settings, and participants, and sometimes these will endure long after you believe your research to be complete. You will share your findings and research stories with others. All the while you will be scratching your head and wondering, just as we have and continue to wonder, am I doing it right? As you will soon read, and experience for yourself, there are many approaches to, and thoughts about, "doing it right." By learning from the experiences of others, and as you practice qualitative research for yourself, you will become more learned in the craft.

Now, a bit about how this book came to be. Ideas for the volume began to take shape leading up to the 2015 Qualitative Analysis Conference held at Brescia University College in London, Ontario, Canada. As organizers for that year's conference, we invited presenters to explore the conference theme: the craft of qualitative inquiry. Fortunately, qualitative researchers are often eager to share their research stories. Even better, they usually find an engaged audience curious to hear about and learn from their experiences. We were not disappointed. There was an excellent response to the conference theme, which spurred animated discussion and debate during and after the sessions. We were pleased and motivated by the conversations and the positive feedback we received about the conference theme.

We proceeded by developing a call for papers, which invited people to contribute to a manuscript on the craft of qualitative research. We asked for people to send us their chapter ideas and draft papers about the actualities of doing qualitative research. Contributors were to select a stage of the qualitative research process and then revisit their experiences with a particular research project. We wanted to know how they went about their research, important decisions they made, and methodological take-aways they found valuable to share. The emphasis throughout was to be on the experience of accomplishing qualitative research.

This book reflects the diverse submissions we received. We realized early on that it would be impossible to address all forms of qualitative research. That said, by keeping the chapters brief and punchy we have been able to include 45 chapters from 55 contributors from all different stages of their careers—from graduate students to emeritus professors. As you move through the different sections of this text, you will find a variety of perspectives, approaches, and experiences covering a range of enduring and contemporary qualitative research issues and substantive topics. The book is Canadian at its core. The vast majority—over 90 percent—of chapters were contributed by Canadians doing research in both Canadian and international contexts. You will also benefit from reading about the experiences and insights of researchers from Poland, the United Kingdom, and the United States.

There are several people who have had a hand in forming the ideas contained herein and in bringing this volume to fruition. Thank you to our research participants, without whom our work would not be possible. Thank you for trusting us with your precious time and life experiences. We hope we do you justice. Thank you to the excellent mentors who have guided us throughout our careers. You have shaped our approach to qualitative research, and we are now fortunate to pass along some of your wisdom and influence to others. Thank you to each of the chapter contributors. The candid experiences and advice you have shared are the backbone of this book. Thank you to Tony Puddephatt for your contributions during the early stages of developing this book. Your assistance in conceptualizing the book's framework, developing a proposal, and responding to initial feedback was invaluable. Thank you to Catherine Andru, Christy Bailey, Lauren Hogan, and Taylor Knipe for your assistance in preparing the manuscript. Thank you to Natalie Garriga, Lily Bergh, and Andrea Gill at Canadian Scholars. It has been a pleasure to work with you. Your professional guidance, flexibility, and constructive feedback throughout the publication process have been much appreciated. Thank you for seeing value in our work and for the opportunity to publish with Canadian Scholars. Thank you to Dorothy Pawluch for connecting the publisher with us in the first place. Thank you to Caley Clements for your thoroughness in copy editing the book. Thank you to the Canadian Social Sciences and Humanities Research Council (SSHRC) for supporting the Qualitative Analysis Conference and the opportunities it has afforded qualitative researchers in Canada and abroad. The financial support provided by a SSHRC Connection Grant in 2015 assisted us in bringing scholars together and, in turn, helped make this volume possible. Thank you to the anonymous reviewers who took the time to assess our proposal and offer valuable feedback on the manuscript. Finally, thank you to you, our readers, for taking a chance on us and this book, and trying your hand at qualitative research. We are excited for you and grateful to have a hand in helping you demystify the qualitative research process.

Steve, Lisa-Jo, and Carrie
March 23, 2018

INTRODUCTION

Invitation to the Craft of Qualitative Research

Steven W. Kleinknecht, Lisa-Jo K. van den Scott, and Carrie B. Sanders

A professor stands before the class holding a yo-yo in his hand. One student asks, "Why the yo-yo?" Some of the other students chuckle. The professor says, "Let me show you." He then proceeds to do yo-yo tricks. "Here's Walk the Dog. Can you do that?" asks the professor. "No," replies the student. "How about Over the Moon? Likely not," the professor states flatly. He goes on, "Maybe you've never seen a yo-yo. You've almost certainly never met a yo-yo master. And, you've probably never read a book on the art of yo-yoing. If you had, it would only get you so far. A book with instructions and diagrams might get you started. A master could tell you and show you all the ins and outs of how to perform tricks. But the fact of the matter remains: you will never become proficient without practice. To become good at it, you must do it." So begins your introduction to doing qualitative research. The lesson is this: to become skilled at qualitative research, you must practice it. This book will help you do that.

In doing qualitative research, your goal will be to acquire an in-depth understanding of some aspect of social life. Unlike quantitative research, the type of data you collect will not be easily reduced to numbers or amenable to statistical analysis. Qualitative data are descriptive statements about dimensions of the social world, such as people and their activities, perspectives, and experiences. Your emphasis will be on how people develop and apply meanings to themselves, others, and objects, and how these meanings impact everyday life. Your approach will be to get close to what is going on in the social world and provide a detailed description and interpretive analysis of it. And you will have several qualitative research methods at your disposal to do so. Say you are interested in studying how people become involved in computer hacking. Taking a qualitative approach, you might begin to hang out with hackers to observe what they do and how they recruit and treat newcomers. You could conduct ad hoc and in-depth interviews with them, asking them to take you through the steps of how they became involved. You could also collect samples of writing, images, and videos from hacker websites and do a qualitative content analysis of what they have produced. Observation, interviewing, and content analysis are three broad qualitative research techniques that could be used separately or in combination to answer your research question.

In thinking about doing such a project, though, many questions likely come to mind. Consider the following: How will you find and gain access to hackers? How will you keep information they share with you confidential? What will you do if a participant tells you something that makes you feel uncomfortable? How might doing this research affect others who are close to you, like friends and family? How should you go about making sense of your data? Is there a right way to finish up your project and bid farewell to participants? How might you share your findings with other scholars, as well as with the broader public? Qualitative research is exciting and can yield fantastic insights. At the same time, working through a project raises a lot of questions and produces its fair share of ambiguity.

Along with supportive professors and classmates, this book is intended to be of assistance as you work through your research challenges. As you carry out your project, you will quickly discover the realities of doing qualitative research. Instead of presenting the research process as recipe-like or formulaic, we emphasize the *craft* of qualitative research. The idea of "craft" highlights the gradual acquisition of skill and proficiency in doing qualitative research by practicing it. We will help teach you this craft by having researchers who have done their own qualitative projects share their experiences with you. You will learn from those at all stages of their research careers, from graduate students to emeritus professors. Some of the authors will have been in your shoes not too long ago. Others will have made a career out of doing qualitative research. You will get a behind-the-scenes look at how qualitative research is accomplished in practice. You will learn about the types of things that can trip you up and propel you forward. We will expose you to some of the messiness of doing qualitative research, while giving you tips, tricks, and general advice on carrying out your own successful projects. We hope to set you on the path from beginner to expert, so that, in future works on the craft of qualitative research, it is you who is sharing your wisdom.

The authors of this book are wise in the craft of qualitative research, but they continue to learn more about it every time they step into the field. They have acquired the ideas they will share with you from professors, mentors, and fellow students like yourself. These ideas have been made real, however, by actually *doing* qualitative research. It is one thing to know how to do something; it is quite another to be able to put that knowledge into practice. The practice-oriented philosophy underlying the pedagogy of great teachers represents the guiding principle of this book. But it is just a book. It can only take you so far. We recommend that you treat it as a handbook: something that accompanies you throughout your qualitative research journey, to which you turn for tips, advice, and practice exercises. It will be useful as you contemplate all stages of the research process from initial conceptions to dissemination of your findings. Instead of viewing this book as a "how-to" manual, it is best to approach your reading of it as food for thought in the accomplishment of qualitative research: something that stimulates your thinking about, and assists you in the doing of, your own research.

Beyond the authors of this text being qualitative researchers, nearly all of us also share the distinction of having participated in the annual Qualitative Analysis Conference (www.qualitatives.ca). This conference—affectionately referred to as the "Qualitatives"—has been an excellent venue for us to come together and share research findings, receive feedback on our ideas, discuss new projects, begin collaborations, and celebrate the value of using a qualitative approach to study the social world. Each year, through our participation in the conference, we learn new research techniques, concepts, and theoretical ideas, and our intellectual curiosity is invigorated. The Qualitatives welcomes researchers at all stages of education and career, from undergraduates to retired professors. It is a Canadian conference at its core, but attracts renowned scholars from across the globe. It has a reputation for being inviting and supportive, and has helped foster vibrant careers and friendships. Many of the ideas presented in this book found their genesis in papers delivered at the conference. If qualitative research excites you, and you are looking to connect with a community of like-minded scholars, come join us.

We designed this book to share many of the same traits as the Qualitatives. First of all, most of the authors of the text are Canadian, showcasing Canada's vibrant qualitative research culture. Second, like the conference, a variety of different disciplines are represented. No matter what discipline you are studying, from sociology and criminology to nursing and health studies, you will find kindred spirits and valuable insights herein. Third, as topics at the conference cover a wide range of qualitative research concerns, we too grapple with these in the following pages. We address ongoing and contemporary methodological issues such as emotionality, bias, subjectivity, power, voice, reflexivity, and new challenges and opportunities posed by digital data sources. Fourth, just as you would experience at the Qualitatives, reading through the chapters will introduce you to the myriad topics we explore as qualitative researchers. We study all dimensions of everyday life, from the mundane to the sensational. The authors recount the lessons they learned in researching groups such as pick-up artists, Inuit, police officers, Mennonites, the homeless, truck drivers, widows and widowers, Hasidic Jews, and sex workers. Finally, we attempt to emulate the inviting atmosphere of the Qualitatives. We have sought to make the tone and writing style conversational and the ideas accessible to help connect with newcomers to our craft. We aim to make the ideas relatable and draw out the human dimension of the art and science of qualitative inquiry.

It is important for you to know that we have the same trepidation and excitement for doing qualitative research that you do. While we have the wisdom acquired from our past missteps and successes, we share with you a journey into uncharted and unpredictable territory, as no two projects are the same. There is a sense of adventure that accompanies each qualitative project. As with any good adventure, you will at times step outside your comfort zone. The discomfort comes largely from a lack of familiarity with the undertaking; so, from this ambiguity also comes the great potential to learn. And as you learn, you will pick up abstract techniques for addressing similar issues in the future.

Over the years, we have discovered that the gifts received from doing qualitative research extend beyond our primary goal of acquiring detailed understandings of others' life-worlds. Qualitative research presents the opportunity to understand and appreciate others' perspectives more thoroughly, while at the same time learning much about ourselves. As we have learned through our own projects, and as our students tell us each year, doing qualitative research can be highly rewarding for both participants and researchers. In-depth interviews, where participants share much of themselves with you, often lead to a human connection at a deeper level than is felt during our daily interactions. As an additional benefit, we believe that doing qualitative research prepares you for much more than research. Even if you never do a formal research project again after taking a course on qualitative methods, you will find doing qualitative research abundantly helpful in fostering your critical-thinking, problem-solving, analytical, and communication skills, which are so much in demand in the modern workplace. As you read this book and carry out your research, take time to reflect on what you have learned. Do not limit your reflection to what you have come to understand about your specific topic, as rewarding as that will be. Give some consideration to what you have learned about the human condition, yourself, and the types of skills you might use elsewhere in your life. Be prepared to apply your imagination and creativity to all aspects of your experience.

As you begin your data collection, you might well be led in new, unforeseen directions. Be ready to adapt your project as it progresses. It is necessary to do this to be responsive to the realities of your participants. Fortunately for us, the qualitative method takes the unpredictable world of human beings into account by encouraging us to remain flexible with our projects. Sometimes this means adapting our topics and questions, while other times it can mean that the steps we planned to follow need to be revised (sometimes on the spot!). While the qualitative research process is necessarily flexible, it does generally align with some key stages. We have divided this book into 10 sections, which follow the general sequence of doing qualitative research. Each section contains four or five chapters addressing different qualitative issues pertinent to the section. The 10 section themes of the book are as follows:

    I. Planning Your Project
   II. Navigating Ethical Dilemmas
  III. Managing Insider/Outsider Status While Gaining Access
  IV. Experiencing Emotions While Establishing Trust and Rapport
   V. Doing Observation
  VI. Doing Interviews
 VII. Collecting Other Forms of Data
VIII. Analyzing Your Data
  IX. Leaving the Field
   X. Disseminating Your Findings to Scholars and Other Audiences

The ideas in each section are not exclusive to a particular moment in doing your research. For instance, during the early stages of your project, you should attempt to foresee potential ethical issues that might arise. At the same time, you should be aware that it is impossible to predict all of the issues that might pop up. Ethics is something to keep in mind from start to finish. Something else we should point out is that some authors, while emphasizing the theme of their section, also touch on different themes in their chapters. This will help you see the big picture of a qualitative project and how the various dimensions of doing qualitative research are intertwined with one another.

Moving you from start to finish, we take you on your qualitative research journey through the different aspects of doing your own project. Each section begins with a brief introduction to the theme and an overview of the chapters contained within. The chapter authors speak to their research experiences, taking a particular angle on the section theme. They address the actualities of doing first-hand qualitative investigation as it happens. In revisiting their experiences, they speak to a wide array of issues by addressing such questions as: What were your first thoughts when you started doing your research? What obstacles did you encounter? How did you overcome them? How did issues of emotionality, power, voice, and reflexivity factor into your research? What lessons did you learn? What important decisions did you make? What would you recommend? They have written about their thoughts, concerns, emotions, encounters in the field, dilemmas they experienced, and tricks they picked up along the way. Their focus is on addressing what is worthwhile about their experiences that is relevant for new researchers to learn about. The authors' lessons are reinforced through "Crafting Qualitative Research Exercises," which appear at the end of each chapter. These thinking and doing exercises offer you the opportunity to reflect on core ideas presented in the chapter and practice the craft for yourself.

We close this introductory invitation to the craft of qualitative research by reminding you that *an expert in anything was once a beginner.* Keep this in mind when challenging yourself with this new undertaking. You will soon be struck by the "realness" of qualitative research. The decisions you will have to make along the way do not always present obvious, black-and-white options. Qualitative data collection comes with all the vagaries and vicissitudes of everyday life. But, once you try it, you will likely agree that it is also a mode of inquiry that respects and is true to the realities of everyday life. By listening and keeping an open mind, qualitative research presents you with the opportunity to look past your taken-for-granteds. Capturing an authentic understanding of social life requires that you take an inside look at how others do what they do. If you want to know how others think and feel, if you want to appreciate their viewpoints, you have to go to them, observe them, talk to them, and examine their cultural productions. There really is no substitute for an approach that is so attentive to people's daily routines and perspectives. While we can tell you this, the value of the qualitative approach is not something you will fully appreciate until you try it yourself. As Alford argues, like any craft, the art of "combining theory, method and evidence ... must be learned in practice" (1998, 19). As newcomers to the practice of qualitative inquiry, we call on you to explore with an open mind and be ever curious about the social world by taking a first-hand look at how it operates. Good luck, and welcome to the craft.

REFERENCE

Alford, Robert. 1998. *The Craft of Inquiry: Theories, Methods, Evidence.* New York: Oxford University Press.

SECTION I

PLANNING YOUR PROJECT

When conducting qualitative research, it is good to begin with a tentative plan. This plan is often expressed in the form of a research proposal. Formulating a plan provides you, and typically your professor or supervisor, with a road map of where you hope your project will go. You want to give your research direction, but the plan is tentative because you will need to be responsive to what you find during your research. We often do not know precisely what will be the most worthwhile angle until we begin our data collection. Moreover, we often do not have an accurate sense of how our participants see themselves and their activities until we meet with them. As an example, when Kleinknecht began his research on computer hackers, he initially defined hackers as those who engage in computer crime. When meeting with hackers, however, he came to learn that hackers are often not engaged in computer crime at all. His initial conception was at odds with how hackers defined themselves: anyone who passionately and creatively works toward the solution to any given problem. As a result, he had to be flexible and adjust when moving forward with his research. Qualitative researchers often come up with findings that were not expected at the outset of their projects. Be prepared to encounter the unexpected, and keep your mind open to insights that challenge your original thinking. Thankfully, the qualitative approach is characterized by flexibility throughout the research process so that we can make alterations and follow new lines of inquiry as we proceed.

To help you through your planning, and subsequent stages of the research process, ask yourself questions. Some important general questions to answer, which will help give structure to your plan, include: What topic am I interested in studying? Based on my topic, what is the research question I hope to answer? What methods will I use to collect my data? How will I develop my sample? What does the literature have to say about my topic? And what pre-existing concepts and theoretical ideas might I start with to help guide my early analysis?

The planning phase is a moment of great novelty. Do you research something you are familiar with or select a topic about which you currently know little? When it comes to figuring out what angle you will take on your topic, do you chart a new path, or do you build on other researchers' ideas? You will want to choose a topic that is appropriate for your discipline and ideally something that you are personally curious about and motivated to research. When brainstorming about a topic, you will find it useful to write down your ideas and keep a file you can return to and revise along the way. To get started, we often advise our students to think about something that is close to home. Consider your personal experiences and interests, such as a team you belong to or a hobby you enjoy. Think about aspects of your family, student, leisure, and work experiences as possible sources of inspiration. Another approach you can take is to think about particular issues, puzzles, or challenges within your discipline that you have read about or have been introduced to through your coursework.

Throughout your planning, keep the ideas of project feasibility and manageability front and centre. Consider questions such as the following: How easy will it be for me to gain access to participants and field sites? What types of ethical issues need to be considered? How much time might it take to complete my project? What types of sensitive issues might arise and how could I deal with them? What biases do I have that might impact my data collection and analysis? What practical obstacles might impede my progress and how could I overcome them? Although many of the problems you will encounter are difficult to anticipate, you should still attempt to foresee those issues that might trip you up so that you feel confident during your research and have contingencies built in so that you are not delayed for too long if they arise.

Reflexivity involves reflecting on how we, as researchers, impact the research process. In the opening chapter, Kalyani Thurairajah focuses squarely on this important qualitative research ability. Discussing her own reflexivity while researching ethnic conflict in Sri Lanka, she uses guiding questions to have you practice reflexivity while reading her chapter. Thurairajah advises keeping a reflexivity journal and making entries throughout the research process. The ideas in your journal will serve as useful data during your analysis.

How does one plan for the unpredictable? In chapter 2, Mark S. Dolson discusses the uncertain and often precarious nature of ethnographic fieldwork. He does so by reflecting on his ethnographic experiences researching homeless, addicted, and mentally ill people in Reykjavik, Iceland. Ethnography relies on researchers immersing themselves in the everyday lives of their participants, often for extended periods of time. Perhaps more so than any other form of qualitative research, ethnographic fieldwork requires the researcher to be flexible and prepared to improvise along the way. Highlighting the emergent qualities of conducting ethnographic fieldwork, Dolson shares valuable advice about making ongoing adjustments and managing adversity.

We often consider how our research impacts our participants; it is also important to consider how your research will affect you. Many of us, however, do not spend a lot of time considering how our research impacts those who are close to us. When Tony Christensen conducted his research on male pick-up artists, he was forced to consider the effect it was having on his relationship with his girlfriend and, correspondingly, their relationship with one another. In chapter 3, he provides sound advice for newcomers to consider regarding the interpersonal toll our research can take on ourselves and those to whom we are close.

The final chapter in this section, written by Chris McCormick, introduces the idea of a pilot study. Researchers sometimes use pilot studies to test some of their ideas and methods before conducting a full-scale project. McCormick presents a preliminary thematic analysis of media coverage of a pathologist's testimony in child homicide cases. Throughout his chapter, he will have you thinking about the planning and analytical choices he made for a media analysis project. By seeing how he makes decisions and develops analytical insights along the way, you are also given an overview of the different steps you might move through in a full-scale project.

1   "The Person behind the Research": Reflexivity and the Qualitative Research Process

Kalyani Thurairajah

INTRODUCTION

Before proceeding to read this chapter, pull out a blank piece of paper and write down everything that makes you who you are. Write about your age, gender identification, race, and ethnicity. Write about your relationship status and your level of athleticism. Write about your religion and nationality, and your educational background. Write down everything that you can think of. And when you are done, continue with the rest of the chapter.

Did you write down everything? Did you write down that you prefer the Leafs to the Habs? Did you write about how you volunteer at the food bank? Did you mention that you have always had a dog and that you don't understand cats? All of these details are pieces that make up a part of your narrative as a researcher, and until you take time to reflect on your own narrative, and how this shapes who you are, it is virtually impossible to truly comprehend the immeasurable data we collect through qualitative research.

Reflexivity in research refers to the practice of reflecting on how you as a researcher are impacting the research process (Burkitt 2012; McCorkel and Myers 2003; Medved and Turner 2011). It calls for researchers to consider why they chose to study a particular question or population. It insists that researchers be cognizant of how their preferences and their biases impacted their decision to conduct research (Dwyer and Buckle 2009; England 1994). Therefore, researchers must learn to recognize their social locations and positionalities. Social locations or positionalities refer to various aspects of your identity. Social locations can be characteristics that place you in a particular situation, or in reference to another. Being a sister or a lapsed Buddhist or being afraid of spiders are examples of social locations. Positionalities help identify our preferences and biases. For example, being a dog lover or a broccoli hater, or a devout believer that *Star Trek: The Next Generation* is the only Star Trek worth watching.

There are a vast number of social locations and positionalities that make up who you are, and it is impossible to list them all; however, as researchers who are engaged in the study of *stories*—as is often the pursuit of qualitative researchers—and the positionalities and social locations of others, it is of immense importance that we take the time to recognize our own stories. Think of a research project that is focused on single mothers. Was your decision to study single mothers influenced by your own history? Or the history of your best friend? Do you already have personal values regarding the benefits and detriments to children being raised by single mothers? How will these views impact how you hear the stories of your participants? Through practicing reflexivity, researchers become conscientious of their own positionalities and social locations, and how they may impact the research process. As such, it is imperative to be reflexive before, during, and after the research process—and to know how to practice this process at all three points.

BEFORE DATA COLLECTION

The exercise that you (hopefully!) completed at the beginning of this chapter is one that you should do before beginning any research project. It offers the researcher the opportunity to take the "pulse" of their current positionalities. While some social locations may remain unchanged over time (e.g., diehard Leafs fan), others are much more dynamic. Some positionalities that may have made your list two years ago may no longer be considered relevant—while new ones may have emerged over the past two years. Therefore, prior to beginning the research process—when you are at the stage when you are *planning* to do research—it is recommended that you take some time to make a list like the one you made earlier.

Once that list is completed, it now becomes important to be reflexive about the specific project you are about to conduct. This involves taking time to reflect on the project that will be completed and considering why you were pulled towards it. Engaging in project-specific reflexivity prior to beginning the project involves the researcher asking some key questions of themself. Keeping a reflexivity journal to answer these questions will be a helpful way to document the evolution of your social locations and their impact over the research process.

At this juncture, the researcher needs to seriously evaluate *why* they were pulled towards a particular research project. What drew them to this topic area? The reflexive process at this stage begins with a free-writing exercise. The researcher is simply meant to write about the topic of study—what they know, what they do not know, and what they hope to find out. In beginning to document their knowledge "starting point," the researcher can then begin to openly acknowledge the underlying assumptions that might be driving their work, and to also begin to draw attention to any biases they may hold.

When I began my doctoral studies, I did not anticipate that I would study anything to do with the ethnic conflict in Sri Lanka. I had no interest in this since I grew up in a very apolitical household; however, during my second semester of graduate studies, I took a social movements course, and while I was learning about collective action and social mobilization, the Sri Lankan Tamil diaspora organized a series of protests in response to the war in Sri Lanka. Suddenly, as a result of my newfound knowledge of social movements, I found myself curious about *why* second-generation diasporic community members were so engaged in homeland politics. I wondered whether they grew up in political households—unlike me—or whether their engagement was born out of their own personal political views. My own experiences directly impacted the questions that I was asking of the protests, and ultimately shaped my dissertation project.

Imagine, for example, that you are given the opportunity to do a research project that examines the efficiency of study spaces on university campuses. Before beginning to do *anything* with this project—including literature review—write down all of your thoughts with respect to study spaces on university campuses. Write down how you understand the topic, and its importance. Write down your questions, concerns, and hypotheses. Take a few minutes and do that now.

If you did the exercise, you probably noticed that you had more to say than you may have thought. There are a number of ideas you may have had, and all of these would have been influenced by your *own* experiences and opinions. By explicitly acknowledging your thought process with respect to this topic, you can then be clearer about *why* you chose a particular direction for the literature review. Without engaging in reflexivity at this starting point, you would not be able to recognize that the pathway your project takes had already been predetermined by your own positionalities and social locations.

DURING DATA COLLECTION

Practicing reflexivity during the data collection process is an ongoing endeavour. While being reflexive prior to collecting data allows us to become aware of how our social locations impacted *why* we pursued a research project, and what biases we hold, we must continue to monitor how the research is affecting us, and how we are impacting the research process. As such, the reflexivity journal becomes particularly important during the data collection period. I suggest that researchers treat this journal much like they treat their field journal—write in it regularly, and do not censor what you write.

The data collection process will differ depending on the methodology that is chosen; however, irrespective of whether the researcher uses interviews or focus groups or participant observations or archives, the reflexive process is the same. There are some key questions that must be asked of oneself during the data collection process:

1.   *What led you to this data collection method?* While the research question should primarily be guiding the data collection method that is best suited for the project, it is important to address how our own positionalities may influence this decision-making process. For example, why did you choose interviews over focus groups? Are you more comfortable with one-on-one discussions than groups?

2. *How did you feel during your data collection?* Just as the emotions of participants may impact the nature of the data that is collected, so too will the emotions of the researcher. For example, did you find yourself feeling excited or disappointed during an interview or when reviewing a historical document? Why did you feel this way? What were you hoping to hear or read?

3. *Which social locations were prevalent during data collection?* While you are made up of innumerable social locations, they are not all equally present all of the time. Some social locations may come to the forefront in certain situations more than others. Just as these positionalities can "lead" in certain social situations, it is important for researchers to pay attention to which positionalities may be coming to the surface during data collection. For example, was your relationship status taking the lead when interviewing single women?

During data collection, researchers must continually ask themselves these three broad questions, and write down their observations. These observations are *also* data that can be used in the analysis process. For example, one of the most important insights I gathered while conducting fieldwork in Sri Lanka happened just prior to the beginning of an interview. The individual and I had just sat down to begin the interview, and I was about to turn the audio-recorder on, when she abruptly stood up. She went to the windows and to the main door, and shut them all—something that is very rarely done when living on a tropical island. She then returned to her seat and said words that would impact my entire Sri Lankan experience: "You never know who is listening. You can't trust anyone. Not your brother, neighbour, or friend."

In writing about this incident in my journal after it happened, I was able to utilize it as a source of data that was independent of the interview itself. Each data collection moment should be treated independently in the reflexivity journal, as the researcher's positionalities do not remain constant throughout the process, and it is vital that researchers monitor how they are evolving through the research process. In looking back at my own journal, I was able to see how my own views and feelings in Sri Lanka were altered after the words of this participant—I found myself more apprehensive than I had been before, and without documenting this moment, I would not have been able to discern what might have accounted for this shift in my mood.

AFTER DATA COLLECTION

At this point in the research process, it is not uncommon to become so engrossed in the data that we have collected that practicing reflexivity is easily forgotten; however, it is vital that we remember to monitor how our social locations impact our analysis, results, and dissemination. With respect to analysis, the process by which we elect to examine our data can be reflective of our own biases. For example, what codes we use in the case of action-coding and thematic-coding can be indicative of whether we have already determined a preferred path for our data. By being reflexive, the researcher can more closely inspect the meanings and values we may have attached to codes. One way to do this is to keep a log outlining what the codes mean, and why we decided to use particular codes. Instead of using the code "knowledge of language" when coding for the ability to understand one's "mother tongue," why did you decide to use "ethnic identity"? To what extent are you moving away from the data and allowing your own social locations to lead the data analysis? By being reflexive in the coding process, researchers can work to ensure that they are being intentional about when they allow the data itself to lead the analysis, and when they as researchers choose to take a front seat in the analysis process.

After the data has been collected and analyzed, the results are used to answer the research question or to tell a story about the research topic; however, as qualitative researchers, we know that the data reveals *multiple* responses to the research question and narrates multiple storylines. As researchers, *we* choose which response or narrative to focus on in our results. Therefore, considering that the researcher may shape or prioritize results, it is of extreme importance that we are reflexive during this point of the research project. One way to do this is to acknowledge all possible results, and then evaluate your thoughts about all of them. Why do you find yourself pulled towards one answer to the research question over the other? Why do you find one particular storyline to be less compelling than another? What emotions do these results evoke for you?

Paying attention to our reactions to our results ensures that we are always aware that we have choice with respect to the results we choose to highlight. Not being reflexive about the decision-making process can lead us to believe that our results are solely borne from the data—which is incorrect. As humans conducting research, we know that we impact the research process from the very beginning. Therefore, it is undeniable that we would impact the research when we near the end with our results. By acknowledging how we impact the results of the research project, we can feel more confident when we disseminate them.

The step of disseminating results—whether it be through papers or book manuscripts or at conferences—also requires reflexivity. The dissemination step is when we share our work with the rest of the world, but for researchers, it is important to define "world." Whom do we decide to share our work with? What led us to pick particular journals or conferences? What audience are we targeting, and how does this impact how we share our work? For example, when I present work at the Tamil Studies Conference, I find my social location as second-generation Sri Lankan Tamil Canadian coming to the forefront. I make certain assumptions about the knowledge base of the audience and, therefore, do not take time to contextualize the history of the Sri Lankan conflict in any depth. However, when I present at the Canadian Ethnic Studies Association Conference, I may find that my positionality as a race and ethnic relations scholar comes to the forefront. I design my slides differently, highlighting different aspects of the literature—even if I am presenting the same research as I did at the Tamil Studies

Conference. I have different expectations of the audience, and I am hoping to gain different insights from presenting at these two conferences. It is important, therefore, that I take time to think about *what* I hope to achieve from each conference, and how this impacts how I disseminate my work.

CONCLUDING THOUGHTS

Reflexivity is a process that requires practice. With each research project, you will find the process much more intuitive—however, the process itself will not be identical with each project. This, of course, is to be expected, as you will evolve over time, and the projects you choose to do (or not to do) will also change over time. Therefore, one cannot skip any of the aforementioned steps by assuming that the social locations you listed for a project you conducted in March will remain the same as the ones you list for a project you conduct in September. For example, as I write this, I sit at a coffee shop in London, England. I have been here for one week and, already, I recognize the addition and modification of what makes me who I am. Where I may have previously defined my relationship with certain British family members in one way, those relationships have already evolved—as has my own understanding of my positionality in the family. I can only imagine how these views will change in six weeks when I complete my stay in the United Kingdom. And I do not know how these views may change one year from now. Your social locations are always changing, and your research interests are always evolving. This is a *necessity* for anyone who is a researcher—as you read and learn and interact with the literature, your perspectives *must* change. And as this happens, so too will the reflexive process.

Grab another blank piece of paper. Without looking at the first list you wrote at the beginning of the chapter, write down all the things that make you who you are. Write down all your social locations and all of your positionalities. Write it all down. Now compare this to the list you wrote at the beginning. Are there any differences? I imagine that the list has changed—perhaps you forgot some things you had previously listed, and perhaps you have added new items to your list. If your list can change over the course of reading one chapter, imagine how it will change from day to day and project to project.

CRAFTING QUALITATIVE RESEARCH EXERCISES

1.   Open up your favourite social media site and pick the third post that you see. What was your initial reaction to this post? How do you understand the motivations of the person who posted this? How does this post impact how you see them? Now think of what you post: To what extent are your posts representative of who you are in your entirety and your world views? What are the

advantages and disadvantages of analyzing people's behaviours and attitudes based on what they post on social media?

2. Ask a close friend *and* a family member to write down how they would describe you. Ask them to write down all of the characteristics that make you who you are—the "good," the "bad," and the "ugly." Do the same about yourself. After all three of you have done this exercise, compare the lists. What items overlap? What were the differences that you noticed? What does it mean that all three of you did not have identical lists? What do these findings mean in terms of research that you choose to do with human subjects?

3. For this activity, go to a public space (e.g., a public park, the library), and do some "people-watching" for 30 minutes. Do not write down what you see, but instead write down what your thoughts are regarding what you see. For example, what did you think when you saw that couple or those toddlers? What did you think about what they were wearing or doing? What conclusions did you draw about who they are, and what were your thoughts about this? After you are done, consider whether you would give these notes to a classmate or professor or stranger on the bus to read. Why or why not? What does it mean that our "private" thoughts may not be our "public" opinions?

4. If money and time were not a concern, what project would you like to conduct? Write down exactly what you would like to study, and how you would do it. Now, be reflexive: What pulled you towards this project? What are your personal objectives and personal biases related to this topic of study?

REFERENCES

Burkitt, Ian. 2012. "Emotional Reflexivity: Feeling, Emotion and Imagination in Reflexive Dialogues." *Sociology* 46 (3): 458–72.

Dwyer, Sonya C., and Jennifer L. Buckle. 2009. "The Space Between: On Being an Insider-Outsider in Qualitative Research." *International Journal of Qualitative Methods* 8 (1): 54–63.

England, Kim V. L. 1994. "Getting Personal: Reflexivity, Positionality, and Feminist Research." *Professional Geographer* 46 (1): 80–9.

McCorkel, Jill A., and Kristen Myers. 2003. "What Difference Does Difference Make? Position and Privilege in the Field." *Qualitative Sociology* 26 (2): 199–231.

Medved, Caryn E., and Lynn H. Turner. 2011. "Qualitative Research: Practices and Practicing Reflexivity." *Women & Language* 34 (2): 109–13.

2

The Role of Unpredictability in Ethnographic Fieldwork

Mark S. Dolson

Abstract knowledge of quantitative and qualitative methodologies, of great books and foreign languages, will not help you reach an understanding of others unless you share in their lives as a fellow human being, with tact and sensitivity, care and concern.

—*Michael Jackson,* Between One and One Another

July 15th, 2013. Reykjavik, Iceland.
I pull up to the Salvation Army's *Dagsetur* (Icelandic for "day shelter") in the old 1996 Toyota Corolla Olaf had lent me as one of the perks of renting her apartment for the next six weeks. As I try and straighten out the already crooked steering wheel, I take a deep breath before exiting, accompanied by a barely audible mutter: "Here I go again…." There's no one around yet, even though it just hit 10:30 am—opening time for the shelter, and drop-off time for the city's homeless shuttle service.

As I approach the front door, not knowing what to expect again, I put my hand on the cold steel handle. An unwanted chorus jolts me as I pull the heavy door towards me: the rusted hinges, each tuned to an A, C, or F#, let out a high-pitched, disharmonic squeak and squeal, and combine with a sharp chink as the lower edge of the door scrapes and gets stuck on the concrete—it scares me every time. As I make my way slowly up the two flights of stairs, I wonder what's in store for me today.

THE OFTENTIMES UNPREDICTABLE NATURE OF QUALITATIVE RESEARCH

As an anthropologist who has been conducting ethnographic fieldwork for over 13 years, it never ceases to amaze me how unpredictable ethnographic research can be. Whether it was conducting fieldwork in a large psychiatric institute in Quebec; a busy pediatric emergency room in a teaching hospital in Ontario; a small Inuit/Settler village in subarctic Labrador; a homeless drop-in shelter for youth in Ontario; or a day shelter for those who suffer from homelessness, mental health issues, and addiction in

Figure 2.1: *Hjálpræðisherinn* (the Icelandic Salvation Army)

Source: Personal photograph.

Iceland, a recurrent theme of all of my field-research projects has been *unpredictability* and *uncertainty*.

In ethnographic fieldwork of any duration, researchers must not only interact with and observe their research participants in a particular context, but they must also constantly grapple with unpredictability and uncertainty. What I mean by this, is that ethnographers, whether professional or novice, must be constantly aware that fieldwork is an uneven social experience through and through: fieldwork not only unfolds through the consideration of one's own experiences, hopes, aspirations, likes, dislikes, biases, and fears, but also how these aforesaid positions on the world interact and intersect with those with whom one is conducting fieldwork—the participants (Campbell and Lassiter 2015). Inasmuch as this is the case, research participants (potential or confirmed) can and will be *unpredictable* in their daily interactions and conversations with you, the ethnographer. Some days research participants will have quite a lot to say, and some days they might not want to talk at all; some will be interested in you, and will express concern and investment in you and your project, while others will avoid you, and may, in some cases, ignore you throughout the duration of your fieldwork!

As I have found in many long-term ethnographic fieldwork situations, when engaged respectfully and patiently, people will want to talk to you about anything *but* the specific details of your research. For example, many ethnographers—including myself—have a script (sometimes rough, but in some cases well structured and thought out) of themes, topics, or questions they want to ask their research participants about during the course of fieldwork. And of course, this all relates back to the original research project or ethics proposal the ethnographer had written either to secure permission from an undergraduate or graduate professor for a project in a qualitative methods course, or to secure funding for an MA or PhD thesis, or even a post-doctoral research project that involves qualitative methods.

My hope with this chapter is that the reader will not only gain insight into the more unpredictable side of ethnographic fieldwork, but will also learn some practical tactics to help ease the potential confusion and ambiguity that can often result from entering the field for the first time. More specifically, I offer advice on how to be flexible and improvise with one's research focus and questions so as to manage the adversity that can arise if there is a disconnect between one's research questions and the social realities of talking and interacting with people in their everyday contexts. Drawing on the ethnographic vignette that opened this chapter, I will illustrate by way of a descriptive example how I grappled with unpredictability and adversity, and how my ability to improvise via the notions of "adversity management" and "negative capability" impacted my post-doctoral ethnographic fieldwork project with homeless, addicted, and mentally ill people in Reykjavik, the capital of Iceland.

BEING FLEXIBLE WITH YOUR TOPIC: THE VICISSITUDES OF FIELDWORK

In 2013, I was awarded a Social Sciences and Humanities Research Council of Canada Post-doctoral Fellowship through the University of Cambridge. My proposed project was to conduct two full summers of ethnographic fieldwork in Reykjavik, Iceland, on the role of the 2008 economic downturn (and subsequent Icelandic banking collapse, which was the largest experienced by any country in economic history) on precariously employed migrant workers.

Specifically, following my research on homelessness in Ontario (see Dolson 2015a, 2015b; Forchuk et al. 2013), I wanted to understand through everyday ethnographic participation the day-to-day strategies of living and making do of migrant workers who had recently lost their jobs and become homeless, and to see what recourse—if any— they had for social services programs (welfare, employment, and housing options). The crux was to understand what gaps—if any—there are in the Icelandic social services system, and to see how they could be reduced to cover migrant workers in Iceland.

Once in Iceland, I spent a great deal of time speaking with many Polish migrant workers at the outset of my fieldwork. In fact, as a point of entry to my fieldwork, I was able to sign up as an official volunteer through *Hjálpræðisherinn* (the Icelandic Salvation Army). For my duties, I was assigned to prepare and serve food to clients of the *Dagsetur*, as well as clean tables, wash dishes, and clean the bathroom. This proved to be an excellent approach to getting to know clients, as I would ask them what kind of food they wanted and bring it right to them at the dining tables. I would then sit down with them and talk about how their days were going. Many were not interested in talking at all, while some would talk quite a lot, discussing family, the hardships of being homeless, and the differences between Iceland and Canada in terms of social programs.

My discussions with participants were going well, despite getting yelled at many, many times for speaking English, being a "foreigner," and for apparently "talking too much" instead of serving food! After another week, I noticed that many of the people who were quite open with me were now coming to the *Dagsetur* extremely intoxicated, and unwilling to talk at all. More aggression followed (yelling and threats), and then I realized that I was very quickly reaching an unforeseen limit—that constantly intoxicated research participants can be sometimes quite difficult to deal with! And then, I met Guðny (pronounced "Gu-thny") and Johannes (pronounced "Yo-hannez").[1] Not long after my first few conversations with them, the entire focus of my research shifted dramatically.

As an ethnographer, my purpose is to facilitate *storytelling* in my research participants; to listen carefully, compassionately, and respectfully, and then, ultimately—when I write up the results from my research—to tell stories *about my participants' stories*. When I got to know both Guðny and Johannes (both elderly Icelanders who have experienced bouts of homelessness over the past 17 years), I quickly realized how compelling and tragic their stories were. A key difference, too, was that Guðny and Johannes *needed* to tell their stories; they *wanted* me to listen, to be moved, and to be shaken by their lived experience of homelessness and exile in their home city. And therein lies a key difference in research participants (and ultimately, the very direction of one's ethnographic research in many contexts): those who *want* their stories heard, who have a desire to share their experiences with only the hope of having a compassionate and listening ear.

Admittedly and realistically, though, this cannot happen each and every time someone sets out to do ethnographic research; however, when it does, it is something to be fostered and cherished. For the rest of my fieldwork in 2013 and all of it in 2014, I spent on average seven hours a day with both Guðny and Johannes. In terms of approach, I would tack back and forth between watching a movie with Guðny—using our shared experience of watching as a point of entry into dialogue—on the *Dagsetur*'s TV and VCR, and sitting and listening to Johannes's stories.

Partway into my second field visit to Iceland, it was resoundingly clear that—due to their willingness to tell me their life stories each day, their intelligence and perseverance, and their patience—I needed to rethink my post-doctoral research by shifting my focus to a more person-centred ethnographic project based on the life histories of Guðny and Johannes.[2] During my preparation for the project, I had made sure to read as widely as I could—in anthropology, sociology, and philosophy—so I could understand as much as possible the literature on the experience of marginalization and disenfranchisement. As an academic exercise, I cannot emphasize this enough, as when it came time for me to switch my topic very quickly, I had an entire tool kit at my disposal to help frame my new-found research approach.

When embarking on fieldwork for the first time, students, like myself, might experience the seemingly jarring disconnect between the focused intentions of a well-meaning research project and the potential lack of investment or interest of one's research collaborators with the research question. If this happens, it does not mean having to return to the "drawing board" and reformulate an entire research project. On the contrary, it means approaching the research situation as a learning endeavour. Listen carefully to what your research collaborators will tell you and learn from them. Rather than frame or contain their experience according to the theoretical or methodological approaches you have learned about in your course-work, be open and flexible to their life experiences, concerns, and interests. More often than not they will be passionate about and invested in issues and matters of concern to them. Much of the information gleaned from ethnographic fieldwork is *emergent*: it arises and unfolds as you go along. And, as such, with patience and re-solve, patterns and commonalities will emerge (albeit potentially different ones than you had started out with) out of the social complexity between yourself and your research collaborators. Receptivity to the incorporation of new research ideas and approaches is key to meaningful ethnographic fieldwork.

CONCLUSION: TOWARDS AN UNDERSTANDING OF ADVERSITY MANAGEMENT IN ETHNOGRAPHIC FIELDWORK

Ethnographic fieldwork, by its very nature, is an unpredictable and uneven social and research experience—an experience that can, in many cases, lead the researcher in com-pletely unexpected directions. For novice researchers, the sheer unpredictability of eth-nographic fieldwork can serve as a source of great frustration and anxiety. In many cases, this is because it is necessary to write a clear, concise, and detailed proposal outlining each and every step of the qualitative research one expects to conduct (ranging from research question to methodology), whether an essay proposal to be based on original research for an undergraduate or graduate class, or an ethics proposal requesting clear-ance for a graduate student or faculty-based research project. However, while important, you can never really anticipate what might happen with the direction of your research once you start engaging with your first potential research participant. And for many stu-dents that I have taught, the disconnect between what was written in a research or ethics proposal and the real experience of conducting ethnographic research can be alarming. Many students get anxious over the inability to control what their research participants say about the intended research and its projected goals and results.

Depending on the focus, the questions asked, and the people with whom one is conducting research, some students might be able to conduct their research with minimal reorganization, rethinking, and reframing; however, based on my own experience, the norm—especially when dealing with longer fieldwork forays—involves at least a moderate level of research project re-evaluation. As such, it is important for students setting out on their first experience with ethnographic fieldwork to think of what I call "adversity management." Adversity management, to me, means having the ability to relinquish control in ethnographic research situations, especially when research participants might not "participate" in the ways you intended in your research or ethics proposal. It means having the ability to manage situations that are literally *adverse*: unfavourable and opposed to what was originally planned.

It also stands for attempting to be comfortable with the unexpected, and trying to make the best of ambiguous situations in which you have no idea what will happen next. Of course, this calls for being socially adaptable and open-minded to modifying your research focus—but it also means trying to be optimistic about research situations that might lead to utter dead ends, just as it did with the migrant workers, who, after a few weeks, were no longer interested in speaking with me about their experiences. Adversity management means having the ability to improvise in uncertain situations. The great English poet John Keats (1795–1821) called the ability to adapt and improvise "negative capability." Keats tells us that this is "when a man is capable of being in uncertainties, mysteries, doubts, without any irritable reaching after fact and reason" (1958, 1). He continues in his highly obtuse prose, stating that "[negative capability] is a glimpsing of a fine, isolated verisimilitude caught from the penetralium of mystery; as such, one who employs negative capability remains content with half-truths and half-knowledge" (1958, 227–28). As I understand it, then, negative capability is the capability to *improvise freely* in situations characterized by contingency and chance—particularly fitting for first-time forays into ethnographic fieldwork.

The bottom line is that adversity management, according to the principles of negative capability, just means "going with the flow" of what your participants are telling you. By chance, fate, or common interest, when you find that your research participants do not want to talk about your research, or if they are interested in something else that is very meaningful to them, and that this interest of theirs could warrant a rethinking and reframing of your project, be open to them and listen carefully to what they have to say. Whether it is the experience of illness, homelessness, unemployment, life tragedies, or other issues, taking a new ethnographic stance according to the principles of adversity management and negative capability means being patient with your participants and being committed to them. It means listening well, and respecting and investing in what your participants have to say. It means caring for them, not as research participants and not as a means to an end, but as people who have feelings, interests, goals, dreams, and fears—just like you. To conclude, then, adversity management means taking risks and embracing going "off script."

CRAFTING QUALITATIVE RESEARCH EXERCISES

1. Building on personal connections, think about bringing together friends or family members to talk about "meaningful school experiences" (e.g., their time spent in grade school or secondary school). This can be done separately via the phone or even in a group (if this is possible). Before you talk to each person about their experiences, write down a list of key aspects that *you* think they might end up talking about. While asking each person about their most meaningful experiences, make sure to take notes that point out both the commonalities and differences between what you thought they would talk about and what each person considers to be a "meaningful" school experience.

2. Within your class, select a small group of three or four students. Each group should then choose a topic from the following list: physical activity, music, or food. Based on your group's topic, each student should separately formulate a series of three research questions. Come together and compare your questions. Have an open discussion about what the commonalities and differences were between each group member's questions. With an aim for flexibility and negotiation, revise a master list of questions that includes the ideas and directions of each group member.

3. Within your class, pair off with an interview partner. Each partner should separately formulate a series of four questions to ask each other about their future plans after university. Come together and conduct your respective interviews. Take brief notes, and listen carefully to what your partner is saying while answering the four questions. After each question is asked, though, prepare to go "off script" and improvise. Referring to your notes, pick up on key themes, topics, or experiences that your partner mentioned, and continue the interview in a more conversational tone. While listening to your partner's responses, take brief notes again and see how the narrative information gleaned adds to, and potentially differs from, the responses to the original four questions.

NOTES

1. In order to protect their identities, I have changed these participants' names.
2. Both Guðny and Johannes were extremely uncomfortable with being digitally recorded. In fact, since Guðny has unwillingly been the centre point of many media stories in local newspapers in Reykjavik, it would cause her great pain to invasively use a digital recorder to capture her words during our more conversational interviews and discussions.

REFERENCES

Campbell, Elizabeth, and Eric Lassiter. 2015. *Doing Ethnography Today: Theories, Methods, Exercises*. West Sussex, UK: John Wiley & Sons.

Dolson, Mark S. 2015a. "By Sleight of Neoliberal Logics: Street Youth, Workfare and the Everyday Tactics of Survival in London, Ontario, Canada." *City and Society* 27 (2): 116–35.

Dolson, Mark S. 2015b. "Precarity, Workfare, and the Social Contingency of Suffering: The Story of a Canadian Street-Youth." *Culture, Medicine, and Psychiatry* 39 (1): 134–61.

Forchuk, Cheryl, Jan Richardson, Karen Laverty, Mirella Bryant, Abraham Rudnick, Rick Csiernik, Betty Edwards, Sandra Fisman, Beth Mitchell, Martha Connoy, Mark S. Dolson, and Kelly Chandell. 2013. "Service Preferences of Homeless Youth with Mental Illness: Housing First, Treatment First, or Both Together." In *Youth Homelessness in Canada: Implications for Policy and Practice*, edited by Stephen Gaetz, Bill O'Grady, Kristy Bucceri, Jeff Karabanow, and Allyson Marsolais, 95–109. Toronto: Canadian Homelessness Research Network Press.

Jackson, Michael. 2012. *Between One and One Another*. Berkeley: University of California Press.

Keats, John. 1958. *The Letters of John Keats 1814–1821*, vol. 1, edited by H. E. Rollins. Cambridge, UK: Cambridge University Press.

3 Collateral Damage: Preparing Your Friends and Family for Your Ethnography

Tony Christensen

> Lying on our bed in front of me, curled into a fetal position, is my girlfriend of three and a half years. The sound of her sobbing is of a type and tone I've never heard before. Her crying is more than sadness; it's anguish. In the events leading up to this moment, a careless choice of words has given her the impression that I think we should break up. I don't want to break up. Or do I? I'm not sure. I wrap my arms around her to console her. As the sobs recede, she asks me what I want. Do I want to take a break? Sow some wild oats? Do I want to live the life of the pick-up artists I had been studying ethnographically for the past several months? This last question crushes me. It angers me. It brings to the surface the fears and truths that I'd been pushing to the side for the past several weeks. My dissertation research was affecting me. Affecting us. Intruding where it was not welcome. Imposing itself because I was unable or, more disconcertingly, unwilling, to keep it at bay. (T. Christensen, unwritten ethnographic reflection)

Shortly after I never wrote that reflection, I quietly ended my fieldwork on a subculture of heterosexual men who self-identified as "pick-up artists" and members of the "seduction community." This research was meant to inform my doctoral dissertation and my exit from this research was wrapped in feelings of failure, shame, guilt, and weakness. It was some time before I would admit to anyone why I stopped my research: I left the field because I felt that, if I stayed, my relationship with my girlfriend of four years would not survive. I felt the death spiral my relationship was entering shortly after I entered the field. I tried very hard to ignore it. I tried to bury our travails by never writing down what was happening in our personal life or my feelings about them, leaving behind an unwritten library of ethnographic reflections. Writing them down would make the problems real. It would force me to recognize that my research was disrupting our life together, turning our relationship into ethnographic collateral damage.

There are a number of reasons ethnographers leave the field. Textbooks and course instructors will speak about waiting for "saturation" to occur, referring to the idea that you are not learning anything new as you go about doing your fieldwork. Other reasons for leaving are more practical. One might run out of time or money, or even have the group they are studying disappear or disband. But to leave because it was bringing your romantic relationship to the point of disintegration did not seem to pop up a lot in discussions with colleagues. To have this happen seemed to be a mark of failure as a researcher. Why had I allowed my home life to compromise my research?

Ethnography can be a greedy institution (Coser 1974), an endeavour that shows no respect for the boundary between work life and private life. Its transgressions will manifest in manifold different ways, but for this essay, I will focus on two particular effects:

1.   It will demand your time.
2.   It will change you.

In discussing each of these issues, I hope to impress upon you the need to talk to those close to you *before* beginning your ethnographic endeavours. Discuss your needs and their needs. Be clear about your goals and their goals and how this research will help achieve those goals. Outline the demands and possible consequences of your proposed work. Talk about what an appropriate level of participation in the group you are studying would be and how far your participation will extend. Listen to their concerns. Most importantly, be honest with yourself and with them about what is important to you. The blunt truth of the experience my girlfriend and I went through was that we had been naive about what the ethnography would demand of us and we had wilfully ignored the changes that were happening. If you do not deal with these matters before you start, the demands of your research might force the issue, often in awkward and painful ways.

Of course, by now you might be wondering why anyone would want to do an ethnography. "Your relationship in tatters! Your personal life a shambles! Beware!" As strange as it sounds, this essay is not meant to scare you away from trying ethnography and, as I point out later, what it requires of you will vary greatly depending on a host of different factors. The experience of novices trying to get their feet wet in qualitative research will be far different from a PhD student embarking on their dissertation research. By telling these stories, I hope to help you approach an ethnography from a position of confidence and with an increased sense of support to make your experience in the field a more powerful and positive one.

MY RESEARCH

My experience with ethnography and its collateral effects on those around me came during my dissertation research. It involved an ethnography of the seduction community, an international subculture of heterosexual men who self-identify as pick-up artists. These men teach other men techniques and tactics for "hitting" on, generating attraction from, and seducing women. To do this research, I spent time with a group of men in a nearby city who belonged to this community. Each month, they would hold meetings where they talked about their experiences hitting on women, and gave each other pointers and suggestions on how to improve their "game." Eventually, they invited me to accompany them as they went about trying to hit on women at local nightclubs using the tactics they had learned.

IT WILL DEMAND YOUR TIME

> It's Friday evening and my girlfriend asks what I want to do. She's been studying for her professional accreditation exam each night after work and Friday is our time to spend together since I'll be in the field on Saturday. I was up until 4:00 am last night. First with the pick-up artists and then writing field notes. I had few hours of sleep before teaching an 8:30 tutorial this morning. I'm exhausted and it's made me irritable. What do I want to do? I'm annoyed by the question. It's obvious! I want to sleep. I'm in bed by 9:00. (T. Christensen, unwritten ethnographic reflection)

At roughly the same time that my dissertation research started, my girlfriend and I moved in together, relocating to a new city about 45 minutes away from the men I was studying. Shortly after we moved in, I was invited to accompany the pick-up artists to local bars and nightclubs. They favoured going out on Thursdays and Saturdays. This entailed spending late nights at various nightclubs, often staying until 1:00 or 2:00 am. After departing the scene, I would make my way to a friend's apartment where I would spend time writing field notes before crashing on his couch. Complicating the matter were the 8:30 am tutorials I had to teach on Friday mornings. This left me with only a couple of hours of sleep on Fridays.

It is easy to see this issue as an artifact of the particular group I was studying. But each group will find its own way to surprise you. A colleague of mine who studied engineers and environmental scientists recounts a story of having to choose whether to dump his child care responsibilities on his spouse on her planned night out because he received notice of an "important meeting" being held only an hour before it began.

As I previously mentioned, ethnography is a greedy endeavour and the first thing it seizes is your time. To understand those that you study, you have to be around them. The more you are around them, the better. But it is not only time that it seizes; it also disrupts the routines you have established with those around you. Ethnographers must adapt to the rhythms of the groups they study. This can require late nights or early mornings. It can require commitments to be dropped at a moment's notice. These demands can leave friends wondering why their formerly steadfast companion no longer seems to have time for them. Family members may have to pick up the slack for neglected household responsibilities and excuse your absence at family functions left unattended. Partners and lovers may feel less important than a new group of strangers who have insinuated themselves into your life.

IT WILL CHANGE WHO YOU ARE

I've just finished having lunch at the campus pub. Throughout the meal, I've been pleasantly chatting with the bartender. I pay for lunch and begin packing up to go. As I get up to leave, she asks me to wait. She reaches down to the credit card terminal and presses a button to spool out a short length of the receipt paper. She tears it off, grabs a pen, and jots something down on it. She hands it to me with a smile, "I really enjoyed meeting you." I glance at the paper bearing her name and cell number. My heart is racing and I'm a bit giddy. This has never happened to me before. I return the sentiment as I shove the paper in my pocket.

Later, in my office, I think about our conversation. How did this happen? At first, I'm convinced that we were just two people who clicked. But as I turn the conversation over in my head, I see the tips and tactics taught by the pick-up artists manifest in what I had said and done. Cold reads and generic truisms used to create a feeling of connection. Selecting stories that portray myself in the image of the male these seduction "gurus" argue women are instinctively attracted to. More disconcerting than the fact that I had done this (and that it seemed to have worked) is that I don't recall making a decision to do these things. The words just seemed to come instinctively. (T. Christensen, unwritten ethnographic reflection)

More subtle and pernicious than the demands on our schedules is the effect doing ethnography can have on our personalities. In spending long periods with a group of strangers with whom they progressively become more intimate, ethnographers leave the field transformed. As Daniels (1983, 196) states, in doing ethnography, "personal values and beliefs are challenged, and attitudes are fundamentally changed." As you spend long periods of time with a group of strangers, trying to grasp how they understand the world around them, it is inevitable that you will absorb some of their world view.

The dilemma you face is that you will want the ethnography to affect you. When I recounted my experience with the bartender to my colleagues, it was viewed as a good thing. They told me that this was a good indication that I was closer to understanding the social world of these men. Having the social world you are studying "rub off" on you can be helpful. Despite their approval, the experience was disconcerting. As these changes take hold, friends and families may perceive them more clearly than the ethnographers themselves. These changes may be welcome, amusing, or bewildering for those close to the ethnographer. This experience raises questions you should ask yourself. How much am I meant to transform myself to fit into and understand the world I am studying? What limits should I place on how deeply I allow myself to be transformed? How deeply can I immerse myself in a world without becoming completely of it? How much of myself is "too much" to give in order to do a good ethnography? Whatever the nature of the changes, they will need to be reconciled by your circles of close family and friends. If they cannot be reconciled, if the changes cannot be accepted, then, again, decisions must be made about what is most important to you. What priorities are you willing to compromise?

BEFORE YOU BEGIN

Choosing to do an ethnography should be understood as a choice to bring a new set of obligations and responsibilities into your life and the lives of those around you. This will require you to reprioritize your existing commitments. In light of this, my advice to you is to reflect on why you are making this choice: What are your motivations for doing this ethnography? How important is it to you? What will the benefits (to you and others) be? How will doing this ethnography change the already existing rhythms of your life? What impact will this choice have on those you have responsibilities to? Critically interrogate your answers to these questions.

As you consider these issues, also consider where you are in your life course. Are you single? Married? Somewhere in between? Do you have children? Are your family members healthy? As in all areas of life, gender is especially important here. If ethnography creates the need for others to pick up the slack created by our research commitments, it is important to examine the division of labour within a relationship. Who is expected to subvert their career aspirations in service to their partner? Who, by default, is expected to take care of the household chores or do the child care? There may be unspoken assumptions made by your partner, your friends, and your family regarding these issues. If you do not discuss these issues and make what has been unspoken open and overt, the demands of the ethnography will bring them into the open, often in troubling and sometimes painful ways.

It might seem obvious to you that friends and family should take precedence over one's research. Why do we need to be with those we study so much? Does it matter if you skip some opportunities to observe those you are studying? As you consider this, consider the stakes involved in the research project. Is it a short project for an undergraduate class? Is it being done with the hopes of helping an underserved or marginalized population? Are you pursuing your PhD, where your research is being reviewed by a committee of experts and will shape your future job prospects? Your reasons for conducting an ethnography will speak to how highly both you and those around you will prioritize it and how much all of you will be willing to sacrifice for it.

Next, you must also consider the point of view of those being studied. Showing them that you are committed to your project and to them is often vital to gaining and maintaining access to the social world you wish to study. A stranger (you) has entered into their social world, asking to watch them and write about them. They agreed to this when they were under no obligation to do so. Your presence is burdensome. They worry about what they should say in front of you. They have to introduce you and explain your presence to others. What are your responsibilities to them in return for this access? Do they not deserve your commitment? How you present yourself to them matters. What do you communicate to them if you decline their invitations to join them after you asked them to let you in?

Once you have sorted these issues out in your own mind, discuss your choice with those most likely to bear the consequences of this choice. Explain why you want to do it, what the benefits will be, and how you suspect it will impact your relationship. Listen to their responses and concerns. You may find them enthusiastic about your choice and a willing participant in the endeavour. You may find them hesitant. You may need to negotiate the boundaries of your participation and reorganize your vision of how you will do your research. This is why sorting out your priorities is a must. You cannot "do it all"; thus, having a clear understanding of what is most important to you and those around you will help you sort out what to sacrifice, compromise, or reorganize as you introduce this new commitment into everyone's life.

Doing ethnography is an incredible experience. There is no better way to gain an understanding of how a group of people makes sense of the world. On the flip side, ethnography is not easy. It can demand a lot of you and the people around you. This essay is meant to give you advice about how to lessen the collateral damage engaging in a demanding ethnography can have on your personal life and relationships. By discussing these issues, I hope to better prepare you, the next generation of ethnographers, for your fieldwork. It is important for you to know that your worries, insecurities, and mistakes are often common experiences shared by even the most seasoned among us. I encourage you to be open about the challenge ethnography, and qualitative research in general, poses to your non-work-related life with your mentors and guides. Promoting open discussions about these matters is an important part of self-care and is integral to preventing burnout and preserving the mental health of our newest practitioners.

I wish you well in your travels.

CRAFTING QUALITATIVE RESEARCH EXERCISES

1. Two ethnographers are in the early stages of planning their research. One will be performing a participant observation study of graffiti artists in a large urban area. The other plans to observe a support group for mothers of young children who have died. In a few short paragraphs, compare the similarities and differences in the demands these ethnographies will place on the researchers' time and the possible effects on their personalities/emotional states.

2. Using the studies described in the previous question, imagine the researcher in both studies is a 26-year-old male PhD student who is living with his partner who works full-time as a physiotherapist. Now imagine that the researcher is a 38-year-old female single parent employed in a tenure-track faculty position.

How do the demographic details of the researcher alter the issues you identified in question 1?

3. You are about to engage in a 12-month ethnographic study of rural evangelical Christians. Brainstorm a list of the various meetings and gatherings (both formal and informal) that you would likely need to be present for (if you are not familiar with what goes on in evangelical churches, Google will be useful to you). Beyond this, think about any other contact you may want to have with those you are studying (e.g., interviews, focus groups). Tabulate how much time you should reasonably expect to spend engaged in research activities each week (do not forget about writing field notes, transcribing interviews, etc.). Now write a few paragraphs detailing the impact your participation in this research would have on your current lifestyle and the lifestyles of those close to you. What about your life and the lifestyles of your friends and family will need to change for this research to be successful?

4. Is ethnography a young person's game? As we move through the life course, we tend have more responsibilities placed upon us. Discuss how one's age makes doing ethnography more or less feasible.

REFERENCES

Coser, Lewis A. 1974. *Greedy Institutions: Patterns of Undivided Commitment.* New York: The Free Press.

Daniels, Arlene K. 1983. "Self-Deception and Self-Discovery in Fieldwork." *Qualitative Sociology* 6 (3): 195–214.

4

The Story of Dr. Charles Smith: An Exercise in Rolling Thematic Analysis

Chris McCormick

INTRODUCTION

In this chapter, I want to outline the planning involved for a research project that entailed analyzing media accounts of the "trials" of Dr. Charles Smith. As an expert witness in pathology, Smith's testimony was responsible for a series of wrongful convictions in Toronto, Ontario, between the early 1990s and early 2000s. The planning for this cultural analysis project will involve using a pilot study to assist in creating a news sample and conduct a preliminary multi-staged media analysis. This pilot study will assist in identifying relevant themes and issues for a larger, more systematic project. To facilitate this, it will use a thematic content analysis with successive readings, thus the "rolling" aspect (mentioned in the title of this chapter). This method is chosen for its flexibility, and is coupled with an introductory interpretive narrative analysis designed to show how planning research by using a pilot study is a recursive, multi-stage process.

THE CASE

This story is about a series of wrongful convictions caused by forensic error, and how the cases were covered in the media. The main character is protagonist Dr. Charles Smith, who was the head pediatric forensic pathologist at the Hospital for Sick Children in Toronto, Ontario, from 1982 to 2003. While often appearing as a star prosecution witness, as time went on the quality of his autopsies was called into question, as were the criminal charges and conviction of various people based on his testimony. Smith was reprimanded with a caution by the Ontario College of Physicians and Surgeons in 2002 because of his work on three suspicious-death cases, and was removed from performing autopsies the following year. The college said he was being "overly dogmatic" and had a "tendency towards overstatement." The Chief Coroner of Ontario ordered a review of 44 Smith autopsies in 2005, and the review was released in 2007. Thirteen of these cases had resulted in criminal charges and convictions, and the review found there were substantial problems with 20 of the autopsies. Subsequently, a full public inquiry into the state of pediatric forensic pathology in Ontario (the Goudge Inquiry, held in 2008) concluded that there were serious problems with the way suspicious deaths involving children were handled.

I first became interested in the case because I was teaching a course on wrongful convictions and wanted to see what a media analysis could contribute to an understanding of how wrongfuls happen. Specifically, I wondered if analysis of media coverage of Smith's cases, before and after his misconduct was revealed, could illuminate the causes of professional misconduct. This would be a rough indicator of the extent of public knowledge of the causes of wrongful convictions, but also perhaps a tool for identifying warning signs of wrongfuls in real time as a prosecution proceeded. I knew I wanted to do an exploratory analysis of a sampling of news items (Hiles 2008), using writing as a method of inquiry (Richardson and St. Pierre 2008) to help develop parameters for a more extensive thematic analysis (Braun and Clarke 2006; Cavender and Deutsch 2007). In addition, because the nature of Smith's deviance was now known retrospectively, it was thought that the media analysis might reveal an underlying "narrative" (Kitch 2003), which might be emancipatory in terms of the stories we tell as a culture.

RESEARCH CHOICES

The first stage in planning a media analysis is to look at general parameters for how crime is mis/represented in the media. For example, Doris Graber (1979) compared homicide stories in television news to official homicide rates and found, unsurprising to our eyes years later, that homicide was overrepresented in the news in proportion to its known official rate as a crime (see also Duwe 2000; Garofalo 1981; Peelo 2006; Sorenson, Manz, and Berk 1998). This technique is often used to study news coverage of other crimes, and shows how people get an exaggerated, sensational view of crime. The putative consequence for viewers, readers, and listeners of the news is an increased sense of fear and decreased locus of control, especially since mis/representation is likely to be skewed toward crimes that are highly violent, sexualized, motiveless, and committed by strangers. So we would need to get some objective statistics with which to compare to media patterns.

However, it seemed to me that simply to focus on exaggeration and distortion was not necessarily the appropriate approach to deal with the representation of the case. To paraphrase Altheide and Michalowkisi (1999), we need to treat the news as a topic to understand how social reality is ordered, maintained, and repaired. This highlights the importance of the "framing of crime" for how a popular audience interprets their world (Chiricos, Eschholz, and Gertz 1997). For example, even though terrorists are more likely to be portrayed as foreigners (Powell 2011), serial killers as roamers (Jenkins 1988), child abusers as pedophiles (Best 1987), and so on, because the main source of information about the world is going to be the media, the media's slant becomes the public's opinion. While the resulting world view might be putatively inaccurate, it is going to be the public's knowledge of the world. In this way, the media has an "agenda-setting" function (Altheide 1997; McCombs 1997), defining the saliency of a few small topics for the larger general population (Sacco 1995), whether it exaggerates or not. Take, for example, the effect of the following:

> "This was a brutal crime against a helpless infant," said district court Judge Joseph Sheard. "The history of Salma's short life is extremely sad, right from her painful entry into the world.... Pathologist Dr. Charles Smith said the force of the fatal fall would be equivalent to an adult plummeting from a three-story building." (*Ottawa Citizen* 1986)

These comments were made at the sentencing hearing for a man convicted of killing one of his twin infant daughters. Charges were also laid against his wife, but they were dropped when he pled guilty to manslaughter. The story becomes one of conviction, not mental illness as a cause, or the plea bargaining as an issue. This thematic narrative becomes part of an overarching story for understanding such events.

Consider the following, a case in which a severely depressed mother killed her children:

> Two baby girls killed by their mom were healthy, a pathologist told a jury. "She was a typical, well looked-after little girl," Dr. Charles Smith testified yesterday about Aparinaa Sriskantharajah, 2 1/2, who along with her sister Apiramil, 1 1/2, was strangled to death by their mother. The eldest daughter was "in good health and obviously well nourished.... She was a healthy little girl." (*Toronto Sun* 1994)

In this case the use of professional knowledge to authorize the prosecution's claim of first-degree murder, rather than say, not guilty by reason of insanity, privileges a theory in court and also in the public's mind. It is a compelling byline in a long narrative of prosecuting parents who kill their children.

Consider the discourse of one last case:

> "Retinal bleeding suffered by a baby girl in September 1986 was traumatic and probably caused by force," a forensic expert testified Thursday. "It was a mechanical injury," Dr. Charles Smith, a forensic pediatric pathologist from Toronto, said in testimony before Youth Court Judge Dolores Hansen.... Smith said also that a head injury that fractured the girl's skull was the result of being hit by force rather than from a fall down the stairs. An Edmonton boy, 16 at the time, was babysitting the child when the incident took place Sept. 3, 1986.... Smith said the injuries to the infant, who is now five years old, are consistent with shaken baby syndrome, in which a child is shaken so violently that blood vessels behind the eyes are ruptured.

"It's the only way we can have a devastating injury occur to a child without leaving a mark," said Smith (*Edmonton Journal* 1990)

The *discursive certainty*, that is, stating what is (meant to be) taken as an absolute fact, in what is now known to be a dated forensic truth is critical in this case, which was eventually overturned. We now know there is no such thing as "shaken baby syndrome," but there is no equivocation in the pathologist's statement that is what happened. *In this way, what role the forensic testimony has in the case is as critical as what role the media's reporting of it has in the public's mind.* The pathologist who can confirm the truth brings justice to murder, with courage and unselfishness; this is not simply about exaggeration, but rather emotional delivery of the facts by a forensic hero. So I knew that I probably would find a qualitative analysis of wording more important than a quantitative analysis of word count, so to speak. The reading would involve looking for themes, identified by the analyst and examined for their effect on the reader.

THE METHOD OF THE STUDY

A lot of decisions are not made solely, or with finality, in the planning stage, but rather in trying to implement a plan. For example, the initial search for media coverage of "Dr. Charles Smith" in the university library's electronic research database, Canadian Newspapers Fulltext, yielded 2,531 items. The results were classified as 108 positive, 490 negative, and 1,933 neutral. The publication with the highest number of stories was the *Peterborough Examiner* (218), while the lowest was the *Stratford Beacon-Herald* (30). The majority of the articles cluster around 2006–08, reflecting the period of the Goudge Inquiry. Smith does not figure in the media much in the two-decade period prior to that when he was doing his work and testifying at trials.

Because of the unwieldy size of the sample that was found, the thought then was to narrow the search to the *National Post* (155 stories); however, the *National Post* largely ignored Smith until after he started to get into trouble, so it would not be a good venue for looking for problems in otherwise straightforward cases. The *Toronto Sun* (172 stories), a tabloid, was then selected; its coverage of Smith's cases started in 1991. The sample was manageable, and would provide a full range of coverage from early to late in his career in order to tentatively generate some themes for analysis. Further, the *Sun* is published in a major city, and while it has been criticized for being sensationalistic and orienting to a low reading level, its subscription of almost 120,000 per week as the seventh most widely circulated newspaper in Canada makes it a prime candidate for framing and agenda setting, especially, it is suspected, for the working class, which Boykoff (2008) calls an understudied segment of society. While the tabloid news might be criticized for being low quality, what is important in analyzing tabloid news is not what kind of people read this news, but what kind of news people are reading.

To conduct the pilot study, the results in the *Toronto Sun* were printed off and subjected to thematic content analysis (Braun and Clarke 2006; Cavender and Deutsch 2007), which I define as reading to look for quotations, emotions, case names, and claims. What is important to stress about this research choice is the explicit disclosure of interpretive decisions taken during the research, such as the size of samples and the naming of themes. This approach highlights the way in which research is done, rather than just the results of that selfsame research. It is also important to stress that you must plan to read through the articles in successive stages so as to build a reflexive thematic analysis, which will help in designing a larger study. The full-blown research could use a more nationally comprehensive sample, or perhaps a comparison with a middle-class newspaper, and so on, but is planned based on what is found within the pilot study. Key to thematic analysis is the impression created in reading; for example, how does it feel the doctor is being represented: as an expert witness, a source of conflict, a discredited pathologist, and so on. The articles can then be reread to fill out what these themes or characterizations "look like," thus the rolling aspect of the thematic analysis. In this case, the sample was read through several times, finding new themes and issues each time.

Moreover, the method of selecting the sample parameters is also about conceptual choices. Knowing in advance the way the story would play out, I thought, what is special about this story? What kind of narrative is it? Is it a story about redemption, truth winning out over injustice? Or is it perhaps a fall-from-grace story, with moral implications? Some narratives are universal, like the cycle of the hero (Campbell 1949), while others, like the funeral narrative, provide comfort and healing in the face of immense tragedy (Kitch 2003). The only way to answer this question would be to read the sample. This would then dis/confirm decisions made in the planning stage, and/or suggest revisions to further refine the study.

READING THE SAMPLE

An initial read-through of the articles published between January 18, 1991, and April 22, 2007, focused on identifying general themes. Colour coding was used to keep track of case names and elements of the pathologist's testimony. The reading was done in successive cycles, as it was focused on developing a rolling series of interpretations. The point here is to outline the process of getting research underway, and to highlight how a serendipitous moment can move the analysis in new directions. This would help in planning the subsequent study.

An initial impression of cycle one was that the articles in the main were very "factual" in their reporting, and the headlines reflect that: "Mother Guilty in Death of Child," "Baby Allowed to Die," "Doctor: Slain Tots Were Healthy," "Doc: Death No Accident," "Sara Never Had a Chance." And, on reflection, that factual character was achieved through very neutral, unemotional language. The pathologist was, or seemed to be, the main witness, and rendered very technical reports. In the narrative cycle of the story, he appeared to represent unselfish personal sacrifice—he is the voice of (forensic) justice. By planning on being sensitive to word nuance, it is easier to see how discursive certainty in the media accounts is achieved, a goal set during the planning stage.

In reading cycle two, I looked for exceptions to certainty and the dominant discourse of guilt provided in the first reading. (In that sense, cycle one became an extended part of the planning stage.) I looked for a resistant discourse, and while there is little that is contrary to the pathologist's evidence, some articles stand out. For example, the prosecutor in a case where a woman killed her two baby girls said the murders were planned, and the pathologist said the children had been healthy; however, the defence lawyer said her client suffered from a "severe depression that grossly distorted her perception of the world and her situation" (*Toronto Sun* 1994). In this way the prosecution and pathologist together create a dominant discourse for a first-degree legal scenario; however, the defence attempts a contrary, resistant discourse based on a medical/mental scenario. This "alternative discourse" creates a resistance to the interpretation offered: that the crime is due to mental illness rather than involving criminal responsibility, but it is only retrievable through looking for a "resistant voice." It is not possible otherwise; this attests to the revelatory power of imagination, rather than what is "revealed in the data." This is the advantage of a heuristic approach that emphasizes discovery, and how "capta" is made available through interpretations. Another way of saying this is that themes are not a given, simply waiting to be found; they are created ("captured") from the reading through the interpretive openness of the analyst. What is seen is that in the narrative cycle, there is now disagreement with the hero.

In a third read-through of the articles, I decided to continue with this theme of the hero and the fall from grace. By 2003, cracks start to appear in Smith's cases, and he begins to be referred to as a "controversial" pathologist. By 2007 to 2012, Smith has long been suspended and his cases are being reviewed. In the media, evidence is now sought for the source of Smith's culpability. Is it a series of mistakes, or due to some deeper problem? He is now "notorious" and "disgraced"; it is at this point that I realized that the narrative cycle here is that of the anti-hero. This is the moment of serendipity for which all the best planning cannot prepare, and also why the research plan cannot be so rigid as to inhibit discovery. While Smith is initially portrayed as the consummate professional, a champion of the children, looking at the media coverage over time shows the pathologist is transformed to become vain and venal. If the hero goes through the transformative phases of separation, initiation, integration, and rebirth, the anti-hero goes through the transformative phases of attachment, regression, alienation, and death (Bonnet, n.d.). Where the hero's story is about redemption, the anti-hero's is about corruption. It is about cynicism and the ego's pursuit of power. This was in part anticipated (because I knew how the story played out), but to see the detail was serendipitous, brought about by the process of an open heuristic reading and grounded thematic analysis rooted in the articles. It is an interpretation with wider significance because it is about the stories we tell (ourselves), stories about the price of arrogance and hubris, that pride goes before a fall, and maybe even about the banality of evil. It is a moral lesson achieved by reading through the long-term media coverage. And, for the public, it is about the triumph of justice, an important ideological point that reinforces the legitimacy of the justice system.

In terms of the study of wrongful convictions, there are issues that are revealed retrospectively that can now be looked for in further research. For example, does the discourse of certainty conceal tunnel vision and a rush to justice? Does a resistant discourse reveal the possibility of alternate scenarios in a case? Does the discourse of certainty in factual reporting create an ideology that forensic truth is justice, and how does this connect with research on true-crime television? Could journalism be more critical if it became more conversant with factors involved in wrongful convictions, such as forensic error and overstatement? How significant is it that those involved in a majority of Smith cases seem to be marginalized people (immigrants, single mothers, people on welfare)? Does this connect with research on the marginalized and their treatment in the media and the criminal justice system? In this way, discourse analysis, media studies, intersectionality, and the study of wrongful convictions all merge in the pilot study and make for the more thorough planning of further research.

CONCLUSION

The programmatic case study discussed here is a heuristic analysis of media coverage of a pathologist's testimony in child homicide cases in a limited sample. It is heuristic because to help in the planning of further research it has to be open to themes that evolve through the reading. It is an exploratory attempt to sort out discursive patterns in media coverage, prefatory to a larger, more detailed analysis. This technique is called a "pilot study," which becomes, by extension, part of the planning process because it is used to identify preliminary themes and issues of sampling and interpretation. Many of these cases came to be known as wrongful conviction cases, so it also begins to show how we could design a study of media coverage that might reveal where justice goes off the rails.

In this pilot study, a media sample of 172 *Toronto Sun* articles, written between 1991 and 2013, was examined using a heuristic, thematic approach. The case coverage was mined to see what it can contribute to a public understanding of the media's role in wrongful convictions. I planned on focusing on the discourse used, and to pay attention to emotional nuance. In looking through the coverage in that time span, we not only see how the pathologist goes from being a prosecutorial victor to a public villain, but also how there is a deeper unexpected narrative of the anti-hero. This finding then points the way to further analysis, a serendipitous moment for which we can prepare but never plan in advance.

Thematic content analysis is used to highlight the stages of interpretive inquiry, and the narrative cycle of the anti-hero is borrowed from literary analysis to enhance the media analysis. The utility of using a pilot study approach is that it quickly gets us looking at materials that can be used to generate more specific research questions for, let's say, a national sample. While it is used here to demonstrate representational issues in the media, it could be used in other method choices as well, such as interviewing and observation. It is a way of testing the water before jumping in for a swim or, to use a different metaphor, reading a restaurant review before tasting the food.

CRAFTING QUALITATIVE RESEARCH EXERCISES

1.   Using the crime statistics for your city, province, or country, create a news sample for a specific crime, such as domestic homicide or child abuse. Compare the amount of news coverage to the amount of crime over a period of time. This is called a "context analysis," and will show how important the news media says a crime is in terms of how often it is covered.

2.   Collect a news sample on a particular crime, such as sexual assault. A context analysis will show that it is highly under-reported in the news as a crime, but in this exercise you are looking at a "content analysis" of what is said about the crimes. Look for themes of responsibility and blame, and who the dominant voices are as indicators of how the media creates an ideology of crime.

3.   Take an example of crime or deviance that is portrayed as a problem in the media. A good example might be immoral behaviour such as prostitution or drug use. In this "snapshot analysis" you are looking at how the problem is portrayed at one point in time, who is doing the defining, and what they say the solution is. For example, is the problem race, class, poverty, individual fault, and so on.

4.   In a "longitudinal analysis," we want to look at news coverage over time and see how a story evolves. Take a disaster, such as the *Deepwater Horizon* or *Exxon Valdez* oil spills, the Westray Mine explosion, or the Lac-Mégantic rail disaster, and look at how one or several news outlets cover the topic over time. In particular, look for thematic issues of corporate and individual responsibility.

5.   Using a "narrative analysis," look at how media coverage of a tragic event of national significance, such as 9/11, evolves over a series of months. Review narrative models from literary studies or anthropology, such as the funeral narrative, and see how there is a cultural story that unfolds to make significance of the event.

REFERENCES

Altheide, David. 1997. "The News Media, the Problem Frame, and the Production of Fear." *Sociological Quarterly* 38 (4): 647–68.

Altheide, David, and Sam Michalowkisi. 1999. "Fear in the News: A Discourse of Control." *Sociological Quarterly* 40 (3): 475–503.

Best, Joel. 1987. "Rhetoric in Claims-Making: Constructing the Missing Children Problem." *Social Problems* 34 (2): 101–21.

Bonnet, James. n.d. "The Journey of the Antihero in Film: Exploring the Dark Side." *Writers Store*. https://www.writersstore.com/exploring-the-dark-side-the-anti-heros-journey.

Boykoff, Maxwell. 2008. "The Cultural Politics of Climate Change in UK Tabloids." *Political Geography* 7 (5): 549–69.

Braun, Virginia, and Victoria Clarke. 2006. "Using Thematic Analysis in Psychology." *Qualitative Research in Psychology* 3 (2): 77–101.

Campbell, Joseph. 1949. *The Hero with a Thousand Faces*. Princeton, NJ: Princeton University Press.

Cavender, Gray, and Sarah Deutsch. 2007. "CSI and Moral Authority: The Police and Science." *Crime, Media, Culture* 3 (1): 67–81.

Chiricos, Ted, Sarah Eschholz, and Marc Gertz. 1997. "Crime, News and Fear of Crime: Toward an Identification of Audience Effects." *Social Problems* 44 (3): 342–57.

Duwe, Grant. 2000. "Body-Count Journalism: The Presentation of Mass Murder in the News Media." *Homicide Studies* 4 (4): 364–99.

Edmonton Journal. 1990. "Baby's Injuries Too Severe to Be Accidental, MD Testifies; Evidence Points to 'Shaken Baby Syndrome,' Pathologist Says." May 4, 1990.

Garofalo, James. 1981. "NCCD Research Review: Crime and the Mass Media; A Selective Review of Research." *Journal of Research in Crime and Delinquency* 18 (2): 319–50.

Graber, Doris. 1979. "Is Crime News Coverage Excessive?" *Journal of Communication* 29 (3): 81–92.

Hiles, David. 2008. "Heuristic Inquiry." In *The Sage Encyclopedia of Qualitative Research Methods*, edited by Lisa M. Given, 389–92. Thousand Oaks, CA: Sage.

Jenkins, Philip. 1988. "Serial Murder in England 1940–1985." *Journal of Criminal Justice* 16 (1): 1–15.

Kitch, Carolyn. 2003. "'Mourning in America': Ritual, Redemption, and Recovery in News Narrative after September 11." *Journalism Studies* 4 (2): 213–24.

McCombs, Maxwell. 1997. "Building Consensus: The News Media's Agenda-Setting Roles." *Political Communication* 14 (4): 433–43.

Ottawa Citizen. 1986. "Man Gets Five Years in Jail for Killing Infant Daughter." May 3, 1986.

Peelo, Moira. 2006. "Framing Homicide Narratives in Newspapers: Mediated Witness and the Construction of Virtual Victimhood." *Crime Media Culture* 2 (2): 159–75.

Powell, Kimberly. 2011. "Framing Islam: An Analysis of U.S. Media Coverage of Terrorism Since 9/11." *Communication Studies* 62 (1): 90–112.

Richardson, Laurel, and Elizabeth Adams St. Pierre. 2008. "Writing: A Method of Inquiry."
In *Collecting and Interpreting Qualitative Methods*, edited by Norman Denzin and Yvonna
Lincoln, 473–500. London: Sage.

Sacco, Vince. 1995. "Media Constructions of Crime." *ANNALS of the American Academy of
Political and Social Science* 539 (1): 141–54.

Sorenson, Susan, Julie Manz, and Richard Berk. 1998. "News Media Coverage and the
Epidemiology of Homicide." *American Journal of Public Health* 88 (10): 1510–14.

Toronto Sun. 1994. "Doctor: Slain Tots Were Healthy." January 22, 1994.

SECTION II

NAVIGATING ETHICAL DILEMMAS

Having read through the chapters in the first section of this book, and perhaps now starting your own project, you are likely beginning to realize the many benefits and opportunities qualitative research offers. Conducting qualitative research can be an exciting process, yet it can also be stressful, scary, and even intimidating. When you first begin to create a research topic and plan how to conduct the research, you will think about many things, such as whom you could speak with and how you will gain access to your research setting. As you think through these aspects of developing your project, you will also try to anticipate possible barriers or challenges to doing the research. It is at this point that you begin to think about the ethics of qualitative research.

In Canada, all research involving human subjects conducted through universities is governed by the *Tri-Council Policy Statement: Ethical Conduct for Research Involving Humans*, 2nd Edition (TCPS 2), which was established by Canada's three federal research bodies: the Canadian Institutes of Health Research, the Natural Sciences and Engineering Research Council of Canada, and the Social Sciences and Humanities Research Council of Canada. The federal government's Panel on Research Ethics has created an online tutorial that covers the guiding principles of the *Tri-Council Policy Statement*. Completing the tutorial, and presenting your certificate of completion, is often required by research ethics boards (REBs) before students can conduct their research. In fact, before you can go out and observe or talk to research participants, in addition to completing the tutorial, you may be required to submit an ethics application to your school's REB or your professor. In this application, the things you will be required to outline include the procedures involved in your project; your processes for recruitment, data collection, and analysis; the potential risks and benefits associated with your project; and your approach to ensuring the confidentiality of your participants. Although the ethics application is submitted at the beginning of your research process, research ethics is something that you will continue to think about, and grapple with, throughout your project.

For example, imagine doing observational research with police. What are the ethics involved in conducting observations during police ride-alongs? During ride-alongs, as the researcher, you must continually think about ways to write field notes that protect not only the confidentiality and anonymity of your participants (i.e., the people you are riding with and observing), but also members of the public who interact with the officers you are observing. Doing these types of observations can raise a number of ethical challenges, such as whether and how to acquire informed consent from everyone being observed. Do you need to acquire such consent? How do you write detailed field notes without disclosing any identifying information that could risk the anonymity of your various participants? Ethical decisions, however, are not something one faces only in the field while collecting data. Researchers are also faced with ethical challenges and dilemmas after they have left the field, and are writing up their findings. For example, in conducting research with police, how might your ethical obligations to your participants shape the way you write and present your findings?

Being "ethical" when conducting qualitative research is something everyone must strive for, yet it is something that is continually negotiated during a research project. Ethics, as illustrated in this section, is an ongoing, processual activity that shapes all aspects of the research process—from research design to analysis to the presentation of research results. While most methods courses will discuss research ethics during the first few weeks of the course, the chapters in this section demonstrate how ethics is something to be mindful of at all stages of your research. You will also find that your own personal ethics will be tested in certain situations. When they are, you might be forced to reconcile your ethics against institutional requirements and your desire to collect useful data. As you go about your research, you will explore what ethics means to you, on the ground.

We begin this section with Kerstin Roger and Javier Mignone's "Living Your Ethics: 'It's' Not Just a Dusty Document." Drawing on their respective research programs, Roger and Mignone examine some of the key challenges they have faced when working with "vulnerable" populations and conducting community-based research. Their chapter beautifully illustrates how ethics is not a static entity to be considered at the beginning of one's project, but is instead a relational process that requires continuous active engagement. They highlight the importance of dialoguing with one's ethics review committee and provide invaluable advice for students and junior scholars working through the ethics review process.

In chapter 6, Katherine Irwin discusses the ethical challenges qualitative researchers face while engaging in ethnographic research with youth. Reflecting on her own personal experiences, Irwin explores how she was able to build opportunity structures in schools through "lunch-bunch" groups, during her study on youth violence. Irwin further discusses how she worked to avoid exploitation and harm in creating these opportunity structures, respecting the decisions of the youth regarding what they wanted others to know about their lives. As such, her chapter elucidates the important role researchers hold in navigating the research process and creating opportunities for empowerment for their participants that is respectful of their voices and experiences.

In chapter 7, Gül Çalışkan discusses the risks—for both researcher and participants—associated with doing qualitative research undercover and conducting interviews with political activists. Reflecting on her personal experiences, Çalışkan recounts how she conducted over

30 interviews with participants undercover, discussing how she actively worked to mitigate risks while conducting her fieldwork. She concludes by providing general safety rules for those who are considering covert research methods.

The final chapter in this section, written by Will van den Hoonaard, discusses the negative impact the social regulation of ethics has had on sociological research in general and ethnographic research in particular. Van den Hoonaard reflects on the way "respect for persons," "concern for human welfare," and "justice" are informed by a biomedical model that cannot be neatly or easily applied to the premises of qualitative research. He then provides strategies for dealing with the challenges raised by the imposition of a biomedical model on qualitative research, and concludes by advancing more realistic expectations for qualitative and ethnographic researchers.

5

Living Your Ethics: "It's" Not Just a Dusty Document

Kerstin Roger and Javier Mignone

INTRODUCTION

As qualitative researchers, we enter into a dialogue with what some call vulnerable populations. They may be vulnerable due to a specific tragedy (e.g., survivors of a one-time trauma), institutionalized abuses over time (e.g., Indigenous communities in the residential school system), or more overarching systemic marginalization related to identity (e.g., gender/LGBT). Individuals, groups, and communities may face very different and wide-ranging challenges based on their socio-economic status, race, and gender, levels of ability/cognition, or language fluency, to name a few examples. Sometimes this mix has been called double or triple jeopardy (Moody and Sasser 2012), or, in a more theoretical sense, intersectionality (Crenshaw 1993). As researchers, we do not always know about the people we are interviewing,[1] although presumably we have a sincere interest in representing them. Further, we cannot always perceive what research participants experience in relation to our research question, regardless of our overall knowledge of their situations; thus, the process we engage in comes with inherent ethical challenges, potential pitfalls, and sometimes serious hiccups.

Consequently, the importance of clearly defining research ethics in those contexts, outlining how to write ethical issues into our research protocols, and carefully thinking about how to implement ethics when conducting research with vulnerable populations is an essential and ongoing practice. Although preparing an ethics protocol is a required research process, it is not a static entity. And so, we might consider a philosophy that many people have referred to as the "ethics of care," first coined by Gilligan (1982). In this sense, ethics becomes shorthand for a complex and dynamic reality of engagement between researchers and study participants that reflects an ethic of care. Reflecting about ethical interactions in research in the context of *caring for others* can lead us to our own ideas about who we are, who our study participants are, and what we (and they) thought they had to offer our study. As you will learn, going into the field and conducting research in an ethical way can lead to many surprising and unintentional impacts—especially when participants feel that as researchers we have power over their story, which can enhance their existing feelings of vulnerability. In this sense, anyone who wants to engage with a vulnerable community as a researcher will inevitably face the very real question of ethics and engagement as a relational and ongoing process.

We take the position in this chapter that an ethics protocol should not primarily be about helping a university to secure its place in potential litigation processes, or in the regulation of what constitutes good research, nor is it about jumping through an onerous but required hoop; rather, we are taking the position that an ethics protocol is primarily meant to support an ongoing dialogue with vulnerable communities and individuals who are participants in our research, and that considering ethical issues is about more deeply understanding how our participants' vulnerability might position them vis-à-vis the research and us as researchers. In fact, true ethics requires us to constantly ask ourselves and our participants if we are proceeding in an ethical way, regardless of many complex factors, including our career-oriented motivations.

Below we present two case studies. The first case problematizes the ethics of conducting research with individuals that may have cognitive challenges. The second case, about a community-based study with a vulnerable population living with HIV, elucidates ethical matters of using innovative dissemination techniques. A discussion of the issues raised by these cases follows. The chapter concludes with advice for students.

CASE STUDY #1: QUESTIONING COGNITIVE CHALLENGE AS AN ETHICAL BARRIER

Over many years, I have conducted research with groups of people who may or may not have cognitive challenges—this is the case of older people who are living with the early stages of dementia or adults across the lifespan with chronic illness. In all cases, they have signed an assent or consent form with a proxy—however, important to me is that they can recognize that I am a researcher; they likely know me by name, but not always; they generally recall what the study is about; and they agree that they have some important things to tell me about their experience in relation to the research question. They are able to speak in full sentences and to carry on an interview with some structure— even if we need to take breaks or reschedule at times. Here, I am describing evidence of an interaction that has a dynamic flow to it, which is suitable for an interview overall; however, as is often required, measuring or assessing (essentially formally testing) a person's cognitive ability in advance of their participation in research and documenting a numeric level of cognitive "ability" has remained a key concern of ethics committees. This has been a well-published area comprising a critical barrier and sincere problem for conducting qualitative research. It was my experience and belief that people with cognitive challenges and/or living with chronic illness are experts of their own experience and should be listened to in the context of research. Engaging with different ethics committees over time, I have discovered that providing a formal numeric measurement of someone's cognitive ability can be seen as equivalent to promising ethical interactions.

This logic concerns me. The ability to assign a cognitive status through a numeric assessment does not necessarily reflect my ethical behaviour. In one case, I was required to prepare a 20-page ethics protocol to include numeric eligibility screens, since people below a certain number were not deemed appropriate for research and, at the same time, my potential behaviour was not the ethical issue. From personal and professional experience, I came to understand that stereotypes about cognition abounded, that ethics committees could act as gatekeepers to important research denying people access who may feel they have a story to tell, and worse, that somehow my being ethical was conflated with their appropriate competency assessment.

CASE STUDY #2: ETHICAL CONSIDERATIONS WHEN USING INNOVATIVE DISSEMINATION TECHNIQUES

This second case relates to a community-based study that sought to understand the caregiving support networks of a vulnerable population living with HIV/AIDS in Winnipeg and Regina, Canada. The study gathered and analyzed qualitative data from 31 participants. Study participants took photographs of people and things that supported them, as well as aspects of their daily lives. They were later interviewed in depth so they could describe what was in the photos and talk about their lives. Participants were assured of confidentiality in compliance with the granting agency requirements, and processes of maintaining confidentiality were approved by an ethics committee of the University of Manitoba. After data collection, study participants saw and then approved most of their photos for use. Each participant could remove photos that he or she did not want used in the analysis. The interviews were audio recorded and later transcribed verbatim.

A novel dissemination approach used in this study was the creation and performance of a readers' theatre based on the interview data. The use of theatre in its various forms as a way of disseminating research findings is captured in the notion of "staging data" (Rossiter et al. 2008) or "data as drama" (Donmoyer and Yennie-Donmoyer 1995), and it has been used successfully within the field of health research.

This case highlights two ethical challenges when conducting research with vulnerable populations, particularly when using innovative data collection and dissemination strategies. One central ethical assumption is that research participants not be identifiable; however, this can contradict the wishes of participants to openly vocalize their experience while being acknowledged for their involvement in the study. This was the case with a number of the participants in this community-based study. In this case, the challenge was handled by writing the readers' theatre script organized by the themes that emerged from the qualitative analysis, and using the actual words of participants as text; however, the quotes of each character in the script were a compendium of quotes from different study participants. Nonetheless, study participants that were interested took part in numerous readers' theatre performances.

The second challenge is to convince the research ethics board at the university that the innovative dissemination techniques are ethically sound. Particularly for the use of this innovative dissemination strategy, the research team communicated early on with the ethics board. While the data collection and initial data analysis was taking place, the research team had careful discussions with the board to explain and adjust the readers' theatre development to fulfill ethics board requirements. In addition, this meant that the board revised some of its earlier positions.

DISCUSSION

Not all ethics review committees are trained in conducting qualitative research in social science research, or in particular methods of qualitative research, or in your research topic. In the example of our case studies, we found the issues we have outlined to be barriers that, without our intervention, may have led to the studies not being conducted. It has been our experience, and that of our colleagues, that ethics committees can follow a standard list of concerns they are tasked to raise, which may not, however, apply to participants in our research, or they may pose false barriers for inclusion in valuable research. For example, the issue of cognition is itself problematic, but a highly relevant topic for research; how someone interacts with a researcher is not inherently "more risky" because of their level of cognition—it is likely more risky because of the stereotypes of the researcher about cognition, or views of cognition in society overall, that then result in ethical issues. To say it simply, the level of a participant's cognition cannot in itself be conflated to result in an "ethical issue." For example, there was a time that women were seen as too vulnerable and fragile to act as reliable research participants (and even more so, as researchers). Shouldn't ethics then be about the researcher and their behaviour towards and care of the participant throughout the study over time, regardless of what the protocol has agreed to, or what the participant's cognition level is? In addition, as shown in the second case study, the challenge of balancing anonymity and confidentiality with the desire of study participants for acknowledgement and recognition requires careful consideration. The onus is on researchers and ethics boards to consider flexible options to deal with these competing goals.

In conclusion, we would only be supporting barriers to knowledge on very relevant topics if we limited the kinds of people who are seen to be eligible as research participants without examining what we need to do, as researchers, to remain ethical throughout the research process. We would have mostly highly functioning and very competent people in all our studies, who likely represent the mainstream in multiple ways, and we would ignore the fruits of important challenges for improved knowledge acquisition. There is already a long history in research of leaving out less visible populations or misrepresenting people who are seen to be vulnerable. Social science research in general, and qualitative research in particular, have historically had the outstanding but not always easily achieved goal of allowing (and making room for) less visible and more vulnerable populations (Denzin and Lincoln 2005). This begins with an ethics protocol, certainly, but it continues on with ethical research practices and continuing practices and questions as we go.

Finally, Marzano (2016) speaks eloquently about the notion of "parrhesiastes," where speaking someone's truth is an unavoidable moral duty of communicating—and to fail is in itself unethical. We believe that as researchers we all have that need to *not fail* at representing our vulnerable populations in an ethical manner. You can surmise that simply getting through the writing of your ethics protocol, and winning the committee's approval to move forward with your research, has not yet begun the essential approach to ethics that we see as one of care, a process of dynamic engagement, interaction, and communication with your selected participants over time as you hope to tell their stories accurately and well.

ADVICE TO STUDENTS

- Be prepared to provide an account for the committee of the potential ethical issues as you see them for your work, beyond what is required in the ethics protocol, with the potential of educating the committee.

- Decide to have a member of your participant community share in advance with you any ethical issues they perceive in your study, before you submit the ethics protocol. Document this process for the committee.

- Decide to have an advisory committee as part of your ongoing study, where members of the selected community participate in working with you to ensure that if and as ethical concerns might emerge, they can mediate or communicate concerns of their community with you.

- Be prepared to reflect, in writing in your protocol as well as verbally to your participants, on your position as a researcher as one who engages in ongoing dialogue with your selected community.

- Engage in conversations with ethics committee chairs before submitting a protocol, in order to discuss potential challenges, particularly when working with novel techniques and vulnerable populations.

- Keep in mind that as researchers (even you, as a student researcher), we have a role in helping to educate ethics committees.

CRAFTING QUALITATIVE RESEARCH EXERCISES

1. Write a fictional letter to a research ethics board where you explain why you will have study participants involved in the dissemination of the findings and how you will deal with their confidentiality.

2. Choose a data collection and/or dissemination process and identify three main potential ethical challenges they may pose and explain how you would deal with these challenges.

3. Find a person who sees themself as belonging to a vulnerable group for any reason and has never engaged in research. Ask them what they think would be risky about participating in research. Document three main issues. How might you resolve those as a researcher?

4. Imagine that you were a research participant on a very personal topic, and you later found out that someone recognized you in an academic paper or conference presentation. Explore your reaction and how you might handle this situation.

NOTE

1. By using the word *interviewing*, we are defining our sample as active participants (not subjects) who are providing the researcher with invaluable information they remain experts in—as opposed to the more traditional view of researchers being in a powerful position vis-à-vis the research question and the subject.

REFERENCES

Crenshaw, Kimberle. 1993. "Mapping the Margins: Intersectionality, Identity Politics, and Violence against Women of Color." *Stanford Law Review* 43 (6): 1241–98.

Denzin, Norman K., and Yvonna S. Lincoln. 2005. *The Sage Handbook of Qualitative Research*. 3rd ed. Thousand Oaks, CA: Sage.

Donmoyer, Robert, and June Yennie-Donmoyer. 1995. "Reader's Theatre as Data Display Strategy: Reflections on the Use of Readers' Theatre as a Mode of Qualitative Data Display." *Qualitative Inquiry* 1 (4): 402–28.

Gilligan, Carol. 1982. *In a Different Voice: Psychological Theory and Women's Development*. Cambridge, MA: Harvard University Press.

Marzano, Marco. 2016. "Uncomfortable Truths, Ethics, and Qualitative Research: Escaping the Dominance of Informed Consent." In *The Ethics Rupture: Exploring Alternatives to Formal Research Ethics Review*, edited by Will C. van den Hoonaard and Ann Hamilton, 106–18. Toronto: University of Toronto Press.

Moody, Harry R., and Jennifer R. Sasser. 2012. *Aging: Concepts and Controversies*. Thousand Oaks, CA: Sage.

Rossiter, Kate, Pia Kontos, Angela Colantonio, Julie Gilbert, Julia Gray, and Michelle Keightley. 2008. "Staging Data: Theatre as a Tool for Analysis and Knowledge Transfer in Health Research." *Social Science and Medicine* 66 (1): 130–46.

Observing Teens: Negotiating Power and Opportunity During Field Research

Katherine Irwin

On the topic of choosing field research settings, Lofland et al. (2006, 9) advocate for "starting where you are"—a productive guide for many new ethnographers. Few who embrace this mantra, however, would think to study where they *were* many years ago; thus, observing teenagers falls well outside of the opportunistic research tradition (Riemer 1977). Ethnographies of teenagers, therefore, are intrusive and force adults to assert themselves into the lives of those with different daily routines, institutional constraints, and culture.

For social justice–oriented researchers (Thomas 1993; Weis and Fine 2001), studying adolescents presents challenges beyond a cultural disconnect. Age is arguably a key vector of oppression working alongside other inequalities. Teens lack autonomy, power, and full citizenship rights. Moreover, parents and adults have considerable control over adolescents, a reality that translates into the possibility that adults, including researchers, can coerce and harm young people (see Best 2007; Raby 2007). When adults who possess power in the form of racial, ethnic, citizenship, and class privileges study youth who lack these advantages, the concerns about coercion and harm become paramount.

In this chapter, I explore the topic of ethics during ethnographic research with teens. Understanding that adults have the power to limit opportunities available to young people and to coerce teens to reveal damaging and hurtful information, I turned to social justice research models, which are specifically designed to grant greater power to youth. Below, I briefly explore the social justice tradition of research with teens and then explain why I could not fully emulate this tradition. Instead, I crafted particular strategies to avoid exploitation and harm during research, and I explain how I used my status as a university-based researcher to funnel resources for and opportunities to teens.

SOCIAL JUSTICE RESEARCH WITH TEENS

Ethnographers have attempted to mitigate harms in research with teens in a number of ways. Some engage in emancipatory research (Weis and Fine 2001), defined as projects that attempt to "interrupt/dismantle oppression" and "sustain justice in the face of ongoing political assaults" (Fine 2006, 83–84). On this score, many ethnographers facilitate adolescents' political action (Clay 2012; Ginwright, Noguera, and Cammarota 2006). Having adolescents gather in safe spaces to discuss the nuances of oppression and injustice that pertain to their lives is also an approach to sidestep harm (Heath and McLaughlin 1993; Lopez and Lechuga 2007; Weis and Fine 2001). Others employ expressive outlets in which teens compose art, poetry, stories, music, dance, or plays to express the realities that teens like themselves confront (Fine et al. 2004; Winn 2011).

I was particularly concerned about power imbalances and harm to study participants when I embarked on an ethnographic exploration of youth violence in Hawaii. Most teens I met while planning the project were working class, born and raised in Hawaii, and of Native Hawaiian, Samoan, Tongan, or mixed Asian and Pacific Islander descent. In contrast, I am a white, middle-aged, middle-class woman from California. *Mainland haloe* (white person from the continental United States) is what most teens called me. The history of takings (e.g., land and sovereignty) and suppression of language, spiritual-ity, and cultural traditions at the hands of American haloes are facts organizing relations between and among people in present-day Hawaii.

At the outset, I had deep, historic chasms to cross. I would have welcomed the chance to engage in social justice research, but there were challenges to enacting this brand of ethnography. My project was funded by an agency under the US Department of Health and Human Services umbrella and stemmed from a partnership between local high schools, community leaders, and a number of university researchers. All par-ties, including high school principals who closely monitored research activities in their schools (see Punch 1986), rigorously reviewed the study design. Engaging in collective action with teens would not have been accepted; thus, my research proposal emerged as more of a critical realist than a social justice project (see Denzin and Lincoln 2011 for a description of these traditions).

While the research was not originally justice oriented, during the course of the project I found ways to incorporate some empowerment and expressive opportunities for teens. Below, I describe a few steps that I took.

BEING OF USE: BUILDING OPPORTUNITY STRUCTURES IN SCHOOLS

I grew up with the understanding that all sociological research should "be of use"—a sentiment akin to Becker's (1967) thesis regarding "Whose Side Are We On?" While embarking on observations—in all the sneaky and semi-covert ways that this can un-fold—I sensed that I could be on adolescents' "side," becoming more than a silent char-acter skulking around the corners of schools. While the original research design was somewhat circumscribed, there were many grant and university resources that could be mobilized for adolescents.

To be of use meant that I was a motivated force in the scene who could ask for funds and personnel assistance when opportunities emerged. Luckily, the original grant application included a promise to build violence prevention initiatives, so funneling resources to create programs for teens was not a hard sell. But the grant was not the only resource at play. The schools, I quickly learned, were poor in terms of funding, but rich with creative staff wanting to expand opportunities for teens. Also, my relationships with students, staff, and administrators at my university could be mobilized to create dynamic programs for adolescents. The trick was to channel resources and buttress the existing strengths within high schools.

As an example of how to marshal academic resources to assist teens, within the first year of the study my colleagues and I met with counsellors at one high school who were fairly bursting with ideas about building teen-centred projects. After a few conversations, we decided to create two support groups—one for girls and one for boys. The counselling groups, which were eventually named the "lunch-bunch," were designed as supportive places for youth to express themselves without judgment, something like Lopez and Lechuga's (2007) work in that we saw these groups as "safe spaces."

Graduate and undergraduate students volunteered to assist with this project, and collectively we added other components to the lunch-bunch program, including camping excursions, therapeutic adventure activities, field trips to nearby universities and colleges, and visits from members of local organizations to discuss leadership opportunities in the community. In addition, each year the teens created public service announcement videos (PSAs); they chose the PSA topics and were the screenwriters, actors, videographers, and editors for each PSA. The students' PSAs were shown at the annual family movie night hosted by the high school.

TEEN ASSENT AND PARENT CONSENT

Building opportunities for teens had ethical downsides. My program provision work increased the probability that teens would forget about my research. More troubling was the possibility that some teens might have seen me as a counsellor rather than a researcher who rushed home after a day in the field to write up notes. Each semester, I explained that I was conducting a study of youth violence, and that I wanted to observe and write notes about teens. I described the purpose of my study: to understand what fighting means to adolescents and learn what teens themselves, rather than adults, think are the greatest challenges and assets in their lives. Their participation in the study, I informed them, was voluntary. In my discussions I also reinforced the idea that teenagers have the right to privacy, which means that they did not have to be a part of the study. I also noted that they were always welcome to join the lunch-bunch activities regardless of whether or not they wanted to be in my study.

Additionally, I announced that if a student wanted to take part in the study, I would need their written assent. In accordance with University of Hawaii human studies protocols, I let them know that I would also need their parents' written consent. While parental consent undermined teens' autonomy, I was legally bound by institutional review board (IRB) restrictions, as are all researchers studying those under the age of 18. Parental consent, therefore, is a non-negotiable aspect of research with teens.

Most lunch-bunch teens did not return parental consent forms, which did not bother me in the slightest. The adult-youth power structure often leaves teens feeling that they cannot say no to adults. Considering this fact, I was concerned that my role as a lunch-bunch organizer might make some students feel obligated to help me. Not returning consent forms, I thought, was an easy way for students to opt out of the study without having to overtly say no to me.

Conversely, I began to think that any student who returned a parental consent form was authentically interested in participation. Many teens in the study lived chaotic lives. A few adolescents were homeless, others had experienced multiple foster home placements, and some lived in one- or two-bedroom dwellings with more than 10 family members. When a teen returned a parental consent form, therefore, I felt that a small miracle had occurred.

Despite my efforts to inform individuals about my research, teens were likely to forget about the observation study. Adolescents' lives transformed quickly, and countless upheavals could occur among the lunch-bunch teens within a single school year. Parental incarceration, drug addiction, running away, family violence, dating violence, death of a sibling or parent, and pregnancy were just a few of the life-changing events that teens might not want researchers to write about, regardless of any paperwork they and their parents had signed previously. The decision to write or not to write about disruptions in these teens' lives haunted me.

After one girl in the study discussed a particularly traumatic event during a lunch-bunch gathering, I made a decision. I would not include any upsetting personal information that teens shared during the lunch-bunch sessions in my publications. I did not want to undermine their trust by writing up the confessions they shared in the lunch-bunch for publication, no matter how rich and deeply moving their stories might have been. I hoped—indeed, I imagined—that lunch-bunch adolescents would read my work one day. How would they feel, I wondered, if they read my summary of their heart-wrenching disclosures made during the lunch-bunch in a publication?

INTERVIEWS AS CONSENT TO PUBLISH

The ethical solution to the problem of difficult confessions made in the field was to schedule formal interviews with the teens, which also required parental consent and teen assent. While adolescents may have forgotten that they were being observed during lunch-bunch activities, talking with me in front of a recorder indicated that formal research was taking place. Before turning on the recorder, I announced my interest in publishing quotes and stories from interviews, and let them know that they did not have to answer any questions that made them feel uncomfortable. I gave them my contact information and encouraged them to get in touch with me if they became concerned about what they shared during the interview. If they wanted, I could delete all or part of their recording, although I could not make changes if one of my written pieces was in press.

Only after taking the above-mentioned precautions did I feel at ease about publishing teens' highly sensitive information. Importantly, many students chose privacy, and some stories will never make it to the pages of my work. Other teens, however, offered difficult personal narratives about family violence, trauma, and devastating losses, with a few announcing that they wanted others to know their story. Youth's lives, one girl said, are important for others to understand.

A core principle underscoring social justice methods with teens is to give young people control during the research process. For me, granting power to adolescents during research meant giving up my chance to offer unmitigated portraits of the many tragedies that unfold for teens. Instead, I was happy to allow teens the choice of which stories they trusted me enough to tell, and which they wanted to keep hidden.

CONCLUSION

I have highlighted some fieldwork dilemmas with teens and noted ways to weave opportunities, structural support systems, and autonomy into a research project. My experiences illustrate that, in cases when researchers have not designed emancipatory projects at the outset, they may have a variety of resources available during the study. We can mobilize our professional networks, contact with undergraduate and graduate students, and college and university seed funds, to name a few assets. Tapping into these resources means that researchers can do more than "take" information from a setting; we can be of use by leaving behind opportunities and support infrastructures, not the least of which is granting choices to young people regarding what they want others to know about their lives.

CRAFTING QUALITATIVE RESEARCH EXERCISES

1. You have the chance to be awarded $5,000 from your college to conduct a one-year qualitative study with high school students in a nearby school. To receive the funds, however, you have to describe the goal of your research and how your work will benefit the high school students. Thinking about this project, discuss whether $5,000 would be enough to accomplish what you hope to achieve. List other resources around you that you could utilize to benefit the teens in your research.

2.   While conducting an observation study of racial exclusion at a nearby high school, you overhear a conversation between two teens in which they use racial slurs to describe other students. The students you overhear have not consented to be in your study. First, discuss some of the ethical dilemmas inherent in using this information in your research. Conversely, discuss some of the ethical dilemmas you might face if you ignore what you overheard.

3.   Imagine that a group of researchers wants to conduct a study of your research methods class. These researchers are outsiders to your school and they are extremely wealthy, older than you, and have considerable political power in the community. List some of the potential harms that may come to you and others if this group is granted permission to observe and take notes about you and your classmates. Will you grant them permission to observe your classroom? Why or why not?

4.   You have just finished a qualitative research project focusing on high school students' experiences with organized sports. One of the teens in your study was eloquent and, as a result, you used this boy's quotes extensively in your final paper. The day before your paper is due, he informs you that he wants you to delete all of the information that he shared with you. Discuss how you will handle this situation. List some of your ethical obligations to honour this student's request.

REFERENCES

Becker, Howard. 1967. "Whose Side Are We On?" *Social Problems* 14 (3): 239–47.

Best, Amy, ed. 2007. *Representing Youth: Methodological Issues in Critical Youth Studies.* New York: New York University Press.

Clay, Andreana. 2012. *The Hip-Hop Generation Fights Back: Youth Activism, and Post-Civil Rights Politics.* New York: New York University Press.

Denzin, Norman K., and Yvonna S. Lincoln. 2011. *The Sage Handbook of Qualitative Research.* 4th ed. Thousand Oaks, CA: Sage.

Fine, Michelle. 2006. "Bearing Witness: Methods for Researching Oppression and Resistance—A Textbook for Critical Research." *Social Justice Research* 19 (1): 83–108.

Fine, Michelle, Rosemary Roberts, and Maria Torre, with Janice Bloom, April Burns, Lori Chajet, Monique Guishard, and Yasser Payne. 2004. *Echoes of Brown: Youth Documenting and Performing the Legacy of Brown v. Board of Education.* New York: Teachers College Press.

Ginwright, Shawn, Pedro Noguera, and Julio Cammarota, eds. 2006. *Beyond Resistance! Youth Activism and Community Change.* New York: Routledge.

Heath, Shirley Brice, and Milbrey W. McLaughlin, eds. 1993. *Identity and Inner-City Youth: Beyond Ethnicity and Gender.* New York: Teachers College Press.

Lofland, John, David Snow, Leon Anderson, and Lyn Lofland. 2006. *Analyzing Social Settings: A Guide to Qualitative Observation and Analysis.* Belmont, CA: Wadsworth.

Lopez, Nancy, and Chalane E. Lechuga. 2007. "They Are Like a Friend: Othermothers Creating Empowering, School-Based Community Living Rooms in Latina and Latino Middle Schools." In *Urban Girls Revisited: Building Strengths*, edited by Bonnie J. Ross Leadbeater and Niobe Way, 97–120. New York: New York University Press.

Punch, Maurice. 1986. *The Politics and Ethics of Fieldwork.* Newbury Park, CA: Sage.

Raby, Rebecca. 2007. "Across a Great Gulf? Conducting Research with Adolescents." In *Representing Youth: Methodological Issues in Critical Youth Studies*, edited by Amy L. Best, 39–59. New York: New York University Press.

Riemer, Jeffrey. W. 1977. "Varieties of Opportunistic Research." *Urban Life* 5 (4): 467–77.

Thomas, Jim. 1993. *Doing Critical Ethnography.* Newbury Park, CA: Sage.

Weis, Lois, and Michelle Fine, eds. 2001. *Working Method: Research and Social Justice.* New York: Routledge.

Winn, Maisha T. 2011. *Girl Time: Literacy, Justice, and the School-to-Prison Pipeline.* New York: Teachers College Press.

7 Doing Research Undercover: Interviewing Protesters[1]

Gül Çalışkan

Being stressed or scared does not help researchers to make good ethical decisions. [The ethical responsibility] is, therefore, an obligation that researchers have, not just to other people, but also to themselves.
  —Stephen Webster, Jane Lewis, and Ashley Brown, "Ethical Considerations in Qualitative Research"

Although it was unknown to most of the world, Gezi Park—the epicentre of Turkey's June 2013 protests—rapidly emerged as a historic site for dissent (Eşkinat 2013). The Gezi events of that year marked a threshold for resistance, social justice, contested citizenship, and activism. The movement created its own vibrant set of actors, a repertoire of dramatic political action, and a new social dynamic that challenged the relevance of previous political norms (Göle 2013).

At the time of preparing my research and ethics proposals in the spring of 2014, the impact of the protests and the government's reactions to them were still fresh. Despite my extensive experience with qualitative research, I felt rather like a novice because I had not handled "above-minimal-risk" research before. For the first time, I felt the need to be cautious about my participants' well-being—and my own.

In the research project, I examined the symbols and humour used in the Gezi protest events, trying to discern their significance as expressions of popular culture and as acts of citizenship. Through a process of narrative analysis, I explored the theoretical and practical dimensions of these expressions (Çalışkan 2014).

DOING UNDERCOVER RESEARCH

When I conducted fieldwork in Turkey, the political climate created by the protests was fresh, the collective memory of the events was still in the making, and the government's surveillance measures were high. Even before I arrived in the field, I knew that these protests had been on such a scale that millions of people had either participated or closely followed the events. Therefore, talking about these events with anyone I spoke with, even casually, would be almost unavoidable. The very magnitude of the events, however, caused the government serious concern and placed the participants under suspicion.

During the summer of 2014, I conducted over 30 interviews with individuals who had played active roles in the Gezi events, either in Ankara or Istanbul. This chapter is about the ethical challenges I faced, and how I negotiated the risks involved at different stages of the research: preparing for my visit, entering the field, making contacts, gaining access, developing rapport, doing interviews, leaving the field, and communicating the results. The project posed greater than minimal risk because there was a danger that the police could confiscate my interview data. I refer to my experience as "doing undercover research" because it was important to maintain the utmost ethical transparency while conducting the interviews in a way that kept the participants invisible to surveillance mechanisms. This negotiation between ethical transparency and a controlled public environment made the experience unique.

THE FORESEEABLE RISKS AND THE MAGNITUDE OF HARM

Any research is a step into the unknown. Doing research can bring social, behavioural, psychological, physical, or economic harm to the participants and others, including the researcher. Chapter 10 of the *Tri-Council Policy Statement* (Interagency Secretariat 2010) is a major source in acknowledging the dynamics of qualitative research. Sometimes, when researchers think about risk, they reflect on the emotional harm it will bring to participants. In my research, there *was* high risk, but the risk was not emotional upset: neither the topic nor the interview questions would cause the participants stress. After all, I was collecting the narratives of the protesters as they experienced the events. These people were passionate about their activism and their experiences during the event— they *wanted* to talk about them. Where, then, did the risk lie?

Assessing how dangerous it was for participants to talk to me was challenging because I had no experience conducting high-risk research. Also, this topic is an emerging area of research, so even though there had been an increase in similar studies, there were few directly relevant publications on methodologies for such research. In any case, I started by assuming that there were two kinds of harm to avoid: personal harm to the participants and myself, and harm to the interests of social activists, minority groups, and individual protesters—and therefore to the future of activism in Turkey. Such dangers might be realized if my presence as a researcher became visible; therefore, I took many precautions. After all, I was acting without the blessing of any research council in Turkey. The Turkish authorities might well consider me an outlaw. This difficulty is related to the fact that conducting qualitative research has never been limited to national boundaries. Research that is global and multinational in scope has been increasing.

I prepared for risks that could develop in worst-case scenarios, such as the emergence of another major wave of protests while I was in the field, or my data being confiscated.

I had to consider if these risks were too high to justify my research project. The potential benefits, I concluded, depended on limiting the possibility of harm in every way possible.

GETTING READY FOR THE FIELD

When I considered the project's ethical acceptability, the following points seemed salient. The population that would participate in this research was vulnerable because of the political context. As a researcher, I was also personally vulnerable to interrogation. To limit risk, I decided that if widespread protests re-emerged, I would not participate in public protests, observe the public protests actively, and, most importantly, conduct interviews with active protesters. I made these choices even before I left, in spite of the fact that the political climate in 2014 was quiet and the possibility of an upsurge in protests unlikely.

As I prepared to enter the field, I had two strong allies. My university's research ethics board (REB) was a solid support. I trusted their experience in developing measures to deal with any problems that might emerge. The second source of support was the university's IT staff, who helped me with all the necessary arrangements to protect sensitive data. My allies helped me plan ways to minimize risk. Their experience and sage advice sensitized me to the issues and enabled me to develop protective measures.

In considering the advice from my various supporters, I generated the following general safety rules for my fieldwork:

- Conduct interviews in public places.
- Delete existing interview data in the digital recorder in case of, for example, police raids.
- Do not become a regular visitor in subjects' circles.
- Do not recontact individuals interviewed.
- Do not provide participants with a personal email address, but only with a university address.
- Use an untraceable, pay-as-you-go cellphone.
- Explain the research to the participants orally.
- Take oral rather than written consent.
- Inform your family about whereabouts at all times.

If you are a student, an additional rule is that your supervisor is privy to all meetings and decisions concerning fieldwork. You should be in constant contact with your supervisor over the entire duration. Let them know, for example, when you enter or leave a site.

Before I wrote the REB application, I attended a workshop on data security and confidentiality given by the IT staff. I met with the REB chair to brainstorm how to construct the REB application, then with the director of the IT centre for an initial discussion. I received substantial feedback on my REB application, which I discussed with the chair. Then, to carry out the measures recommended, I worked with the IT centre and research office to get the equipment necessary to secure my data during interviews and when transmitting the files.

The aim was to eliminate any possibility of disclosing private information, regardless of the situation. I developed ways to exclude all identifiers throughout the whole process—from contacting potential participants, to conducting interviews, to transmitting information, to writing up the research.

CONDUCTING THE FIELDWORK

As mentioned, I developed ways to exclude identifiers. While preparing for the research, I was aware of many activist groups that had formed during or since the protest. The contact information for these people was public; many had a digital presence. Some of these (now) public individuals and groups were my initial contacts. When I arrived in the field, I contacted them by phone, explained my research, and asked if they were interested in participating.

In all recruiting activity, I preferred oral communication. When email was used, I was brief and generic, simply suggesting a brief meeting or phone conversation to explain the research. I used an untraceable phone for all research-related calls. I did not give anyone any other phone numbers, such as those of my parents, or even the phone number of the residence where I was staying. To achieve anonymity, I handled the consent processes orally and did not carry documents that could identify participants as research contacts.

Using numbers and pseudonyms protects the identity of participants. I assigned a number to each participant and used it for data, transcriptions, analysis, and field notes. Once I conducted an interview, I destroyed any scrap of paper that could identify the person I had interviewed. While drafting the research results, pseudonyms protected participants' confidentiality while describing their experiences and insights. I ensured that it would not be possible to track down who they were. Participants could identify themselves, but other readers could not identify them. Also, if a participant decided mid-interview that they no longer wished to participate and wanted their data pulled from the project, this would easily be done. I would be able to identify all of their material by the numbers and pseudonyms assigned to their interview recordings.

To conduct the interviews, I chose public places; however, due to potential surveillance, the most public areas were not necessarily safe places. For instance, many public cafés frequented by tourists, such as the big Starbucks at Taksim Square, were being watched. Sometimes it was the activist who was being followed. Therefore, I chose interview locations that were public enough that I could remain anonymous, yet intimate enough that the participant would feel safe. A café, restaurant, or a bookstore with regulars was the participants' choice most of the time. In a few cases, the participants were ordinary citizens who did not have any connection to an activist group or civil organization. Initially, I did not plan to have meetings in homes, but deemed it to be safe in particular cases.

After the fieldwork was done, a safe exit from the field and return trip home were also important. To ensure safety, I took several measures. The laptop I carried during the research period was encrypted, and I used an electronic folder with a secure password. The electronic files were stored in encrypted electronic devices. I used a digital recorder for interviews. The interviews were downloaded to a secure university domain on the same day they occurred, then erased from the recorder. I avoided taking extensive handwritten notes, and destroyed any such notes once I had saved my general field notes in a secure file. I arranged for my connection to the university server to be removed before I left the research site. I did not cross borders with any sensitive data or even access to such data.

HOW TO APPROACH SAFETY PLANS

This experience of preparing for sensitive research confirmed for me, once again, that a researcher can never anticipate everything that will happen. I appreciated how important it is to be flexible while following ethics measures. There were situations in which I needed to be creative—I needed to adjust some rules to the situation. Other rules were no help; they were needless. There were situations that I did not anticipate, where I had no measure in place. I even made mistakes.

Here is an example of how the rules changed or emerged as I went along. One day, after I had already conducted interviews with two activists, I was visiting a house that fellow anarchists were squatting in for a third interview. Suddenly, there was a police raid on the house. I panicked: I quickly deleted the interviews, took out the batteries, and hid the recorder under a pile of wood. But the police, it seems, had only come to tell the group about complaints received from neighbours. They checked our IDs and left. I realized that I should have met the activists in a place outside the group's turf—somewhere that was not a site of their activism. The biggest lesson I learned was not to visit places frequented by certain activist groups. But then, this is against the nature of qualitative research, where we are accustomed to following leads; we observe events, activities, projects. In the end, the political climate was quiet when I was in Turkey. Although it turned out that I was, perhaps, over-cautious, I would be just as vigilant if I were to do this research again.

WHITE NOISE: AN UNEXPECTED SHIELD FOR THE RESEARCH

Being heard and accounted for in their activism for social justice was the main reason these people agreed to give me an interview. Their involvement in the resistance was also the very reason I had to protect them from any possible harm that talking to me could cause. It was my ethical responsibility to make their stories and perspectives known, while, at the same time, protecting both them and myself from any adverse consequences. Anonymity and confidentiality were essential.

The 2013 uprising was still on the minds of my participants. These events were talked about widely and openly. I had many casual conversations that were at least partially helpful for building my contextual analysis. Even though surveillance levels were high, the social change efforts remained prominent a year after the protests. The activists were very much involved in creating and mobilizing their social change and social justice projects. Activist groups were debating and responding to the question of "what now?"—how to move forward from here. While carrying the momentum of their efforts into the immediate future, many participants believed that the passing of time would reveal the long-term impact of events in the summer of 2013. Several dozen new publications documented the protest events, which confirmed that the uprising was taking its due place in the historical record. Moreover, these accounts were still being published. A very active thinking process was going on.

The strong presence of the protest events in people's lives and in the media acted as a kind of shield for my research effort. The high levels of concern over Gezi by both the public and the government provided a white-noise cover for my research, which actually helped me to avoid the very risks I had anticipated.

CRAFTING QUALITATIVE RESEARCH EXERCISES

1. Thinking about the nature of qualitative research and research ethics review, study chapter 10 of the *Tri-Council Policy Statement*. What are the three most important lessons you can take from it? What are the two aspects that are not clear to you? What is one challenging question you think chapter 10 does not address in relation to the nature of qualitative research?

2. Generate and reflect on a research topic that would involve "above-minimal risk." Explain why you would consider it above-minimal-risk research. What safety plan would you come up with for this research?

3. In relation to the research topic you came up with in question 2, go over each general safety rule suggested here to see if it applies to the fieldwork your

proposed research requires. Discuss why or why not. Are there any safety rules that are not included but would be relevant for this particular research?

4. If you were conducting the research you came up with in question 2, what would be the difficulties in navigating between anonymity, confidentiality, and ethical transparency?

NOTE

1. This paper is dedicated to Turkey's Academics for Peace.

REFERENCES

Çalışkan, Gül. 2014. "Symbols and Humor as Works of Justice and Citizenship in the Gezi Protests of Istanbul." *Global and International Studies Initiative.* http://wp.stu.ca/gisi/2014/03/30/symbols-and-humor-as-works-of-justice-and-citizenship-in-the-gezi-protests-of-instanbul/.

Eşkinat, Doğan. 2013. "Gezi Park: Negotiating a New Left Identity." *Insight Turkey* 15 (3): 45–49.

Göle, Nilüfer. 2013. "Protests and Politics: Turkey after the Gezi Park." *Insight Turkey* 15 (3): 7–14.

Interagency Secretariat on Research Ethics, Canada. 2010. *Tri-Council Policy Statement: Ethical Conduct for Research Involving Humans.* Ottawa: Government of Canada.

Webster, Stephen, Jane Lewis, and Ashley Brown. 2014. "Ethical Considerations in Qualitative Research." In *Qualitative Research Practice: A Guide for Social Science Students and Researchers*, 2nd ed., edited by Jane Ritchie, Jane Lewis, and Carol Nicholls, 77–110. Los Angeles: Sage.

8 Social Regulation and Ethics in Research

Will van den Hoonaard

The social regulation of ethics in research continues to have a remarkable, albeit negative, impact on sociological and ethnographic research. This regulation can create imaginary ethical issues; often, too, it ignores ethical issues that are central to research in sociology and ethnography. Students find themselves standing in this tide of ethics regulation, with water pulling them this way, that way. The whole process can be quite perplexing, especially for those who are stepping into the ethics tide for the first time. My chapter explores the origins of these perplexities, and outlines a number of key issues that attend to sociological and ethnographic research.[1] I see several opportunities, in the face of these perplexities, for students and other researchers to gain a more profound understanding of conducting sociological and ethnographic research.

THE GENEALOGY OF THE SOCIAL REGULATION OF ETHICS

It is no surprise that the very genealogy of the social regulation of ethics in research would cause bewilderment among social scientists. Premised on misfired experiments in psychology and biology, the review of ethics in research had a singular biomedical angle. What followed from that perspective was the sole reliance on deductive or hypothesis-driven research, and the use of individually signed consent forms. No less significant was the drive to institutionalize mandated research ethics review. Mission creep began to occupy areas of research thought to be impervious to social regulation, such as conversations with research participants, unobtrusive observations in the field, or linguists inquiring about anyone's unusual accents. Receiving research grants is now conditional on ethics approval from a formally recognized body (such as research ethics boards). Even research journals now insist on proof that the research has "gone through ethics." As if this process of ethics colonization has not gone far enough, many researchers in the social sciences now take the perspective of their "colonizers" and are "othering" their own research, and adopt the same perspective towards their own research as those who privilege the biomedical angle on research. Other researchers who might disagree with formal research ethics review are trying to find ways around the social regulation of ethics in research. As one can see, this whole context makes it problematic for those coming into the field to acquire a frank and sincere appreciation of ethics while conducting research. It is not a climate that nurtures reflection—a necessary component of doing ethical research.

When one reads the 467 paragraphs in Canada's ethics codes, the *Tri-Council Policy Statement: Ethical Conduct for Research Involving Humans* (CIHR et al. 2014), only 10 refer to research paradigms outside the biomedical framework. Significantly, three out of four paragraphs that warn researchers of potential dangers are related to "naturalistic observations." Such explicit warnings characterize social science inquiry as a special source of ethical worry.

The colonization of research ethics by the biomedical paradigm and the diminishment of ethical issues that social scientists face have led to the homogenization of research methods, and the pauperization of social research itself. Rather than availing themselves of the rich diversity of qualitative methods, researchers now typically limit their choice to one or two research strategies, i.e., the ones that resonate the most in the minds of members of ethics committees, such as the interview method. Moreover, arraigned against a wide tapestry of research topics, the social regulation of ethics encourages safe, non-controversial, and antiseptic topics—a pauperization of topics in research. We also find a decline of covert research, the virtual collapse of participant observation, and a decline in the study of subcultures. All of this has led to making social research bland, and a reluctance to produce anything in an unflattering light. Many opt for doing library research to avoid review by ethics committees.

KEY ISSUES IN SOCIOLOGICAL AND ETHNOGRAPHIC RESEARCH

The three guiding principles of ethics codes—respect for persons, concern for human welfare, and justice—already point to a landscape foreign to qualitative researchers. "Respect for persons" is a broad principle which, for the most part, is undone by ethics codes highlighting the fragility and vulnerability of research participants. For example, if you were to work with me as a research participant, some ethics committees will require you to ask the permission of one of my adult children before interviewing me—someone who is over 70 years of age.

"The concern for human welfare" is another general approach that can lead social researchers in diverse directions. Does that mean that our research should be mainly policy-oriented research so as to improve human welfare? Once you step outside the biomedical framework, it is difficult to put a finger on this ethical principle. This concern foreshadows worries about the vulnerabilities of research participants. Taking a human-centred approach, one can see that describing someone as vulnerable is potentially an insult. It is a deep disparagement of the human condition to view humans as vulnerable.

Moreover, the concepts that ethics committees work with are quite expansive in that regard: it does not take long to assign vulnerability to many people who otherwise do not see themselves as vulnerable or at risk. It is common for ethics committees to invent the perspective of research participants.

"The concern for justice" is not what many qualitative researchers think it is. In the original medical research context, this concern revolves around a methodological position that no one is potentially left out of the research. If everyone is to benefit from gene therapy (to take one example), it is important that no one be excluded from the research. Medical researchers must include all relevant populations. It would be unjust to exclude them from the research: the concern is primarily one of proper sampling.

It is not only these three principles that make qualitative research an exceptional and troublesome category of research. The vigorous growth of the ethics regime has led to the shrinking of conventional qualitative research into smaller niches of social research. Qualitative research encompasses many methodological approaches such as participant observation, social action research, interviews, life histories, visual sociology, and so on. The existence of many varieties of qualitative research makes it difficult to assert what the defining core of qualitative research is. The interdisciplinary adoption of qualitative research exacerbates a worrisome trend that opens qualitative research to divergent interpretations with the inevitable adoption of the biomedical ethics regime. No one is suggesting that divergent interpretations are per se the problem, but if those interpretations do not cohere around a common stock of knowledge of the historical roots of qualitative research, qualitative researchers open themselves up to foreign incursions of their own terrain. The contemporary emergence of neo-positivism, even under the guise of "mixed" methods, for example, constitutes a major distraction for qualitative researchers. The current insistence by universities and other research agencies on mobilizing "applied" knowledge leads to a particular, narrow approach where the definition of what constitutes a social problem is a deductive, not inductive, claim.

The ethics review of research is increasingly involving many more layers of regulatory engagement. This "vertical ethics" involves the research ethics board (REB), departmental committees, university research offices, and sometimes, too, the (Canadian) Interagency Panel on Research Ethics. Journals are entering this layered fray: articles involving research must demonstrate that the research was "ethical." Differences among all parts of the vertical ethics regime hamper the smooth flow of research and publication.

PREMISES

Inductive research remains a far cry from the way ethics committees view "normal" research. Application forms for introducing one's research to ethics committees imply a commitment to stating hypotheses, with the attendant review of the literature. The researcher needs to avoid giving the impression that he or she will be doing a detour through the "literature" while collecting data. In the end, members of ethics committees will be expecting a statement about "generalizability" of one's findings, while it is more common for qualitative researchers to be wanting to find "transferability" of concepts: how can one transfer a concept (such as "becoming an ex") in one setting to another setting?

Ethics committees count on researchers indirectly affirming the core values inherent in ethics codes. The need to use consent forms, to be signed by each research participant, expresses the value of individualism and individual autonomy. The need to collect research data pertaining to each individual makes it problematic for ethics committees to understand the collective aspects of qualitative research: researchers are seeking *patterns* of doing things and are simply not engaged in scoping out each individual's character and habits. In this connection, ethics committees put a lot of attention on the individual interview itself. Reliance on interviews as *the sole* method of research has become quite standard now.

Both anonymity and confidentiality remain the top concerns of ethics committees. While qualitative researchers and ethnographers attach value to these two concerns, they also realize that in some cases (such as when conducting research in small communities or settings) anonymity remains a difficult, nay impossible, goal to achieve: everyone in a village knows whom the researcher visited and talked with. Confidentiality seems easier to achieve, although my wife and I recall reading a study about how professors write in which we were able to easily name the research participant by reading quotes and expressions that we identified as belonging to that colleague. Interestingly, the researcher had switched the gender and discipline of the participant.

The extensive routinization of research ethics review has meant that terms that have frequently not been used in social science research are now commonly accepted. Such acceptance skews research in a medical direction. Terms like *autonomy, subject, protocol, confidentiality*, and *research risk* accentuate a foreign approach to social research. The term *protocol* is reserved for the use of a research measurement that is consistent and not subject to interpretation. Many social scientists see the contortion of their research approach to the medical model as unethical, but are not able to convince ethics committees of that fact.

Finally, we come across the notion of "data" as defined in ethics regimes. Social scientists are used to having a broader view of data than is customary in ethics review regimes. The former see data as part of the social interactions of research participants with others, including with the researcher themself. There are no "autonomous" data; humans are all interconnected. The latter offers a simplified view of what constitutes "human subjects" and "data" and does not see data in a holistic sense. This crucially different view of data constitutes a significant gap in the social regulation of research. Not unrelated is the issue of data retention. Qualitative researchers often retain their data over a long period. Researchers devote a particularly long time from the conception of their research, to the collection of data, to their publication. A time span of 15 years is not unusual. The mandate to destroy data before the analysis and writing have run their course is not ethical.

STRATEGIES

The first-time interaction between a researcher and an ethics committee might be unpredictable and uncertain. The one who wants to initiate the contact must show deference. One side might be frustrated and impatient, and show fear. They might end up experiencing shame when problems are found. The process of "going through ethics" has been the subject of anticipatory socialization. The system rewards deference and the researcher cannot afford to engage in even a quiet resistance; docility on the part of the researcher is desirable.

Some researchers, not satisfied with the status quo, will engage in performative language ("I believe in ethics") to lend strength to their application. Still others maintain rituals, such as making a supreme effort to avoid finding out who is on the ethics committee, while others plagiarize or copy successful applications. These rituals create a sense of certainty about a good outcome of their application to the ethics review committee. "These habits sustain secondary adjustments," especially prevalent when practices deviate from institutional regulations, but do not directly challenge staff or institutions. The main dictum that covers all applications is "don't give ethics committees cause to worry."

FADS/FETISHES

Like other bureaucratic routines, ethics regimes fall into habits that rise to be fads and then fetishes. They standardize application forms, and create checklists and the consent form. Some practices become fetishes: the demand for anonymity, confidentiality, and member-checking. An ethics pointillism becomes the watchword. In the end, the right to conduct research morphs into a privilege, provided that the researcher has passed ethics review. The phrase "trust but verify" embodies a suspicious attitude—hardly useful for a mutual development of appreciation of ethical guidelines.

WHAT ETHICS COMMITTEES CANNOT OR WILL NOT SEE

The biomedical paradigm misconstrues the character of qualitative research in several ways: (a) it is impossible to know in advance the extent and nature of the data to be collected; (b) qualitative researchers avoid having, as much as possible, any advance knowledge of a social setting, leaving review of the literature to a later stage of research; (c) qualitative researchers see signed consent forms as problematic because the relationship between the researcher and the research participant entails very different assumptions than in biomedical research; (d) there is no discrete stage of analysis because analysis takes place continuously from the beginning of data collection to the end; (e) the qualitative researcher does not "invent" the viewpoint of the "social actor," which implies an avoidance of pre-formulated questions and issues; and (f) given the close collaborative relationship between the researcher and the research participant in the social setting and that the researcher brings so much of themself into the research, qualitative researchers object to using the term *human subject*.

ETHICS FORMALISM VERSUS ETHICS REALISM

The reader can now infer that there are problems with each of "Ethics Greatest Little Hits": free and informed consent, confidentiality, anonymity, conflict of interest, no harm, preserving human dignity. Various settings undermine the notion that there is "free and informed" consent. People do not lead autonomous lives and therefore do make decisions with an eye on others in their lives. As humans we are always mindful of others who mean a lot to us. Confidentiality or anonymity, as already demonstrated, is sometimes impractical or impossible to maintain in qualitative research. Moreover, participatory action research sometimes disavows anonymity, while in other instances, research participants want their "voice" to be heard in any research. Ethics policies contextualize conflict of interest in terms of members of ethics committees making decisions about research applications that implicate them. What is missed is corporate sponsorship of research, and the researcher's underlying assumptions about the goals of the research. The biomedical paradigm highlights the concern that no harm should come to the research participant when he or she participates in research. For social researchers, this is a notoriously difficult notion given humans' web of interdependence. The research participant may not directly experience harm, but even by merely participating in research, can harm be telescoped to the whole social group? The exaggeration of harm is still an unresolved aspect of the work in ethics committees. Ethics policies have no secret lock on what human dignity entails. Their very assumptions about vulnerable people, such as the elderly or disabled, seem to deny these people the dignity that comes with being a human being. These policies hold no premise on how to treat people with dignity.

UNFORESEEN OPPORTUNITIES

Bioethics-based regimes are expanding across the world. Social science research is having to find smaller niches to conduct research according to its own precepts. A careful examination of ethics committees' application forms constrains the view of the larger, often more meaningful ethical issues in qualitative research. For now, it will be a challenge to find unforeseen opportunities in prevailing ethics regimes to mark out a meaningful ethics approach in qualitative research. It might be too much to ask social researchers to "burst the bubble" and step out of their customary knowledge to develop a relationship with ethics committees and, at the same time, gain a deeper understanding of the studied social world.

CRAFTING QUALITATIVE RESEARCH EXERCISES

1. Can you spot the difference when one speaks of *ethics* versus *ethical review?*

2. Are there times when conducting covert research is unethical?

3. You are promising anonymity to a research participant, but the participant wants their involvement in the research to be specifically recognized. What do you do?

4. Can you think of any research participants whom you can describe as indubitably vulnerable?

NOTE

1. I refer readers to my 2013 book, *Essentials of Thinking Ethically in Qualitative Research*, which I co-wrote with Deborah K. van den Hoonaard. Another volume, *The Seduction of Ethics* (2011), is mainly an ethnographic study of research ethics committees.

REFERENCES

Canadian Institutes of Health Research, Natural Sciences and Engineering Research Council of Canada, and Social Sciences and Humanities Research Council of Canada. 2014. *Tri-Council Policy Statement: Ethical Conduct for Research Involving Humans.* www.pre.ethics.gc.ca/pdf/eng/tcps2-2014/TCPS_2_FINAL_Web.pdf.

van den Hoonaard, Will C. 2011. *The Seduction of Ethics: Transforming the Social Sciences.* Toronto: University of Toronto Press.

van den Hoonaard, Will C., and Deborah van den Hoonaard. 2013. *Essentials of Thinking Ethically in Qualitative Research.* Walnut Creek, CA: East Coast Press.

SECTION III

MANAGING INSIDER/OUTSIDER STATUS
WHILE GAINING ACCESS

Gaining access to your field site can be intimidating, regardless of your start position. The chapters in this section speak to the various experiences you might have based on how closely you are already aligned with those who populate the world you are trying to access. While we are excited when embarking on a new project, we are all also spending a good deal of emotional energy thinking about the best way to approach those we wish to study and whether they will welcome us or not. Whether or not you are an insider or outsider—whether those in your field site consider you one of them or not—will affect not only your experiences gaining access, but also your methods, data, and even your analysis.

You may think that coming into your field site with insider status is preferable. Indeed, this offers some significant advantages, but there are also some disadvantages. In terms of advantages, you may already be familiar with the norms of the site, such as how to dress and act appropriately, and the issues that are most relevant to your participants. You will already have spent enough time in that site to know how to frame your research. One disadvantage might be that, having spent so much time as an insider, you might not see something an outsider would see with fresh eyes. It can be hard to make the familiar strange. You may also uncover some things about your friends or colleagues that you wish you had not known. Another challenge could be that participants already assume you know a lot of basic information. Fruitful data can materialize when participants try to explain things to you as an outsider, and you might miss out on that as an insider. For example, when van den Scott was interviewing participants about their experiences with airline travel in Nunavut, she had to ask them to describe the airport to her as if she had never seen it so that she could learn what they consider important to communicate about that space. At first participants were vague about the airport, telling van den Scott, "you know," but after she asked them to describe it to her as if she were an outsider, she learned how the airport feels like a gateway to the South for them. It also became clear how important the airport's lack of a secure area is to socializing. The space encourages visiting with friends and recounting the experiences someone just had on a trip, or the expectations of upcoming travel. This makes air travel in Nunavut feel more like a bus service would elsewhere.

Conversely, there are some advantages and disadvantages to approaching a field site as an outsider. The explanations that participants give newcomers can yield great data. You come to the scene with fresh eyes and might see things in ways that would be unexpected for an insider. Having said that, an outsider also has to develop trust-based relationships from scratch. It is easy to accidentally violate a norm, but also easier to gain forgiveness as an outsider. Some groups are reluctant to trust outsiders and other groups can be difficult to access for a variety of reasons.

Both insiders and outsiders have to reflect on how to treat their participants and their data ethically. The chapters in this section are unanimous in encouraging you to adopt an attitude of respect and learning in your field site. You are there to learn from your participants, not to be the expert. These chapters also emphasize the importance of reflexivity, of taking the time to think about your own biases, whether you are an insider or an outsider or somewhere in between. What preconceived ideas do you have? What is your social location, your social perspective? How might that affect your analysis? Always attend to your own biases, as those are part of the work as well. The chapters in this section will help you navigate insider and outsider relationships with your field site. They offer insights and some great tips and tricks with regards to dealing with the messiness of research.

In chapter 9, Lesley J. Bikos provides an inside look at the challenges she encountered while doing research on policewomen in Canada. She had previously been a policewoman, and so approached her research with a particular kind of insider status. In addition to other excellent advice, such as choosing a research topic about which you feel passionate, she urges you to consider how your relationships with participants will be ongoing and how that might impact you and your work. She outlines some pros and cons of insider status and encourages you to spend time interrogating your own biases attached to your status.

Next, in chapter 10, Matthew S. Johnston shares what it was like to approach a close-knit community as an outsider. He is a straight, white, cisgender man doing transgender research. He writes about the challenges around access, particularly around assumptions that researchers may make when attempting to gain access. The group that he studies is a marginalized group with a challenging history. He could not trust the assumptions of the research ethics board to keep his work ethical—his participants, however, knew exactly what kind of ethical behaviour they wanted in a researcher. Being willing to learn from your participants, building genuine trust-based relationships, being open to learning more about yourself in the process, and being brave enough to step outside your comfort zone are the cornerstones that guide his work with trans people.

In his chapter on researching truck drivers, Michael A. Fleming engages in outsider research with a hidden and little-researched population. He discusses his experiences overcoming "contact barriers," issues around accessibility and lifestyle, and "cultural barriers" (in this case a reluctance to engage with a researcher whose legitimacy in that hyper-masculine culture is in question). Fleming found that respecting the drivers' working realities and time as well as their knowledge about their own world helps to reach across these barriers.

Cathlene Hillier and Emily Milne have both conducted research in schools, one as an insider and one as an outsider. Their chapter compares and contrasts their experiences in the same field site. Outsiders may find that legitimacy is more of a challenge, but they also can feel less threatening and obtain explanations of things that might not be clarified for someone in the know. An insider, however, can often fit in quickly and easily, but may face challenges around their previous roles in that setting. Hillier and Milne encourage you to keep reflecting on the experiences you are having throughout the research process and offer some handy tips for fitting into a field site to respectfully gather the best data possible.

9 An Insider's Perspective on Research with Policewomen in Canada

Lesley J. Bikos

Congratulations on your choice to explore the world of qualitative methodology. The connections we make and the personal growth we achieve as researchers, while simultaneously empowering participants to voice their own experiences, makes this methodology rewarding for both the researcher and participant. As a former policewoman, I conduct research that investigates the experiences of police officers in Canada. This chapter focuses on my experiences conducting a study with 15 policewomen in Southwestern Ontario. My status as a former officer provided me the opportunity to conduct research as an insider, an important factor in my ability to gain access to a notoriously difficult population to study. Based on my research experiences, this chapter will explore the pros and cons of insider research, with the goal of offering you practical advice as you move forward in your own projects.

My first piece of advice is to choose a research topic you feel passionate about. Forget about scholarships, marks, and how to get a good job to pay off your student loan. Passion for your work will get you through the long and sometimes tedious processes that research requires. A good way to begin is to brainstorm about topics that interest you—research can and should be fun! Now that you have thought of a research topic, think about whether you are a member of the population you wish to study. If your answer is yes, then you are an insider researcher who shares language, experiences, and an identity with the population you are studying (Asselin 2003; Kanuha 2000). If your answer is no, then you are an outsider researcher. You will no doubt have guessed that an outsider researcher is someone who researches populations they are not a member of (Adler and Adler 1987). There is debate amongst qualitative researchers about whether insider and outsider researcher roles are dichotomous roles. Some researchers argue that there is a space between the two distinctions that applies to both insider and outsider research. There is not enough room in this chapter to cover the insider/outsider debate; however, Dwyer and Buckle's (2009) work offers a great analysis if you wish to know more. For the purposes of this chapter, we will concentrate on the experiences of the insider researcher.

THE BENEFITS AND RISKS ASSOCIATED WITH INSIDER RESEARCH

Some groups, such as police services, are reluctant to come under the scrutiny of outsiders. This can make recruiting participants difficult, particularly in a police service where the norms of silence and loyalty to the group are paramount, with the potential of severe social and professional repercussions for those who violate them. My insider status assisted with this obstacle, as my contacts within the group gave me the ability to recruit participants directly, without the knowledge of co-workers or the police administration. This greatly contributed to the success of the study, as many participants indicated they would not have consented to being interviewed by an outsider. Insider research also gave me the opportunity for ongoing access to participants in the event I wished to ask more questions at a later date. This is helpful as your study progresses, as you may wish to inquire about themes that emerge in interviews with other participants. While not impossible as an outside researcher, the connections you have as an insider make gaining and maintaining access to your participants an easier process.

The ease of building rapport and trust with participants is another positive aspect of insider research. For example, as a former policewoman, I can engage in "cop talk" and have a deeper level of understanding of the culture than an outsider would. This creates an easy flow to the interview, which becomes more like a conversation. In my experience, this often results in more robust data, as both the researcher and participant feel relaxed and connected; however, this type of rapport can also create a situation in which assumptions are made about the shared meaning of words and behaviours between the two parties. Be aware of this when interviewing and ask your participant to explain their meaning if it is not clear. This offers some protection against the loss of valuable data and/or the misinterpretation of your participant's experience. Still, overall, insider research sounds amazing, right? These are people you know or at least share common ground with—how hard can it be? Well, it can get a little complicated, as experience taught me.

Once I began the interview process it became clear that this was harder than I thought, and I had the advantage of prior interview experience as a police officer. Given my connection to the policing institution, I understood the potential for an emotional reaction while listening to other women's stories. Despite this awareness, I underestimated the extent to which their stories would affect me. I was honoured, but unprepared for the depth and breadth of some of their stories detailing misconduct, sexual harassment, discrimination, and bullying by their co-workers and supervisors. Of course, there were also participants who had positive experiences, but those were the minority. I found it hard to hear about the lack of support and the barriers policewomen were experiencing, and I became increasingly alarmed as I began to understand the depth of what I was taking on. My attachment to the group as an insider provided data that outside researchers would likely not be privy to; however, it also meant that this work became more than just a study to meet graduate school requirements. This is the cost of insider research and one you should think carefully about. Many of the women outright asked me to champion their cause, feeling powerless due to their precarious position in the institution. At times, I felt overwhelmed by the pressure and unsure if I was up to the task. The pressure was more intense because these were women I knew, or came to know, on a deep level as a result of my intimate connection to them.

Another reality you should be aware of is that interviewing friends and/or family can be tough. Do not be surprised if someone you thought you knew shocks you in an interview, altering your view of them. For example, I am a feminist who studies gender, policing, and work/occupations. As such, I understand how gendered institutions, such as police services, can create a competitive atmosphere that divides women. This means that women may reproduce their own oppression by using against each other the same tactics—such as name-calling, bullying, and social isolation—their male counterparts use against them. Listening to policewomen degrade each other in interviews was frustrating. There were many moments when I wanted to point out the irony of their complaints of harassment by male colleagues, as they displayed the same behaviour towards each other. Indeed, in one interview I did point out the contradiction, feeling comfortable that I knew the participant well enough to offer my opinion. My display of judgment jeopardized the rest of the interview, destroyed the rapport, and made our relationship uncomfortable for a time. I apologized and we carried on; however, it was a lesson learned. The challenge for an insider researcher is to find a balance between the role of insider and researcher. As the researcher, you are there to listen without judgment and allow thoughts to come organically from your participants. You must try to conceal your opinions, or you will isolate participants and possibly taint the data if they feel your disapproval. It is important to be aware of your facial expressions and body language, and keep your opinions to yourself!

Another area that is important to consider is your ongoing relationship with participants after the interview is complete: this is not a typical "ask questions, get answers, see you later" kind of operation. These are potentially friends and family from a subculture of which you are a member. At the very least, participants are members of the same group as you, making post-research contact more likely. Consider that the access insider research provides flows both ways. Although you may gain access to participants through your status as an insider, they also have ongoing access to you. Further, participants may have access to others in the subculture whom you may be interested in interviewing, therefore, your reputation within the group is pivotal to your ability to continue your work. All of these factors combine to make the relationship between the insider researcher and the participant a reciprocal one that may differ in its intensity from the outsider experience. For example, I was unprepared for the questions participants had about my own experiences as a policewoman, which required a certain amount of vulnerability on my part that was tricky to navigate. Yes, they were willing to give me access to their experiences, but many expected the same commitment from me due to my membership in the group. These do not have to be cons per se, but be aware that insider research requires emotional energy that may differ from outsider research. On the positive side, I developed strong bonds with other policewomen that have become important both personally and professionally.

Speaking of your reputation, remember that it is likely that participants will read your study once you are done. This can cause stress for the researcher, who may experience an inner conflict as they attempt to balance the dual role of researcher and group member (Adler and Adler 1987; Brannick and Coghlan 2007). For example, participants recounted stories that, as a researcher, I knew were important, particularly if the goal was to expose the barriers policewomen identified; however, the stories were often critical of the institution and highly controversial, which I knew had the potential to generate a negative reaction from the subculture that could isolate future participants or jeopardize the already precarious position of policewomen. The roles of former officer and academic often collided for me in ways I had not anticipated. The officer in me struggled to find a way to report the findings without breaking the cardinal rule of policing: loyalty. However, the academic in me understood that these stories were important to reveal as examples of how the culture of policing negatively impacted the participants' lives. There was a period of deep reflection as I struggled to understand my role: Would I be viewed as a champion fighting for a healthier, more equitable workplace or a traitor to my former profession? If my fate was the latter, I knew it meant my work in that field was over. I also knew this was a risk I had to take if the goal was to improve the lives of policewomen in Canada. My final decision was to report the issues in a careful, balanced way that exposed the reality of the participants' experiences using discretion and respect for the participants' wishes. The insider researcher must maintain a delicate balance, as there is the potential that an intimate relationship will come to an end if a participant feels betrayed or misrepresented.

ADDRESSING OBJECTIVITY IN INSIDER RESEARCH

This brings me to the crucial question insider researchers must address: How do you research a topic that is personal and still produce credible work? The issues of bias and objectivity are heatedly debated within sociology, particularly for those who are insider researchers. You may find, despite your best attempts, that there will be those who argue that your study is not valid because you are too intimately connected to your work. I strongly disagree. True, my own experiences create a bias, but that does not change or lessen the experiences reported by other policewomen. While it is true that their interviews are filtered through me, all studies, including quantitative studies, have human input of some kind that incorporates an element of our lived experiences. My goal was a valid and reliable study that honoured the experiences of the participants. I feel confident that I produced a study with integrity by acknowledging my personal biases and reducing their impact to the best of my ability by using a careful study design, recruitment techniques, and extensive reflexivity. Let us take a look at some of the methods I employed that may be useful to your own work.

First, I suggest you make a list of all the potential biases you may have in relation to your topic. This will assist you in anticipating ways bias may occur and help reduce their impact. For example, I created an interview guide with neutral, open-ended questions to allow participants to express what *they* thought was important for me to know, rather than direct questions that may lead them in a particular direction. It was also important to interview officers I did not know from police services I had not worked in. The challenge, as we discussed, is gaining access to those officers. To solve this problem, I employed convenience and snowball sampling to recruit 15 participants from five different police services in Southwestern Ontario. My insider status made this type of recruitment possible, as officers who knew me were willing to vouch for my trustworthiness and promote the study to other officers with whom they had connections.

Other important ways to mitigate bias concerns are bracketing, memoing, and field notes. Bracketing is a simple process of writing down your thoughts, feelings, and assumptions before you begin your research—you already began this practice when you made your list of potential biases (Dwyer and Buckle 2009). Memoing, which entails making notes of your thoughts as you review your transcripts, is frequently used during the data collection and interpretation stages of research. Field notes are made as soon as possible after the interview; they include reflective comments on your feelings and observations. You can also use these processes to make notations on emerging themes, connections, and areas you wish to explore further in subsequent interviews. I constantly used these methods as reflection tools while collecting and analyzing the data, which was important because it assisted in my ability to see how my biases may affect the interpretation of results.

Finally, I reveal in my written work my position as a former officer to allow the reader to understand the potential biases of the study. Remember, the goal is not a perfect, completely objective study—that is impossible. Your goal is to be upfront about who you are, why the work is important, the methods you employed, and who the participants are. If you carefully think through the potential biases, design your study with those in mind, and continue to reflect on them throughout the research process, you will have a solid, credible study that accurately represents your participants' experiences.

Insider research is valuable in terms of richness of data and access to participants, but it also has a price for the researcher who is intimately connected to the population they are studying. For me, the cost was worth it and I will continue my work within the subculture. As you go forward, understand there will be times when you question why you chose your topic and whether it will make a difference in your participants' lives. Good research is like a ripple in a pond—you never know what positive long-term impacts it may have, such as policy changes that improve the lives of your participants.

Care about your work, care about your participants, and put in the effort to provide the most credible work you can. In my experience, participants were empowered simply through telling their stories, some for the first time. Similarly, I was inspired by their stories of strength and resiliency. That, in itself, makes the work I do worth it.

CRAFTING QUALITATIVE RESEARCH EXERCISES

1. Make a list of groups you are or have been a member of that you may wish to research someday. These can be related to employment, hobbies, religious pursuits, and so on. Write down your preconceptions about each group you have chosen. For example, as a member of a sports team, you may have the preconception that competitiveness is what drives members of a team to work hard and develop their skills. You have now completed a bracketing exercise.

2. Conduct a short five-minute interview with a friend or peer on a topic that you have in common, such as a favourite course or experience. While interviewing your subject, take notes on your questions and their responses. Now carefully read your transcript while making notes of your thoughts and intuitions. Compare these with any preconceptions you may have had before you began the interview. Is your data different than you expected? Similar? Are there places where your own bias may have influenced your interpretation? These are important questions to reflect on. You have now completed a memoing exercise.

3. Using the list of potential groups to study from question 1, consider how you would gain access to those groups. Make a list of the sampling techniques you wish to use. Remember to think of potential gatekeepers. Now make a list of the pros and cons of using your sampling framework. Finally, make a list of the potential harms to you and your participants that your insider research could cause, for example, confidentiality if you are interviewing members of the same group. What are some ways you can mitigate these? Be sure to reflect on how you will navigate the sometimes conflicting roles of group member and researcher.

REFERENCES

Adler, Patricia, and Peter Adler. 1987. *Membership Roles in Field Research*. Newbury Park, CA: Sage.

Asselin, Marilyn E. 2003. "Insider Research: Issues to Consider When Doing Qualitative Research in Your Own Setting." *Journal for Nurses in Staff Development* 19 (2): 99–103.

Brannick, Teresa, and David Coghlan. 2007. "In Defense of Being 'Native': The Case of Insider Academic Research." *Organizational Research Methods* 10 (1): 59–74.

Dwyer, Sonya Corbin, and Jennifer L. Buckle. 2009. "The Space Between: On Being an Insider-Outsider in Qualitative Research." *International Journal of Qualitative Methods* 8 (1): 54–63.

Kanuha, Valli Kalei. 2000. "'Being' Native versus 'Going Native': Conducting Social Work Research as Insider." *Social Work* 45 (5): 439–47.

10 Politics and Tensions of Doing Transgender Research: Lessons Learned by a Straight-White-Cisgender Man

Matthew S. Johnston

INTRODUCTION

Navigating the contentious "outsider status" in qualitative research can be quite cumbersome and emotionally draining (Bucerius 2013), as seen, for example, in cases where researchers learned about Indigenous peoples, immigration reform, ethnic and migrant populations, and women (Armitage 2008; Blix 2015; Watts 2006; Wray and Bartholomew 2010). The literature on outsiders has yet to fully explore the experiences of allies doing research on LGBTTQIA+ communities, let alone answer the following question: What obstacles and successes would a straight-white-cisgender man,[1] whose gender and sexuality have remained relatively stable throughout his life, encounter when he undertakes research on transgender people? In attempting to respond to this question, I describe my experiences doing doctoral research on transgender prisoners and students, and negotiating the role of being a gendered outsider in a community where trust is—for good and strong reasons—very delicate and difficult to earn when you are privileged and share very little in terms of your gender identity. My goal is not to provide readers with a strategic manual on how to do research on trans people if you are not trans, but rather to offer some points of reflection to consider throughout any research process when we are engaging with people whose marginalization and modes of resistance and empowerment may be adversely affected by how we disseminate our findings.

COMMUNITY ACCESS IS NOT SIMPLE

Common barriers to conducting graduate-level research on trans people include difficulties related to securing funding, institutional support, cultural competence, and adept mentorship and expertise to help with the development of a research question that holds practical utility, does not demean or pathologize trans people, and is meaningful to the transgender community (Rachlin 2009). The ethical standards and best practices to follow when conducting research on transgender populations are still roughly delineated because few LGBTTQIA+ community agencies have their own research ethics boards

(REBs), and must partner with faculty members in order to access a university REB (Martin and Meezan 2009). Yet, given that the general purposes of REBs are to weigh the potential harms to participants against the potential benefits to them or society, and to promote the redesign of research to ensure that participants are not overly exploited or subject to coercion, REBs can be prone to rejecting proposals dealing with sensitive topics and vulnerable populations because they deem the research and the researcher to be too "risky" (Haggerty 2004). Even if the research proposal is not rejected, as is eventually often the case, we can never assume that the ethics application process actually prepares us to approach our participants with an adequate level of care, respect, empathy, and gratitude. This is especially true if we identify very little with them, or do not yet have the education or life experience requisite to understanding how our research impacts those who have experienced gendered harm and violence. To put it simply, REBs cannot teach us how to be ethical; the people we study, however, can.

The trans people I met, interviewed, and exchanged letters with not only taught me about the stigmas and oppressions they endured and the positive experiences they enjoyed while studying at a university or being incarcerated, but they also made me come to terms with my own gendered insecurities, assumptions, and painful life experiences that I often did not adequately reflect on during the research process. Gatekeepers in the trans community took on a very special meaning. Yes, I required friends to help convince other members of the trans community, a notably small and interconnected population that can be difficult to recruit (Rachlin 2009), to trust that I—a straight-white-cis middle-class man—was doing research in order to improve trans lives and give accounts of their marginalization and perseverance without a hidden agenda. I also needed friends to help me believe that I was a reflective and good person committed to addressing any concerns that I was not fully invested in discovering and responding to participants' needs because of my different background and my eagerness to complete doctoral research. It is my advice that anyone engaging in research about trans people from a position of heteronormative privilege do their best to confess their difference and naïveté, and, if necessary, apologize for their capacity to unknowingly use heterosexist or heteronormative language that reproduces problematic assumptions about trans people. Despite my best efforts to use the correct pronoun when referring to authors of trans studies whose gender identity may have changed more than once during their life, I made mistakes and, when this occurred, it was best just to say I was sorry.

KNOW YOURSELF BEFORE YOU GET TO KNOW OTHERS

We cannot enter a research site where the territory is unmarked and new to us with the perspective that we always/already have the know-how because of our degrees, education, and status we carry as researchers. Even in familiar territory, we cannot assume expertise. This lesson was brought home to me when I completed my MA thesis on a hospital security job I had worked. The research revealed to me many nuances about hyper-masculine culture I had overlooked when I was immersed in the job setting (Johnston 2016a). Granted, you may have a family member, friend, relative, or spouse who identifies as trans when you begin the research (I did not); however, we must understand that, in a subjective world, others will have conflicting and intersecting perspectives on what trans people need. I recall a colleague, who is not trans but identifies within the spectrum of LGBQ and has a female-to-male trans partner, telling me about her experience of being informed by members in trans organizations that she was "not trans enough" to take on some of their important projects. Of course, my knee-jerk reaction was to think, "What chance do I have?" With this in mind, there is little point in pretending that the elephant in the room does not exist—it most certainly does. To my own detriment, I tried at times to ignore my gender status because of the bond and connection I shared (at times) with the trans people I was meeting and learning from. Not all trans people welcomed me, and some who did made me feel that I had overstayed my welcome. Until the world becomes truly equal and past harms are reconciled, many trans persons will be frightened or skeptical about letting allies in, especially if they have experienced pervasive neglect, victimization, marginalization, abuse, and stigma throughout their childhood and adult lives (Stryker and Aizura 2013).

As graduate students, we have to negotiate our uneasiness and discomfort when working with a community we do not really know (no matter how much we have read) because our dissertation and thesis are at stake. However, for the participants, what is most at stake is the quality of their life and the belief that you will not say things or disseminate findings that cause unnecessary unrest and turmoil in a community that is often highly politicized, and, like other contemporary social movements (Gavrielides 2008; Nagle 2016), prone to contention and battles from within (Halberstam 1998) despite the many accomplishments they have made in building a better and safer world for trans people. Little did I know during my initial supervisor meetings that I would be asked upfront if I was "a straight-white-cis boy," or interrogated during a Skype interview just after I accepted my doctoral offer and asked, "So why the jump from masculinity studies to trans?" In spite of my belief at the time, I would not characterize these statements as judgments of myself given that my supervisor did not know me then. Rather, I believe these comments shed light on how trans people have been publicly misinterpreted and misrepresented (Martin and Meezan 2009), in part because they have participated in projects where they felt the results were distributed in ways that disempowered them or made them feel as though the research was conducted solely to promote the career or opinion of the researcher (Rachlin 2009). Even though some trans people experience high rates of victimization, mental suffering, exploitation, and suicidality, not all trans research has to be negative, nor should we assume that research is always the needed and appropriate intervention. It is imperative that we do not privilege our own perspectives and interpretations over the voices of the trans people who make up our data.

TRUST RARELY COMES EASY, AND WHEN IT DOES...

If there is suspiciousness on the part of the trans community related to allowing cis people to do research on them, be sensitive to the idea that our visible features can trigger trauma, past abuses, wariness, or a general discomfort. It is well documented how trans people are treated by gender normative people in disturbing ways, and that trans people face dark life circumstances more often than people who do not identify as trans (Stryker and Aizura 2013). I may have been abused throughout my life, physically and verbally, but within the context of doing trans research, it was important for me to weigh considerably how others' harms carry different and more complex meanings and political implications than my own. I had to recognize that I still have quite a lot to learn even though, at times, I regretted not getting the chance to really elaborate to my friends, teachers, advisors, and participants how I felt some of my past sufferings and victimizations made me a special candidate for helping another vulnerable population. In my study of transgender students (Johnston 2016b), a trans woman told me during our Skype interview about her experience of being sexually assaulted. I was not ready for this, and in the drama and tension of the moment I did my best to listen empathetically to her and share my condolences and sympathies. We cannot expect that such trust will always be built over the course of a two-hour interview. This is why Rachlin (2009) insists that outsider researchers of trans populations must expect to give before they take, and be aware of the time, volunteerism, and personal resources needed to build adequate levels of trust, expertise, knowledge, and education.

That said, I was fortunate enough to gain very quickly the trust of a trans man who had just started his transition. With my permission, my doctoral supervisor gave him my phone number because he had information to share with me regarding how trans people are treated inside the Canadian prison system. While our initial phone chat started as an information-gathering exercise, our conversations evolved throughout the year, especially after he moved to the city where I was residing. We became friends, and he was quite forthcoming about the personal distresses and crises he was experiencing leading up to his surgical procedures, not to mention the difficulties he had trying to pin down his sexual preferences and identities.

My supervisor was intended to be a mentor to him throughout this time, but I learned from my friend that when he would try to call my supervisor for help, sometimes his reply would be something to the effect of, "I am really busy, why don't you talk to Matthew?" I did not admit this to my friend or supervisor, but I felt deeply uncomfortable, unprepared, and unqualified to take on the responsibilities of counselling my friend about issues where I lacked any kind of expertise whatsoever. I listened to him as best I could, but as the stresses of the PhD program and conflicts I had with my committee began to take over my life and almost destroy it, it was not long before I found myself letting my cellphone go to voice mail every time I saw that my friend was calling. I was not able to communicate very well to him the pain I felt while trying to balance my life, or the pressure I felt when trying to counsel a person much older than myself, whose safety I was very concerned about when he was on the brink of a mental breakdown.

The lesson I take from all this is that we can never be *fully* prepared for or knowledgeable about human needs that arise when others are suffering, let alone react perfectly to them. Research will teach you about yourself, teach you how to be a better person, and teach you what you can do next time you or others make a mistake. Try to be kind and forgiving to yourself and others with the understanding that research is social and, therefore, will create meanings, emotions, and realities you never thought possible.

HOPE FOR THE FUTURE

Looking back, I understand that navigating the tensions and demands of doctoral student life may have gotten in the way of showing some of the people I worked with and learned from how much I cared about helping the world—hindsight is, after all, 20/20. But what I take, and hope you will take, from my experiences is that it is okay to make mistakes in the research process. In fact, expect that you will. And know that if people hurt you or make you feel like you are an outsider, it is often because they too have been made to feel that way. This is the vulnerable core of the human spirit. Throughout trials and tribulations related to my research, I met a lot of good people, had many positive interactions, and learned about myself, and I now hold a plethora of knowledge and insights into transgender issues and social movements that I could not have gained had I not been willing to step outside of my box, take risks, and put my inspirations and beliefs into action. There will be good and bad experiences when doing this kind of research, and I feel that, sometimes, as critical sociologists, we give too much credence to the word *critical*. You are still enlightening the world when you emphasize what society is doing well, and, moreover, you can empower the LGBTTQIA+ movement by revealing how its members find light in darkness when their lives become entangled by the myriad of unjust social forces, inequalities, and structures at work. While I have completed one study on trans students, the project I have undertaken on trans prisoners is still ongoing as I continue to build networks of support and learn about trans prisoner life through letters my wife and I exchange with incarcerated trans friends. Newman (2016) makes a powerful point when he encourages people who study or participate in social movements to really ask themselves what they are getting out of doing the research. In my own naïveté, perhaps I glossed over this query while trying to mobilize my research skills in ways that help trans people. How you find your answer is up to you, but in knowing yourself better and reflecting deeply about your motivations, rest assured that trans people will be more willing to share theirs.

CRAFTING QUALITATIVE RESEARCH EXERCISES

1. Consider analyzing on Twitter a recent social movement you might be interested in researching that you are not fully immersed in or do not directly

identify with (e.g., #BlackLivesMatter, #WeBelieveSurvivors). Before reading a few tweets that use an applicable hashtag, jot down some notes on how your identity, gender, social status, and/or potential privilege may shape how you understand the messages being communicated within the movement. Reflect on how members might perceive your relationship to them, and brainstorm some ways you could acknowledge your status to the community in subsequent research papers or during interactions.

2. Suppose you are doing a research project that involves interviewing people, and one participant contacts you frequently after the interview because it is clear they want to pursue a friendship with you. Is this something you would be comfortable with? If so, how might you negotiate the professional boundaries and time commitments you may be struggling with while still doing your best to ensure that their feelings aren't hurt? Think up some possible scenarios and obstacles that could test your comfort levels, ethics, and personal boundaries, and how you might react to such challenges.

3. Imagine you have finished your data collection, and are "leaving the field." You have built relationships of trust with your participants and they have shared sensitive information about themselves and confided in you, an outsider to their community. How might they feel if you suddenly disappear from their lives? Are you able and willing to continue to offer support and contact if needed? If not, how might you provide resources to ensure that they are supported emotionally?

NOTE

1. *Cisgender* is a subcultural term that generally refers to people who are not transgender and whose gender identity closely reflects and stays within the parameters of the sex they were assigned at birth. *Transgender*, on the other hand, refers to people whose gender identity or expression of gender does not neatly fit what society expects based on their birth-assigned sex.

REFERENCES

Armitage, Janet S. 2008. "Persona Non Grata: Dilemmas of Being an Outsider Researching Immigration Reform Activism." *Qualitative Research* 8 (2): 155–77.

Blix, Bodil H. 2015. "'Something Decent to Wear': Performances of Being an Insider and an Outsider in Indigenous Research." *Qualitative Inquiry* 21 (2): 175–83.

Bucerius, Sandra M. 2013. "Becoming a 'Trusted Outsider': Gender, Ethnicity, and Inequality in Ethnographic Research." *Journal of Contemporary Ethnography* 42 (6): 690–721.

Gavrielides, Theo. 2008. "Restorative Justice—the Perplexing Concept: Conceptual Fault-Lines and Power Battles within the Restorative Justice Movement." *Criminology and Criminal Justice* 8 (2): 165–83.

Haggerty, Kevin. 2004. "Ethics Creep: Governing Social Science Research in the Name of Ethics." *Qualitative Sociology* 27 (4): 391–414.

Halberstam, Judith. 1998. "Transgender Butch: Butch/FTM Border Wards and the Masculine Continuum." *GLQ: A Journal of Lesbian and Gay Studies* 4 (2): 287–310.

Johnston, Matthew S. 2016a. "Men Can Change: Transformation, Agency, Ethics and Closure during Critical Dialogue in Interviews." *Qualitative Research* 16 (2): 131–50.

Johnston, Matthew S. 2016b. "'Until That Magical Day … No Campus Is Safe': Reflections on How Transgender Students Experience Gender and Stigma on Campus." *Reflective Practice* 17 (2): 143–58.

Martin, James I., and William Meezan. 2009. "Applying Ethical Standards to Research and Evaluations Involving Lesbian, Gay, Bisexual, and Transgender Populations." In *Handbook of Research with Lesbian, Gay, Bisexual, and Transgender Populations*, revised ed., edited by William Meezan and James I. Martin, 19–39. New York: Routledge.

Nagle, John. 2016. *Social Movements in Violently Divided Societies: Constructing Conflict and Peacebuilding.* New York: Routledge.

Newman, Saul. 2016. *Post Anarchism.* Cambridge, UK: Polity Press.

Rachlin, Katherine. 2009. "The Questions We Ask: Conducting Socially Conscious Research with Transgender Individuals." In *Handbook of Research with Lesbian, Gay, Bisexual, and Transgender Populations*, revised ed., edited by William Meezan and James I. Martin, 261–79. New York: Routledge.

Stryker, Susan, and Aren Z. Aizura, eds. 2013. *The Transgender Studies Reader 2.* New York: Routledge.

Watts, Jacqueline. 2006. "'The Outsider Within': Dilemmas of Qualitative Feminist Research within a Culture of Resistance." *Qualitative Research* 6 (3): 385–402.

Wray, Sharon, and Michelle Bartholomew. 2010. "Some Reflections on Outsider and Insider Identities in Ethnic and Migrant Qualitative Research." *Migration Letters* 7 (1): 7–16.

11 Researching Truck Drivers: Difficult Data Collection and Proving Oneself amidst a Culture of Suspicious Masculinity

Michael A. Fleming

Truck driving is among the most commonly reported occupations for Canadian men. In 2011, Statistics Canada calculated that there were over 250,000 truck drivers nationwide, yet the nature of truckers' work renders invisible much of what they do and how they do it. There has been relatively little sociological interest in the world of long-haul trucking, but existing research has uncovered a common social reality. Truck drivers are entwined in a complex web of occupational realities and cultural images that shape and influence both their working and personal lives. Masculinized images of truckers' work in music and in film mask the tedium, stigma, and scrutiny many truck drivers experience on the job. My research over the last decade has been rooted in the complex social reality of truck driving. Crafting qualitative research with truck drivers, however, has required that I rethink my role as a sociologist in terms of both my accessibility to, and legitimacy in the eyes of, hidden, hesitant research participants. I have become aware of the existence of "contact" and "cultural" barriers that, if left unaddressed, would have severely limited my ability to capture truckers' social lives in the course of my research. These barriers, as well as the strategies I have developed to overcome them, are the focus of this chapter.

The first step in qualitative research design is examining what is already known about a hidden population. This process not only helps establish one's own research goals, but also provides insight into potential roadblocks in the data collection process. Some of the earliest sociological insight into the work lives of truckers has been presented by drivers-turned-sociologists (Ouellet 1991; Rothe 1991), as participant observers with unrestricted access to the work worlds of truck drivers. The success of this research was shaped by truckers' willingness to invite researchers into the intimate spaces of their lives in general, and, in more specific instances, into the cabs of their trucks (Agar 1986; Hollowell 1968). Such groundbreaking qualitative research into truckers' work worlds has consistently found that truckers identify with and are influenced by elements of the occupational mystique of truck driving (Blake 1974), a series of images and public perceptions of freedom and independence that is largely ideological. For many truck drivers, trucking becomes akin to a master status. The demands of the job often force trucking into the centre of truckers' lives, as well as the lives of their families. As one driver told me, "Trucking is a job that you have to love or you won't last and it's a job your wife has to love or your marriage won't last" (Fleming 2002). It is also a world in which hegemonic masculine traits of independence, toughness, and hard, physical work are personally and professionally valued. I have found that truck drivers often adhere to the values of hegemonic masculinity at the expense of their economic, physical, and psychological well-being. As another driver simply stated, "Truckers don't cry" (Fleming 2002). It is, perhaps, evidence of the occupational mystique of trucking that of all the truck drivers portrayed in popular media, one would be hard pressed to see them loading or unloading their truck, waiting for a load, or even simply driving.

My first exposure to the fascinating world of long-haul truck drivers came during the summer of 2000, when I was afforded the opportunity to travel along on multiple long-distance trips with a long-haul driver. As a young sociologist about to begin graduate school, I had found my research topic. As would become clear shortly after, however, finding research participants would prove to be more difficult. I am a firm believer that we, as sociologists, have to work hard for good data. This is the social reality I have dedicated my professional life to understanding. I have interviewed dozens of drivers and company owners and have travelled in excess of 15,000 kilometres with truck drivers throughout North America, and none of the data I have collected has been easy to obtain.

For me, working hard has meant finding ways to overcome contact and cultural barriers that have threatened to shut me out of my research participants' worlds. I have encountered and developed research strategies to overcome two types of barriers while engaging in qualitative research with truck drivers. Contact barriers are largely reflective of the nature of the work truckers do and are alleviated through creative accessibility strategies. Cultural barriers are reflective of the ways drivers' work environments engender skepticism and reluctance, and are largely overcome by gaining legitimacy in the eyes of research participants. While undoubtedly challenging and, at times, excruciatingly time-consuming, I have found interviewing truck drivers to be thoroughly exhilarating. The truck drivers I have had the privilege of spending time with and learning from have proven themselves to be paradoxically very difficult yet incredibly willing informants. I hope much of the insight offered here will be useful to qualitative researchers seeking to uncover the private worlds of similarly situated subjects.

OVERCOMING CONTACT BARRIERS THROUGH ACCESSIBILITY: "IF MY WHEELS AIN'T TURNING, I AIN'T EARNING"

Gaining access to hidden populations presents a series of difficulties for qualitative researchers. So, how many sociologists does it take to find a truck driver? Difficulties finding truck drivers to talk to—what I have called *contact barriers*—reflect the nature of the work truck drivers do. The solution involves finding a balance between accessibility and objectivity. One strategy I have employed has been to secure the support of company management who can facilitate access to employees in a wide range of ways. Aligning myself with trucking management has worked to alleviate some of the accessibility problems. Many truck drivers, however, have learned to be suspicious of anybody asking questions about how and why they do the work they do, and are particularly suspicious of anybody who appears to be aligned with company management. Given the level of mistrust between truck drivers and trucking management, this approach is always tempered with the fear of my perceived lack of objectivity eroding truckers' willingness to become research participants.

This is, indeed, a relationship that has to be managed effectively. In some instances, trucking management does not fully understand or respect the boundaries of anonymous, ethical research. Unfortunately, there are no guidelines that can be universally applied to negotiate these relationships. In my experiences, for example, management offers to provide interview space on company premises were not useful, yet providing an opportunity to speak with drivers in informal ways—introducing my research at the end of company meetings or even talking informally with drivers in the company lunch room—worked better. Finding the balance is a matter of trial and error, which can seem overwhelming in the early stages of a research project. All of this can be very frustrating when faced with limited time in the field, quickly dwindling research budgets, and the demands of graduate supervisors.

Securing access to potential participants, however, is only one element of accessibility. Securing interviews requires that we develop a thorough understanding of the lived realities of the populations we seek to engage with. I learned very early in my research career that truckers live by the adage of "if my wheels ain't turning, I ain't earning" (Fleming 2002). Successful truck drivers pay continual attention to time—time use on the road, as well as time spent at home. For many truckers who are paid based on the number of kilometres driven, time spent not driving is money lost. Interviewing truck drivers takes away their limited free time, and I quickly learned that drivers' willingness to spend time with me was a privilege. Similarly, it became clear to me that truckers' days revolve around distance not hours, and that it is very difficult to predict what a driver's schedule may look like from one day or week to the next. The process of making initial contact with truck drivers (with or without the support of company management), determining their interest in participating in my research, scheduling a tentative interview, and completing it can take weeks. Even the best planning and firmest commitments can be undermined by the routine reality of mechanical breakdowns, loading problems, weather delays, and personal circumstances.

My most successful strategy challenges the way we tend, as sociologists, to think of accessibility. I have adopted an "open door and last minute" policy. I have conducted interviews in the middle of the night in the cab of a truck sitting at a loading dock; in crowded truck stops along the highway; at repair facilities at all times of day and night; and in truckers' homes, company headquarters, and even shopping malls. In this regard, securing successful interviews is as much about my accessibility as it is about drivers' accessibility. While researching the trucking industry, I have learned that securing interviews and maintaining relationships with research participants often requires stepping outside of my comfort zone. More often than not, my willingness to recognize the demands of truckers' working worlds has been rewarded with incredibly rich and forthcoming interviews. My accessibility is, in itself, a key element of their vetting process.

OVERCOMING CULTURAL BARRIERS THROUGH LEGITIMACY: "IF YOU'RE COMING WITH ME, YOU'D BETTER PACK YOUR WORK GLOVES."

Truck drivers, like many hidden populations, are skeptical of the motives of researchers who show up with the single-minded purpose of data collection. These cultural barriers can seriously undermine researchers' ability to secure access to participants. In attempting to overcome cultural barriers, the question I have had to ask myself is how to convince reluctant truck drivers to talk to me when so many of their encounters with the non–trucking world are stigmatizing, and so many of the demands of the work they do are steeped in ideological images of independence, isolation, and skepticism. While every hidden population is going to have a different set of cultural barriers that has to be understood, well-crafted qualitative research undertaken by researchers with a deep understanding of their participants, and a desire to gain their trust, is paramount. This is what I mean by gaining legitimacy.

Truck drivers are often in the unenviable situation of having a lot to say, but nobody to say it to. The truck drivers I have interviewed see themselves as rugged men, self-reliant doers of hard work. In the trucker's world, my academic credentials are of diminished value. At best, they are ignored or tacitly respected. At worst, they actually work against my credibility in the eyes of participants who, in various cases, have responded with attitudes ranging from hostility to intimidation towards my position. I have been put in my place, figuratively and literally, on several occasions by truck drivers who have had to deal with the popular perception that the only people who drive trucks are those who cannot possibly do anything else. One driver told me at the outset of an in-cab interview that if I was looking for someone to "fill me full of bullshit" then I was wasting his time, and he would have no difficulties throwing me out of his truck. Similarly, I have also been asked on several occasions why "anybody from the university would have any interest in what truck drivers do." I have been exposed to a wide range of foul language, dirty jokes, and disparaging comments about management, law enforcement, politics, and academics, and I have been asked if I brought my work gloves. One truck driver who denied my interview request clearly told me that if I wanted to know about truck drivers there was nothing stopping me from becoming one.

The question I have had to come to grips with, then, is how I become legitimate in the eyes of participants. First, overcoming cultural barriers requires that qualitative researchers learn a considerable amount about the pressures and forces that shape their research subjects' lives. Second, and equally important, though, is not using our knowledge to overshadow the knowledge that our research subjects can share with us. It has been my experience that truck drivers are not looking for, and do not need, someone to explain to them what they are doing wrong. This is their world, they know it, and if I am not respecting that, they will make sure I know it. My role as a researcher is to collect and organize truckers' experiences in their words. Ensuring that the truck drivers I work with know and understand my role is central to becoming a legitimate ally. Ultimately, despite what is often a frustratingly slow research process, the majority of the truckers I have asked to interview are not resistant to participating in research. These are, after all, people who spend much of their working lives alone and have considerable time to reflect on the nature of the work they do, and it is important that as a qualitative researcher, this depth of knowledge is respected.

FINAL THOUGHTS: FINDING BALANCE IN ACCESSIBILITY AND LEGITIMACY

Trucking is not for the faint of heart; truck drivers spend their working lives navigating myriad procedural and literal roadblocks, collectively carrying the load of contradictory images of masculinity and occupational mystique, and struggling to overcome the stigma attached to the work they do. Crafting qualitative research with truck drivers requires dedication, commitment, and willingness to renegotiate how we view accessibility and legitimacy in the research process. It is easy to assume that responsibility for overcoming occupational and cultural barriers is the implicit responsibility of research participants; they should, we convince ourselves, be thrilled to be participating in our research projects. Well-crafted qualitative research, however, recognizes that, in fact, we must strive to find creative ways to make ourselves accessible to, and legitimate in the eyes of, our research participants. We have to truly value the time our research participants are willing to share with us and not lose sight of the fact that they are the experts. We are simply there to organize and share their stories. This is both why we engage in qualitative research and why we value the stories we are told. Renegotiating what we mean by accessibility and legitimacy is not easy, there is no single path forward, and the process can be fraught with frustration. Qualitative research, however, is seldom engaged in under ideal circumstances. Renegotiating accessibility and legitimacy has been a vital step in my research. Despite it all, the time I have spent with truck drivers is one of the greatest privileges of my academic life.

CRAFTING QUALITATIVE RESEARCH EXERCISES

1. This chapter discusses strategies used to overcome contact and cultural barriers in qualitative research with long-haul truck drivers. What are some other occupational groups that may pose similar difficulties for qualitative researchers? How could you overcome the contact and cultural barriers of those groups?

2. Are there reasonable limits to the accommodations that qualitative researchers should make to gain access to their intended research subjects? At what point would you decide to draw the line for the sake of conducting qualitative research?

3. Forming a bond with research participants is an important process of crafting and completing qualitative research, yet becoming too close to research participants may limit one's objectivity. What are some of the strategies you could use to find a balance between access and objectivity? Do you feel that the balance made by Fleming was appropriate? Why?

4. In this research, Fleming could have chosen to align himself more closely with trucking company managers, but chose not to. This slowed down the progress of the research considerably, but increased his legitimacy in the eyes of his research participants. Do you feel this was an appropriate decision? Could the relationship with trucking company managers have been handled differently?

REFERENCES

Agar, Michael. 1986. *Independents Declared: The Dilemmas of Independent Trucking.* Washington, DC: Smithsonian Institution Press.

Berger, Peter. 1963. *Invitation to Sociology.* New York: Anchor Books.

Blake, Joseph A. 1974. "Occupational Thrill, Mystique, and the Truck Driver." *Urban Life and Culture* 3 (2): 205–21.

Fleming, Michael. 2002. "Just Buying Themselves a Job: The Work Lives and Work Ideology of Owner-Operator Truck Drivers." MA thesis, University of New Brunswick, Fredericton, NB.

Hollowell, Peter. 1968. *The Lorry Driver.* London: Routledge and Kegan Paul.

Ouellet, Lawrence. 1991. *Pedal to the Metal: The Worklives of Truck Drivers.* Philadelphia: Temple University Press.

Rothe, J. Peter. 1991. *The Trucker's World: Risk, Safety, and Mobility.* New Brunswick, NJ: Transaction Publishers.

Statistics Canada. 2011. *Table 3: The 20 Most Common Occupations among Men Age 15 and Over and the Proportion of Men in the Total Work Force, May 2011.* https://www12.statcan.gc.ca/nhs-enm/2011/as-sa/99-012-x/2011002/tbl/tbl03-eng.cfm.

12   "You're an Alien to Us": Autoethnographic Accounts of Two Researchers' Experiences in an Organizational Setting

Cathlene Hillier and Emily Milne

INTRODUCTION

In qualitative research, we are asked to be reflexive of our experiences in the field and to account for the biases we may have prior to entering a study (Savvides et al. 2014). The source of our biases is mainly attributed to past experiences and our own cultural and political positions. This notion of bias contributes to the debate on whether it is better to be an insider or an outsider in the field of study (Bridges 2009). In the organizational setting of schools, where we conducted research for four years, the term *alien* was used to describe those considered foreign to teaching experiences. Alternatively, another label used is *backyard researcher*, which refers to someone researching something with which they are closely associated, such as a teacher researching teachers (Leigh 2014). This chapter is an autoethnography of the accounts of two researchers conducting a study in schools with parents and teachers: one who is considered an insider (a certified teacher and parent) and one who is considered an outsider (not a certified teacher or parent). Drawing on field notes and interviews conducted with 27 elementary school teachers and 57 parents, we ask: What are the advantages and disadvantages to being an insider or an outsider in the research process? After a reflexive analysis of our experiences, we conclude with strategies for conducting interviews and maintaining access in an organizational setting from each perspective.

THE INSIDER/OUTSIDER STATUS OF RESEARCHERS

Merton (1972, 21) defines insiders as "members of specified groups and collectivities or occupants of specified social statuses" and outsiders simply as "non-members." Seemingly, insiders have a greater advantage than outsiders in ethnographic research. Insiders may possess comprehensive insight into the group being studied (including context-specific terms and organizational processes); be seen as "one of them" and have a more equal relationship with participants; have expedient access to the research site (and to in-group activities); and build rapport and legitimacy faster (Bridges 2009; Chavez 2008; Labaree 2002; Savvides et al. 2014). Yet, the literature acknowledges that outsiders can do all of the above *in time* (Bridges 2009). Additionally, outsiders are per-ceived to delineate a clear distinction between the researcher and the researched (Chavez 2008) and ask for more description and explanation of concepts and processes to ensure correct interpretation of responses (Bridges 2009). Outsiders may also see broader pat-terns as well as the taken-for-granted, which an insider may miss.

The disadvantages associated with the outsider role are that access and building rapport are more difficult and, until they have spent a significant amount of time in the field, which is not always possible when interviewing, they may lack true contextual un-derstanding (Chavez 2008; Savvides et al. 2014). Insiders may have bias in being overly positive and seeing things through "rose-coloured glasses," or their familiarity may result in failure to recognize patterns in responses (Chavez 2008, 475). It also can be more dif-ficult for the insider to draw the line between researcher and participant, and they may be asked to take sides in political or moral issues (Labaree 2002). Moreover, there is the chance that informants may fear judgment from the insider (Bridges 2009).

Considering an organizational perspective is important when discussing the in-sider/outsider status of researchers. Particular workplaces, in our case schools, develop professional subcultures and have shared meanings and ways of doing things (Kelly 2014; Labaree 2002). Additionally, school-university research partnerships have been portrayed as difficult relationships, especially when participants feel that the university does not understand school processes (Coburn, Bae, and Turner 2008).

OUR RESEARCH IN SCHOOLS

To understand insider/outsider relationships with participants, we draw on field notes and interviews with 27 teachers and 57 parents from two schools in Southwestern Ontario. In 2012 and 2013, we spent 10 weeks at two elementary school sites, conduct-ing interviews, writing field notes, and interacting with parents and educators. Our access to research sites and participants was granted as a result of our involvement in a larger study on summer learning. We assigned pseudonyms to protect participant confidentiality.

We present our findings in the form of an autoethnography—a "self-narrative—to give an analytical account of our personal experiences doing research in schools (Ellis, Adams, and Bochner 2011). Autoethnography is an effective tool to reflect on our influ-ence in the field and our analysis of the data afterwards (Savvides et al. 2014).

Milne's Experience: The Outsider/Alien

I was perceived as an outsider in two ways during our study: I am not a teacher or parent. Upon reflection, my position as an outsider allowed me to appear less threatening and elicit detailed responses.

A drawback of being an outsider is that you may be labelled as such by gatekeepers. My suitability as a researcher was questioned by school administrators during our initial negotiations to gain access to school sites. It was as if I was incapable and untrustworthy because I was not a certified teacher. I was informed on a few occasions that I was an "alien," and that it would be impossible for me to get teachers to open up to me during interviews and to understand the work and experiences of teachers. As a result, the school administrators recruited a retired superintendent—an "insider"—to accompany me to the schools and co-interview teachers.

I quickly learned, however, that the presence of the insider created its own challenges. I was informed by teachers that they felt judged when the insider walked into their classroom and felt guarded during interviews when the insider was present. For example, during an interview, Jack (a teacher) shared that he was apprehensive to invite parents into his classroom. He liked to joke and be silly, and was worried that parents would not view this behaviour as professional. The insider began questioning Jack about what he believed was appropriate versus inappropriate teacher conduct. The tone of the conversation changed; Jack became defensive and uneasy.

Jack: Personally because I'm a goofball, [having parents in the classroom] would change my teaching. I would tone things down. I'd be more serious, and I wouldn't be as open.
Insider: Is there a reason why you would make that change in your own personal behaviour? And what do you mean if there are parents in the room you're not a goofball?
Jack: I'm a really anxious person by nature. I just understand that there are expectations from some parents and I would be professional.

I shared my experiences with the school administrators (or gatekeepers) and I was able to continue my interviews without the insider's supervision. I learned from this experience. Moving forward, I prefaced interactions with teachers by describing that I was just trying to learn about their work, and that I had no background in teaching and, therefore, had no basis to judge or evaluate them. Using this approach, I found that teachers welcomed me into their classrooms, and were at ease during interviews and spoke openly. My outsider status became an asset; I was perceived by participants as less threatening than an insider (especially one with high status).

I am also not a parent. This fact often came up during interviews with parents, either because I mentioned it (e.g., "I am not a parent, so can you explain …") or the interviewee asked directly. I found my outsider status in this regard was also beneficial. Interviewees would provide great detail and explain things in different ways to help me understand because they knew I did not have child-rearing experience. The following excerpt is an example from my interview with Clara:

Clara: Having a special-needs child, like you have to tell your story to so many people on so many different levels that at some point … you don't have any kids, right?

Milne: No, not yet.

Clara: I'm trying to think of an analogy that would best describe it. Have you ever been in the hospital for an operation?

Overall, I believe that my outsider status was an advantage because I approached interviews and framed questions in a way that put the interviewee in the position of expert.

Hillier's Experience: The Insider/Backyard Researcher

I am an insider in this study because I previously taught for eight years in Ontario schools and I am a mother of three children.

After hearing that Milne was called an "alien," I tried to use my insider status to my advantage. My approach was to try to fit in, and be useful and approachable. I frequented classrooms in order to develop a rapport with teachers and offered a helping hand. I assured the teachers that I had been an elementary school teacher prior to becoming a sociologist. Teachers appreciated my ability to contribute to classroom learning with little guidance and supervision, and, as a result, I believe they were more willing to be interviewed. I feel that sharing my teaching background and establishing a collegial relationship encouraged participants to be open about their classroom practice because there was less suspicion of judgment.

There was also a downside. I often had to ask teachers to elaborate on their answers because, based on our similar backgrounds, they would often reply, "you know what I mean." Teachers frequently used acronyms during our interviews (e.g., LTO, ELL, ELP), and discussed curriculum documents and ministry policies. Although I was familiar with these terms and documents, I should have asked for clarification to better understand the meanings and definitions from their point of view.

Additionally, I found that due to my experience sometimes I said too much and possibly aided respondents with their answers. Despite my efforts to avoid this, there were a few occasions where this happened. One example is when I was talking to Beth about why she has not incorporated the Ontario Ministry of Education (2009) *Aboriginal Perspectives* teacher's tool kit in her teaching:

Hillier: Well, sometimes with these curriculums that are written up, it's separate from the Ontario curriculum. It's like an added resource, and teachers don't know about it or they do what they've always done, right? So they don't necessarily look up this new resource.

Beth: And it was never pushed upon us to use that either. It's an Ontario curriculum document. So that's the sad part about it, right?

Hillier: It's not mandatory, right? It's like extra resource for teachers?

Beth: That's right.

This is an instance where I was providing Beth with excuses rather than allowing her to articulate her own response. In addition, as many qualitative researchers can attest, it is difficult to shut off our own connections to the subject matter and even to participants. Another example, below, comes from my field notes after an interview with Jane (a parent).

> Today I interviewed Jane who has received mixed messages from her doctor versus her daughter's teacher. This is her first experience with schooling as a parent and she is finding it difficult. She sees her daughter struggling and yet the teacher is telling her not to worry. I felt for Jane; I remember my own frustrations with the struggles my eldest child had in school. When the interview was over, I gave her ideas on things she could do to help build her daughter's literacy.

These field notes show that it was challenging for me, at times, to separate my role as an interviewer from my role as a teacher and parent of a child who struggled with learning to read.

CONCLUSION

Kelly (2014) suggests that, when possible, studies should include researchers with diverse backgrounds to ensure that participants' interests are well represented. Certainly, insider and outsider positions each have their own benefits and challenges. Milne found that as an outsider her ability to conduct research in the field was questioned by gatekeepers; however, she was able to leverage this status by appearing non-threatening to participants and eliciting detailed descriptions. Hillier easily fit in and established rapport, facilitating her ability to recruit participants and create a safe interview space. Yet, her insider status also created personal challenges in separating her roles as researcher, teacher, and parent during interviews.

We conclude by sharing suggestions for future researchers based on our own experience and what we have learned along the way:

- *Be familiar with the topic, as well as roles and experiences associated with the topic:* This can be achieved by reviewing published academic literature, policy documents, the company/organization website, and local news and media stories related to the topic before conducting interviews. However, be aware of the gap between academic knowledge and information, and personal lived experience.
- *Continue to reflect upon your interview schedule:* Does my interview schedule have the right flow (e.g., do I need more lead-up questions or dialogue with the participant to better set the stage for the interview before we begin)? Are

my questions framed in a way that informs my broader research question (e.g., are questions being received and interpreted the way I intended)?

- *Transcribe and begin analyzing interview data as you continue to conduct interviews:* This will allow you to contextualize your findings with existing research, check your interviews for emerging themes and patterns, and determine if your insider/outsider status influences respondents' answers. As Kvale (2009, 242–43) notes, ensuring validity requires that we let the "object speak" and allow the "object to object" at any point in the interview, regardless of our own views.

- *Ensure that you, as a researcher, fit in to the research environment:* This may seem obvious; however, how you look and act when entering the field can either invite open/uninhibited interviewee dialogue or push people away. *Dress* appropriately for the environment. For example, educators often wear semi-casual attire. Business formal would be appropriate attire for interviews conducted at a legal or government organization. Similarly, use *language* appropriate to the environment. If you are interviewing people with little or no education background, make sure you use language that is accessible. Demonstrate appropriate *body language and demeanour,* such as care and sensitivity when appropriate. If you are seen as judging the participant, or as unengaged or inauthentic, this may result in an unfruitful interview.

Overall, while there are advantages and disadvantages to being an insider or an outsider in the research process, we stress that being sensitive and approachable to participants is crucial for both insider/outsider roles in qualitative research.

CRAFTING QUALITATIVE RESEARCH EXERCISES

1. Experience both the insider and outsider status in research: Interview someone about a hobby, game, or sport that both of you share an interest in. Then, interview someone who is involved in a hobby, game, or sport that you know nothing or very little about. Which role did you find easier in the interview process? Why?

2. Practice reflexivity in research: After conducting the two interviews outlined in question 1, reflect on how your insider or outsider status might have influenced the interviews in some way.

3. Choose one of the disadvantages of being an insider and one of the disadvantages of being an outsider outlined at the beginning of the chapter and brainstorm with a classmate ways to overcome these disadvantages.

4. One of the arguments for insider research is "you have to be one to understand one." Do you think this is true? Why or why not? Can you think of a setting where it would be difficult for an outsider to gain access and truly understand the group being researched? Can you think of a setting where it would be difficult for an insider to see the broader patterns of the actions and/or responses of the group to which they belong?

REFERENCES

Bridges, David. 2009. "Education and the Possibility of Outsider Understanding." *Ethics and Education* 4 (2): 105–23.

Chavez, Christina. 2008. "Conceptualizing from the Inside: Advantages, Complications, and Demands on Insider Positionality." *The Qualitative Report* 13 (3): 474–94.

Coburn, Cynthia E., Soung Bae, and Erica O. Turner. 2008. "Authority, Status, and the Dynamics of Insider-Outsider Partnerships at the District Level." *Peabody Journal of Education* 83: 364–99.

Ellis, Carolyn, Tony E. Adams, and Arthur P. Bochner. 2011. "Autoethnography: An Overview." *Forum: Qualitative Social Research* 12 (1). http://www.qualitative-research.net/index.php/fqs/article/view/1589/3095.

Kelly, Peter. 2014. "Intercultural Comparative Research: Rethinking Insider and Outsider Perspectives." *Oxford Review of Education* 40 (2): 246–65.

Kvale, S. 2009. *InterViews: An Introduction to Qualitative Research Interviewing*. Thousand Oaks, CA: Sage.

Labaree, Robert V. 2002. "The Risk of 'Going Observationalist': Negotiating the Hidden Dilemmas of Being an Insider Participant Observer." *Qualitative Research* 2 (1): 97–122.

Leigh, Jadwiga. 2014. "A Tale of the Unexpected: Managing an Insider Dilemma by Adopting the Role of Outsider in Another Setting." *Qualitative Research* 14 (4): 428–41.

Merton, Robert K. 1972. "Insiders and Outsiders: A Chapter in the Sociology of Knowledge." *American Journal of Sociology* 78 (1): 9–47.

Ontario Ministry of Education. 2009. *Aboriginal Perspectives: A Guide to the Teacher's Toolkit*. Toronto: Queen's Printer for Ontario. http://www.edu.gov.on.ca/eng/aboriginal/Guide_Toolkit2009.pdf.

Savvides, Nicola, Joanna Al-Youssef, Mindy Colin, and Cecilia Garrido. 2014. "Journeys into Inner/Outer Space: Reflections on the Methodological Challenges of Negotiating Insider/Outsider Status in International Educational Research." *Research in Comparative and International Education* 9 (4): 412–25.

SECTION IV

EXPERIENCING EMOTIONS WHILE ESTABLISHING TRUST AND RAPPORT

Conducting research comes with a heap of ups and downs, successes and failures, and plenty of introspection. When you embark on research, you are embarking on an emotional journey, the beginning of which can be particularly thorny. In this section, you will read about the emotional journeys of five researchers, at various stages of their careers, as they navigate the roller coaster ride of establishing trust and rapport.

It can feel devastating to encounter a barrier in your research plans. Keep in mind that this experience, in and of itself, is part of your data. What kinds of barriers are you encountering? What might they tell you about the unsaid side of your research question? How does the social setting throw up barriers? These are important questions that can offer insight. It is also important to recognize that while, on rare occasions, some barriers can end a project early, most only present relatively minor bumps in the road. Part of learning the craft of qualitative research is learning how to manage these obstacles when they arise.

Keep in mind that your participants, both potential and actual, are on an emotional journey themselves. It can be intimidating to become the focus of a research study. Sometimes social science researchers are confused with those who make documentaries or exposés. Your participants might be concerned with how they or their group will be portrayed, even if it is under the umbrella of confidentiality. It makes sense for your participants to question your motivations. Wouldn't you if someone wanted to study you or some aspect of your life? Be prepared to help set participants' minds at ease. It is worthwhile to point out that you are not there to judge their way of life; your goal is to present things as they are—an authentic account of how people go about their everyday lives.

Reflexivity is a theme that has been and will continue to be repeated in this volume. That is because reflecting on your experiences is vital to doing good and ethical research. Part of reflexivity is thinking about any discomfort you or your participants might feel. This is a valuable exercise both for your conduct as you build trust and rapport, and for your analysis. Rapport and trust are integral to the research process, but can often be fraught with fears, elation, and other heightened emotions. Take heart in the fact that we all experience an emotional journey when we step into our research and that this can be an important part of the process.

Justin Wright shares a unique perspective in his chapter on applied social science research. In his work with the military, he has had to negotiate the kinds of constraints you might run into if you decide to become a researcher with an organization other than a university. Doing applied research means finding a balance between your own integrity and the needs of the organization for which you work. Wright shares how he has to take positionality into account in different ways and shares the emotional experience of encountering the kinds of things one cannot prepare for in advance, such as heightened emotions expressed during interviews by participants. He works to give military members a voice while navigating the "lived experience" of doing qualitative research in an organizational setting.

In chapter 14, Colleen McMillan brings to the foreground the variety of emotions an autho-ethnographer may experience while doing research. To conduct autoethnography, you must be prepared to be reflexive, that is, to engage with your various roles, biases, and ways of viewing the world, and to think meaningfully and mindfully about your relationship to the research. McMillan brings her social work background and experiences to bear in her discussion of the emotions of autoethnography and their relationship to ethics, which includes the boundaries of what therapy is, what research is, and whether the two can intertwine.

In his chapter on personal reputation and its relationship to research settings, Steven Kleinknecht discusses his experience interviewing Old Order Mennonites. He already had a reputation when entering this field site, one based on his grandfather's work as a teacher in this community. This pre-existing reputation, therefore, influenced how he had to approach building trust and rapport, including taking into account the higher emotional stakes involved. He was not only taking his grandfather's reputation in hand, but also found himself in the situation of presenting as a researcher to people who already knew him in a different role. Kleinknecht offers creative tricks for navigating the taken-for-granteds and reconciling the kind of role conflict he encountered in the field.

Thaddeus Müller's chapter confronts something researchers do not talk about very much—rejection and failure. We have all experienced this at some level. Müller's chapter will reassure you that this is normal and that there are many things that influence our experience as researchers. He also offers some great tips to keep in mind as you conduct your work. Pay attention to how your participants might feel about the environment where you are trying to talk to them. Be aware that many have a healthy distrust of researchers or may not be sure of your motives or your relationship with policy-makers. Müller acknowledges the discomfort and emotional strain of rejection and offers excellent suggestions for how to reflect on your research attempts and hone your strategies to maximum effect.

In chapter 17, Magdalena Wojciechowska relates her challenging experiences as she worked to gain the trust of members of the female escort industry in Poland. Wojciechowska found that some of the most important qualities for navigating the emotional ups and downs of access include resourcefulness, creativity, steadfastness, and not underestimating one's social networks. She also stresses that we must be aware that our participants are also engaged in an emotional journey, one potentially fraught with self-consciousness and power dynamics. Ultimately, Wojciechowska argues that the most important thing is to retell the stories of her participants in ways that uphold the trust-based relationships she has formed.

13 Using a Qualitative Approach in Applied Military Personnel Research[1]

Justin Wright

INTRODUCTION

As a social scientist employed with Defence Research and Development Canada, I conduct applied social science research with military personnel. My research aims to provide my primary "client," the Canadian Armed Forces (CAF), with empirical evidence in as timely a manner as possible. Military leaders use this evidence as one of several sources of information when making decisions about how best to look after the well-being of serving CAF members and their families.

Working in military personnel research has its share of constraints that are typical of any large organization. For example, research topics are based on the needs of the organization, and not necessarily my own research interests. Despite these constraints, my experience has taught me that qualitative research makes a valuable contribution to the military's efforts to support its people. I have also learned that in an applied research environment, it is just as important to understand my own relationship to the research and to the organizational context in which that research happens. Nancy Taber (2012) describes this relationship between a researcher and their research as "positionality." She suggests that by reflecting on our own positionality as researchers, "we [are] better able to explore how *who we are* continually interacts with *how we research*" (Taber 2012, 78). My aim in this chapter is to reflect on my own experiences doing applied social science for the military to show how the craft of qualitative research in this context works and why it is so important.

I began my public service career as everyone does: by closely studying the language of my "letter of offer" and a few other documents about values, ethics, and oaths to uphold the principles of the Government of Canada. To a new public service employee just out of graduate school, these documents and forms send an explicit message about the nature of the work arrangement into which I had entered. As a social scientist, this also meant that I had to rethink my relationship to the craft of social science research itself. For example, something that was expressed to me very early on was the importance of remaining politically impartial. As political leadership of the government changes, the workforce of the public service remains constant. This is to make sure there is continuity in service provided to Canadians and that this service is delivered to all Canadians fairly and equally, regardless of political affiliation. For a public servant doing research, however, the need for impartiality also means there are limitations on academic freedom—applying my knowledge as a federal scientist to support partisan views would benefit some Canadians but disadvantage others.

When examining the relationship between *who I am* and *how I do research* in my job, my professional obligations supersede, but do not exclude, my personal values and perspectives. This implied tension between personal and professional identity should not be overstated—thankfully, my professional and personal perspectives are not frequently at odds—but is still one of the key differences between the experience of doing research as a public servant and as an academic.

POSITIONALITY IN PRACTICE

The above provides a glimpse into the ways in which my positionality as a social scientist has to be reconciled with my professional obligations as a public servant, regulated by a complex framework of policies and legislation. But this is only half the story. As a new researcher working in applied military personnel research, a large part of my initiation involved learning how to interact within the military organization. In the beginning, this meant learning organizational acronyms, language, and structures, and recognizing the differences between military ranks; this led to an awareness of how I should address different rank levels appropriately, and figuring out how I could approach and navigate the military chain of command. With experience, I began to recognize the underlying values, narratives, and ways of making meaning (Giddens 1991; Kegan 1982; Strong et al. 2008) shared among military members, all of which provide insight into military culture and, most importantly, its expectations about research; thus, I learned how to interact with the military—both as the "client" and the subject of research—through sets of socially determined rules and organizational behaviours.

A good example from my experience doing qualitative research is gaining access to military participants for a study and excusing them from their workday to participate. The importance of the chain of command and of military leadership's role in looking after their people is deeply entrenched in the CAF. Even with institutionally delegated authority to conduct research with military members, I still require permission from a participant's immediate chain of command to have access to participants. When conducting qualitative research, it is therefore virtually impossible for a CAF member to participate without at least one person in her or his chain of command being aware.

When designing qualitative studies for the military, moreover, there is often an expectation to try to include as wide a cross-section of the sample population as possible, depending on the aim of the study. As an example, I ran a series of focus groups with members who are employed in one of a dozen technical military occupations that were eligible for occupational training at civilian colleges. The aim of the study was to see if civilian training led to any differences in early military socialization, as compared to traditional training through military schools. The personnel in my sample were working on bases across the country, which posed a significant, albeit common, methodological challenge. The usual approach in this situation is to rely on local military points of contact to help recruit participants and organize focus group schedules and spaces. Identifying local points of contact often means relying on the "client" of the study—that is, the military unit or authority who has requested the research—to reach out through, and sometimes across, the military chain of command. This arrangement is practical, in that it allows effective and timely local coordination, and it is also in keeping with the importance that is placed on engaging the chain of command when gaining access to personnel.

This approach also has the potential for other impacts on the research process. For example, by the time individuals are approached to participate, the direction to recruit volunteers has already passed through several layers of the chain of command and, much like the "telephone game," parts of the message are reinterpreted or lost altogether. As a result, the members I met with often had an incorrect understanding of the aim of the research and why they had been specifically identified to participate. To ensure informed consent and voluntary participation, I had to allow for additional time before the focus groups started to discuss the study with the participants, as well as the steps I would take to protect their identities in the analysis and reporting of my findings; thus, the way the military is organized—in this case, the manner in which access to military personnel is controlled through the chain of command—was somewhat out of sync with my professional obligations to those members in ensuring their free and informed consent. Although these checks and balances demonstrate how sometimes the context in which qualitative research happens is subject to competing rules and responsibilities, they also define the space in which applied military personnel research becomes possible, and ensure that participants and the organization are protected from harm.

My analysis and dissemination of qualitative research findings are also different in this context. Military personnel research is described as "client-driven," meaning that my research efforts are always directed towards specific organizational priorities. The nature of this arrangement means that military decision-makers usually prefer quantifiable and generalizable evidence when making decisions that may impact policies and processes. Qualitative research tends to be portrayed to military decision-makers as useful for "scoping out" a problem, or as part of a larger effort to develop or validate quantitative research instruments.

My first encounter with this view of qualitative research came while I was still in the midst of conducting focus groups and interviews for a project. I was asked by my client to attend a meeting of senior military officers and provide a summary of my initial findings from the focus groups. The meeting was attended in a small boardroom by a handful of brigadier-generals/commodores representing the Navy, Army, Air Force, and the Canadian Forces Recruiting Group. Eventually, my turn came on the agenda and

I took the podium. I began by explaining the larger study and the extensive conceptual work and model that I had developed, followed by the methodology for the focus groups and interviews I was still running. Before proceeding into a summary of my preliminary results I noted that, so far, I had only collected data from Air Force and Navy personnel, and therefore could not speak about the experiences of Army personnel at that time. It was at this point that the Army general leaned back in his chair, tossed his pen down on the table and crossed his arms, clearly signalling his loss of interest. I gave my presentation, and even received a few positive comments from the meeting's chair (a "two-star" major-general). As my final PowerPoint slide clicked over, the Army general immediately launched into a critique of the value of all the "anecdotal" information I had collected, and concluded by asking when they could expect to "see some numbers."

The reaction of the Army general is not unique among the military research clients with whom I work, which is informed by the "applied" nature of military personnel research. Every decision that military leadership makes has second- and third-order consequences related to publicly funded resources and operational effectiveness. Because accountability to the public is paramount, any scientific evidence that is used to inform decisions about policies and processes must be taken to represent as complete a picture within the organization as possible. This situation, therefore, creates the organizational conditions in which decisions informed by generalizable data are considered more justifiable. This institutional reality has led to a perspective that qualitative research is therefore less useful for decision-makers.

Qualitative research, however, does play a vital role in applied military personnel research, despite the manner in which it is sometimes understood. The development and validation of many of our quantitative research instruments and measures have relied on rigorous qualitative work to ensure they reflect the lived experience of military members as closely as possible. Perhaps most importantly, however, qualitative research serves the key function of giving voice to military members.

One of my earliest and most memorable research experiences was an interview I conducted with a young soldier concerning his time in Afghanistan. I was fortunate enough to be involved in a book project that aimed to profile military members who had been recognized for their actions during the early years of the Afghanistan mission. The idea behind the book (aside from adding to the historical record) was to let soldiers share their stories in their own words, and thereby provide some examples of what it means to put Canadian military values into practice. The interview was conducted at the soldier's base, where he had been excused from his regular duties to participate. I met with him in an unoccupied conference room that had been arranged for the interview. In truth, he was not much younger than me and, dressed in his uniform, he was the epitome of military discipline and professionalism. As I was less than a year on the job and as this was my first real interview with a military member, I was more than a little unsure of myself. In rapid succession, I introduced myself, explained the book project again, reviewed the consent form with him, had him sign it, and gave him an opportunity to ask any questions before we started. I recall avoiding eye contact with him by staring at a checklist in my hand that contained all of the steps of the approved interview protocol that I was supposed to follow. In short order, I had switched on the tape recorder and jumped right into my prepared list of questions.

The soldier listened to my first question patiently, and then sat quietly for several long moments until I finally looked up and met his eye. He waited another moment, and then the first thing he said to me was, "I have PTSD [post-traumatic stress disorder]…. Talking about this is still very hard, and I don't know if I will get through it. But I owe it to my friends, who didn't make it home with me, to tell this story." The experience of those words was a defining moment for me as a researcher, and still elicits a gut reaction in me today. In that moment, any thought of the policies or rules, the oaths or the codes of conduct that I was working under simply vanished. I listened and watched in awe as this person shared his incredible story with me, at times visibly struggling to continue, but determined to see it through.

One of the actions recommended to our team during the project's ethics review was to try and prepare for the possibility of interviewing members suffering with PTSD or other operational stress injuries. Those preparations included consultation with medical professionals, attending military conferences on mental health, taking suicide awareness training, and developing an information package detailing available organizational resources that would be provided to participants. We also spent a great deal of time discussing how far our obligation towards our interview participants extended and the point at which our ethical responsibility would be satisfied. All of these actions and discussions, although important and helpful, originated and were carried out within the same organizational context that regulates military personnel research. In other words, how we went about studying and preparing for members with PTSD—how we defined and understood the issue—was also impacted by the same organizational context in which we worked. My experience in this first interview, however, demonstrated to me how these types of preparations will always be limited, because rules and policy can never be a substitute for lived experienced.

My interview with the soldier was a defining experience for many reasons. It helped to dispel some of my own assumptions about the people who choose to serve, allowing me to eventually alter my positionality as a researcher. One of the key lessons from this experience, upon reflection, has been that, although the rules that regulate military personnel research are necessary to safeguard the underlying principles of public service and the military members themselves who participate, the "lived experience" of doing qualitative research with military members entails a much more authentic act of exchange and meaning-making (Ellis, Adams, and Bochner 2011; Strong et al. 2008). That is, the rules that regulate the business of military personnel research should not be assumed to wholly dominate the particular moment of collaboration, meaning-making, and exchange that is shared between researcher and participant during qualitative research. The context (including the rules) defines the space in which this exchange may occur, which in turn creates the potential for the military member's voice to be heard. Giving military members an opportunity to have their voices heard and being able to incorporate their perspective into the evidence researchers provide to senior decision-makers illustrates the significant contribution that qualitative inquiry makes to applied military personnel research.

CRAFTING QUALITATIVE RESEARCH EXERCISES

1. As a qualitative researcher, it's important to understand your own positionality—that is, how *who you are* interacts with *how you research*. Take some time to reflect on your positionality. Think about and write down where you come from, what you believe in and value, your culture, your heritage, and your personal characteristics. Now using what you've written, consider how these aspects of who you are might influence the way you would approach doing qualitative research. Pay particular attention to not just your strengths but where you may need to be more mindful.

2. Imagine presenting the results of a qualitative research project about student life to your university's administrators. During the presentation it becomes clear that they consider the results "anecdotal," not generalizable to the student body, and therefore of minimal use to their goal of improving the student experience at your school. Write down some points you could make to counter this perception about the value of your qualitative findings.

3. Imagine that you are planning a qualitative research project that could involve potentially vulnerable participants. This might be a project with children, or with those suffering from a mental illness, or perhaps members of a marginalized group. Consider some of the risks these individuals might face by participating in your study and then write down what steps you would take to try and mitigate them.

NOTE

1. This chapter is under Crown copyright. The opinions expressed in this chapter are solely those of the author, and do not reflect the position of the Department of National Defence, the Canadian Armed Forces, or the Government of Canada.

REFERENCES

Ellis, Carolyn, Tony E. Adams, and Arthur P. Bochner. 2011. "Autoethnography: An Overview." *Historical Social Research* 36 (4): 273–90.

Giddens, Anthony. 1991. *Modernity and Self-Identity: Self and Society in the Late Modern Age.* Redwood City, CA: Stanford University Press.

Kegan, Robert. 1982. *The Evolving Self: Problems and Processes in Human Development.* Cambridge, MA: Harvard University Press.

Strong, Tom, Nathan R. Pyle, Cecile deVries, Dawn N. Johnston, and Allison J. Foskett. 2008. "Meaning-Making Lenses in Counselling: Discursive, Hermeneutic-Phenomenological, and Autoethnographic Perspectives." *Canadian Journal of Counselling* 42 (2): 117–30.

Taber, Nancy. 2012. "Beginning with the Self to Critique the Social: Critical Researchers as Whole Beings." In *An Ethnography of Global Landscapes and Corridors*, edited by Loshini Naidoo, 73–88. IntechOpen. https://doi.org/10.5772/35336.

14 Navigating Emotions While Establishing Trust and Rapport in Autoethnography

Colleen McMillan

How do emotions help or hinder a researcher when doing an autoethnographic study? How does one negotiate the slippery slope of ethical behaviour when this method depends on the authenticity of emotions to engage with one's subject? This chapter will explore these questions and more in the context of using this highly reflective, reflexive, and rewarding qualitative research method. Let's start with a definition of what autoethnography is as described in the literature.

Autoethnography is a genre of writing, research, and clinical work that merges the personal into the cultural, placing the self within a social context (Reed-Danahay 1997). As such, content is written in the first person and makes central dialogue, emotion, and self-consciousness, and aims to understand how institutional stories are affected by history, social structure, and culture (Ellis and Bochner 2000). Known widely for her pioneering work with this qualitative method, Carolyn Ellis (2004) offers us this definition: "[autoethnography is a] research, writing, story, and method that connect[s] the autobiographical and personal to the cultural, social, and political" (xix). Maréchal (2010, 43) adds that "autoethnography is a form or method of research that involves self-observation and reflexive investigation in the context of ethnographic field work and writing." As a newer qualitative method, autoethnography continues to evolve, which makes it an exciting and forgiving research approach for beginning researchers. This is best illustrated by how Adams, Jones, and Ellis (2015, 12) normalize the messiness of ethnography when they say, "social life is messy, uncertain, and emotional. If our desire is to research social life, then we must embrace a research method that, to the best of its/our ability, acknowledges and accommodates mess and chaos, uncertainty and emotion."

The critical message here is to embrace the emotional chaos autoethnography offers. It is initially hard to resist the innate urge to neatly categorize emotions and roles, but doing so will remove the richness of this method. Allow yourself to shift toward an intentional place of vulnerability, to become a human canvas for the myriad emotions that will colour your research journey with the vibrancy this method promises.

THE ROLE OF REFLEXIVITY

As you embark on autoethnography, a first step is to identify and reflect upon the myriad roles you already assume: student, sister, child, friend, teacher, parent, tutor, mentor, among many others. Within each of these roles there lies a multitude of embedded narratives entangled within the relationship, cradling smaller and more nuanced stories that may not be obvious until they are staring at you. The immediacy of such moments can catch you in unexpected ways, poking your vulnerabilities and raising the issue of reflexivity.

The concept of reflexivity is defined as "the process of examining oneself as researcher and the research relationship" (Hsiung 2008, 212). It involves examining one's "conceptual baggage," meaning one's assumptions, biases, and beliefs around how knowledge is constructed and who is considered a knowledge holder. While a guiding principle of qualitative research is to be intentional about practicing reflexivity, the complexity of human relationships eclipses even the most experienced interviewer, leading to blind spots, which is not a bad thing. One of the joys of autoethnography is giving yourself permission to experience emotions that seep unnoticed into the relationship. This is especially true as you work toward establishing the essential premise of trust, a prerequisite for entry into recessed content held by the person you are interviewing. The reciprocal nature of autoethnography means that you may become aware of information stored within yourself, which may come as a surprise. Allowing such information to freely surface will allow you to become more attuned to yourself as a research instrument. Reflecting upon *why* such emotions or feelings are now surfacing is critical to developing authenticity and trust in this relational method.

Honouring the concept of "voice" is another guiding principle valued by qualitative research; when using autoethnography, this means making your own voice visible in addition to your participant's in a respective, equitable way. This marks a shift from ethnography, where the voice of the interviewer is absent in the text. Referred to as "silent authorship," this type of writing was once considered to be the mark of mature scholarship (Charmaz and Mitchell 1996). Shifting from ethnography to autoethnography creates space for the interviewer to be heard in addition to the participant; however, writing with voice also means making transparent emotions that surface during the relationship-building part of the interview, a critical part of attaining the depth needed to fully understand an issue. Several examples will illustrate this last point.

IS IT RESEARCH OR THERAPY? WHEN EMOTIONS AND ETHICS INTERSECT

Can therapy sessions ever merge into research? Alternatively, can research interviews be experienced as therapeutic? This question is explored by Kvale and Brinkman (2009) in their book *InterViews: Learning the Craft of Qualitative Research Interviewing*. They suggest that an interview becomes therapeutic when a "change through an emotional personal interaction [occurs] which can lead to increased understanding and change" (41). Can such a proposition happen in both research and therapeutic interviews? Despite the postmodern slant of this question, it was, ironically, Freud who approached the therapeutic interview as a research method: "It is indeed one of the distinctions of psychoanalysis that research and treatment proceed hand in hand" (1963, 120).

As a clinical social worker and qualitative researcher working in health care, I regularly work with people who are experiencing painful issues, including trauma. Several years ago, I had the opportunity of working with Helen, a white, Western-educated woman who was hit by a taxi while visiting her adult son in Shanghai. Despite being perilously close to death, Helen lived, but upon her eventual return home she was given the diagnosis of posttraumatic stress disorder (PTSD) by her physician. Helen refuted this diagnosis. Helen's feminist standpoint rejected what she saw as a label, neatly categorizing her experience into a box without taking into account how the intersection of social location and race, specifically that she was white and had money, allowed her to live.

Our work began rather routinely, characterized by my slowly building rapport with the goal of establishing trust. My professional training initially allowed me to suspend my emotions, making space for me to be unequivocally present to hear about Helen's daily struggles of resistance as she defied being seen as "sick" by others. At the beginning, Helen's stories were individualized, meaning that the majority of our time was spent exploring *her* symptoms. This part of the relationship was effortless because it allowed me to remain in my familiar role of expert. And then Helen's stories changed, and I felt the ground shift under me.

Her stories grew larger. They reached into meta-narratives of gendered violence against women. They spoke to preferential standards of health care, depending on whether your skin was brown, yellow, or white, or whether you had cash or spoke English. As Helen's stories of trauma collected cultural and societal meanings, I could feel the circumference of my professional space become smaller and smaller, until, one day, the lines defining professional distance and personal experience crossed.

If you have ever watched the tide roll into a beach, then you also know that the tide eventually returns to the sea. The first time these lines intersected I managed to hold on to my inner voice that spoke to emotions of vulnerability and surprise. What is happening here? I asked myself. Yet, I managed to quiet this inner script under the guise of professionalism, reassuring myself it was likely a one-off occurrence and that my clinician self would steadfastly return. The predictability of the next couple of sessions confirmed my standpoint as the professional. Helen had regressed, feeling fatigued due to recurring and intrusive nightmares of abandonment. Trust was firmly rooted in our relationship at this time and I felt emotionally attuned to Helen and her struggles. As I unpacked Helen's description of her nightmare, I stumbled across a feeling of incongruence within myself that, if unaddressed, would be counter-therapeutic and actually do harm. Helen's stories of gendered trauma had entered my consciousness and lived experiences of being a woman. I was aware that at a subconscious level my inability to reconcile these conflicting emotions was being detected by Helen. Charmaz and Mitchell (1996, 212) succinctly capture this dynamic when they write, "we act as if we can cover up confusion, as if ignorance does not show." No longer could I ignore what was now an ethical issue, one that held the potential to erode the rapport we had worked so hard to establish.

Opening oneself up to possibilities when faced with challenges can also open up new frameworks of thinking and doing. I went back to the tide metaphor, and remembered reading advice about what to do if ever caught in a tide: go with the current and do not try to swim against it. Swimming against the current of what felt authentic was, in fact, unethical conduct within the context of my relationship with Helen. Simply put, while making my emotions visible to Helen went against my social work training, not doing so placed Helen at risk by rupturing the trust we had worked hard at creating.

While this case makes explicit the importance of reflexivity and truly knowing oneself, the following two examples illustrate how *not* making emotions visible can result in the same outcome: the preservation of trust within a relationship. Regardless of the choice you make, it is imperative that you "check in" with your internal set of values and beliefs to avoid being perceived as disingenuous.

Several years ago, I used the qualitative method of photovoice for a study that explored the concept of autonomy and connection experienced by adolescent girls who displayed disordered eating behaviours (McMillan 2010). Girls between the ages of 9 and 12 were asked to take photos of concepts related to connection, disconnection, dieting, acceptance, and mutuality. Each week we would spend a Saturday afternoon together as a group, talking about the concepts, doing artwork, playing games, and sharing snacks. As the girls developed relationships with each other and with me, conversations evolved to become more layered, complex, and complicated, reflective of a deepening rapport within the group.

Over the course of four months, stories disclosed by two of the girls moved me into emotional terrain that see-sawed between feelings of duty, urgency, responsibility, resignation, and, finally, permission to release. Mary was a vivacious 12-year-old girl who liked pink nails, pink hair ribbons, and high-topped Nike sneakers. On the demographics questionnaire, Mary's body mass index score was slightly higher than the norm for her height. She usually arrived late to the group due to a schedule that was bookmarked by photo shoots and meetings with modelling agencies, as Mary's mother believed she had potential to become a teen model. She also typically arrived hungry and would ask if we could have snacks early. This pattern continued for several months, during which time I noticed Mary stuffing her knapsack full of snacks when I was out of the room. Upon leaving one afternoon, Mary dissolved into tears in response to my wishing her a good weekend. Between sobs, she shared that she hated going to modelling appointments as her weight inevitably came up as a booking obstacle. As a solution, Mary's mother placed her on a low-caloric diet, which left her hungry much of the time. Mary made me promise I would not tell anyone, as she craved the attention and closeness to her mother that resulted from the modelling appointments. This scenario was further complicated by two additional layers: I knew the physician who told Mary and her mother of the research group, and I had seen Mary's sister as a client two years earlier for a different kind of eating disorder. Her sister was also in modelling.

On the other hand, I had Chelsey: a quiet, thin 11-year-old with eyes defined by large dark circles. Chelsey and her younger sister lived with their grandmother, whom I never saw during the four months of the study. One Saturday I arrived an hour early to prepare for the group and Chelsey was waiting outside of the locked door shivering in the crisp November air. Her eyes asked me not to question her so we simply went into the building together and I gave her the task of cutting construction paper. Several times, Chelsey's grandmother did not come to pick her up after our group finished. Rather than risk embarrassing her, I would ask if she would like a drive home, which was simply accepted with a head nod. Once in the car, Chelsey transformed into a different girl, one that was animated and full of questions. During one of these drives home there was a longer than normal pause and I instinctively glanced at Chelsey to see tears dropping onto her lap. As I pulled into the parking lot, I saw a colleague of mine who worked for Children and Family Services entering the front door of the apartment building. I stopped the car. The deafening silence gave way to a sharp closing of the car door, and I never saw Chelsey again. I did, however, start to receive emails from her a few weeks later, detailing experiences that were beyond her ability to process. Words that felt too shameful in person found their way to the keyboard.

HOLDING AND RELEASING

As you read through each case, you may have asked yourself the following question: Did the presence of emotions not complicate things and create messy ethical dilemmas? Absolutely. Emotions such as caring, acceptance, compassion, and concern granted me entry into deeply personal recesses of each person's life, allowing me to build a space defined by trust and safety. By doing so, I entered terrain that was slippery, unfamiliar, and terrifying at times. Was it my intrapersonal uncertainty that contributed to Helen's nightmares of abandonment? By agreeing to Mary's request for confidentiality was I maleficent toward her disordered eating? And, finally, by asking questions, instead of trying to remain respectful through silence, could I have prevented Chelsey from being removed from her grandmother's care? Had I remained objective, protected by clean, discreet boundaries, I may have neatly retrieved my data without finding myself in these emotional swamps of relational quandaries. I would be exiting the relationship with data that was superficial, empty, and void of meaning.

Giving yourself permission to relinquish control of your emotions during an interview can open doors for both you and your participant to sojourn together into deeper internal crevices that cradle meanings that would never find their way into a research question. For example, my time spent with Helen pushed me to examine my own personal narratives of cultural and societal trauma against women, and my efforts to hold these emotions separate mocked me as I strove to be authentic. Another lesson I learned was not to underestimate the importance of silence in building rapport without first knowing how words may have been violent or hurtful in someone's past. Filling the extended periods of silence with words when driving Chelsey home rather than simply accepting her need to "to just be," might have felt violating to her. My own anxiety around this space threatened the seeds of trust that were planted in the silence of those car rides.

Holding on to preconceived ideas of how to act during an interview can reduce a rich, personal exchange into a performance, leaving both parties feeling unsatisfied. While one must have some sense of where an interview might go, being authentic with one's emotions will grant you entry into places of silence, or conversation, wherever the greatest of meanings reside. You will know when you arrive through the emotion of connection—to your participant, to the research issue, but also with yourself.

CRAFTING QUALITATIVE RESEARCH EXERCISES

1. Identify how many roles you play in several of your close relationships. Pick one of these roles and reflect on how you typically communicate with the other person. Now add another layer—what are the issues that you do not talk about and why? Compare your answer to another relationship. What is the difference and what does this say about who you are?

2. Identify a relationship where your emotions have changed or evolved over a period of at least six months. Create a timeline and mark on the timeline what emotions you experienced according to what was happening in the relationship. Identify the intersections and whether there is a pattern or any association. Once you have plotted these intersections ask yourself the following question: Where was the concept of trust at these points in time?

3. Position yourself in a situation like the one with Mary, where a multitude of items concurrently collide in a single moment—ethics, confidentiality, trust, values, and responsibility. How would you negotiate through this and preserve the relationship with Mary while doing so? What resonated with you while reading this case and is that emotion still with you now?

4. Identify an emotion that others use to define who you are as a person. Give an age to that emotion: how old is it? Now interview that emotion. You might start by asking how it has helped or hindered you in relationships. If that emotion has helped you, how could it be an asset when building rapport or trust during autoethnographic interviewing?

REFERENCES

Adams, Tony E., Stacy Holman Jones, and Carolyn Ellis. 2015. *Autoethnography: Understanding Qualitative Research*. New York: Oxford University Press.

Charmaz, Kathy, and Terence R. Mitchell. 1996. "The Myth of Silent Authorship: Self, Substance, and Style in Ethnographic Writing." *Symbolic Interaction* 19 (4): 285–302.

Ellis, Carolyn. 2004. *The Ethnographic I: A Methodological Novel about Autoethnography*. Walnut Creek, CA: AltaMira Press.

Ellis, Carolyn, and Arthur P. Bochner. 2000. "Autoethnography, Personal Narrative, Reflexivity: Researcher as Subject." In *The Handbook of Qualitative Research*, edited by Norman Denzin, and Yvonna Lincoln, 733–68. Thousand Oaks, CA: Sage.

Freud, Sigmund. 1963. *Therapy and Technique*. New York: Collier.

Hsiung, Ping-Chun. 2008. "Teaching Reflexivity in Qualitative Interviewing." *Teaching Sociology* 36 (3): 211–26.

Kvale, Steinar, and Svend Brinkman. 2009. *InterViews: Learning the Craft of Qualitative Research Interviewing*. London: Sage.

Maréchal, Garance. 2010. "Autoethnography." In *Encyclopedia of Case Study Research*, vol. 2, edited by Albert J. Mills, Gabrielle Durepos, and Elden Wiebe, 43-45. Thousand Oaks, CA: Sage.

McMillan, Colleen. 2010. "What the Body Stories of Girls Tell Us about Autonomy and Connection During Connection." PhD diss., Wilfrid Laurier University, Kitchener, ON, Canada.

Reed-Danahay, Deborah R. 1997. *Auto/Ethnography: Rewriting the Self and the Social*. Oxford, UK: Bloomsbury Academic.

15 Personal Reputation as an "In" to Field Research Settings

Steven W. Kleinknecht

REPUTATION AS A FIELD RESEARCH CONSIDERATION

Having grown up surrounded by the Old Order Mennonites, I have been intrigued by the simple life they appear to lead. Biking along the back roads near my village, it was not uncommon in the summer to see bonnet-clad women with plain, dark-coloured ankle-length dresses working in the flower and vegetable gardens, children playing games with each other in the yard, livestock milling about in the pasture, and fathers and sons working the fields. Although tractors, electricity, and the telephone are now common amenities among these people, they belie the Old Order Mennonites' sense of simplicity as evidenced by their plain dress, horse-drawn transportation, and general suspicion of technology. Despite living in the same area as these Mennonites, I later realized that I really never got to know any of them or to understand their way of life. This became even clearer as I embarked on an ethnography of cultural continuity among the Old Order Mennonites.

While I soon discovered that I had much to learn about the Old Order way of life, it was also certainly the case that my lifelong geographical proximity to this community offered several methodological advantages. Not only did it place me in the heart of Ontario's Old Order Mennonite country, it also meant that I had a history in the community. Or, more importantly, my family had a history in the community and our family name was well regarded. As one would expect with traditional groups, personal and family reputation forms a strong basis for judging whether or not one can be trusted. In this regard, my family name was key in helping facilitate access. My grandfather, Frank Kleinknecht, had taught many of the now oldest members of the Old Order community. Having this as an "in" to the Old Order community was both advantageous and, as I quickly came to understand, problematic.

As a qualitative researcher, a good reputation can be key to finding an "in" to our research settings. When potential research participants know nothing about the researcher's personal reputation, they consider other aspects about you, as the researcher, to situate you within their realm of understanding. Like anyone, they do this so that they might better know what to expect from you, how an interaction with you might proceed, and if you can be trusted. In these instances, when personal reputation is unknown, the reputation of our discipline, or people fitting the researcher identity more generally, impinges on our efforts to conduct a study. In this vein, the stereotype of the lab coat–wearing scientific researcher has done us no favours; however, what we do offer as qualitative researchers is a sympathetic ear, an open mind, and lots of time to understand how our participants feel, act, and see the world. The opportunity to explain our approach to participants is perhaps the highest card we can play as qualitative researchers.

Now, for groups that are familiar with us personally, the element of reputation takes on a different dimension. Our participants can at least partially transcend the "scientific researcher" stereotype and consider our personal reputation when agreeing to participate and offer intimate details about their experiences and perspectives. Having lived near the Old Order Mennonites for most of my life, I was counting on my personal reputation to ease the process of acceptance into their community. In this chapter, I will describe how I have come to think about the benefits and problematics of personal reputation in the field. I will explore the variously intertwined issues of developing trust and rapport, dealing with taken-for-granteds, and the role conflict of being both a real person—and sometimes friend to the participants—and a social scientist. I will draw on my research experiences with the Old Order Mennonites as a reference point.

DEVELOPING TRUST AND RAPPORT

When researching a group of people that are already at least somewhat familiar with you personally, through reputation, one might be hasty to assume that trust and rapport are pre-established. While having a good reputation going into the project likely aids in the development of trust and rapport, it is by no means going to be immediate or constant. As with any sustained qualitative project that puts one near their communities of interest, trust and rapport are constantly being negotiated. For me, in my research with the Old Order Mennonites, rapport was partially pre-established, but most certainly developed as I invoked and provoked stories of my grandfather.

As I found more and more that people in the Mennonite community knew my grandfather, and saw him in a positive light, it became a useful icebreaker to open the interview with a line such as "You might know my grandfather, Frank Kleinknecht?" To which most people would respond with something like, "Ah, you're Frank's grandson! Your grandfather was a wonderful man." Or, "Let me tell ya a story about Frank …" Or, "My sister was so interested when she heard that your grandfather was the old Frank Kleinknecht. Because she really liked him as a teacher." Or "He liked the name Barbara apparently. I remember my sister saying that. He said, 'You know what we would name a girl if we had one? Barbara. You know what we would name another girl if we had another girl? Barbara.'" This was a great aspect of the research. Not only did it allow me to foster rapport with participants and help keep our discussions congenial, it allowed me to learn more about a man I had much respect and love for.

But, it was not always win-win. On one occasion when meeting with an older conservative Mennonite man, I found the interview was getting to be a little dour, so I thought it might be a good time to invoke the ghost of Frank to get the interview back on course and set a lighter tone. So, at the right moment, when there had been a pause in the conversation, I said,

Steve: I was wondering, you must've known my grandfather? Frank Kleinknecht?
Old Order Mennonite: Nope.
Steve: He was a schoolteacher back in the '50s and '60s around here …
Old Order Mennonite: Nope.
* *Silence* *
Steve: Okay, so you were just telling me about Mennonite theology …

And so we continued our interview.

At times I felt a sense of guilt for building on my family's well-regarded reputation in the community. Sometimes it felt that I was using and, though I hate to think it, abusing, my grandfather's good name to secure me brownie points. Perhaps it even led to me finding out more about the community than I might have had they not so trusted me and respected my family. Of course, developing such intimate familiarity with a group that trusts you not only on professional grounds, but also personal grounds, adds a dimension to the research that some of us, myself included, might not be all that comfortable with. Such feelings of uncertainty are not uncommon in qualitative research. There are a lot of unknowns, awkward situations, and on-your-toes moments we must face. I find some solace in knowing that my participants' trust in me helps to set them at ease. My aims are to better understand a group's way of life and learn more about how the social world operates. If personal reputation can assist me in these endeavours, my mind is less burdened and my research that much better.

NAVIGATING THE TAKEN-FOR-GRANTEDS

As researchers, a number of the things we take for granted in our everyday lives cannot be taken for granted when we don our analytical caps. While in many ways we all share common cultural understandings, there is usually much more going on within people's lives than meets our often ethnocentric eye. While we know that we, as researchers, need to attune our gaze to the perspectives of those we are attempting to understand, our participants will most likely continue to work with their taken-for-granteds.

For research participants, the issue of "taken-for-granteds" arises when they presume that you have more familiarity with their life-worlds than you really do. Although it is sometimes difficult to interject when our background knowledge of the group is being taken for granted by participants, we know that it is imperative for us to do so. This issue becomes amplified when the group knows you personally. And why would it not be? Probably part of the reason you are allowed to be there and why they feel somewhat comfortable with you is because they feel that they know you. Maybe you are from their area or you have a reputation that is well respected by members of the group.

The Old Order Mennonites that I was studying knew I grew up in the area, that my grandfather had taught them or many of their parents and grandparents, and that I had a good reputation, or, more specifically, I had a good name by way of a positive family reputation. The types of taken-for-granteds that arose on the part of my familiarity to the group were numerous, but revolved around having a good understanding about the Mennonite way of life, knowing the geographical area, and knowing who was related to whom. This led to some complications, which could have been somewhat damaging to the study, or at the very least embarrassing, had I let their assumptions take root. Let me demonstrate with a taken-for-granted moment from my Mennonite research when an Old Order woman assumed I knew which church was theirs:

Old Order Mennonite: Our church is the one just heading into Creekside.

Steve: Okay, I know where you mean … Actually, are there not two Mennonite churches on the way into town?

Old Order Mennonite: Oh yes, but make sure you come to ours and not the Dave Martins. Ours is the one on the left, the Daves are on the right coming into town.

Steve: I guess that would be a problem if I went to their church?

Old Order Mennonite: Oh, yes. They would not be too happy if you walked in. They would likely not be physical towards you, but they would wait until you left before they would start their service. They're not very friendly, and you would be made to feel very unwelcome.

Steve: That's good to know.

In this moment, had I let our assumptions persist in order to save face, I would have awkwardly ended up at the wrong church. At the same time, the example illustrates how the participant assumed I knew the area well. It was often taken for granted that I knew more about their culture than I did. Things that seemed superficial and common knowledge to them were of great interest to me. In this vein, I found myself probing for more information, which again was met with quizzical stares. My ignorance was baffling, but sincere.

I have come to learn that, to do worthwhile qualitative research, we must question both our own taken-for-granteds and those of our participants. This can be awkward, though, when we research close to home. Stating what we do not know in front of friends, family, or acquaintances is sometimes more difficult than doing so in front of strangers we might never see again. Knowing that all sides take things for granted during research allows us to watch out for those moments and reflect on their impact during data collection and later analysis. When it comes to managing participants' assumptions, an on-the-spot strategy is to interrupt a perceived taken-for-granted with a question. For instance, we can follow up participants' quizzical looks with self-deprecating humour such as, "Yes, it's true, I really do know that little, which is why I'm here." Or, building on this, you can play to the participant's role, and perhaps pander a bit to their ego, through a statement like, "You're the expert on what it is you do in your everyday life. I'm here to learn from you."

MANAGING ROLE CONFLICT AND LEAVING THE FIELD

For me, accessing the Old Order community at least partially because of my ancestral reputation was personally problematic. I had a hard time reconciling the role conflict generated by being both researcher and friend to the participants. First and foremost, I did not want to abuse the good name and close relationships that my family, and particularly my grandfather, had built up over the years. In addition, as I carried out the research, my respect and admiration for the Old Order community had only grown. As many qualitative researchers have found, the personal bonds we develop with participants who share many hours and close, personal experiences with us makes it difficult to write about the community without questioning not only "Am I doing the group justice," but also, "Am I doing my friends and family justice?"

When building on and developing personal ties with participants, it is always a dilemma to filter out as many personal biases that might encroach on one's analysis as possible. To reconcile this discrepancy is not an easy task. Our perspectives are tied to our experiences and the stocks of knowledge we have generated. With this in mind, I attempted to distinguish between my roles as both analyst and friend to the Mennonite community as I conducted my research, while fully recognizing that they are not wholly separable.

Sometimes researchers might wish to escape their past research and certain participants they have met along the way; however, truly leaving the field and severing ties with participants is not a real option when personal ties were pre-established with the community. Fortunately, I have been able to stay on good terms with everyone I have met during my research. At the same time, I have learned that foregoing such relationships for the sake of science is not all that necessary.

CONCLUSION

I have come to a greater appreciation of qualitative research by grappling with the various dilemmas brought on by having a pre-existing personal reputation in my field site. The advantage that my family reputation provided for me in offering a way into the Mennonite community is perhaps best summed up in the following comments made by an Old Order woman: "It helped a lot [knowing you were Frank Kleinknecht's grandson], and I probably would've let you come anyway, but when you said your name was

Kleinknecht, I thought, 'He'll be okay' *laughter*." We invest a great deal of ourselves any time we conduct a qualitative study. I think we up the ante when the research takes on a personal tone. A good personal reputation can set the scene for you, get you some ins, partially establish an element of trust and rapport, and have participants be more at ease with you and your research. At the same time, personal reputation, and assumed familiarity with the group's way of life, leads participants to take for granted that we know more about them than we really do. Potentially interesting surface issues might be glossed over, and living up to one's reputation can be a constant concern. Whether recognized or not, the reputations of our personal past and discipline are at play in our qualitative research projects. When it is clear that reputation is on your side, be aware of the biases it creates, see how it can work for you, and for your own piece of mind, try not to abuse it.

CRAFTING QUALITATIVE RESEARCH EXERCISES

1. Consider a qualitative research project you might be interested in doing that builds off your personal connections. Perhaps it is a project that draws on a sports team you belong to, co-workers, your family, close friends, or classmates. Write down some of the obstacles you might encounter in having to manage your ties to these people and collecting in-depth, personal insights from them about their perspectives, feelings, actions, and experiences. Remember, your relationship with these people will continue after your project is complete.

2. A research participant who is also a close friend has told you a secret about herself that is relevant to your topic. Consider whether or not you will use this information as data in your project. What should you do in this situation? How might you present the data in a research paper if she says that it is okay for you to use it? What issues might arise if you decide to include it or not to include it?

3. Spend 10 minutes doing an unstructured interview with a friend or a classmate you know well. Make a controversial topic the focus of the interview. Then, with the interviewee, discuss and write down some advantages and limitations that arose because you were doing an interview with someone you know well— both from the point of view of the interviewer and the participant.

16 "You Are Not Allowed to Be Here...": Ethnography of Rejection, Shame, and Hurt

Thaddeus Müller

> I am in a medical marijuana dispensary in Toronto and introduce myself as a Dutch professor interested in drugs policy. He says: "How did you get in, are you a member?" I reply that his colleague had let me in and that I am not a member. "You are not allowed to be here and I also have no time for you. I am running a business. Just go online, you can find all information you need there."

It is quite common that researchers get rejected during fieldwork. During my 30 years of experience as a fieldworker, I have encountered dozens of rejections, which can be painful, even for a seasoned researcher. Sometimes we refer to this in our publications, but we hardly reflect on it in an extensive way (Hennink, Hutter, and Bailey 2010; Lofland et al. 2006; Warren and Karner 2005). By focusing on this topic I want to give a more complete portrayal of the practice of qualitative research that novice researchers can use in preparation for entering the field (Johnson 1975; Lareau and Shultz 1996; Müller 2013). Here I will use examples from my own career and I will also present some strategies I have used in dealing with rejection.

The first time I did an interview I was 19 years old and felt very uncomfortable. It was like doing something "deviant." I expected that people had no interest in talking to me. But I was wrong. I learned over the years that if you show genuine interest, people tend to like to talk to you, especially people who are introduced to you by a third party, which is also known as a "warm" introduction. But during "cold" introductions, as in a situation when researchers approach a person unknown to them, rejection is quite common.

A rejection in "normal" social life can be painful because you might feel that this is a rejection of yourself. And when you are self-conscious and have some insecurity about who you are, you might think it is all about you. But that is, in general, not the case in fieldwork. The three most common motives I have encountered for refusing an interview are "being busy," "distrust," and "self-interest."

BEING BUSY

During research on the user's experience of a central city square in Rotterdam, it was fairly easy to interview those sitting on benches and those hanging around with friends. But people who walked hurriedly through the square tended to refuse an interview, mostly because they had no time. I could have ended the interaction after their refusal, but after some time I decided to walk with them through the square and prolong the interaction. Even during those few extra minutes, people would share important information. It turned out that most people who refused an interview did not like the square because of its design and the presence of teenagers. Their refusal was also an indication of how they related to the square, as they did not see it as a place for social encounters. Once in a while they became so enwrapped in the conversation that they would take more time to explain themselves, talking to me at the side of the square.

I had a similar experience while researching "social cohesion" in a high-rise building of over 100 units in Tilburg. I walked from door to door and invited people for a focus meeting. When people refused, I prolonged the conversation and asked for the reason. This would say a lot about the people living in their flat and their time to socialize. It turned out that at least half of the people were heavily involved in organizing their lives between work (e.g., working night shifts), family (e.g., single parents), volunteer work, care (e.g., senior parents), hobbies, and dealing with their health (e.g., hospital). I learned that being that busy hardly left time for "social cohesion," a finding in itself.

Casually, I would also ask if they liked living in the neighbourhood. In some cases, this would trigger conversations from five minutes long to over an hour, during which some inhabitants would reveal that they had actually had some friendly fleeting contact in the flats. Sometimes people changed their minds and decided to come to the focus meeting. In this case I also learned something different: because of the many rejections, I could better identify with the discontent of active citizens who complained about the limited involvement of other inhabitants.

When the motive for a rejection is "being busy," a rejection is not always a (full) rejection. It pays to take a rejection not too personally and not to be too civil all the time as a researcher—to use what I would like to call the "salesperson strategy." But it will take some time to be able to use this strategy. We all learn to stick to the rule "not to bother people one does not know." But you can learn to see making contact as an exciting game. It can become adventurous because you never know what to expect. It might lead to new and challenging information about the social worlds we study.

DISTRUST

Distrust is quite a common motive for not participating in research, especially when it is related to criminal, deviant, or transgressive behaviour (Adler 1993; Ferrell and Hamm

1998; Liebow 1967). In these cases, respondents might think that you are, for instance, a police officer or a journalist (with the intention of portraying them in a negative way). In some cases, the researcher is able to directly change a situation of distrust into one of trust. When I talked to a former PhD student of Diederik Stapel, a fraudulent social psychologist who faked the research and the data in at least 55 articles published in top-tier journals, she distrusted me because she did not want her narrative published in the media. An email from my university account solved that problem. When I did a study on youth hanging around and littering, some of them would smoke pot and put away their joints in my presence. They thought I was connected to the police. When I said that they could smoke a joint in front of me and that it did not bother me, the ice was broken.

In some cases, respondents firmly believe that you are "the enemy" and the only thing that can help is "social endurance." Be patient and polite, and hope that over time they will change their mind because they learn to know and trust you. One example of "silent rejection" comes from my research in Tilburg. I sensed there was some passive resistance towards me by the personnel of the housing corporation. Their silent rejection consisted of avoiding me and not responding to my requests for an appointment. I was interested in their perspective on the neighbourhood. But they were not my main respondents, which were the inhabitants of the neighbourhood. After some months of research in the neighbourhood people started to greet me, including the personnel of the housing corporation. While I was eating my lunch in the community centre, one of them approached me and said in a friendly way, "You are still around. We thought you would be one of those people who do their project and leave the neighbourhood within two months and we would never see you again." I stayed there for two years and developed close relationships with some of them.

SELF-INTEREST

Though a rejection after a cold introduction can be expected, when it happens several times in a row, it is more difficult to deal with it and one might become disappointed, get drained, and start losing hope. But a rejection, after a relationship is established, can actually have a deep impact. This is not only because of the time one has invested in building up the relationship, but also because your self or your self-presentation is at stake, as I will show in the next examples, in which self-interest is the driving motive for rejecting the researcher.

While doing research in a multicultural neighbourhood, after months of negotiations, I was able to get a meeting with the board of a mosque. I was excited by the prospect. When I entered the room there were five men sitting across the table and nobody smiled. They made it clear that they were angry with the local municipality because of cuts to their subsidies. They said that they would talk to me if I could help them get the subsidies back. I responded that I could not help them. They then replied in a polite and determined way that they did not want to talk to me anymore. I was angry and felt used. I had lost so much time trying to interview them. I stayed calm, stood up, shook the hand of the chairperson, said goodbye, and left.

When such a situation occurs it is important to reflect on it to learn and to be better prepared next time. I asked myself two questions: (1) Should I have stopped earlier; did I force the situation? and (2) Why did they think I was part of the local municipality? Maybe in this case I should have stopped earlier, but "social endurance" did help me quite often in creating an opening with other groups. For instance, it took more than half a year to negotiate a focus group with a group of Somalian men. They did not see the need to talk to me. Finally, they said that if I would pay 50 euros for snacks they could consume during the meeting, they would come. This indeed happened and resulted in a lively meeting and several enduring field relations. The answer to the second question was that when I reflected on my public presentations, I was always in the presence of someone from the local municipality, whom, for instance, introduced me before a presentation of the research findings. Though verbally it was stated that I did not belong to the municipality, my co-presence with them was an indication of the opposite. I decided to minimize my co-participation with representatives of the local municipality during public meetings.

In the previous examples, the rejections did not jeopardize the research. And I could also neutralize the failure of the rejection with two lines of thought: (1) I did my utmost to gain access and I am not to blame for their non-participation, and (2) there are more fish in the sea; there are always others to be interviewed.

Rejections by gatekeepers, persons who control access to a group or a place, can be more problematic (see also Burns 2015; Gilliat-Ray 2005). In two instances, I experienced the rejection as truly painful because of the negative way I was labelled by an alderman and an active citizen in two different locations. During that period, I worked as an urban sociologist for an architecture firm and this led two people to believe that I was only into research for the money and did not care about the people I studied. Both experiences hurt me deeply. To understand and deal with my reaction, I reflected on my emotions. The fact that I could not change their "labelling" made me feel powerless. I felt shamed by these people who corrupted my reputation. Because of my reflection I could relate better to the anger and frustration of those who experience degradation and stigmatization.

Years later, the activist came to me at a meeting. She said that for all that time she had been wrong about me. She had learned in recent years that my deep research involvement showed that I cared about people. That made me feel good. The alderman disappeared into anonymity after he was sent away by the local council.

FINAL WORDS

Rejection is part of doing field research and is quite common in "cold" introductions. A range of strategies can be used to deal with rejections. In each case, it is important to reflect on the rejection. The first question one might ask is whether the method of approaching individuals needs to be changed. This might include the phrasing of the introduction, the location of the first interaction, and the way one presents oneself, such as clothing and demeanour. It is worthwhile to experiment with the method and see which one works best.

The second question refers to the emotional experience of the rejection. How emotional is the impact and why is the impact so emotional? Reflecting on the experience of being negatively labelled opened up new perspectives on the social worlds I studied. To be labelled in this way, to feel powerless and shamed, made me more sensitive to how it feels to be rejected, stigmatized, and excluded. For instance, it was easier to understand the resentment of active citizens when they talked about persons not wanting to participate in neighbourhood activities.

The third question is related to the topic we study. What does the rejection tell us about the researched social world? In the examples I have given, the rejections reveal insights into the relations and interactions we observe. For instance, they say something about the social experience of a public square, the time one has for "social cohesion," and the distrust of marginalized persons towards certain professions.

The rejections also show us that the power dynamics between the researcher and the researched are not always in favour of the first. Though research ethics boards make it look like researchers are in control, the rejections show that the researched have agency, decide whether participation is in their own interest, and use the researcher to their advantage.

But, as I have explained, a rejection is not always a rejection. With what I have called the "salesperson strategy" one can prolong the contact and gain more data. "Social endurance"—being a bit more assertive and persistent—is crucial in this strategy. Another advantage of this stance in fieldwork is that it makes it less difficult to accept the failure of the rejection and say, "I have done my utmost. I have to respect their decision not to participate." After some time, one learns that making contact and gaining access can become an exciting process that can develop into unexpected field relations and provide challenging insights in the studied social world.

I have just had three negative experiences in a row while visiting the dispensaries. It does not really bother me too much but the tone of some people throws me off and wears me out. I feel like quitting for the day. But I decide to try another one. The next guy turns out to be very nice. He talks to me for almost 20 minutes and has a ton of information on the dispensary business. I cannot believe my luck. In the end he gives me his email in case I want to know more.

CRAFTING QUALITATIVE RESEARCH EXERCISES

1. Think of a social situation in which you used to feel insecure and explain why you felt like that.

2.   Think of a social situation in which you applied the strategy of social endurance and reflect on the outcome of this behaviour.

3.   Think of a social situation in which you have applied or could apply the "salesperson strategy" and reflect on its effectiveness or ineffectiveness.

REFERENCES

Adler, Patricia A. 1993. *Wheeling and Dealing: An Ethnography of an Upper-Level Drug Dealing and Smuggling Community*. New York: Columbia University Press.

Burns, Emily. 2015. "'Thanks, but No Thanks': Ethnographic Fieldwork and the Experience of Rejection from a New Religious Movement." *Fieldwork in Religion* 10 (2): 190–208.

Ferrell, Jeff, and Mark Hamm, eds. 1998. *Ethnography at the Edge: Crime, Deviance and Field Research*. Boston: Northeastern University Press.

Gilliat-Ray, Sophie. 2005. "Closed Worlds: (Not) Accessing Deobandi Dar ul-Uloom in Britain." *Fieldwork in Religion* 1 (1): 7–33.

Hennink, Monique, Inge Hutter, and Ajay Bailey. 2010. *Qualitative Research Methods*. London: Sage.

Johnson, John M. 1975. *Doing Field Research*. New York: Free Press.

Lareau, Annette, and Jeffrey Shultz. 1996. *Journeys through Ethnography: Realistic Accounts of Fieldwork*. Boulder: Westview Press.

Liebow, Elliot. 1967. *Tally's Corner: A Study of Negro Streetcorner Men*. Boston: Little, Brown.

Lofland, John, David Snow, Leon Anderson, and Lyn H. Lofland. 2006. *Analyzing Social Settings: A Guide to Qualitative Observation and Analysis*. Belmont, CA: Wadsworth/Thomson.

Müller, Thaddeus. 2013. "In Praise of Ethnography: Towards a Rich Understanding of Crime and Deviance." *Kriminologisches Journal* 45 (2): 144–59.

Warren, Carol A. B., and Tracy Xavia Karner. 2005. *Discovering Qualitative Methods: Field Research, Interviews, and Analysis*. Los Angeles: Roxbury Publishing Company.

17 Doing Research on Behind-the-Scenes Phenomena: Entering the Female Escort Industry

Magdalena Wojciechowska

PLUNGING INTO THE UNKNOWN

My first serious field research, conducted in Poland, which I often recall in terms of a rite of passage, dealt with how female escorts see themselves—and are seen—within their professional context. Why such subject matter? After having read a novel undertaking the issue of prostitution, I wanted to gain an actual understanding of this phenomenon as experienced by those partaking in the "unknown" I intended to explore—I was simply curious. And so, equipped with tricks of the trade that researchers are sometimes encouraged to embrace regardless of context (see Roman 2016), I started "digging." While many of these tools were helpful, I had little literature on the subject matter to guide me, which presented some problems, and emotional distress, which I shall address below.

Soon enough I realized that a striking contradiction between the legal status of and the legal attitude towards prostitution reveals not only moral objections to the phenomenon at hand but also its sensitive and behind-the-scenes nature.[1] Indeed, it is a rather hermetic universe, operating on the fringes of "normal" society. But, this was not as much of an obstacle to my research as the way women socialized within "normal" society perceived their money-earning activity. The feeling of shame drove most of them to operate behind the judgment-free walls of escort agencies, making them suspicious towards outsiders, but also highly dependent on men willing to buy sex and those facilitating the exchange at hand. The above contradiction unveils the specific interactional context within the prostitution sphere in which escorts can easily be cast into the role of the subordinates. It also makes it even more difficult for a female researcher to gain access.

My first intention was to build a research design based on previous empirical endeavours (e.g., Prus and Irini 1980), but—at that time—Polish context-specific qualitative studies on escort agencies were scarce. Then, I thought I would jump into the deep end—I made over 100 phone calls to women posting information on sexual services they provided. To my surprise and dismay, none of them consented to be interviewed; some gave me valuable advice: *Find another way*. And so I did.

GAINING ACCESS: WHEN RESEARCH SETTING CALLS THE SHOTS

Realizing the specific context of the paid sex industry, I somewhat deconstructed my imagery and adapted to the conditions imposed by the research setting; thus, I turned to men, who ultimately granted my access to five escort agencies.

Escort agencies are usually located on the outskirts or discreetly integrated into the city landscape; no standing out or excessive advertisement, and fairly far from frequented areas, parking lots, and bus stops. They appear as regular, indistinctive houses in the neighbourhood, "minding their own business." As a client, you take a cab rather than go there by car. So I went to the nearest cab stand to seek advice. In this way, I collected some insightful data on how escort agencies operate, as well as co-operate with other agents,[2] which further facilitated my research design. I was also given several phone numbers for regulars, ex-escorts, and escorts,[3] as well as yet another piece of advice: *You need an inside guy who will vouch for you.*

Escort agencies may be selling sex in the shadow economy and be otherwise officially registered as massage parlours or strip clubs—one of the reasons they do not value publicity. Still, these operate legally, and require services most other companies would need, such as garbage removal or electricity. With this in mind, I turned to a friend working for an insurance company, who introduced me to a male colleague providing such services to several escort agencies. He was quite reluctant to endorse me at first, claiming such behaviour would be seen as unprofessional. Instead, he offered to tell one of the insiders he knew socially about my project. And that was good enough, since some time later I found myself in an escort agency office with my gatekeeper, the insurance agent, and three bodyguards working for the "club."[4]

This first entrée, although relatively brief, gave me a great deal of insight into how men support one another within the universe of escort agencies. I took the role of a "pet" researcher (Adams 1999) and played the game. For instance, I was the only one sitting the whole time, was referred to as a "nice girl" (e.g., "What does such a nice girl like yourself want to find here?"), and was invited to give a few examples of questions I would ask if "granted permission to speak with the escorts."[5] I would respond with examples of subtle interactional and discursive scripts revealing the specific context of my research setting and offering guidelines as to how to act therein.

Did I feel threatened, offended, or patronized? I did, in a way. But, I expected nothing else—my gatekeeper made me aware that I would be checked to confirm I represented no threat to the business. I passed the test. Still, to my dismay, I was not promised any results—my phone number was to be given to those women who wanted to share their stories. *Let's see how lucky you are,* I heard before we left. And, as it turned out, it was, indeed, a matter of luck.

One of the things I have learned is that one should never underestimate one's social network. At some point in my venture, I was to such an extent emotionally involved and conceptually focused on the research that it became the sole subject of almost every casual conversation I had—and it paid off. A university colleague, familiar with my project, introduced me to her acquaintance, an ex-bodyguard still socially involved in everyday activities of two escort agencies; she did not mention, though, that he was a sociology graduate. We first met over a glass of beer, as he insisted on getting to know each other before scheduling an interview. This time, I was the one to share what I had learned so far; he simply listened. At some point he said, "You haven't seen any real stuff yet, just the front stage; if you wanna see the back stage, I can help you with that" (see Goffman 1959). And so he did. Only this time, I was introduced as his "friend," which gave space for constructing different meanings of my presence, and eventually resulted in seeing me as a potential working girl.[6]

WHAT ARE EMPTY STORIES FOR? DEVELOPING RAPPORT AND WINNING TRUST

It is one thing to be let in, and another thing to become entrusted with the emotional space of the informants. Many women in this study willingly narrated the physical— "formal"—dimension of their money-earning activity; few, however, verbalized how they experience and see themselves within their professional context. It took a while before I was entrusted with the feeling of entrapment in their bodies—symbolic bridges between normality and deviance—or shown the tangible proof of male domination these carried. The importance of developing rapport and learning from one's faux pas became clear in my first interview with an escort living and working at the same site.

She was the one to let me inside; there were no men around. We shook hands and she offered me a beverage. I was able to tell that she did not trust me, as she put on the "costume" (Goffman 1959) she would wear in front of her clientele. We looked as if we had nothing in common, but it was not my intention to change the way I would dress for any other interview. When she showed me her room, she said, "This is where I work; sit wherever you like." There were two chairs and a large bed; I sat on the latter. She seemed pleased with my choice. Why? Because I demonstrated that I am not repulsed by how she makes a living. Indeed, our understanding of people's concerns, and how we behave accordingly, is of key importance when it comes to investigating delicate issues (see Adler and Adler 2012). For example, I assumed our encounter would last up to three hours, but I stayed there for almost eight. I had three cups of tea during that time. To my astonishment, she asked me at some point: "Does this place put you off?" What had I done wrong? I did nothing—and that, in a way, was the point. The woman I interviewed had a similar number of beverages, and she left the room twice whereas I not even once; thus, she assumed I was afraid of going to the washroom escorts use.

Why would she, and other women in this study, want to share their stories if doing so was such an emotional challenge? I was an outsider who offered to listen, as well as to *hear*. For instance, we never spoke about prostitution per se, since it was not what they were doing. What were they doing then? They were working to pay off their debts, provide for disabled children or sick parents, escape from abusive husbands—it was never a matter of choice, but one of necessity. Of course, what one could see here on the analytical level, is how these women rationalize undertaking the activity that an outsider might find disgraceful; still, prior to analyzing the data, we need to collect the stories. Before tears and genuine laughter came, there were some humorous stories of Catholic priests frequenting the place or "what happened to my friend" stories, as well as "girly" discussions regarding nail polish. Such empty stories, not to mention outwardly irrelevant chats, may seem of little importance. Still, these provide the informants with a form of security blanket and the researcher with yet another context-appropriate discovery mechanism. And, most importantly, these, I believe, facilitate developing rapport.

This first interview was not our last—we met again in person and via Skype. She also gave me a hand in establishing contact with other escorts and offered some insightful comments on my final conclusions. Why would she do that? *You don't judge*, she once told me.

IS WITNESSING DIFFERENT TO BEING TOLD? EMOTIONAL BURDEN

Being exposed to stories of suffering that impose emotional distress on the researcher seems unavoidable when we engage in face-to-face contact concerning sensitive issues (see, e.g., Melrose 2002), and "there are no proven techniques that would fully prepare one for the effects of exposure to suffering and social injustice" (Roman 2016, 21). I knew that when I first entered the field. I was also aware that with time I could become somewhat "desensitized" (Campbell 2013); thus, I naively assumed I had the issue at hand covered. But, what happens when you actually witness pain and humiliation, and all you can do is to keep on watching?

When my gatekeeper, the sociology graduate mentioned earlier, took me to an escort agency for the first time—so I could see some "real stuff"—he intentionally left me alone for a while, to see what would happen. Since one of the escorts must have assumed I was a future employee, I was introduced to the rules and offered some tips as to how to work with the johns. This experience made me realize how it must feel to be somewhat deracinated and abruptly confronted with the previously unknown perception of one's body, a substantial aspect of one's self—a perception imposing systematic and automatic sexual intercourse with strangers, now to become part of one's everyday reality.

On yet another occasion, I witnessed a blood collection procedure, which is exactly what it sounds like—a part of regular examinations by a doctor (gynecologist) co-operating with an escort agency. Of course, these medical appointments are not held in private; instead, they take place in a room where the women are herded like cattle, and which anybody can access. I remember an interactional episode when an escort was ridiculed as her colleagues found out she has used a piece of sponge to work during menstruation, which she could not remove afterwards; being too embarrassed, she did not ask for help until the examination day.

Witnessing how a human's body is symbolically transformed into a machine reduced to its functions made the depth and the extent of the previously verbalized suffering almost tangible. My first thought was to somehow "save" those women, but this is not our job. The feelings of anger and helplessness eventually resulted in cyclical pullouts from the field—I needed emotional space to reflect on further steps I would take. Was it necessary? I believe so, since the quality of the research (as well as our welfare) depends on our ability to manage emotions (see Rubin and Rubin 2012), and that was my way of caring for my emotional well-being.

A CONCLUDING NOTE

I remember being asked on a number of occasions whether sex workers would want their occupation to become a legitimate profession, mostly for the purposes of safety. "They wouldn't like that," I replied every single time. "I don't see why, this would help them," some stated. But, as I realized at some point of this venture, most of the women who shared their stories would rather suffer alone than be exposed to the critical social gaze. They do not wish to be "saved," but to survive. Still, there is one simple, yet vital thing we can do—we can retell their stories, hoping that doing so will contribute to the understanding of their everyday lives. Will it make any difference? I do not know, but it is worth trying. As for me, retelling their stories—and, most importantly, seeing how people responded to what they heard—turned out to be one of my coping strategies: it contributed to my emotional strength, empowering me to go on.

CRAFTING QUALITATIVE RESEARCH EXERCISES

1. Consider a qualitative research project you might be interested in doing that, most likely, would expose you to stories of suffering. To do so, you can watch a documentary on a sensitive social issue first, for example, *Whores' Glory*. Reflect on how your emotions may affect the quality of your research, as well as your welfare. Is there anything you can do to manage your emotions?

2. Think about a qualitative research project you might be interested in doing that would deal with informants' intimate/painful/shameful experiences. Then reflect on some commonly used terms/expressions that the potential research participants might be sensitive to (e.g., terms that are offensive, blunt, inaccurate).

Write these down and think about how you can replace, or better yet, avoid, such potentially sensitive expressions.

3. Imagine that you have consented to be interviewed on a very delicate subject matter based on your personal experiences. Then consider how the researcher should behave in order to make you feel comfortable during the encounter at hand. Is there anything specific they could do (or should not do) to win your trust?

NOTES

1. In Poland, where prostitution is not recognized as a legitimate profession, offering sexual services in return for financial gain is legal, unlike any form of pimping or forced prostitution. Still, many aspects of the paid sex industry, such as operating escort agencies, are tolerated by public institutions.

2. Cab drivers themselves are paid for recommending certain places, bringing clients, informing about indoor, non-institutionalized prostitution, and other small courtesies.

3. All but the latter—who told me that by giving me their phone numbers cab drivers violated their trust—consented to be interviewed.

4. I had not met the actual owners of any of the escort agencies where I collected data, only those who introduced themselves as managers ("bosses") and regular bodyguards.

5. For anonymity purposes, women often chose on-site accommodation.

6. Although the bodyguards knew the purpose of my visits, some of them, as I was told, believed I was looking about prior to being hired.

REFERENCES

Adams, Laura L. 1999. "The Mascot Researcher: Identity, Power, and Knowledge in Fieldwork." *Journal of Contemporary Ethnography* 28 (4): 331–63.

Adler, Patricia A., and Peter Adler. 2012. "Keynote Address: Tales from the Field; Reflections on Four Decades of Ethnography." *Qualitative Sociology Review* 8 (1): 10–32.

Campbell, Rebecca. 2013. *Emotionally Involved: The Impact of Researching Rape.* New York: Routledge.

Goffman, Erving. 1959. *The Presentation of Self in Everyday Life.* Garden City, NY: Anchor Books.

Melrose, Margaret. 2002. "Labour Pains: Some Considerations on the Difficulties of Researching Juvenile Prostitution." *International Journal of Social Research Methodology* 5 (4): 333–51.

Prus, Robert, and Styllianoss Irini. 1980. *Hookers, Rounders, and Desk Clerks*. Salem, WI: Sheffield Publishing Company.

Roman, Alexandru V. 2016. "Studying Corruption: Reflections on the Methodological, Practical, and Personal Challenges." *Qualitative Sociology Review* 12 (3): 6–27.

Rubin, Herbert J., and Irene S. Rubin. 2012. *Qualitative Interviewing: The Art of Hearing Data*. London: Sage.

SECTION V

DOING OBSERVATION

The best tools you take into the field with you are your observational skills. You need to look around and make sure you stay engaged with your field site, observing everything going on around you. While in the field, you can take jottings to remind yourself of what you have seen. Once you leave the field site, you need to get to a computer or notebook as soon as possible and write down everything you remember seeing, hearing, smelling, and even tasting. This is called "taking field notes." You can also journal about your personal reactions and thoughts, which is called "memo writing."

As you do observations, keep in mind everything you have learned so far about the importance of reflexivity. You will be making choices about what to write down. You may be the kind of person who notices smells more than someone else, or your attention might automatically be drawn more to people who resemble you or your family and so you might remember more about what they have said and done. You will also come into your field site with your own understandings about the social world, which may be different from those you are observing. Remember to reflect on your positionality, or social location, as you take field notes. You will also encounter an array of emotions and reactions to what you see going on around you. It takes practice and skill to navigate your own responses and to be aware of any power dynamics that might be in play.

When writing your field notes, remember to ask yourself what knowledge you may have brought into your field site with you. You might also take time to think about what knowledge you may be lacking. Keep an attitude of learning and be willing to look at familiar things in new ways. Your field site has much to teach you and figuring out how to see and hear, and then record, those lessons is integral to your work as a qualitative researcher. Be mindful not to ascribe unknown motivations to behaviours you observe.

The best advice we can offer you is to write everything down. You will not know at the start of your project what may emerge as important later on. If you do not capture as much as you can remember right away in your field notes, that data can be lost forever. In addition to the benefit of writing robust field notes, intensive memo writing can help you sort through the emotions, power dynamics, and underlying social processes in play. This can be time-consuming, but it is well worth it! As you practice doing observations, pay attention to your own role in the field. Try to capture all of the nuances that you can when you sit down to record your observations. And, of course, keep reflexivity at the forefront of your mind.

Crystal Weston and Carrie B. Sanders discuss the importance of *emotional knowledge* when taking field notes. One's own social location, as well as the emotionality of the process, shapes each stage of the research process. Weston and Sanders take us through their experience doing research within police services. Working in an organizational setting comes with its own set of challenges. They found that having a non-technical description of their work helped them explain their presence to officers who were unsure whether to trust them and to see their presence as legitimate in the field. They also discuss how they dealt with a particularly emotional experience in the field and, in the end, used it to gain a further window on the emotion-work of the police themselves.

In chapter 19, Scott Grills reminds us that the tensions we may feel while conducting observations are not only to be expected, but are also forms of data in and of themselves. These discomforts, particularly around roles, may help bring our attention to situations of dominance that we could otherwise miss. Interactions balance on *role claiming* and *role rejection*, and within these interactions we must maintain our integrity as researchers, while behaving ethically in the field. Grills reminds us that processes of domination, of subordination and superordination, are always a part of the interaction order and that we need to be mindful of this as we collect observational data.

In his chapter on observing interactions in public settings, Kritee Ahmed emphasizes how fraught interpretations of others can truly be. He guides the reader through the ways in which observing interactions on public transit helped him to realize that a researcher cannot always know the ways in which the world is ordered for those they are observing. We all see things through lenses, through the ways in which we understand and organize information in the world. There are dominant ways of ordering representations and, as Peter Berger (1963) argued, we need to make the familiar strange so that we can see these preconceived ways of understanding the social world. Ahmed also stresses that we cannot know what others are thinking, and what other interactions have led to the one on display. We must always be aware that we have only partial data.

Krystal Kehoe MacLeod highlights the importance of good field notes and offers advice to new ethnographers taking their first field notes. To do this, she uses her experience as part of a team conducting *rapid ethnography*, an approach that some health scholars use to gain a sort of shorthand picture of a setting over a set amount of time. Essentially, this means spending a few hours in the same location several times during a set interval of time. She writes about the challenges of writing good field notes in situ and offers some tricks for taking down jottings which can later be fleshed out to create detailed, nuanced, and reflexive field notes. You may find it heartening that she finds that experienced researchers are not always better than novices at writing field notes.

REFERENCE

Berger, Peter L. 1963. *Invitation to Sociology: A Humanistic Perspective.* Garden City, NY: Doubleday.

18

"Going Through the (E)motions": Attending to Social Location and Emotionality in Observational Studies of Police

Crystal Weston and Carrie B. Sanders

Antipathy and distrust of the academic researcher is endemic to most police departments.... The outside researcher in police organization[s] is therefore rarely asked in by police administrators and even more rarely welcomed by the rank and file if he should somehow succeed initially in getting through the door.

—John Van Maanen, "On Watching the Watchers"

INTRODUCTION

Van Maanen's experience of conducting research on police in 1978 is similar to our own experiences in Canada today, where policing research is described as a "barren landscape" due to challenges associated with gaining access, collecting data, and reporting findings (Huey and Ricciardelli 2016, 122). Underlying and connecting each of these challenges are elements of emotionality. Our experiences conducting observational research on police have been fraught with feelings of frustration, alienation, discomfort, fear, excitement, and elation. These emotional experiences, we argue, have shaped every aspect of the research process—from gaining access, to collecting and analyzing data, to disseminating results.

In field research, we enter a social world and attempt to record the behaviours, conversations, and interactions we see in detailed field notes (van den Hoonaard 2014). Field notes are thickly descriptive, fully narrative, and attempt to define "the world from the perspective of those studied" (Shaffir and Stebbins 1991, 5). They attend to participants' language, actions, and interactions within their situational contexts, while identifying important processes occurring within the field (Charmaz 2006).

While many qualitative textbooks discuss the importance of writing descriptive field notes, what is often missing is the importance of attending to the "emotional dynamics of fieldwork" (Blee 1998). This *emotional knowledge*, we argue, is invaluable for (1) making sense of the social world under investigation, and (2) understanding how, through the dynamic interplay of emotions in the field, researchers and participants "jointly shape knowledge" (Blee 1998, 381). In what follows, we draw on our own experiences to illustrate how our social location and emotionality shape all aspects of the research process—from gaining access to interpreting data and disseminating findings.

NEGOTIATING ACCESS AND SOCIAL LOCATION: OBSERVATION AS A PRIVILEGE

Our social location as female academic researchers shaped our experiences and interactions in the field—both facilitating and constraining our ability to not only gain but also maintain access to our research site. Police services represent "bounded and formal institutions" that have organizational rules, policies, procedures, and cultures that govern action and membership (Warren and Karner 2010). Given our social location as academics, the organizational sense of discomfort over our presence was evident when we first attempted to gain entry. Many police services have internal research offices that require us to enter into contractual research agreements. These documents outline agreed upon objectives and goals of the research and notify us that any findings outside these agreements must be reviewed and approved by the organization. As a representative from a police research office explained,

> The purpose of our review of your work is to ensure the protection and privacy of persons and entities that, through your association with the service, have informed or are in some way referenced within your document, as required of us under the Freedom of Information and Protection of Privacy Act (FIPPA). Essentially, as prescribed and/or prohibited by law under FIPPA, a researcher's only legal recourse to access information from an institution that falls within the meaning of private and/ or personal information (per s. 2) is by way of entering into a research agreement that includes requirements stipulated under s. 10 of the Regulation. (Field notes)

These agreements required us to submit all working papers to the service for review and *written approval* before submitting any manuscripts for publication. After a number of meetings, we came to a mutually agreed upon solution: the service would be sent drafts of all manuscripts prior to submission, and they would have two weeks to review and provide feedback, but we, as the researchers, maintained control over final interpretations of the data.

Once we agreed to the terms outlined in the research agreement, we received access to the research site. The negotiation process involved in these research agreements provided invaluable insight into the role emotionality (such as fear and vulnerability) plays throughout the data collection and analysis processes. By maintaining field notes of our experiences, we were able to see ways that police services engage in organizational risk management. Further, by attending to the emotional dynamics involved in the research agreement negotiations we began to see how knowledge is co-constructed and shaped by the actions of our participants.

NAVIGATING OBSERVATIONS AND THE EMOTIONAL DYNAMICS OF FIELDWORK

Organizational approval, however, marks only the first layer of observational research. Once in the field, we had to learn how to navigate our environment and our relationships. For example, we quickly learned the importance of hierarchy within the police service and its impact on our actions in the field. We learned that professional attire (such as dress pants and suit jackets) was appropriate for interviews and observations with "white shirts" (i.e., those in administrative roles, such as inspectors and police chiefs), while street clothes were more appropriate and acceptable for observations with front-line patrol.

During our fieldwork, we adopted an observer-as-participant role (Gold 1958). Our presence and intentions as researchers were known to the officers. We attended shift briefings, calls-for-service, and social outings. As young, female academics with little experience in the daily realities of police work, our status as "outsiders" was evident, as neither of us had personal policing experience (Warren and Karner 2010). We found that our social location and how we presented ourselves—as external researchers—impacted what our participants would and would not say. We often faced cultural skepticism toward our research (Foster and Bailey 2010). For example, during an early ride-along the officer we were riding with asked, "So I know you said your study is on police technology, but what is it really about? What do you really want to know?" We quickly learned how important it was to have a layperson description of our research goals and objectives ready and to review these prior to the start of any ride-along.

Our presence infringed on the usual privacy of the patrol parade room and patrol cruiser and, for some in the organization, created a sense of discomfort. As outsiders, we often felt ourselves being "tested" to see how we reacted in certain situations. For example, as policing is predominantly male, we were often faced with sexist jokes. When these jokes were shared we would notice the officers looking to see our reaction. While in the field, we found ourselves having to engage in emotion work—not only in our interactions with police officers, but also during our observations of calls for service, as we quickly came to realize that our own emotional displays in the field were expected to "comply with organizational rules concerning emotional expression" (Bakker and Heuven 2006, 426). As a result, during ride-alongs, we often experienced emotional dissonance, wherein we displayed emotions that aligned with those we saw in the field, but were in contradiction to the emotions we felt.

While smiling and nodding along became commonplace, one ride-along incident struck an emotional chord that proved challenging for Crystal to contain and process:

> A call came over the radio that a young male was seen taking clothing from a donation bin in the neighbourhood. As we drove to the scene, the officer I was riding

with commented that "stealing from the charity bin isn't really theft." The officer triggered the cruiser lights as we approached a young male walking away from the bin. The male was respectful and co-operative as the officer took his identification and ran it through the police computer system. Inside the car, the officer told me that he had come across this individual before, and that he was an Armenian orphan with a traumatic past of extensive abuse. The officer ordered the young man to empty out the duffel bag and backpack he was carrying, and a number of sweaters, dress shirts, and jeans were pulled from the bags. The young male admitted he had taken them from the donation bin.... The officer told him that he would need to return the clothes, and followed him in the cruiser back to the clothing bin at the edge of a park.

The young man fumbled as he pulled clothes out of the bags and threw them back. He paused and told the officer that several remaining items, including the backpack, had not come from the bin but already belonged to him. The officer ordered him to throw all of these belongings into the bin as well, leaving him with nothing but the clothes he was wearing. The young man co-operated, and apologized to the officer and waved as he walked away from the scene. The officer commented, "With a background like his, how could you not be messed up."

I felt horrified watching this young man forced to throw everything, including his own prior belongings into this bin, knowing he was walking away empty-handed and with nowhere to go.... I felt anger and disgust that the officer—knowing the individual's difficult background—could make him throw away everything that he had. (Field notes)

Despite the objections that she felt to this interaction, she believed that she needed to disguise her discomfort and present a supportive appearance in order to maintain rapport and access to the field.

As demonstrated by Crystal's field notes, emotionality and social location are integral to field research and must be attended to, as they shape the research process (Kleinman 1991). In being attentive to our own feelings and reactions, we are not "hidden" in our ethnography. Rather, we acknowledge that researcher observational presence is an element of the research process, and emotions are not detached from observational research data. As Fine (1993, 281) explains, the emotions we experience in the field influence "what we see, how we get along with others, and the strategic choices that we make in our ethnographies." Documenting emotional responses following fieldwork provided two important functions. First, it provided a place to debrief about the emotion work embedded within our observations. Second and more importantly, it illuminated the impact of this experience on Crystal, identifying the intensity—but also the anomaly—of this observation. Despite its emotional impact, the incident was not representative of her other experiences in the field and therefore did not justify inclusion in her central findings.

By being analytically aware of our emotional experiences in the field, we began to be attentive to police officers' emotion work. In fact, the longer we stayed in the field, the more we recognized that the dissonance between felt and displayed emotions was also experienced by police officers. The following field note excerpt illuminates this emotion work:

> While out for coffee, one officer shared that he'd just given a ticket. He said the sergeant had been on his back to increase ticket numbers. I asked what the ticket was for, and the officer hesitated and said, "Failing to signal a lane change." He continued, "I know, I was so embarrassed, I walked away with my face hidden in my coat." (Field notes)

Like researchers, officers are also expected to constrain feelings of discomfort. In another instance, Crystal stood with an officer waiting in a rundown single-room occupancy building for an ambulance for one resident. She remarked,

> "It seems like this job would be very emotionally draining." He said, "You know, my wife thinks I'm a horrible person, but I just don't give a shit. You can't, you'd go crazy." (Field notes)

While sharing experiences of emotional dissonance does not mean that we could fully understand what it is like to be a police officer, experiencing this containment process allowed us to better understand the daily realities of officers.

EMOTIONALITY, POWER, AND THE CONSTRUCTION OF KNOWLEDGE

After concluding observations, documenting field notes, and journaling personal thoughts or reactions, emotionality and social location continued to shape the analysis and interpretation of research findings. For example, when Carrie shared a research manuscript with the participating police service, she faced organizational discontent. The police service objected to her inclusion of the research agreement in the description of her methodology. In the service's review of her manuscript, it was noted that

> the inclusion of your Research Agreement in your methodology section [is] not germane to your findings or discussion. Bear in mind that these references could also be seen as either a detractor or as introducing controversy or bias. Further, as you note in your conclusion, your role as a researcher may have significant impacts. How you behave in the field may limit other researchers access to the service. As you have expressed so well in your reflections and conclusions, there is indeed a

unique relationship between researcher and participant that begs to be recognized and respected. Along with such relationships come obligations and expectations.

This comment was followed by a one-page outline of the regulations falling under FIPPA, where the agreements she would be breaking if she did not make the suggested changes were highlighted. Further, the service identified the ramifications associated with breaking these laws, warning: "You may want to remove the following words/phrases as they could potentially result in lawsuits, with possible costs extended to you." In the end, in fear of losing future research access, Carrie removed the discussion from her manuscript.

The disjuncture between police and academic culture is evident in this tension of knowledge construction. Academia encourages self-reflexivity during the research process and acknowledging elements that shape findings (such as Carrie's inclusion of the research agreement in her methodology section). From an academic standpoint, including this discussion in her methodological description is not only appropriate, but also highly regarded, as it provides important insight into the construction of knowledge; however, to the police organization the inclusion of the agreement appears threatening. Fear and vulnerability exist on both parts. Organizations fear how knowledge may be constructed—how it will be written—and potential reputational consequences. The researcher too experiences fear in this process, as resisting organizational influence on one's findings is not necessarily as tentative as the agreement would suggest. Researchers must balance professional commitments and cultural influences. The institutional power of police organizations—and their ability to grant and deny research access—can shape what is written about them, as researchers write with the organizational gatekeepers as potential readers in mind. Fear of jeopardizing future research opportunities illustrates how scholars and research participants jointly shape knowledge.

CONCLUDING THOUGHTS

In this chapter, we reflect upon the ways in which our social location—as women and academics—and emotional experiences in the field were important objects of analysis that enabled a deeper understanding of the social world of policing. Conducting observations, and being attentive to our emotional experiences in the field, helped us contextualize the daily realities of patrol work and develop a deeper appreciation of, and insight into, the emotional complexities involved in policing. Emotion work influences not only the collection of data, but also, more importantly, the analysis, interpretation, and dissemination of research findings. As such, emotional reactions and experiences are important sources of data and knowledge that draw attention to our buried assumptions about our research field and participants that, in turn, push us to a deeper appreciation for, and understanding of, our fields of study (Blee 1998).

CRAFTING QUALITATIVE RESEARCH EXERCISES

1. Go to your student centre or another well-populated space on campus, and sit down on the floor with your legs crossed. Try to position yourself close to where other people are socializing or where there is a lot of activity—and where sitting is not the "norm." While sitting there, do not move or interact with others; just sit still and observe how others are reacting to you and how you feel while doing this. Stay in this position for 10 minutes before returning to your classroom to write extensive field notes. When writing your field notes, begin by visually presenting where you positioned yourself and what was physically located around you. Then write thickly descriptive notes about the activities and interactions that were occurring around you, as well as your emotional reactions and feelings while doing the exercise. After you finish your field notes, reread them to see what analytic insights are gained from your emotional reactions. For example, how might your own emotional reactions provide insight into concepts such as deviance or stigma?

2. Policing has been identified as a "bounded" research site that poses significant challenges around gaining access for researchers. What are two or three other organizations that are "bounded" institutions? What do you anticipate as challenges for gaining entry into each of these organizations? How might you overcome these challenges?

REFERENCES

Bakker, Arnold, and Ellen Heuven. 2006. "Emotional Dissonance, Burnout, and In-Role Performance among Nurses and Police Officers." *International Journal of Stress Management* 13 (4): 423–40.

Blee, Kathleen. 1998. "Managing Emotion in the Study of Right-Wing Extremism." *Qualitative Sociology* 21 (4): 381–99.

Charmaz, Kathy. 2006. *Constructing Grounded Theory: A Practical Guide through Qualitative Analysis*. London: Sage.

Fine, Gary. 1993. "Ten Lies of Ethnography: Moral Dilemmas of Field Research." *Journal of Contemporary Ethnography* 22 (3): 267–94.

Foster, Janet, and Simon Bailey. 2010. "Joining Forces: Maximizing Ways of Making a Difference in Policing." *Policing* 4 (2): 95–103.

Gold, Raymond. 1958. "Roles in Sociological Field Observations." *Social Forces* 36 (3): 217–23.

Huey, Laura, and Rose Ricciardelli. 2016. "From Seeds to Orchards: Using Evidence-Based Policing to Address Canada's Policing Needs." *Canadian Journal of Criminology and Criminal Justice* 58 (1): 119–33.

Kleinman, Sherryl. 1991. "Field Workers' Feelings: What We Feel, Who We Are, How We Analyse." In *Experiencing Fieldwork*, edited by William Shaffir and Robert Stebbins, 184–95. Newbury Park, CA: Sage.

Shaffir, William, and Robert A. Stebbins. 1991. *Experiencing Fieldwork: An Inside View of Qualitative Research*. Newbury Park, CA: Sage.

van den Hoonaard, Deborah. 2014. *Qualitative Research in Action*. 2nd ed. Don Mills, ON: Oxford University Press.

Van Maanen, John. 1978. "On Watching the Watchers." In *Policing: A View from the Street*, edited by Peter K. Manning and John Van Maanen, 309–49. Santa Monica, CA: Goodyear Publishing Company.

Warren, Carol, and Tracy Karner. 2010. *Discovering Qualitative Methods: Field Research, Interviews and Analysis*. 2nd ed. New York: Oxford University Press.

19 Reconsidering Relations in the Field: Attending to Dominance Processes in the Ethnographic Encounter

Scott Grills

The pleasures, challenges, and discomforts of qualitative research are found in the doing, and in the practical, everyday life experiences of the observer and the observed—of researcher and participants. This chapter offers some observations about practical problems of disquiet, mistrust, and conflict that can arise in field settings in the context of the relationships that develop over time between the researcher and those in the field.

At the risk of asserting the obvious, to effectively undertake field-based observation the researcher needs to find a social location from which to observe. Quite apart from how researcher access and initial entry into the field is facilitated (e.g., prior relationships, via gatekeepers, personal experiences), every social location that a researcher occupies offers up a mixture of insight and blindness (Rosaldo 1993). It cannot be otherwise, for the social locations that we hold allow us to see some aspects of the social world more clearly than others. The magician sees the performance differently than the audience (Prus and Sharper 1991), the chef offers a different perspective than the front-of-house staff (Fine 2008), and serious amateur sports enthusiasts experience their activities distinctly from professional athletes (Stebbins 1992); however, all of these roles provide an exceptionally useful observational vantage point that allows for the ethnographic gaze—for the ability to tell a story that would not otherwise be told.

In considering the observational location in the field and the research enterprise more generally, ethnographers have long attended to (1) the importance of the identity of the researcher in the field, (2) the need to learn *from* those in the field, and (3) the ethical requirement to limit harm (e.g., Shaffir and Stebbins 1991); however, considerably less attention has been placed on field relationships and the generic social processes that accompany potential conflicts therein. In his book, Athens (2015) argues for the importance of attending to the processes of domination and subjugation in everyday life. These are distinct yet related social processes. Domination is played out in the roles we play in our interactions with one another and the corresponding subordination and superordination that go with them. It is one of the ways in which the subjugation of human actors occurs.

One of the truly fascinating things about domination is that it is rarely accomplished in the most explicit and direct ways. Rather, domination activities occur as an ongoing, mundane, regularized feature of everyday life. Consider the student/teacher relationship in university and college settings. Even in the most collegial and open of classrooms, the faculty member engages in domination activities through such everyday work as creating syllabi, determining tasks at hand, grading, and the accompanying determination of the subcultural value of students' efforts and work. This pragmatic reality takes nothing away from the emergent, negotiated, ad hoc qualities of everyday life, but it does remind us of an important aspect of everyday life—that dominance and domination practices may be in play whether or not overt conflict is present. This is an important consideration as one undertakes the practical work of doing field-based qualitative research.

The research roles that we construct and shape influence the practical doing of qualitative research. As Goffman (1959) taught, the work of impression management is rather central to role performance and this is most certainly the case for research roles. However we come to them, the research roles we adopt are lived in the world of everyday life and are therefore contested and contestable. As a practical matter, what does this look like?

DOMINANCE ENCOUNTERS IN THE FIELD: AN EXAMPLE

One extended ethnographic study I undertook involved more than three years of intensive participant observation research with the Christian Heritage Party of Canada (CHP) and the Communist Party of Canada (Marxist-Leninist) (CPC-ML). While very different subcultural settings, from my perspective, this was one larger project with two distinct field sites. I was interested in how people who were involved with more marginal and somewhat stigmatized political movements both experienced deviance designations and engaged in stigmatizing others at the very same time. Such stigma contests needed to be understood in the context of all of the subcultural complexities that come with party-based political activities.

In both settings (CHP and CPC-ML), the idea of people associated with universities doing ethnographic research was not a foreign concept for some participants. Since both groups included university students, had a campus presence in some post-secondary settings (though not always overt), and counted university faculty as active members, my interest was consistent with what at least some members of the setting understood to be reasonable and understandable activities for a sociologist in their midst. This is one of the advantages of openly approaching a group about one's research intentions—it affords subcultural members to enter into a research relationship with the researcher on more authentic and transparent terms.

However, that very same openness and transparency can also serve to routinize and reaffirm the different social location held by the researcher relative to more fully committed subcultural participants. Even where the researcher holds various sympathies in common or shares world views with participants, the commitment to doing research and telling ethnographically based and sociologically interesting stories establishes the researcher's everyday activities as distinct from and (for some audiences) potentially at odds with the interests of subcultural members.

These were, after all, partisan settings. It is not surprising that members would be interested in the question "Are you with us?" and would engage in various strategies to, in some way or another, test myself and others. Haas (1977) found this in his study of high iron steel workers as they evaluated his goodness of fit to be trusted on the high steel. Wolf's (1991) work with the Rebels outlaw motorcycle club also addresses this ongoing testing of loyalties (in this case, the researcher was a biker first and an anthropologist second). In my case, it was what I was *not* that helped fuel a dominance encounter—I was not a member of either party, I did not accept the request from both parties to let my name stand as a candidate in local elections, and, at the end of the day, I was not "one of them" as I returned to my everyday life in another community and to patterns of relationships that did not overlap with my field sites. While I might be "their sociologist" and a participant observer, I was not a full member in any sense of the term. And this, in and of itself, may be defined as problematic. As the following quotation from my field notes indicates, the challenges faced by researchers can include intense domination encounters and involve attempts to denounce the other:

> I don't know how you can do this without joining us. All I know is that there are two forces in this world: the saving blood of Jesus Christ and the hand of Satan. If after hearing the Word of the Lord here tonight you can still hide behind the lies you have learned in those universities then you have declared yourself very clearly. I just hope that when people hear what you write, that they hear the evil that you represent. (CHP member, Grills 1998, 83).

For novice researchers, there is an instructive and hopefully helpful reminder in the above interaction. No matter how much work we put into developing our research presence, or strive to adhere to ethics guidelines, or how respectful we attempt to be of the world views of others, we cannot control how we are seen, the attributions that are made by others, or how our purposes and intentions will be framed and reframed by participants. But *it is all data*—evidence grounded in the everyday activities of members that tells us something about the people, perspectives, and practices that help to frame and define a local culture. It is rather crucial that researchers attend to instances like this one—dominance encounters where the research site itself becomes contested ground.

This should not surprise us. For if the study of social life, to paraphrase Cooley (1918), is the study of social process, then the act of doing research needs to be framed in process terms as well. It is not just a question of how best to do qualitative research, but it is rather central that we ask how it is done with others—as a mutually accomplished joint act. The best of field research shares all of the aspects of generic social processes found in human group life. Put another way, it would be somewhat foolhardy to suggest that the very same processes that we may claim are central to accomplishing our lives together are not in play as we are engaged in the work of qualitative research. So we should expect all of the relational, emergent, conflictual, and perspectival qualities of everyday life to shape the practical everyday accomplishment of research activities. Simply put, ethnographic research is based on joint action and as such brings with it all of the complexities that accompany the same.

Given that all social acts have the potential for co-operation and/or conflict (Mead 1934), and that, as students of everyday life, we are interested in all forms of human relationships (Blumer 1986), it is perhaps helpful to attend to some of the rather fundamental ways in which conflict-related processes may be found in the research process. I would suggest that we can profitably draw upon Athens's conceptual framing of domination and subjugation and attend to key ways in which research roles can become contested during the practical accomplishment of research activities and in the context of a *dominative engagement*. I will focus briefly on the two key stages of role claiming and role rejection in this process (Athens 2015, 175–201).

ROLE CLAIMING

One useful question that we can ask about roles and their performance is how they relate to issues of superordination and subordination or where one stands in an interaction sequence. We would make a serious mistake to assume that these are features of the roles themselves—that dominance is simply a product of occupying a certain role. Observing child-parent interactions in a checkout line, or student-teacher encounters in a high school classroom provides ample evidence that subordinate status in a specific interaction is not role-specific. The cry, "You are not the boss of me" from a four-year-old aptly demonstrates the attempt of the child to occupy the superordinate position in an encounter. Likewise, when members of a high school class coordinate joint acts to systematically subvert the classroom encounter they are adopting a superordinate position relative to the teacher and effectively using power to subvert authority (e.g., Bonner 1998; Prus 1999).

If we are mindful of this rather fundamental aspect of role relationships—whose collective or more singular role interests are to define the interaction sequence—then we can more fully appreciate these dynamics as they are in play in the *everyday accomplishment of research*. For example, even while deeply interested in the perspectives of others, those conducting ethnographic interviews may claim the superordinate role in the interaction sequence to ensure its continuance. More experienced interviewers may be able to accomplish this without strong public displays. But simple statements like, "Perhaps we can return to the earlier question" or "I was wondering if we can turn our attention now to …" affirm that the researcher may be the one whose role is dominant in the interaction sequence in that it is the researcher's interests that drive the encounter. On the other hand, those engaged in more observationally based work may deliberately and strategically adopt more subordinate postures so as to facilitate an unfolding of everyday life. My point here is important, but also fairly simple: given that subordination and superordination processes are in play in the interaction sequences that accompany the research relationship, we need to be intentionally mindful of their presence as we approach these interactions and select from lines of action that respect the empirical world we seek to understand.

ROLE REJECTION

In interaction sequences, those in positions defined as subordinate by others (and perhaps themselves) have a choice to make. Do they accept their subordinate position and co-operatively engage in the projects, agendas, and activities advanced by those holding the more dominant roles? If not, how might they choose to resist more passively or aggressively, or some combination thereof? This is what might be colloquially referred to as *donkey power*: we can dig in on a variety of matters and by so doing *reject the subordinate role* in any interactional encounter, no matter how fleeting or comparatively sustained. If the research act requires the participant to willingly (if even fleetingly) accept a subordinate role (e.g., to answer questions, serve as an informant, help the researcher learn the ropes), then the potential rejection of that subordinate position may place aspects of the research at risk.

In field research, it is rather essential that the researcher's agendas not be subordinated to the interests of the group to the point that the research cannot be accomplished. The ongoing negotiation of the interests of the researcher and the various interests of those whose lives we seek to understand more fully is captured, in part, by the *research bargain*. It is within this developed and shared understanding that the potential conflicts present in the research agenda are worked out, and that a more co-operative, collegial, and quite close research relationship can develop over time. But I wish to stress that negotiating the research bargain is an ongoing feature of any extended research project—over time new concerns arise, unanticipated consequences come to light, and participants come to develop new and modified understandings of the research and the researcher. The successful negotiation of the emergent research bargain may be rather crucial to maintaining the research role and the continuance of the project.

During my research with the CPC-ML, the protection of participant identities and assurances of anonymity were rather central to the project. For example, some adherents and members worked in occupations in which they feared reprisals from employers and/ or co-workers should their communist involvements become more widely known (e.g., journalists, public school teachers). I needed to find strategies to assure members that I would protect the identities of participants as I came to know them over time. Initially this was relatively unproblematic. Regulars at a CPC-ML bookstore that operated in a community with a university were, all in all, quite supportive of my research, and would lend me reading materials and become engaged in the interview process, at times challenging my questions helpfully, offering their own additional insights and suggesting others whom I needed to meet. My research position in the setting was fully overt relative to the *regulars*; however, since this was a public setting I could not reveal my status as a researcher doing participant observation to the casual passerby—to do so would violate the research bargain that I had previously made with others. As researchers we cannot expose our respondents to potential harm by revealing to others that they are willingly participating in a research project. For all practical purposes then, my research location involved both overt and covert elements, often at the very same time. This is a delicate balance and one that has the potential to produce role rejection.

One rainy evening I was sitting in the CPC-ML bookstore talking with three members about evidence they saw of US imperialism in a variety of unconventional settings. The cold, unheated room was smoke-filled from pipes and cigarettes. Our conversation was interrupted by the entrance into the bookstore of an individual who, by all outward appearances, was living on the streets. He was known by the party members, but he was also known to me—he had been living rough on the grounds of a university where I taught and he sat in on my Social Problems class at my invitation. This unanticipated encounter produced a short breach in the interaction sequence—the newcomer appeared to know all in the room, but assumed that my role as a sociologist was concealed from the party members. He announced my status as a professor who taught sociology, told them I was spying on them, and that I would reveal who they were. The response of the party members present was simply to inform him that they knew about my research and that I was "their" sociologist. Had I opted for a covert research strategy this brief encounter may have had a very different ending, for under that circumstance the newcomer would have been revealing a potentially damaging secret.

This brief interaction sequence is illustrative of how quickly and spontaneously role rejection can occur. The individual entering the interaction sequence sought out and occupied the dominant position in the interaction sequence—by *outing* me to others, challenging the legitimacy of the research role, and ensuring that the prior conversation and interaction was ended. No matter how co-operative or facilitating of the research enterprise participants may be, the possibility of role rejection remains a hazard in the field.

IN SUM

The ethnographic research tradition is a rich one. It provides insights into human group life that are otherwise unavailable to us. There is no substitute for going where the action is if we are interested in what people do and the subcultural worlds in which they live. But by so doing we place ourselves on the line in ways that other social scientists may not. While exceptionally valuable insights can be gained by survey research, content analysis, and experimental designs, ethnography places the researcher fully in the midst of everyday life. As such, the ethnographic research act includes all of the perspectival, negotiated, emotive, and emergent qualities of life in the making. Therefore, it is rather crucial that those approaching the field attend to potential sources of conflict that may be present as they embrace and negotiate research roles in the setting at hand. Rather than viewing instances of tension and unease as entirely unwelcome, I would encourage us to see these as useful openings that may provide opportunities for understanding the setting in ways that might have been otherwise concealed. For, at the end of the day, if we are to respect the nature of the empirical world, we need to know it as fully as is reasonably possible, and that demands that we be attentive to both co-operation and conflict and learn from each.

CRAFTING QUALITATIVE RESEARCH EXERCISES

1. How are role claiming and role rejection related ideas? Do you agree with the author when he claims that dominance is not simply a product of occupying a certain role? What argument would you develop to support your position? How do the roles researchers choose relate to this issue?

2. This paper suggests that domination activities occur as an ongoing, mundane, regularized feature of everyday life. Drawing on a setting with which you are familiar, consider how domination happens within it. What would be the best ways for a researcher from outside the setting to see this domination happening in everyday life?

3. How can field research be covert and overt at the very same time? What do you see as some of the risks and benefits of covert participant observation?

REFERENCES

Athens, Lonnie H. 2015. *Domination and Subjugation in Everyday Life*. New Brunswick, NJ: Transaction Publishers.

Blumer, Herbert. 1986. *Symbolic Interactionism: Perspective and Method*. Berkeley: University of California Press.

Bonner, Kieran. 1998. *Power and Parenting: A Hermeneutic of the Human Condition*. Houndmills, Basingstoke, UK: Macmillan Press Ltd.

Cooley, Charles H. 1918. *Social Process*. New York: Scribner's.

Fine, Gary Alan. 2008. *Kitchens: The Culture of Restaurant Work*. Berkeley: University of California Press.

Goffman, Erving. 1959. *The Presentation of Self in Everyday Life*. Garden City, NY: Doubleday.

Grills, Scott. 1998. "On Being Nonpartisan in Partisan Settings: Field Research among the Politically Committed." In *Doing Ethnographic Research: Fieldwork Settings*, edited by Scott Grills, 76–94. Newbury Park, CA: Sage.

Haas, Jack. 1977. "Learning Real Feelings: A Study of High Steel Ironworkers' Reactions to Fear and Danger." *Work and Occupations* 4 (2): 147–70.

Mead, George Herbert. 1934. *Mind, Self, and Society from the Standpoint of a Social Behaviorist.* Edited by Charles W. Morris. Chicago: University of Chicago Press.

Prus, Robert C. 1999. *Beyond the Power Mystique: Power as Intersubjective Accomplishment.* Albany: State University of New York Press.

Prus, Robert C., and C. R. D. Sharper. 1991. *Road Hustler: Hustlers, Magic and the Thief Subculture.* New York: Kaufman and Greenberg.

Rosaldo, Renato. 1993. *Culture and Truth: The Remaking of Social Analysis.* Boston: Beacon.

Shaffir, William, and Robert A. Stebbins. 1991. *Experiencing Fieldwork: An Inside View of Qualitative Research.* Newbury Park, CA: Sage.

Stebbins, Robert A. 1992. *Amateurs, Professionals, and Serious Leisure.* Montreal: McGill-Queen's University Press.

Wolf, Daniel R. 1991. *The Rebels: A Brotherhood of Outlaw Bikers.* Toronto: University of Toronto Press.

20 Minding the Gap at the Limits of Observation[1]

Kritee Ahmed

INTRODUCTION

Think about your commute on public transit to the university. You get on the bus. You pay your fare. You look for a seat. You look out the window. The bus stops. An argument develops between the bus driver and another person. In that moment, what are you thinking? What are other passengers doing? How does the argument shape your perception of public transit workers and how they *should* behave? Was your perception already shaped by past knowledge or experience of public transit?

While these questions presume that simple observations are enough to interpret moments, passengers' observations on transit are not the same as lengthy ethnographic observations. Unlike passengers on a bus, practitioners of observational methods systematically and regularly observe with purpose (Adler and Adler 1994, 377). Nonetheless, DeVault (2004, 6) indicates that observers are also "insiders" that are "embedded in social relations, and therefore a practitioner of the very methods of coordination [studied]." As such, those relations may blur the distinction between observant researcher and average observing person. Moreover, Fine (1993, 279–81) underscores that researchers are also not perfectly observant and miss details; they are not entirely unobtrusive and their presence frames what is observed. Researchers must therefore recognize that even with purposeful observation, all observations come with their own limitations, resulting in gaps in the type of ethnographic picture painted (Fine 1993).

In this chapter, I argue that knowledge as experience and discourse fill gaps in the ethnographic picture, rendering phenomena knowable. How phenomena are known affects how one acts in relation to them (Townley 1993, 520–23). To demonstrate this claim, I draw from a pilot project that was conducted within an 11-day period and was not meant to be exhaustive. The project focused on the perception and representation of the public transit worker working for the Toronto Transit Commission (TTC). From observations on TTC vehicles, I outline three examples highlighting the role of extant knowledge in "filling in the gaps" within incomplete ethnographic pictures. These examples illustrate the operation of everyday sense-making processes, and emphasize the (re)production of knowledge and discourse via "filling in the gaps."

Tips and Tricks: Describe all that you see, smell, and hear as well as your reactions (Emerson, Fretz, and Shaw 2011, 24–25). Try to keep your reactions and analysis separate but be ready to deconstruct *all* your notes. Take jottings too. These are part of your initial notes and provide more detail about events occurring and can act as prompts to recall events later (Emerson, Fretz, and Shaw 2011, 29).

FRAMING THE ETHNOGRAPHIC PICTURE

Notions of good customer service increasingly affect the TTC's organizational discourse (Ahmed 2016; Toronto Transit Commission 2012). Concurrently, worker foibles have been captured in photos and videos by members of the public (Ahmed 2016). A Toronto newspaper even compiled a top 10 list of "employee blunders" (*Toronto Sun* 2012). These perceptions and representations might also be read alongside broader attacks on and typically negative representations of public sector workers (Camfield 2011). The above typify the types of knowledges that might be used to "fill in the gaps" and may intersect with a person's experiences of transit. For me, user experience matters in this project because I regularly use the TTC. Like a typical passenger, I am subject to such circulating knowledge.

Through observing, my research question eventually became focused on observable roles and responsibilities of public transit operators and converged with an insight on customer expectations of transit operators found in a 2010 TTC Customer Service Advisory Panel report: "Operators are expected to act as a tour guide, policy enforcer, fare collector, and custodian, while providing information, directions, and special assistance. All of this and much more is expected while, at the same time, they are to operate the vehicle in safe manner—Paying [*sic*] attention to the road at all times, adhere to the speed limit despite a tight schedule, and practice defensive driving" (O'Brien et al. 2010, 2–3). This comment led me to consider the development of worker role expectations and the effects of failed role performances. It also led me to wonder whether passengers and workers sustain or reproduce particular worker narratives through these roles.

INTERPRETIVE FRAMES

Media scholars Trinh T. Minh-ha (1991) and Stuart Hall (1992) help make sense of interpreting observed moments. TV programs, films, and ads come bundled with messages to decipher, though there is never a guarantee that a message will be decoded as intended (Hall 1992). The decoding of a message articulates one's experiences of reality via other messages or ideologies (Minh-ha 1991, 93–94; Hall 1992). Crucially, this suggests that no observed moment is predetermined nor does decoding guarantee a link to something particular; the observer produces meaning as much as the producer (Minh-ha 1991, 94; Hall 1992, 129–30). Ultimately, moments may be read through discourse and knowledge.

Discourse can be understood as a group of statements around a certain topic that structure contextually the "true and appropriate," thereby producing what is known and knowable (Mills 2003, 64–66). Experience and discourse as forms of knowledge are inflected with power, rendering some things visible while obscuring others, enabling governance by legitimating certain forms of action and intervention (Townley 1993, 520–23).

In sum, discourse and knowledge help to interpret moments when one is privy to partial details. Interpretation, whether intentional or not, operates to uphold certain ways of organizing and ordering the world. If observers consume partial contexts or partial moments, they may interpret them by drawing on other sources of knowledge to complete their (ethnographic) picture. A researcher's descriptions and interpretive capacity provide a lens on how moments *could* be read and understood generally by researchers and average observers alike. This suggests that, in this case, one's interpretations are subject to preconceived understandings of public transit (workers) *before* entering a public transit vehicle, which may derive from media representations, experience, or other forms of knowledge.

FINDING THE GAPS THROUGH FIELD NOTES

To explore my claims, I discuss three moments from my field notes that highlight how knowledge operates to fill the gaps of what cannot be known through observation, and how the positionality of the researcher and passenger merge.

Excerpt 1: On the Bus

In this example, I overhear a partial conversation. The only statements overheard in the conversation are those made by the bus driver:

> Ahead of me, I notice that the bus driver is in conversation with someone at the bus stop. He closes the door and opens it. There is a conversation that is happening. *Why?*[2] ...
>
> Driver: "You think I should get a real job?"
>
> Driver: "Get a job at McDonald's."
>
> The door closes and opens at least once more during this conversation. I'm uncertain of the exact timing.
>
> Driver: "Learn to use a computer."
>
> The door closes.
>
> One passenger starts laughing loudly, raises his hands and starts a slow clap. The lady sitting beside the clapping gentleman, I notice, has a smile on her face. An older lady is standing ahead with two large bags, talks to the passenger sitting next me. I'm not focused on what she's saying, but I soon start to realize that she says, "I think he wants a seat!" There is standing room on the bus only.

Tips and Tricks: If you have a mobile phone, you may want to write a draft text message, email, or use a note-taking application. I did this in excerpt 1. You can rewrite your jottings into something more substantive later.

Despite my best intentions, my own interpretative and observational capacity interjects and muddles the field notes. My partial and incomplete observations suggest a case of bad customer service and rude behaviour, but the reactions of fellow passengers disrupt that reading. What shaped that initial interpretation? The reading of good service ("the customer is always right") draws on white, middle-class ideas of respectability that dictate the right way to behave, which might be well known to passengers. Where does this understanding of customer service come from? Could the driver be speaking in their own defence? Crucially, the incident highlighted interpretive gaps in observation and how known discourses such as customer service may work to complete a picture.

Tips and Tricks: If you are on a crowded or moving vehicle, you might not be able to take any notes. Take a mental note of everything relevant. As soon as you can, write out your observations.

Excerpt 2: On the Bus, Again

Three people get on at [the stop]. One is a kid, one is a woman, and another is a man. I hear the man saying to the driver, "I'm a little short ... just going [several stops ahead]." Regardless of the confession, the man is permitted to get on the bus. They sit across from me. The kid turns to the man and high fives him. *Did they scam the driver?* The lady with them pushes the kid down to sit back.

Did they scam the driver? My question demonstrates my own expectation and assumption that operators must enforce fares. It highlights how the operation of good customer service discourse and role expectations might help to interpret what should be considered appropriate on-the-job conduct.

Excerpt 3: On the Subway

A large group of children are on the subway with a few adults. I assume this to be a school group.

The kids gets off at [the subway station]. A TTC worker, not sure the type of worker he is, gets off at the same stop. The chimes go off to indicate the closing of the doors rung [*sic*], and they start to close on the kids; not all of them have left the train. One of the adults stands in the doorway to make sure that the children can get out. The doors are held until they get off. The chimes ring again and the doors close.

The incident above made me question why the conductor closed the door so quickly even though everyone had not alighted safely; however, I could have otherwise asked why the adults did not prepare the children more appropriately to get off the train. This incident highlighted the operator's role to ensure safe travel, but perhaps this may have been in tension with train timeliness. I cannot be certain of the intent behind the operator's action and am left with partial awareness of that intent. The observations demonstrate the role partial information may play in affecting readings of observed moments. Limits and gaps might be filled with already known narratives and discourses.

CONCLUDING THOUGHTS

The examples presented here help illustrate that no account of a phenomenon can pin down its meaning for both the observer and all the others in the scene (see Rosaldo 1993; Said 1989). This reinforces claims about the imperfections of observational methods (Fine 1993). All three excerpts underscore my presence and positionality as researcher *and* passenger to shape observations (Fine 1993, 279–81). The interpretive gap created by this was seemingly filled by pre-existing information of customer service discourse associated with worker conduct, as well as my own expectations and experiences. They indicated that I was subject to the same social relations as passengers when embedded in the observation (DeVault 2004, 6).

Excerpt 1 highlighted the unobservant ethnographer who lacked observational details (Fine 1993, 279–80) opening the interpretive space to "fill in the gaps" through extant knowledge perhaps to vilify the driver for "bad" conduct. The acts of interpretation and decoding are inflected with power, making some things more visible than others (Townley 1993, 520–23), (re)producing particular meanings when drawing from discourse and knowledge as well as experience to decode a moment (Minh-ha 1991, 93–94; Hall 1992). This may affect how one might act based on that decoding (Townley 1993, 521).

I learned that interpretations of particular observed public service worker "blunders" (big or small), including my own, may be filtered through knowledge and discourse to reproduce dominant negative readings of the public servant in everyday situations, affecting action related to public servants. Crucially, my own observations suggested how partial information as well as multiple understandings and misunderstandings operate to produce and/or sustain representations of public transit workers and public servants.

CRAFTING QUALITATIVE RESEARCH EXERCISES

1. Get into two separate groups. The first group's mission is to observe other students in a busy part of the university. Take detailed notes related to the people you observe. What patterns did you observe? Take notes about only what you see. The second group's mission is to observe the first group. How do they present themselves while observing? How did other people react to them while they observed? Why is it significant that we see *how* we observe as much as *what* we observe?

2. Look at excerpts of my field notes above and consider the following questions:
    a) What are some of the assumptions I make that are not discussed in the chapter, but are visible to you?
    b) How do the notes uphold dominant ways of knowing the world?
    c) How do dominant ideas of gender and race filter through or remain invisible in the notes?
    d) How could these notes have been made better?
    e) Would you write them differently? How so?

NOTES

1. Thanks to Lorna Erwin, Katherine Bischoping, James Braun, Mark P. Thomas, and Alix Holtby for their important support through different stages of this project.
2. Italics in the notes indicate my own thoughts and questions, intended to be separate, as they emerged from observation, though, as my notes indicate, my thoughts did not always remain separate.

REFERENCES

Adler, Patricia A., and Peter Adler. 1994. "Observational Techniques." In *Handbook of Qualitative Research*, edited by Norman Denzin and Yvonna S. Lincoln, 377–92. Thousand Oaks, CA: Sage.

Ahmed, Kritee. 2016. "Engaged Customers, Disciplined Public Workers and the Quest for Good Customer Service Under Neoliberalism." In *Engaging Foucault*, vol. 2, edited by Marjan Ivković, Gazela Pudar Draško, and Srdan Prodanović, 46–62. Belgrade: Institute for Philosophy and Social Theory. http://instifdt.bg.ac.rs/wp-content/uploads/2016/02/Engaging-Foucault-vol.2.pdf.

Camfield, David. 2011. "The 'Great Recession,' the Employers' Offensive and the Public Sector Unions." *Socialist Studies* 7 (1/2): 95–115.

DeVault, Marjorie. 2004. "What Is Description? (One Ethnographer's View)." *Perspectives (ASA Theory Section Newsletter)* (January 2004): 4, 6, 18.

Emerson, Robert M., Rachel I. Fretz, and Linda L. Shaw. 2011. *Writing Ethnographic Fieldnotes*. 2nd ed. Chicago: University of Chicago Press.

Fine, Gary A. 1993. "Ten Lies of Ethnography: Moral Dilemmas of Field Research." *Journal of Contemporary Ethnography* 22 (3): 267–94.

Hall, Stuart. 1992. "Encoding, Decoding." In *Culture, Media, Language*, edited by Stuart Hall, Dorothy Hobson, Andrew Lowe, and Paul Willis, 128–38. New York: Routledge.

Mills, Sara. 2003. *Michel Foucault*. London: Routledge.

Minh-ha, Trinh T. 1991. *When the Moon Waxes Red: Representation, Gender and Cultural Politics*. New York: Routledge.

O'Brien, Steve, Matthew Blackett, Robert Culling, Susan Davidson, Yves Devin, Tyson Matheson, Roy Morley, Sue Motehedin, Krisna Saravanamuttu, Kripa Sekhar, and Julie Tyios. 2010. *TTC Customer Service Advisory Panel Report*. Toronto: Customer Service Advisory Panel. https://web.archive.org/web/20100827063546/http://ttcpanel.ca:80/wordpress/wp-content/uploads/report.pdf.

Rosaldo, Renato. 1993. *Culture and Truth: The Remaking of Social Analysis*. Boston: Beacon Press.

Said, Edward W. 1989. "Representing the Colonized: Anthropology's Interlocutors." *Critical Inquiry* 15 (2): 205–25.

Toronto Sun. 2012. "Top 10 TTC Employee Blunders." September 27, 2012. http://www.torontosun.com/2012/09/27/top-10-ttc-employee-blunders.

Toronto Transit Commission. 2012. *Modernizing the TTC*. Toronto: TTC. https://ttc.ca/PDF/Modernizing%20The%20TTC/Modernizing_The_TTC.pdf.

Townley, Barbara. 1993. "Foucault, Power/Knowledge, and Its Relevance for Human Resource Management." *Academy of Management Review* 18 (3): 518–45.

21 Tips and Tricks for Writing Reflexive Field Notes When Doing Team-Based Rapid Ethnographic Research

Krystal Kehoe MacLeod

INTRODUCTION

My first foray into hands-on research was as a student conducting team-based rapid ethnographies as part of the major collaborative research initiative "Re-imagining Residential Long-Term Care," funded by the Social Sciences and Humanities Research Council. As a member of this research team, I participated in site visits to long-term residential care homes, commonly known as nursing homes, where we toured the facilities and grounds; conducted key informant interviews; spoke informally to workers, residents, and family members; and observed the daily happenings of life. In line with a feminist political economy approach, the research team was interested in the context set by the conditions of work because, we argued, this influences the conditions of care. Our intention with this project was to capture the experiences and perspectives of care providers and residents. To do so, we employed a variation on the traditional ethnographic method. We collected data using a large and diverse team of researchers who were present in the field for short periods of time—a few hours for a "flash" visit to a few days for a "rapid" ethnography at each research site. Our research team included students as well as junior and senior academics trained in a variety of disciplines, including sociology, medicine, social work, history, media studies, philosophy, architecture, health policy, nursing, anthropology, economics, and political science, from four Canadian provinces, the United States, the United Kingdom, Sweden, Germany, and Norway. Our study used the "fresh eyes" of many researchers to collect data in several short bursts and then facilitated team collaboration in order to analyze the data. Each team member aimed to capture data in a way that was detailed enough to accurately, yet succinctly, reflect their experiences in the field; the large amounts of data we each collected were made accessible to all team members so we could share, discuss, and learn from each other's experiences.

As I stepped onto the scuffed tile floor of the first nursing home we visited, I had a notepad holstered on one hip, a new pen on the other, and no idea what I was going to write down or how I should go about doing so. I approached this initial site visit thinking that the purpose of writing field notes was simply to create a written record of what I observed so that I could remember it later. As it turns out, writing field notes *is* about that—in part—but there are many other considerations that factor into the preparation of a written account of one's research experience, especially in a team-based research project. Now, after visiting four long-term residential care homes—two in Ontario and two in Norway—I am better positioned to share some of the lessons I have learned about how to use detail and reflexivity to enrich ethnographic field notes.

THE WHAT OF WRITING FIELD NOTES

My impulse to record my visual observations in my field notes was a good start, but in order for my notes to be a holistic reflection of my experiences on site, I realized that I needed to move beyond what I could *see* to also write about the conversations I had during my fieldwork and offer details about the sounds and smells I experienced during the day and night. The opportunity for me to read other researchers' field notes following our first site visit was a benefit of working as part of a research team that included experienced ethnographers. Upon reviewing the notes prepared by the seasoned ethnographers who visited the same site as me, I saw what details they included and excluded and how this compared to what I deemed worthy of recording. While my notes focused on the things I had experienced, some of the most useful field notes from my colleagues also included observations about the things that they had *not* experienced. As it turns out, the absence of smells, cries, dirty laundry, or visitors in a nursing home can tell you a lot about what life is really like in a particular facility. Reflecting on what is absent is an important component of field notes that is often overlooked in lieu of things that are more noticeable.

Recording my thoughts and feelings about what I was experiencing at the time of data collection, called "memoing" (Groenewald 2008), is another important component in the preparation of useful field notes. Recording memos while in the field helps the researcher engage in reflexivity during the data collection phase of their research by encouraging them to take "two steps back" (Bourdieu 2004) from the subject of their research. The first step back is the observation of the research participants and the next step back is the researcher's reflection on the observation itself. My memos recorded my preliminary thoughts about my research methodology and its strengths and limitations; possible relationships, patterns, tensions, or contradictions I noticed in the data; the impact of my or other researchers' positions or presence; the impact of the research participants; and the importance of the research context (Finlay 2002, 225; Guillemin and Gillam 2004, 275). I used these reflexive memos to add nuance to the observational data I included in the field notes that I wrote at the end of each shift in the field.

THE HOW OF WRITING FIELD NOTES

The writing of my field notes started with the jot notes I hastily recorded during my time in the field in order to help me recall the details of, and my reflections on, my experiences.

I found that remaining focused on my tasks of observing, participating, and recording, and giving equal energy to each of these, helped me carve out the time to take down the detailed jot notes I needed to be able to write accurate and comprehensive field notes later, which included reflexive memos as well as robust descriptions. Sometimes a little creative problem solving was also necessary to deal with obstacles that hindered my efforts to write jot notes or memos. For example, ethnographic research at nursing homes kept me busy. Between observing mealtimes; participating in recreational activities; speaking to residents, families, and workers; and conducting formal interviews, I found it very difficult to stop and jot down the details of what I was seeing, hearing, and thinking, as well as what was absent. Heeding the advice of an experienced ethnographer, a trick I used was to sneak away to a private place (e.g., a restroom, an empty kitchen, a common room) at frequent intervals to do my jotting and memoing—though admittedly this was easier said than done. A student researcher on my team documented a similar struggle to jot notes while in the field, describing a situation at an Ottawa nursing home in which she felt forced to "hide" from a resident in order to get some time alone:

> I walk down the long hall and duck into the large dining room, and hide behind the door in the dark to try to write down everything that has happened in the last hour. About two minutes later, I hear shuffling sounds and look through the crack in the door to see J using her slippered feet to pull her chair slowly down the hallway past the dining room. This is the last time I see J on the shift. (Yes, I basically just hid from a resident; feels pretty terrible.)

Once my shift in the field was complete, it was time to turn my jottings into reflexive field notes as part of the "meaning-making process" of working through my own interpretation of my experiences and then sharing these with others (Scales, Bailey, and Lloyd 2011). Sharing reflexive field notes amongst team members is fundamental to the success of the rapid ethnography method. A limitation of spending only short bursts of time in the field at each site was that individual researchers were not able to see recurring patterns emerge over time at a single site. Instead, our team of researchers consolidated our reflexive field notes from the many sites we visited and used them as a tool to engage in "collective reflexivity" (Bourdieu 2004) by looking for patterns across all of our data. In line with Bourdieu's (2004) recognition of reflexivity not as a solitary, individual-istic process (nor the sole domain of the "expert" researcher), but rather a process that is collaborative, interactive, and inherently social, we worked together to identify the conditions that were most promising for promoting the dignity and respect of both care providers and residents.

The writing of reflexive field notes to be shared with a large research team was not without its challenges. One researcher on our team confided in me that she felt conflicted about incorporating some of the reflexive thoughts contained in her memos into field notes that would be accessible to other members of the research team. She explained that, for her, writing shared field notes required a kind of careful and precise composition that she found much more time-consuming than writing field notes for private use. I found that there was no simple trick for negotiating to what extent I was comfortable sharing my personal reflections with my research team; however, learning to balance the desire to keep one's reflections private with the need to share in order to engage in collective reflexivity is a particularly relevant concern for students who may find themselves working closely with their supervisors or other academics that they wish to impress on research teams.

The pressure felt by students new to ethnography to produce field notes up to the standard of experienced ethnographers was a concern raised by graduate students on this project in parallel with the acknowledgement that our positioning as students sometimes influenced how we wrote our field notes and what types of reflexive thoughts we included or omitted. As a student researcher, there is value both in sharing your reflexive thoughts with your team members through your field notes and in giving yourself permission to keep portions of your field notes private if this is what you need to do in order to reflect honestly on your data and methodology. In this research project, I found the team's diversity comforting in that our research team comprised a wide variety of academics with various disciplinary backgrounds at different stages of their careers and included many students. In fact, some of the most experienced researchers on the team were as unfamiliar with the ethnographic method as the students. Furthermore, because rapid and flash ethnographies are a relatively new, and still somewhat controversial, variation on the traditional ethnographic method, the majority of the researchers on the team were inexperienced "rapid ethnographers." This created camaraderie amongst the team members, which resulted in a view of this research project as a shared learning experience. This helped reduce anxiety about the need to produce reflexive field notes of a predetermined calibre.

TESTING OUT MY OWN ADVICE

At the time of writing, the research team in this study had completed 27 rapid or flash ethnographic site visits over seven years. An advantage of the long duration of this particular project has been the opportunity for me to test the recommendations for writing useful field notes that grew out of my initial fieldwork experiences. At a flash ethnography visit to a residential long-term care facility in Simcoe County late in the project, I was determined to use all the tips and tricks outlined above to facilitate the writing of my most comprehensive field notes to date. How did I fare? Finding the time to jot notes and memos during a hectic day of observing and participating was still a challenge—even when I knew up front that this was my goal. It would have been impossible for each team member to remember the vast amount of information we were exposed to during this one-day site visit and so we all felt acute pressure to jot quickly but accurately throughout the day. Despite my best intentions, I was so busy during the site visit that I was only able to sneak away once to a restroom, following an interview with a resident, to scribble some longer, though still rushed, memos.

As a method of doing better work, I took numerous photos throughout the day that I used to help turn my jottings into more comprehensive field notes and memos later that evening. During the visit, I made an explicit effort to record data about smells, sounds, feelings, and my interactions with residents, workers, and other researchers—things that could not be captured well in photos. I collected materials (forms, brochures, presentation slides) that administrators at the site offered, which I used with caution to supplement my notes. When doing so, I was careful to reference the source of the information to avoid assumptions about organizational information being more credible than interview or observational data (Becker 1967), especially given the frequent contradictions we noted throughout the project between how things were *supposed to* work in long-term residential care homes versus how they *actually* worked in practice. I elaborated on my jottings and reflected more extensively on my memos in the evening immediately following the site visit to create my field notes. It was important to do this as soon as possible following the day of observations because I wanted the details to be fresh in my mind and not get diluted by other information. Finally, I tried not to worry about being candid when writing the first draft of my field notes; I did not censor my reflexive comments as I endeavoured to capture a comprehensive and holistic account of both my experiences and my reflections on them. While I was comfortable sharing my field notes in their entirety with my team members, it would have been an option to keep certain portions of them private if I had been concerned about sharing some of my raw thoughts and reflections with a broader audience.

CONCLUSION

My experiences as a student researcher conducting rapid team-based ethnographies in long-term residential care settings have taught me many things about writing field notes, one of which is that more experienced researchers do not necessarily write better field notes. Creating the most useful account of your research experiences is about being open to recording things other than "sights" (often the most significant things are those you smell, hear, feel, or do not see at all); reflecting on your observations using memos and incorporating these thoughts into your field notes; and taking the time away from observing and participating to jot, take photos, and collect organizational materials. While the team-based rapid ethnography methodology has certain limitations, it offers an excellent forum for collective reflexivity that can provide important data. Writing detailed and reflexive field notes that accurately and succinctly capture a researcher's experiences in the field is an essential skill for students participating in flash, rapid, or other more traditional forms of ethnography.

CRAFTING QUALITATIVE RESEARCH EXERCISES

1. Spend 20 minutes as an observer-participant in your nearest building lobby, grocery store, gym, etc. After the first 10 minutes, take 2 minutes to write a purely descriptive field note. After the next 10 minutes, take 2 minutes to write a reflexive field note. Compare the notes. Which note was easier to write? Why? Which note offers the more accurate account of your research experience? Why?

2. Spend 5 minutes thinking about your favourite place in your neighbourhood or on campus. Write a one-page description of that place from memory—try to include sights, sounds, smells, and feelings. Next, go visit this place in person and spend 5 minutes observing. Write a one-page description of your observations, again including sights, sounds, smells, and feelings. Analyze the differences in the two descriptions. What were the challenges in writing these two notes?

3. Pretend you and a partner are members of a research team. Spend 15 minutes observing the same location on campus. Feel free to interact with people on site and your research partner as you would if you were doing research during a real site visit. Make jottings while you are observing; make them as detailed and reflexive as possible. Upon concluding your observations, spend 30 minutes writing field notes and then share them with your research partner. How do your notes compare? Were there observations that one partner made that the other did not? How did you decide what to record and what to leave out of your notes?

4. Spend 10 minutes observing a busy place on campus. Jot down the most noticeable sights, smells, and sounds. Now, think about what kinds of things are *not* there: can you identify anything significant that is missing or absent from the site you are observing? Think about things like gender, race, class, and age—are any of these significant to what you are observing?

REFERENCES

Becker, Howard S. 1967. "Whose Side Are We On?" *Social Problems* 14 (3): 239–47.

Bourdieu, Pierre. 2004. *Science of Science and Reflexivity*. Cambridge, UK: Polity Press.

Finlay, Linda. 2002. "Negotiating the Swamp: The Opportunity and Challenge of Reflexivity in Research Practice." *Qualitative Research* 2 (2): 209–30.

Groenewald, Thomas. 2008. "Memos and Memoing." In *The SAGE Encyclopedia of Qualitative Research Methods*, vol. 2, edited by Lisa M. Given, 505–6. Los Angeles: Sage.

Guillemin, Marilys, and Lynn Gillam. 2004. "Ethics, Reflexivity and 'Ethically Important Moments' in Research." *Qualitative Inquiry* 10 (2): 261–80.

Scales, Kezia, Simon Bailey, and Joanne Lloyd. 2011. "Separately Together: Reflections on Conducting a Collaborative Team Ethnography in Dementia Care." *Enquire* 6: 24–49.

SECTION VI

DOING INTERVIEWS

We like to encourage our students to think of qualitative interviews as being akin to "conversations with a plan." Making your interviews conversation-like, but with some guiding questions, goes a long way towards creating a comfortable interview environment. In this type of atmosphere, participants feel more at ease sharing the type of frank, rich details we rely on as qualitative researchers. Capturing a fine-grained understanding of people's everyday lives is our scholastic reward for carrying out well-conducted interviews. The benefits of qualitative in-depth interviewing, though, go deeper than that. This technique, which permits participants to talk about things that matter to them, can be highly rewarding for researchers and participants alike. In their qualitative research methods text, Bruce Berg and Howard Lune (2012, 128) liken a well-developed in-depth interview to reading a good book: "Even after several hours, there is often a feeling that only minutes have passed." This is a common experience for researchers who focus on generating a conversation-like, comfortable interview atmosphere, which places the experiences and perspectives of participants front and centre.

How conversation-like your interviews will be depends on how much structure you give them. Qualitative researchers often conduct semi-structured and unstructured in-depth interviews. With a semi-structured interview, you develop a set of questions you plan to ask each participant, but you are also prepared to introduce new follow-up and probing questions, and occasionally discard some of your prepared questions on the spot to suit your participants' experiences. You might approach an unstructured interview with an overarching question or some important themes you would like participants to touch on. The more unstructured the interview is, the more the interview will feel like a conversation.

Flexibility is a hallmark of qualitative research. Being flexible while interviewing means being responsive to what your participants say and do. You will do a lot of "on-your-toes" thinking during interviews. For instance, despite your best efforts to construct worthwhile questions, you can expect that some of your questions might not make sense to your participants or that there might be more worthwhile questions to ask. Here it is important to anticipate the unexpected—that is, be prepared to follow lines of inquiry in response to what your interviewees have to say and insights they feel are useful for you to understand. After all, it is difficult to know ahead of time precisely what will be important to your participants. With each subsequent interview, you can make adjustments based on insights from your past interviews, following up on useful leads and hunches you have along the way.

There are many things you will consider when preparing for and conducting an interview, from planning where to carry out your interviews, keeping your questions open-ended, and avoiding complex questions, to introducing a recording device, managing ethical issues, and wrapping up your interviews. Perhaps the most crucial aspect of the craft of qualitative interviewing can be distilled down to this oft-shared advice from veteran qualitative researcher, Robert Prus: *make the participant the star of the show*. This means giving participants your full attention, listening intently to what they say, reflecting on what is said, and asking useful probing questions that build on the dialogue. In line with this advice is a refrain that qualitative researchers commonly use during interviews, which is, "That's interesting. Can you tell me more about that?"

Appealing to people's humanness by honouring their desire to be understood, treating them with respect, and remaining non-judgmental can go a long way towards fostering rapport during interviews. The chapters in this section build on this type of advice to help prepare you for some of the ins and outs of conducting qualitative interviews.

What if we were to ask participants to bring a symbolic object with them into the interview, and then asked them to reflect on what the object means to them? In chapter 22, Kathleen Steeves and Deana Simonetto take up this question, emphasizing the benefits of using objects as a visual interview guide. More than simply conversation starters, the authors demonstrate the utility of incorporating a visual component in developing rapport, helping with recollection, acquiring richer data, and creating a positive interview experience.

As interviewers, our attention is often focused on *what* our participants tell us. In chapter 23, Deborah K. van den Hoonaard draws on her research with older people—widows and widowers in particular—to highlight the value of paying closer attention to *how* participants say things. By actively considering how participants engage in impression management during interviews, we are presented with deeper insights into participants' sense of self.

In chapter 24, Taylor Price and Antony Puddephatt explore the strengths and weaknesses of different communication technologies in conducting long-distance interviews. To do so, they use media synchronicity theory to analyze their experiences of conducting long-distance interviews with open-access journal editors. If you are using a form of communication technology, such as email or Skype, to conduct interviews, the ideas in this chapter will help you consider methodological issues. These include which technologies are better suited to recruiting participants, developing rapport, addressing sensitive questions, reducing attrition, achieving a mutual understanding between researcher and participant, and acquiring detailed responses.

As Ellen Rose indicates in chapter 25, some qualitative interviews emphasize having participants reflect on and interpret their experiences. In phenomenological interviews, however, the emphasis is on eliciting concrete stories of participants' lived experiences. If this is your goal, how can you take participants back to particular moments in time and space and have them experience these moments anew? Using data from her research on online instructors, Rose provides several insightful tips to help accomplish this. Walking us through the process of conducting a phenomenological interview, she begins with her thoughts on where to hold interviews and how to prepare for them, considers how to evoke particular instances and events, provides examples of probing questions to help participants explore different aspects of their experience, and offers advice for helping to keep participants focused on specifics.

Sometimes our research takes us to different parts of the world. This can create opportunities for developing cross-cultural insights, while also presenting some unique cross-cultural challenges. In chapter 26, Abhar Rukh Husain discusses interviewing in the context of international research. As her case study, she recounts her experiences with interviewing Bangladeshi female temporary workers. As a Bangladeshi Canadian woman and feminist scholar doing research in Bangladesh, she notes how her ambiguous status as both insider and outsider impacted the interview process. In doing so, she presents us with an opportunity to consider how we might navigate issues pertaining to status characteristics (e.g., gender or class) and power dynamics to help foster collaborative interviews.

REFERENCE

Berg, Bruce L., and Howard Lune. 2012. *Qualitative Research Methods for the Social Sciences.* 8th ed. New York: Pearson.

22 "Show and Tell": Using Objects as Visual Interview Guides in Qualitative Interviewing

Kathleen Steeves and Deana Simonetto

INTRODUCTION

Show and tell is an activity many of us have memories of from grade school. This childhood ritual involves bringing in an object and explaining to the class its significance. Steeves remembers taking her baby sister in for show and tell in kindergarten, with her mother's help, of course. Perhaps you also recall that having a favourite object in hand helped you open up, share stories, and talk about yourself in the classroom. What we learned in kindergarten is that significant insights can be gleaned about an individual or group when asked to talk about an object that is important to them. As in show and tell, we suggest that researchers can incorporate objects into interviews as a "visual interview guide"—a method that can add to the quality and experience of gathering qualitative data. This strategy can help answer research questions around attitudes, perspectives, experiences, identities, social relationships, and other activities and behaviours. In this chapter, we offer a case study of our experience employing objects as visual interview guides. In our project on identity work, we asked women to bring their charm bracelets to our interviews in order to discuss the meanings these objects elicit. Through this process, we learned that the "object as a visual interview guide" approach has several benefits, including facilitating rapport with participants, assisting participants in remembering past events, enriching the quality of interview data collected, and allowing the interview to be a positive experience for everyone involved.

OBJECTS AND INTERVIEWS

We are not the first to suggest using tangible objects as part of qualitative data collection in order to glean more in-depth information from participants. Other researchers have used objects including photos (family photos, cartoons, pictures of people, historical events), artifacts (clothing, tools, buildings), keepsakes (jewellery, trophies, collectibles), and documents (personal journals, publications, government documents) to encourage participants to talk about their lives (Clark-Ibanez 2004; Collier and Collier 1986; De Leon and Cohen 2005; Harper 2002; Nordstrom 2013). In photo elicitation interviews, researchers use photographs to help participants recall events and people from the past and collaboratively talk about the emotions, experiences, and relationships these pictures invoke (Clark-Ibanez 2004; Collier and Collier 1986; Harper 2002). For example, Harper (2001) used historical photographs and aerial views of farmland to interview farmers about the changes they experienced in their identities and communities with the growth of farming technology. These historical photos became a starting point from which participants could explain the changes that had occurred over time; they helped participants recall a time in their lives and express deeper parts of the human consciousness that words alone could not access (Harper 2002).

In a variation of this method known as "photovoice," researchers may ask participants to take their own photographs and bring them into an interview (Wang, Cash, and Powers 2000). Clark-Ibanez (2004), for example, gave students their own disposable cameras to use to take pictures of people and things that were most important to them. During the subsequent interviews, students used the photographs they had taken to reveal unique and unexpected information about their lives—information that may not have been included otherwise. This technique empowered and engaged the students in the interview process. When employing this method, fewer direct interview questions are needed because significant meanings and information flow from participants' connections to the culture, place, or history represented by the image (Clark-Ibanez 2004, 1511). In a similar fashion, we encourage researchers to bring objects into the interview setting to engage participants and generate high quality interview data.

TOWARDS EMPLOYING "OBJECTS AS VISUAL INTERVIEW GUIDES": A CASE STUDY

Entering the field to interview a new population can be intimidating for novices and experienced researchers alike. Constructing the interview around an object your participant owns (like a bracelet, a scrapbook, sports memorabilia, or a coin collection) takes the pressure off everyone involved. This allows the conversation to naturally gravitate towards topics your participants will be excited to talk about. As researchers, we discovered this principle first-hand when we entered the field to talk to women about their charm bracelets and discover what these pieces of jewellery say about the wearer's identities and relationships. For this project, we asked women to bring their own charm bracelets to the interview so that we could discuss them. We interviewed eight women, focusing on the stories that emerged from the charm bracelets themselves. Here, we discuss three benefits to this approach: developing rapport and remembering the past, collecting rich data, and enhancing the quality of participant experience.

Developing Rapport and Remembering the Past

The goal of conducting in-depth interviews is to have people share their experiences, perspectives, ideas, and feelings in ways that are meaningful to them. Starting with an object to "break the ice" allows participants to begin in a place they are comfortable with. The object helps create a connection between the participant and interviewer and encourages the development of a more natural conversation where participants control the pace. For example, here is the beginning of Steeves's interview with Carly. Notice how the conversation starts:

Steeves: Ah—okay, so first of all just when did you, so you say this is from the '70s?
Carly: Right.
Steeves: How did—did someone give it to you?
Carly: Yes, my first husband gave me this bracelet, I don't, I'm trying to think what the first charm was. Um, it might have been the engagement charm.
Steeves: Oh. Which one is that?
Carly: This is—the love birds.
Steeves: Oh, that's cute.
Carly: Oh, the valentine's charm I should say.
Steeves: Yeah, okay. So the two birds in the heart. Ah. Excellent. Did you wear this at the time—like you would have worn this all the time?
Carly: Oh yeah. I wore it a lot, yeah.
Steeves: Any more today, do you still wear it?
Carly: No.
Steeves: Okay.
Carly: Yeah, it catches on everything [laughter].
Steeves: Yeah, it's a little bit dangly.
Carly: You spend 25 bucks on a pair of (panty)hose [laughter].

Within seconds of starting the interview, Carly discloses that she has been married before and quickly describes the first charms on her bracelet. The conversation then abruptly turns to laughter as she imagines the mishaps that could occur between her bracelet and a pair of pantyhose. The nature of this object helped break the ice and set the atmosphere for an enriching interview.

Being able to refer to the charms on the bracelet also helped participants remember things from their pasts that they may not have thought about referencing without the prompt. Topics came up that we, as the interviewers, would not have known to ask about without the charm bracelet. For example, Carly had a hard time remembering the significance behind a church-shaped charm on her bracelet when initially asked about it. Later on, near the end of the interview, the topic had changed but Carly suddenly remembered and brought the conversation back to this charm instead of answering Steeves's question:

Steeves: Oh, I love it. Do you think that the meaning of the charms or the bracelet as a whole has kinda changed over time? How has maybe the meaning …

Carly: I know what this is! [pointing at the church charm]—confirmation at [name] Church! It's coming back to me!

Over the course of the interview, Carly remembered and got to share experiences from her past that she might not otherwise have recalled without the prompt of the object in the interview.

Collecting Rich Data

Using an object as a visual interview guide may allow new themes to emerge, adding to the quality and substance of interview data. For example, our charm bracelet participants led us to consider a process we may not have discovered had we not been using this visual interview guide. Over and over again, our participants taught us that meaning is not inherent in objects themselves, but is socially constructed. We were able to see first-hand how the same object can hold different meanings for different people, and were reminded that, as researchers, we should not presume to know what that meaning is going to be before we ask. When a participant showed us their bracelet, we sometimes found ourselves (the researchers) prioritizing our own assumptions about what charms must be the most important, or what each would mean. In reality, often the charms *we* thought might be the most meaningful were actually treated as pedestrian by our participants, while others we were perhaps quick to mentally disregard actually elicited the most lengthy stories. Examine, for example, the dynamics of this conversation between Simonetto and Lisa, in which they discuss three different charms on Lisa's bracelet:

Lisa: [pointing to a charm on her bracelet] This one is the faith, hope, and charity.

Simonetto: Can you explain that more?

Lisa: No. [Simonetto and Lisa start laughing at the abruptness of Lisa's response.] In my mind it is a religious thing. They always go together faith, hope, and charity. And when we were younger, I don't even know.

Simonetto: Would you say you tried to pick charms that represented a time of your life or part of who you are?

Lisa: Absolutely, there is that one [referencing a charm] which is the astronomical sign, there is this one [pointing at another charm], which is a typewriter, and in high school I took that arm of studies, back in the day. It was a secretarial thing, I took shorthand, and typing and office management and all that in high school so when I graduated from high school and trying to think what I was going to do and I knew I wanted to go to university. In those days there weren't a whole lot of girls going to university … [Lisa continues telling the story stemming from the typewriter charm for another few minutes.]

In this example, Simonetto's initial probes around the significance of the "religious" charm are dismissed by Lisa; however, moments later a typewriter charm (which would not, on the surface, seem to have a special significance) catches Lisa's attention and generates the unsolicited story of an entire season of her life. Again, using an object as a visual interview guide allowed participants to exert agency in guiding the interview and talking about each part of the object as much or as little as they liked, sharing their own stories and meanings. This exercise also reminded us, as researchers, to check our own taken-for-granted assumptions at the door and prioritize the meanings participants themselves attribute to objects and life events.

Enhancing the Quality of Participants' Interview Experiences

Most researchers hope that taking part in their study is a positive experience for their participants. Using an object as a visual interview guide can help make interviews fun and less intimidating for everyone involved. The charm bracelets our participants brought with them started conversations around events and relationships that were fun and nostalgic for them to remember, bringing up memories they were eager to talk about. For example, Bree brought three charm bracelets to her interview (her grandmother's, her mother's, and her own). When Steeves pointed out one bracelet that was especially full of charms, Bree immediately replied: "This is my mom's. My mom, she was, my mom was my best friend and we always—wherever we went, we always bought charms." Looking at the bracelet as a whole served to remind Bree of her mother, and talking about it was like sharing a piece of this special relationship, and person, with us. At the end of her interview, Lisa similarly reflected on the experience of getting to talk about her childhood charm bracelet. Simonetto asked: "Is there anything about your charm bracelet that I didn't ask you but you felt was important?" to which she replied,

> I don't think so, other than for me it's very nostalgic after so many years and to go back and look at it so many years removed. But we talked about that—it's nice to be nostalgic and like I said, every one of them brings back good memories … good times, good people. It's the remembering … when I look at this one [her bracelet] I remember, remember, remember.

It was clear through her posture and response that talking about her charm bracelet was an enjoyable, near therapeutic, nostalgic experience for Lisa because of the meanings attached to this object. We believe that being asked to share about any variety of significant objects can be a very energizing and positive experience for participants, which, of course, makes it fun for the interviewer, too.

CONCLUSION

The practice of show and tell has an equally long tradition in kindergarten classrooms as in our experiences of everyday life. We go on a trip and bring back souvenirs and pictures to show others and facilitate a conversation about our experiences; we converse using digital objects like images and emojis on social media; and in the tangible world, we sometimes question each other about the meaning of a tattoo, necklace, or t-shirt. Employing "objects as visual interview guides" as a method of qualitative interviewing can be a beneficial and natural way to start conversations with participants around something that is of great interest and importance to them. At the same time, this method allows researchers to glean rich insights about participant identities, relationships, and life experiences. As you seek to gain practical experience interviewing, ask your participants to bring in and discuss a tangible object that is important to them. Perhaps this will be the outfit they wear to their favourite sporting event, their collection of stamps or coins, or their trophies or scrapbooks. Engage in the rewarding, rich experience of using an object as a visual interview guide to enhance the quality of your data and the quality of your interviews. Give it a try.

CRAFTING QUALITATIVE RESEARCH EXERCISES

1. Partner with another student. Take an object out of your backpack/pocket/ purse/wallet and have your partner do the same. Ask each other the following questions about the object of choice (feel free to probe for further information as you interview each other and make up a question of your own):
   a) Where and when did you get this object? Was it a gift or did you purchase it for yourself?
   b) Describe how you use this object in your everyday life in as much detail as possible.
   c) What meaning does it have to you?
   d) Does it remind you of any events or people in your life?
   e) Would you be upset if you lost this object? Why/why not?

   After the discussion, write a brief summary of what you learned about your partner. Did anything about their answers surprise you? Was the meaning you might attribute to the object different from the meaning they gave it?

2. Develop a research question that interests you—perhaps it is to guide a project on identity work, sports and leisure, or work and occupations, or an entirely different area. What types of objects could you use to gain insight into this question and enhance the interview process? Create a list and defend your choices.

3. Take one object and ask at least five different people (friends and family, colleagues or fellow students) the following questions about it:
    a) What is this? What would you do with it?
    b) What specific memories or experiences does this object bring up for you?

    In your mini-interviews, make up a few questions of your own, or probe for more detailed responses. Record the responses you are given and compare them. How were the meanings and experiences the object generated similar and different for different people?

4. Consider the challenges, limitations, or problems that might arise in the process of employing an "object as a visual interview guide" method. Write a paragraph about the strengths and weaknesses of this approach.

REFERENCES

Clark-Ibanez, Marisol. 2004. "Framing the Social World with Photo-Elicitation Interviews." *American Behavioral Scientist* 47 (12): 1507–27.

Collier, John Jr., and Malcolm Collier. 1986. *Visual Anthropology: Photography as a Research Method.* Revised and expanded. Albuquerque: New Mexico Press.

De Leon, Jason P., and Jeffrey H. Cohen. 2005. "Object and Walking Probes in Ethnographic Interviewing." *Field Methods* 17 (2): 200–4.

Harper, Douglas. 2001. *Changing Works: Visions of a Lost Agriculture.* Chicago: University of Chicago Press.

Harper, Douglas. 2002. "Talking about Pictures: A Case for Photo Elicitation." *Visual Studies* 17 (1): 12–26.

Nordstrom, Susan N. 2013. "Object-Interviews: Folding, Unfolding, and Refolding Perceptions of Objects." *International Journal of Qualitative Methods* 12 (1): 237–57.

Wang, Caroline C., Jennifer L. Cash, and Lisa S. Powers. 2000. "Who Knows the Streets as Well as the Homeless? Promoting Personal and Community Action through Photovoice." *Health Promotion Practice* 1 (1): 81–89.

23 Interactional Strategies of Interview Participants and Their Sense of Self

Deborah K. van den Hoonaard

I have spent most of my research life conducting interviews with older people—widows (2001), widowers (2010), older women, retired baby-boomer women. The people I have interviewed are not simply vessels of experiences and answers to mine for data. They are human beings who bring their identities and sense of self into the interview situation. By analyzing not only what these research participants say, but also *how* they say it, I have discovered how they see themselves and wish to be seen. In this chapter, I recount how I used an active interview approach (Holstein and Gubrium 1995) to add depth to my understanding.

Older widows demonstrated their fears that they might not be competent interview participants by asking, "Am I doing it right?" and treated the interview situation as one of hostess and guest, with which they were familiar and comfortable. Their strategies shone light on the fact that older women are often seen as uninteresting and likely to talk too much.

In contrast, older widowers used the interview to claim their status as *real men.* They interrupted me, called me by a diminutive name, emphasized their heterosexuality by focusing on relationships with women and referring to themselves as "bachelors," and claimed an inability to carry out traditionally feminine tasks such as cooking and cleaning. These strategies reflect the lack of masculinity scripts (Spector-Mercel 2006) available to older men, in general, and widowers, in particular.

"AM I DOING IT RIGHT?"

In 1995, I interviewed 27 older widows in New Brunswick, Canada, using a symbolic interactionist perspective that recognizes widows as experts in their own lives. I developed a very open-ended interview guide and presented myself as an interested and sympathetic listener rather than an expert. I was familiar with the challenges of women interviewing women identified by feminist researchers (see Oakley 1981; DeVault 1999) and was determined to minimize any status differences between us. The women welcomed me into their homes and were generous in sharing their stories with me, stories that demonstrated both the challenges they faced and their creativity and strength.

As I began to analyze the transcripts, I noticed that I had spent a fair amount of time reassuring the research participants that they were doing "interview participant" correctly and that they had meaningful and important things to say. Phrases such as "Am I supposed to be doing this?" and "Does that answer your question?" appeared throughout the transcripts.

Noticing these questions of uncertainty, what Marjorie DeVault (1999) refers to as a "dance of orientation," led me to carefully look through the interview transcripts for other indications that the women were concerned about their ability to be *good* interview participants. These included concerns that they might be talking too much—"gabbling," as one of them put it—or really did not have anything to contribute: "Well, I don't know what kind of an input I've put into it, probably not very much." They also worried that I might think they were selfish, immature, or a "little crazy." Comments like "I hope I'm not whiny," and "maybe I'm just a sentimental slob," were scattered throughout the interviews.

> **Tips and Tricks:** Pay attention to what the participants say that is not directly related to the topic of the interview. These parenthetical remarks often provide clues to important issues about their sense of self.

Finding Familiar Roles

Some participants transformed the context to one with which they were more familiar by adopting the role of hostess. They gave themselves and me roles they understood—hostess and guest. Some women established this social context by inviting me to lunch before the interview or offering tea and cookies at the outset of our interview.[1] The following example, from an interview transcript, is characteristic of the more common trajectory, which reflected this participant's anxiety about her participation; she offered coffee or tea as she began to feel comfortable. About a half-hour into the interview, she suddenly decided to offer me refreshments:

> And my daughter's very proud of the fact that she has six brothers.... *Well, how about a tea and a piece of pie?*

This offer came in the middle of a response, seemingly out of nowhere. As the interview progressed, the woman's responses continued, but interspersed with her answers are the questions of a hostess:

> Anyway, he got sick.... He had the ticket all bought, ready to come, and my daughter was talking to him—*no sugar?*—and they decided they would go down and get him.

Later in the interview, this participant offered to refill my tea, again without skipping a beat in her response.

Tips and Tricks: Always accept hospitality offered by participants. It demonstrates that you see them as equals and puts them at ease.

Another strategy the women used to convert the interview into a more familiar woman-to-woman social encounter was to ask me questions about myself. Hence, we shared common experiences with children and identified people we both knew, a common way that Maritimers place each other socially.

By paying attention to the women's approach to the interview situation, I was able to analyze their efforts to transform the research encounter into one with which they were familiar and their desire not to talk negatively or off point. These patterns communicated aspects of their experience as widows and of the precariousness of older widows' identity. The women reflected the low status of older women and the widespread belief that older women, and older widows, in particular, are uninteresting and have led ordinary lives.

"I WAS THE MAN"

When I carried out a similar study with widowers in 2002, I knew that they would be different. I also knew that, although women are more forthcoming in an interview, men are more likely to talk expansively with women than with other men. I did not foresee, however, that the men would go to great lengths to establish themselves as masculine through the way they presented themselves and interacted during the interview. They did this through taking charge and interrupting my questions, referring to me as "girl" or using a diminutive of my first name, lecturing me, emphasizing their heterosexuality, and claiming limited capacity to cook and clean.

Taking Charge

Although I have spent most of my life in Canada, I am originally from New York City, where interrupting people is how you talk. At the same time, one of the most basic rules of interviewing is to give participants ample time to answer questions, never to interrupt. I was, therefore, surprised and dismayed to see that the transcriptionist had noted many places where the widower and I were talking at the same time. How could I have made this basic mistake? It was only when I looked more closely that I saw that I had not interrupted the widowers—they had interrupted me! This interruption began with the very first question of the interview. I originally used the same question that had worked well with widows:

> What I would like for you to do now is tell me your experience with being a widower. You can start where you like and end where you want...

After a few interviews, it became obvious that the men were not allowing me to complete the question. They began talking before I was finished. Because qualitative interviews are flexible, and the researcher can modify the interview guide along the way, I shortened the first question to "What's it like being a widower?" or "Tell me about being a widower."

> **Tips and Tricks:** When the wording of a question is not working, change it. Later, think about why it did not work and if it can add insight to your analysis.

Another way the men asserted their dominant position was to refer to me as "girl," "dear," or to use the diminutive of my name, "Deb." One man used this terminology when he wanted to change the subject or was getting emotional, which moved him out of masculine space. He controlled the pace of the interview with comments like, "Let's get going here, *Debbie, dear*" and "What else have you got up your sleeve there, *girl?*" Another widower controlled the tempo of the interview by referring to me as "girl" or "Deb" when he wanted to close off a subject.

Men demonstrated they were knowledgeable by lecturing me about things not related to the topic of our interview. These topics included: Winston Churchill, how to ripen pears, the military, getting extra frequent-flyer points, the Great Depression, social justice, and men's slavery to testosterone. Some were likely emphasizing knowledge associated with their age cohort, but in a number of the interviews, their didactic tone was striking. I note the tone because sometimes the words on the page of a transcript do not reflect the condescending tone one can hear in the men's voices.

Claiming Heterosexuality

One topic the men explained deserves special mention: specific differences between men and women. Many of their comments about women, especially old women, were decidedly negative. The most frequent context for speaking of women in a derogatory manner involved the men's thoughts about remarriage. The participants commented that they would only be interested in younger women because women their own age were unattractive and asexual:

> I'm 75 years old [and] I look pretty good.... To me, a 70-year-old woman is an old lady, and I don't feel like going out with an old lady.

These men, if interested in remarriage, were only interested in younger women.[2] Their comments both desexualized old women and established their own sexuality.

> **Tips and Tricks:** Go along, as much as possible, with the tone and approach your participants take. Later, you may find their self-presentation useful in your analysis.

Another way the men brought attention to their own heterosexuality was to refer to themselves as bachelors. I was at first puzzled when they referred to themselves as bachelors. I could not imagine that women would claim the title *old maid* or *spinster* even though they did not like the term *widow*. After much thought, I concluded that the men used the term *bachelor* as a tool of impression management (Goffman 1959) that preserved their identities as heterosexual and reinforced their status as men. A few men underlined the connotation of being a bachelor by seeing themselves as "a lone wolf" or a "free agent" compared to other widowers who "become female when their wife [dies]." According to one man, widowers become [like] women when they lose their wives and "sit and die." Others suggested that a man who does not live up to the masculine ideal is like a woman (Edley and Wetherell 1995).

Although only two men explicitly referred to sexual intimacy during the interviews, many talked about being surrounded by interested women. They said they knew they were widowers because women reacted to them differently. Regardless of their thoughts about remarriage, most of the widowers raised the issue of finding a new partner early in the interview without a prompt. The ubiquity of this topic kept the spotlight on their heterosexuality and identity as men.

Minimizing Competence in Feminine Tasks

Finally, the men claimed their masculinity by insisting that they had limited cooking and cleaning ability. Even if they knew how to cook, they claimed they were not very good at it: "I can heat things up. Sometimes I overheat them and they come out absolutely solid." Those who could, cooked primarily masculine foods like turkeys, roasts, and meat and potatoes. They linked cooking with masculine activities such as being a soldier during the war. One man was most emphatic in associating his cooking with masculine activities:

> Oh yeah, I enjoyed cooking … and I've played senior hockey. I've played senior basketball … volleyball … softball … nine years coaching hockey.… I'd say, "Hey, come on home; I'll cook you a steak."

The men similarly described their housekeeping abilities as limited and unrewarding. They insisted that they had a low standard of cleanliness and pointed out that their standard was lower than their wives' had been:

> I'm starting to get a little bit tired of housework.… I don't always do a good job of it. Sometimes I just give it a lick and a promise every couple of weeks.

Considering the confidence with which the men talked about most aspects of their lives, their insistence that they cooked plain, masculine food and knew how to clean, but not too well, was striking. The men were using impression management in their discussion of household duties. Only feminine tasks were beyond their capacity to master.

CONCLUSION

These examples demonstrate how, by being attentive to our participants' interaction strategies, we can enrich our analysis and add depth to our findings. As Howard Becker (1998) noted, when we do research, we should ask, "I have these data. What question do they answer?" By allowing the data to suggest questions, I discovered my interview participants' strategies of impression management. This approach required that I be attentive, not only to the words on the page of the transcripts, but also to the way research participants spoke and their tones of voice that communicated uncertainty on the part of older widows and dominance on the part of older widowers.

> **Tips and Tricks:** Think about how your participants see you. They respond to you, not just as an interviewer, but as a person of a particular age, gender identity, racial group, and so on.

In more recent studies of widows and retired women baby boomers in 2015, the women's impression management reflected a changing social context. In these recent interviews, both groups of women established themselves as doing everything they can to take care of themselves. They used phrases like "you have to put yourself out there" to demonstrate that they were not sitting around waiting for support; rather they have conformed to current neoliberal thinking that individuals are responsible for themselves. The social context has changed and the results are different. Nonetheless, the impression management that interview participants engage in has not changed, and when we attend to it, our analyses are much richer.

CRAFTING QUALITATIVE RESEARCH EXERCISES

1. One way to become sensitive to impression management is to think about our own behaviour. Notice how you present yourself to different types of people, those older or younger, with different gender identities, a co-student versus a professor. Note the type of language you use, stories you tell, and topics of conversation you raise. What aspects of your identity do you emphasize with different types of people?

2. Think about a group you might consider conducting an interview project with. Consider what aspects of identity or social status might influence the

way group members might interact with you as an interviewer. How might they use impression management to influence your idea about what kind of people they are?

3.   To hone your skill at analyzing impression management, watch people being interviewed on public affairs shows. Notice how they address the interviewer, how they dress, their posture, and the phrases and comments they make that are not directly related to the questions asked. What kind of person do they want the interviewer and audience to think they are? Notice if they act differently when being interviewed by a woman or a man.

4.   Look at an interview transcript and see if you can identify impression management in the transcript. Now, listen to the recording of the interview and note whether or not you can hear efforts at impression management more clearly than you could when you were reading the transcript. You can also look at the script for a movie and then watch the movie to see how much more you can learn about a character when you can hear and/or see them rather than when you have only read their lines.

NOTES

1.   I accepted the lunch invitations but discovered that widows often told stories that I had to ask them to repeat during the interview. It might have been easier to ask to have lunch after the interview although we did establish rapport during the meal. Few widowers offered refreshments.

2.   Research shows that widowers who remarry often choose women who are younger than their wives.

REFERENCES

Becker, Howard S. 1998. *Tricks of the Trade: How to Think about Your Research While You're Doing It*. Chicago: University of Chicago Press.

DeVault, Marjorie. 1999. *Liberating Method: Feminism and Social Research*. Philadelphia: Temple University Press.

Edley, Nigel, and Margaret Wetherell. 1995. *Men in Perspective: Practice, Power and Identity*. London: Prentice-Hall Harvester, Wheatsheaf.

Goffman, Erving. 1959. *The Presentation of Self in Everyday Life*. New York: Doubleday.

Holstein, James A., and Jaber F. Gubrium. 1995. *The Active Interview*. Thousand Oaks, CA: Sage.

Oakley, Ann. 1981. "Interviewing Women: A Contradiction in Terms." In *Doing Feminist Research*, edited by Helen Roberts, 30–61. London: Routledge.

Spector-Mercel, Gabriela 2006. "Never-Ending Stories: Western Hegemonic Masculinity Scripts." *Journal of Gender Studies* 15 (1): 67–82.

van den Hoonaard, Deborah K. 2001. *The Widowed Self: The Older Woman's Journey through Widowhood*. Waterloo, ON: Wilfrid Laurier University Press.

van den Hoonaard, Deborah K. 2010. *By Himself: The Older Man's Experience of Widowhood*. Toronto: University of Toronto Press.

24 "Opening Access" to Open Access Editors: Communication Technologies in Long Distance Interviewing

Taylor Price and Antony Puddephatt

INTRODUCTION

Qualitative research has been transformed by the digital revolution, providing new opportunities and dilemmas for researchers. New online research methods are often compared to more traditional methods, identifying advantages and shortcomings (Mann and Stewart 2000; Salmons 2014). Two major challenges of online interviews are gaining rapport and encouraging in-depth answers. In this paper, we reflect on our interview-based research project that explores the perspectives and experiences of the editors of open access scholarly journals. Drawing on our research experiences, we consider how the use of technology relates to the pragmatic accomplishment of long distance interviewing. "Media synchronicity theory" provides a way of conceptualizing communication technologies based on the immediacy of feedback. We draw on media synchronicity theory to help understand how different mediums of communication compare with one another (Dennis, Fuller, and Valacich 2008), especially with regard to developing rapport, as well as achieving clarity and depth in interviews. We conclude with some ideas that might prove useful for other scholars in doing more effective long distance interviews.

THE TECHNOLOGICAL CHALLENGES OF LONG DISTANCE INTERVIEWS

Our research explores the experiences of editors of open access journals in the social sciences and humanities in Canada. Publishing using open access enables the articles to be freely accessible to anyone with the Internet (Suber 2012; Willinsky 2006), which poses a threat to the profit motives of major publishing companies. As such, the open access movement has faced a great deal of resistance, especially in the social sciences and humanities (Eve 2014). As scholars strive to publish in high-ranking journals, there is a disincentive to publish in relatively new, and often lower-status, open access journals. Further, open access journals are often unfairly lumped in with "predatory journals," which prey upon naive academics, publishing their work without scholarly peer review. These are some of the problems the editors of open access journals face as they try to compete in fields still dominated by traditional subscription journals. Given these issues, why do these editors choose open access at all? What does open access mean to them? What are the major obstacles in these projects, and how do they strive to overcome them?

While we had solid research questions in mind, we knew that we faced a challenge in gaining access to these editors, building trust and rapport, and collecting detailed information about their experiences. This is largely because our research population is highly dispersed across Canada, making in-person interviews difficult. We realized that long distance interviews were the answer, yet neither of us had any experience in this regard. We decided that we would conduct interviews through Skype, telephone, email, or face-to-face meetings, depending on our respondents' preferences. We discovered that each of these communication mediums poses unique challenges. Far and away, the biggest differences were between face-to-face, Skype, and telephone on the one hand, and email on the other. While the former strategies yielded rich data, email presented the most significant difficulty in this regard, as respondents would often provide only short, glib, and seemingly disinterested responses. In our telephone and Skype interviews, a sufficient level of rapport could be built up naturally. In contrast, it was much more difficult to generate this in our email interviews. This was due mainly to the lack of give-and-take interaction and physical and verbal cues, making it difficult to determine if and how to follow up in cases when respondents gave unusually short answers.

For example, near the end of one email interview, Taylor asked his interviewee to recall one of their toughest experiences in open access editing:

Taylor: What was the hardest day or week you had as an open access journal editor?
Email respondent: Whenever I learn a new HTML program.

Obviously this answer is not terribly helpful. We might compare this to the answer he received to the same question when it was posed in a Skype interview:

Taylor: So what would you say was the hardest day or week that you had as an open access editor?
Skype respondent: [leans back, sighs, looking up] I would actually say that the hardest time I've had was actually finding my way around the online editing system itself … just the mechanics of learning about the software, what you could do, the mechanics of inviting people in or writing letters.… We're a dual language journal and, when we first started, the French side of it was basically non-existent, which was really frustrating. So we did a lot of work.… There are defaults within the system that you try to struggle against, which, in fact, don't make an awful lot of sense but they're default ones, and then if you want to make any kind of modification it involves reprogramming various things and stuff like that, which can be a real mess.

Both of these editors had an issue with their publishing platforms, but the email interviewee did not seem willing to expand on the specific problems experienced. In contrast, the Skype respondent demonstrated his passion and willingness to help us understand his experiences.

With our email respondents, it was often difficult to know how to proceed. For example, to understand the challenges an open access editor might face, Taylor asked the following question:

Taylor: Has your journal experienced any major challenges? How did you approach resolving these problems?
Email respondent: None.

This answer is obviously lacking as well. Further, not being in a shared interactional space with the respondent, Taylor was not sure how to respond. He did not want to unduly push a point that the respondent had no interest in, so moved on to the next question. The methodological literature did not adequately prepare us for effectively responding to short answers lacking description over email. Perhaps there is no "right move" in this particular situation. Still, understanding the underlying issues as a logical relation to the type of medium used can help identify the root interactional dilemmas they introduce, and how to prevent them from arising in the first place.

MEDIA SYNCHRONICITY THEORY AND ONLINE QUALITATIVE INTERVIEWS

With the above issues in mind, we now turn to consider some of the existing literature about online communications in qualitative research. We then introduce media synchronicity theory as a useful conceptual framework to better understand the root issues at play. Hodkinson (quoted in Mann and Stewart 2000, 127) states that:

> generating an atmosphere of rapport online can be a problem, and given the lack of tone or gesture and the length of time between exchanges it can lead to something of a formal, structured interview…. The best words I can think of to separate off-line from email interviews then, are FLOW, and DYNAMICS, both of which, in my view are liable to contribute to greater depth and quality of information in an off-line interview than over email.

Indeed, the level of flow and dynamics of a face-to-face conversation is not afforded by email, and one cannot expect to get the same form of interaction here. In defence of email interviews, the flow and dynamics of a face-to-face conversation are not called for in every research situation. For example, some have found that sensitive research on people with disabilities can be well suited to email, because the respondent can take as much time as necessary to accurately realize and convey their experiences (Bowker and Tuffin 2004; Illingworth 2006).

Still, email interviews also have clear disadvantages. For example, attrition is a serious problem, since respondents may exit the research situation without notice; therefore, the researcher must actively "work to retain participants throughout the process" (Kazmer and Xie 2008, 263). To do this effectively, researchers must read into their respondents' answers to figure out how to proceed. This ambiguity is compounded when interviewers have never met the interviewee, and have no interpersonal context to enable an educated guess. Perhaps the respondent typically communicates with short responses, they may be temporarily distracted, or they may actually be losing interest.

But why does email often pose the most challenges in gaining rapport and achieving a mutual understanding? In other words, what are the key underlying issues across different technological mediums that affect the research interview so drastically? Media synchronicity theory is useful to help understand how different types of information are made present or absent across different communication mediums (Dennis, Fuller, and Valacich 2008). For example, a given communication technology may or may not transmit text, sounds, and physical gestures from participants. The more information that is available in communication at one time, the "richer" it is, while mediums that transmit less communicative information are considered "leaner" (Daft and Lengel 1986).

On a spectrum of lean to rich media, email would fall on the lean side, Skype on the rich side, and the telephone somewhere in between. The concept of "synchronicity" refers to the degree of instant feedback available. As such, synchronous mediums allow continual interactional cues and turn-taking, enabling "convergence," as participants in the exchange might learn from and adapt to others' viewpoints dialogically, in real time. Asynchronous communications, such as written letters, television broadcasts, and emails, do not allow for instant interactive exchange. As such, these mediums are best for the goal of "conveyance," by presenting complex ideas in thoughtfully

Table 24.1: Comparing Communication Technologies Using Media Synchronicity Theory

Asynchronous: the speaker and receiver need not be temporally co-present (e.g., email).	**Synchronous:** communication where feedback is immediate (e.g., telephone).
Lean: one or few forms of sensory stimuli are utilized (e.g., text messaging).	**Rich:** multiple forms of sensory stimuli are used at the same time (e.g., Skype).
Conveyance: presenting ideas in a pre-scripted way (e.g., company memos).	**Convergence:** explaining ideas through a process of joint dialogue (e.g., conversation).

organized ways, and allowing recipients to read and reread the material as necessary. In other words, there are no interruptions to "get in the way" of a well-rehearsed and -presented message. This chapter, for example, uses an asynchronous medium of communication. Hopefully, this way, we could more logically organize the material we are presenting, and it is easier for you to digest at your own pace. The shortcoming, however, is that we do not know how you are reacting, and lack the ability to reply to your questions about or challenges to our ideas as they arise. We also do not benefit from your input.

Certainly, using asynchronous communication mediums such as email can "negatively impact convergence processes by increasing delays that impede the rapid development of shared understanding" (Dennis, Fuller, and Valacich 2008, 583). As we explained, more synchronous mediums improve processes of mutual understanding by increasing the flow of information between people (Dennis, Fuller, and Valacich 2008, 581). If misunderstandings are present, these can be worked out in real time. Yet conveyance has its place too, and generates information that might, at times, be a more accurate and careful reflection of a participant's actual views. For example, doing interviews through email allows one to "type what you mean to say, not the first thing that comes to mind" (Illingworth 2006, section 4.4). Salmons (2014, 79–80) argues that in qualitative research, the "degree of richness or leanness does not matter; what matters is the appropriateness of the technology to the style of interview." In other words, paying attention to how the richness or leanness of a communicative medium may improve or suppress conveyance and convergence are important, as both goals have their advantages depending on the research questions.

Still, our experience is that convergent mediums are crucial to the development of rapport and hence the very willingness of participants to put effort into the interview process at all. Further, we encourage people to use more than one communicative medium in the interviewing process, in recruitment, rapport-building, and the delivery of the actual interview. If email is a preferred method of a respondent, then other, more convergent forms of media communication might be utilized beforehand to maximize rapport prior to the interview. Consider, for example, the answer obtained from Taylor in an email follow-up *after* a Skype interview had already taken place:

Email respondent: I had a few more thoughts on monetizing open access publications. We talked about submission fees, which don't fit with our philosophy since it discourages submissions from communities or developing countries that may not have access to funds specifically for publishing. The other options are ... [goes on to list several other funding options, and their pros and cons, in detail].

Now, suddenly, the email response seems quite rich and informative, since the interviewer and respondent had developed a good rapport during their previous Skype interview. If there is no real interactional history between the interviewer and interviewee(s), a richer medium than email might be used prior to the interview to help develop the rapport that email does not allow.

CONCLUSION

Using media synchronicity theory has been useful in reflecting about the craft of our research. In conducting long distance interviews, researchers benefit from understanding the concepts of convergence and conveyance, and how these two results are likely to emerge from different rich or lean mediums of communication respectively. Our early attempts at email interviews, for example, showed the difficulty of achieving convergence, since email is a "lean" medium that is much better suited to the goal of conveyance. Convergence, or the collaborative co-construction of ideas through an interpersonal encounter, can be difficult for those with little history of interacting (Dennis, Fuller, and Valacich 2008, 590). Yet this is crucial at some point if we are to expect our respondents to put their trust and enthusiasm into the interview process at all.

The need to ensure convergence with the use of rich, synchronous media is much like Shaffir's (1999) injunction that qualitative researchers must spend some time simply "hanging around" to gain familiarity and trust, setting the scene for more robust data collection down the line. When it comes time for the official in-depth interview, one may have a better conception of a respondent's personality, helping direct probing and follow-up questions more naturally through email, should this medium be chosen at all. Conversely, a preliminary conversation also allows respondents to gain a better understanding of what the researchers are expecting. By spending some time using convergent technologies early on, the benefits of leaner mediums to accurately convey complex ideas are more likely to be realized.

CRAFTING QUALITATIVE RESEARCH EXERCISES

1. Lean mediums such as email are good at achieving conveyance, while richer mediums, such as telephone or, preferably, Skype, are best for achieving convergence. List some research topics where the use of lean mediums might be preferred. In contrast, what topics would be better suited to rich mediums?

2. Create a mock schedule of questions about students' experiences of the class so far. Choose two students who you do not know very well to mimic doing an interview with strangers. Do one of the interviews using a rich medium such as Skype. Do the other interview (using the same questions) via email. With both mediums, feel free to ask follow-up questions as necessary. Once you have transcribed the interviews, compare them. What are the main differences you notice in the quality of data obtained?

3. An interviewee states that they prefer to be interviewed through email, a lean asynchronous medium. As the interview progresses, your interviewee takes longer intervals of time to respond to your questions and gives shorter and shorter responses. Brainstorm ways to improve the enthusiasm of your interviewee and to prevent participant attrition.

4. Look online for qualitative data related to a topic of interest to you. Consider lean, asynchronous data sources that are better at conveyance (e.g., official reports, organizational statements, travel diaries) and richer, synchronous sources of data that are better at convergence (e.g., interviews, web chats). How do these different forms of qualitative data serve to inform your topic, and what are their relative strengths and weaknesses?

REFERENCES

Bowker, Natilene, and Keith Tuffin. 2004. "Using the Online Medium for Discursive Research about People with Disabilities." *Social Science Computer Review* 22 (2): 228–41.

Daft, Richard, and Robert Lengel. 1986. "Organizational Information Requirements, Media Richness and Structural Design." *Management Science* 32 (5): 554–71.

Dennis, Alan R., Robert M. Fuller, and Joseph S. Valacich. 2008. "Media, Tasks, and Communication Processes: A Theory of Media Synchronicity." *MIS Quarterly* 32 (3): 575–600.

Eve, Martin Paul. 2014. *Open Access and the Humanities: Contexts, Controversies and the Future.* Cambridge, UK: Cambridge University Press.

Illingworth, Nicola. 2006. "Content, Context, Reflexivity and the Qualitative Research Encounter: Telling Stories in the Virtual Realm." *Sociological Research Online* 11 (1).

Kazmer, Michelle M., and Bo Xie. 2008. "Qualitative Interviewing in Internet Studies: Playing with the Media, Playing with the Method." *Information, Communication and Society* 11 (2): 257–78.

Mann, Chris, and Fiona Stewart. 2000. *Internet Communication and Qualitative Research: A Handbook for Researching Online.* London: Sage.

Salmons, Janet. 2014. *Qualitative Online Interviews: Strategies, Design, and Skills.* 2nd ed. Thousand Oaks, CA: Sage.

Shaffir, William. 1999. "Doing Ethnography: Reflections on Finding Your Way." *Journal of Contemporary Ethnography* 28 (6): 676–86.

Suber, Peter. 2012. *Open Access.* Cambridge, MA: MIT Press.

Willinsky, John. 2006. *The Access Principle: The Case for Open Access to Research and Scholarship.* Cambridge, MA: MIT Press.

25 Conducting Phenomenological Interviews

Ellen Rose

Ruth's office is a warm, comfortable space, decorated with brightly coloured pictures. She strikes me as a warm, friendly person, although I notice that she immediately positions herself behind her desk rather than in the chair next to mine. We chat for a few minutes, then I turn on the tape recorder and begin the interview with a few simple questions about her experience as an online instructor: how long has she been teaching online, what courses does she teach? She answers easily, smiling. Then I ask her to focus on a particular, recent time when she was instructing online and to tell me about that experience. She responds with generalities. I prompt her again to focus on a specific instance or experience, and again, frowning slightly, she responds with general statements: "Usually, I ..." This goes on for what seems like a long time but is probably only a few minutes. I notice that she is no longer smiling; her body has turned away from me, toward her computer, and her gaze lingers for longer and longer periods on the computer screen ...

Several years ago, I undertook a joint research project that involved conducting phenomenological interviews to gain insight into participants' experiences as online instructors (Rose and Adams 2014). The above anecdote is from a research journal that I kept at the time. Later, reflecting on what went wrong with this interview, I realized that the research participant was herself an experienced qualitative researcher. She probably thought she was giving me exactly the kinds of responses I wanted: general statements about her beliefs, attitudes, and practices as an online instructor. Indeed, her responses would have served me well if this had been a "normal" qualitative research project, but within the context of a phenomenological inquiry, the interview did not yield much in the way of useful data, and, unfortunately, we both left it feeling dissatisfied.

Why was this an unsuccessful phenomenological interview? Like all qualitative research, phenomenological research aims to obtain rich information about the attitudes and experiences of particular people. It relies on what Polkinghorne (2005, 137) calls "languaged data," usually collected in semi-structured, open-ended interviews.

However, whereas the questions asked in a typical qualitative interview are intended to provoke research participants to reflect upon and interpret their experiences, the questions asked in a phenomenological interview are designed to elicit responses that are "prereflective"—in other words, that capture what an experience is like, prior to the research participant's analysis of, reflection on, or judgment about it.

The difference can be best illustrated with some examples. A typical open-ended, interpretive question in a qualitative interview with online instructors might be, "How do you find the experience of teaching online compares with the experience of teaching face to face?" Normally, research participants will respond to such general questions with generalities, such as, "I find that teaching online can be challenging because I can't see my students' faces." Occasionally, a respondent might go on to give a specific example, but as Stake (2010) points out, the qualitative interview does not necessarily or even typically involve asking for such stories directly.

The phenomenological interview, however, is structured around the goal of eliciting stories and anecdotes, which are known, collectively, as "lived-experience descriptions" (Van Manen 1990, 54)—that is, recollected stories of human experience "as-we-live-through-it in our actions, relations, and situations" (Van Manen 2007, 16). When I first began conducting phenomenological interviews, I called these anecdotes "nuggets" because they seemed to me to be like the chunks of gold that a miner might find shining forth amidst otherwise grey rock. Below are sample lived experience descriptions that I collected during phenomenological interviews with two online instructors:

It's late at night and I am in the living room; my kids have gone to bed and my husband is downstairs watching TV, and I'm upstairs, and it's quiet. All the kids are sleeping, and it's just the light in the living room on upstairs, and I can just hear the background TV noise downstairs. And so it's just me. It's quiet, it's dark, it's late, it's winter. The window is right beside me; it's a huge picture window, and it is black. And I worked all day, and I'm online at night: check emails, answer the questions, check the papers, and I'm popping in and out of the discussion. It's the same kind of routine every night. (Jan)

I was sitting at my desk in front of my computer with a whole bunch of books immediately around my computer, and I'm kind of caged in between the bunch of books and the computer. And I was thinking, "You're good. You know this material." I found myself nervous to enter the classroom because what if I can't answer what they ask? But then I thought, "Okay, I can't even get nervous if I can't get in." So I type my password and wait. I'm looking at the screen. Tick, tick, tick, tick. You know that little circle that goes round and round that shows you that it's chugging? So, it's chugging once; chugging twice; chugging three times. Just as it was chugging the fourth time, ding!—my computer makes a chime noise. So I literally threw my hat. Hot damn, we're in! And, as it opened up the course, I could see four students had emailed me and three or four had posted in this forum. Then I said to myself, "Come on, off to work." (Kara)

As these examples illustrate, in drawing forth a lived experience description, the interviewer does not ask the interviewee to reflect objectively upon an experience but essentially to return for a moment to that time and space, to experience it anew (which is why lived experience descriptions are often related in the present tense). Clearly, this is a very difficult movement to enact; in an interview situation, it is always much easier to obtain interpretive data, such as the research participants' general views and judgments, than to elicit concrete stories and anecdotes. Even in phenomenological interviews conducted with the explicit intention of eliciting such nuggets, one can generally expect to obtain very little in the way of actual lived experience descriptions.

However, while the rest of the information garnered during an interview is certainly useful, it is the lived experience descriptions that comprise the primary source of raw data with which the phenomenological researcher works. There is no science to eliciting such nuggets; however, I have discovered several strategies that a researcher can use to increase the likelihood that participants will respond to questions and prompts with specific anecdotes and stories rather than generalities. I present these in the next section of this chapter.

TECHNIQUES FOR ELICITING LIVED EXPERIENCE DESCRIPTIONS

One of the first decisions that confronts the phenomenological researcher has to do with where the interviews should take place. My own experience illustrates some of the complexities that complicate this seemingly simple decision. When I first began conducting phenomenological research, I assumed that, since the purpose of the interview is to elicit concrete stories and anecdotes, I should interview people in the settings in which their stories would be situated; however, conducting interviews in participants' workplaces and homes proved to pose both ethical and logistical challenges. I then prioritized comfort, seeking to create a warm conversational connection by conducting interviews in coffee shops and faculty lounges; however, these public spaces did not afford the necessary quiet and privacy. Settling on quiet, distraction-free spaces—unused classrooms or offices—I next experimented with bringing elements into the interview site that might help research participants connect with their experiences. For example, in interviews I conducted for a study of the experience of onscreen reading (Rose 2011), I brought my laptop computer into the room; however, it soon became apparent that the computer did little to help interviewees recollect their experiences of reading onscreen because those experiences were intimately bound up not simply with the technology but also with the specific physical and social context in which that technology was situated—for example, stretching out on a sofa in a busy living room to read a novel or hunching over a desktop computer to read an academic article in the middle of the night. Over time, I have found that the most successful interviews are conducted in an uncluttered neutral space in which research participants are removed from distractions and able to imaginatively return to the time and place of a lived experience.

Once the challenge of deciding where the interview should take place has been addressed, the next step is preparing for the interview. As with any qualitative interview, the interviewer should formulate in advance a set of open-ended questions. I have found that a good number is half a dozen; when I arrive at an interview with a list of more than 10 questions, I find that they can actually become an obstacle to the kind of free-flowing conversation in which I hope to engage my interviewees. Perhaps it is fair to say that being prepared for a phenomenological interview also means being ready to let the research participant take the interview in unexpected directions.

When conducting the interview, I have found it helpful to briefly explain that my purpose is to elicit stories and anecdotes rather than opinions and interpretations, and then to set people at ease by beginning with a few simple, easily answered questions. After five minutes or so, I gently shift gears, asking the research participant to think back to a particular instance or event related to the research question. This might be the most recent instance—for example, "I'm going to ask you now to think about the last time you read a book or article onscreen"—or it might be the most vivid instance—for example, "I'm going to ask you now to think back to a specific time when you were teaching online that was, for you, particularly memorable."

With that specific instance evoked, my goal is to guide the interviewee into a full consideration of every aspect of it, using the following types of probes: "What was it like? Can you tell me what happened? What happened next? Just walk me through it. What did you do? Can you describe that a little more? What else do you remember about this event? How did it feel?" Attentive listening is key here, particularly because *how* people describe an experience—the language they use—can be very telling. Often, rather than posing a new question, I ask participants to clarify words or phrases, using probes such as, "That's an interesting way to put it. What do you mean by that? Why do you describe it in that way?"

During this process, it is natural for people to lapse back into generalities. In such cases, I have found Van Manen's (1990) four life-world existentials very helpful. According to Van Manen, there are four "fundamental existential themes which probably pervade the lifeworlds of all human beings" (101): lived space, lived body, lived time, and lived human relation. As individuals begin to draw away from the specific instance and lapse into generalities, I use the existentials to gently guide them back to specifics: "Can you describe where you are as this is happening? How and where are you positioned, physically? What time of day is it? What is your experience of the passage of time? Are there other people around you?" Framing questions in the present tense often helps interviewees return imaginatively and vividly to the specific experience.

While such probes are extremely valuable, it is also important to remember that perhaps the best aid to memory is silence. Rather than leaping to fill what seems like an awkward pause, I try to allow the interviewee a few uninterrupted moments to recollect and reconstruct the details of a specific experience.

Generally, a phenomenological interview will take about an hour; however, it is wise not to attempt to constrain the interview to that time frame. I wrapped up the interview with Ruth after 40 minutes when it became clear that it was causing her confusion and anxiety. Conversely, the interviews with Jan and Kara both stretched to an hour and a half of animated discussion.

Finally, it is good practice to follow up with a second interview at a later time. In a phenomenological interview, interviewees not only give their time but also share intimate aspects of their personal experience. For this reason, as Van Manen (1990, 98) observes, the participants in a phenomenological inquiry tend to care deeply about the study: "Accordingly, the researcher develops a certain moral obligation to his or her participants that should prevent a sheer exploitative situation." Inviting interviewees to participate in a second interview following the interpretation of the data extends the conversation and allows the researcher to confirm with participants that their experiences have been used and represented appropriately and accurately. Further, a follow-up interview can help the researcher validate the research by ascertaining that he or she has succeeded in capturing, from the specific stories and anecdotes, the invariant dimensions of the experience being studied. One touchstone of success is the "phenomenological nod" (Van Manen 1990, 27). For example, when I shared my interpretations with participants in my study of the experience of onscreen reading, several immediately responded that I had captured "exactly what it's like."

WHY PHENOMENOLOGY?

Phenomenological research is a challenging, time-consuming, but ultimately rewarding process. In this chapter, I have focused on the process of eliciting lived experience descriptions in phenomenological interviews; the process of interpreting those stories and anecdotes, with reflective techniques such as bracketing and reduction, and then representing those interpretations in a vivid, evocative prose, merits a separate chapter.

Phenomenological research faces at least two common objections. First, it may be argued that the project of eliciting prereflective lived experience descriptions is, in a sense, doomed from the start, because the moment we begin to speak about something we are also, of necessity, making judgments about it.

Second, questions may arise about the practical utility and relativism of a form of research based on the idiosyncratic stories of a few individuals, given that we live in a society that privileges what Heidegger (1966, 46) called "calculative thinking"—thinking and research that reduces the life-world to something that can be completely known and explained through measurement and quantification.

Neither of these objections diminishes the importance and necessity of phenomenological research. Phenomenology as both a philosophy and a research practice arose as a challenge to calculative thinking, which it seeks to counter by providing not a rational or technical but a "feeling or emotive" (Van Manen 2007, 21) way of knowing. Rather than studying the world objectively, as something that is separate from us, phenomenological researchers begin from the premise that all phenomena are experienced by *somebody*. In this way, "doomed" as the project of phenomenological research may be, it serves as a worthwhile and necessary corrective to the calculative thinking that dominates many other modes of research.

CRAFTING QUALITATIVE RESEARCH EXERCISES

1. Write a lived experience description in which you recollect in detail, without judgment or interpretation, your most recent or memorable experience of eating ice cream. Make sure to write about all the dimensions of the experience, including lived space (where are you? what is going on around you?), lived body (how are you positioned? what kinds of sensory experiences are involved?), lived time (what time of the day is it? how do you experience the passage of time?), and lived human relation (are there other people around you? how does their presence affect the experience?).

2. In conversations with friends, begin to pay attention to the kinds of prompts and questions that provoke them to relate stories and anecdotes. Record the prompts in a journal. When you feel you have a good sense of the kinds of prompts that help to guide a conversation away from generalities and toward specific stories, try your hand at deliberately eliciting lived experience descriptions in a conversation with a friend.

3. Interview three or four people about what it is like to fall asleep. Prepare by developing a list of six to ten questions that will help elicit lived experience descriptions and by finding a quiet, neutral space in which to conduct the interview. Consider audio-recording the interviews so that you can review them later, analyzing what worked well and what could be improved in the future.

4. Try to put yourself in the shoes of someone who is participating in a phenomenological interview on the experience of having lung cancer. Reflect upon and write down some of the feelings you might have about participating in such an interview. What are some of the challenges you might experience? What concerns might you have?

REFERENCES

Heidegger, Martin. 1966. *Discourse on Thinking*. New York: Harper and Row.

Polkinghorne, Donald E. 2005. "Language and Meaning: Data Collection in Qualitative Research." *Journal of Counseling Psychology* 52 (2): 137–45.

Rose, Ellen. 2011. "The Phenomenology of Onscreen Reading: University Students' Lived Experience of Digitized Text." *British Journal of Educational Technology* 42 (3): 515–26.

Rose, Ellen, and Catherine Adams. 2014. "'Will I Ever Connect with the Students?': Online Teaching and The Pedagogy of Care." *Phenomenology and Practice* 8 (1): 5–16.

Stake, Robert E. 2010. *Qualitative Research: Studying How Things Work*. New York: Guilford Press.

Van Manen, Max. 1990. *Researching Lived Experience: Human Science for an Action Sensitive Pedagogy*. London, ON: Althouse Press.

Van Manen, Max. 2007. "Phenomenology of Practice." *Phenomenology and Practice* 1 (1): 11–30.

26

A Reflection on Challenges and Negotiation in the Context of International Fieldwork

Abhar Rukh Husain

INTRODUCTION

Interviewing is an important method of data generation for all critical researchers, including feminists. The class, ethnicity, and social and cultural situations of the researcher and the research subject are particularly important concerns within the interview scenario. The relational situation of the interviewer and interviewee along these and other axes of differentiation can substantially influence the dynamics of the interview process and affect the type and quality of the data generated. In other words, it is important for researchers to be attentive to the context of their interview research.

I am a Bangladeshi Canadian woman who has been living in Canada since 2004. For my doctoral dissertation, I researched Bangladeshi female temporary workers' experiences on their migration journey. My objective was to go beyond a simplistic understanding of their experiences with migration brokers and their employers in the destination country, as these have been rendered by the media, especially Bangladeshi newspaper reports. I wanted to unravel the complexity of their migration journey. To this end, in 2010–11, I conducted open-ended interviews with 34 Bangladeshi female temporary workers who had returned from the Middle East. I also interviewed important institutional actors, including recruiting agents, state officials, brokers, and migrant rights activists who were either directly or indirectly involved in the women's migration process.

This chapter is based on my experiences of doing interviews in Bangladesh. More specifically, I expand upon the challenges and dilemmas I faced while interviewing my informants. It is my hope that my experience will help novice social researchers understand the importance of identifying and addressing the challenges of doing interviews in their particular research contexts.

EXPERIENCES AND CHALLENGES OF INTERVIEWS

Returning to Bangladesh to do fieldwork was not quite the same as returning "home" for me. By then I had lived in Canada for over six years, and "home" was Canada. I love

Canadian hockey, basketball, and jazz; the voices of Celine Dion and Bryan Adams take me away. At the same time, I take inspiration from the writings of Nobel Laureate Bengali philosopher and poet Rabindranath Tagore. I occasionally participate in Bengali cultural events in Toronto; I sing and recite poems with my friends, and I absolutely love Bengali food, especially fish curry with white rice. I seem to live on a bridge between Canada and Bangladesh—I belong in both countries but do not belong anywhere in an "authentic" way.

During my fieldwork, I had to continually negotiate the subjectivities of my "hyphenated" (Banerjee 2002, 117) sense of home. I was both "insider" and "outsider" in Bangladesh, the country where I was born and grew up. As a result, I often assumed an ambiguous status in the context of my fieldwork scenario. I was an insider by dint of my Bengali ethnocultural belonging. My Bengali parentage, growing up in Bangladesh, my fluency speaking and writing Bangla, and my Bangladeshi nationality by birth made me an insider. Nonetheless, my "Bangladeshiness" was not strong enough to gain the trust of my female informants. Even though I thought we would get along because of the commonalities in our ethnocultural and national roots, not to mention our common gender, it was not as easy as all that. My independent and unmarried status and my relatively short hair do not fit the stereotypical image of a traditional Bengali woman, and this concerned my informants. I was asked uncomfortable questions about my marital status; many women sounded skeptical about the prospect of my getting a good husband and having children if not done sooner rather than later. One of the recruiting agency proprietors with whom I spoke during the fieldwork did not seem happy when he heard where my *desh* (ancestral home in the village) was. I could see, for a few seconds, deliberate unfriendly signals in his body language. In Bangladesh, people often like to know about a stranger's ancestral roots; this is an important way to find out about the person. Sometimes they overtly express regional prejudices against those who do not belong to the same district. Clearly, this was the situation with the recruiting agency proprietor; he constructed me an "outsider" as I did not come from the same place as his ancestors.

At the same time, my privileged social status due to my educational background, my "transnational" privilege over resources and opportunities, combined with my upper-middle-class status in Bangladesh, constrained me from completely appreciating the multiple struggles encountered by my female informants in their everyday lives in Bangladesh.

Given the non-existence of any pure insider or outsider category, whether and how I was an insider or outsider, or both, my fieldwork can always be contested. Ultimately, what counts is my fieldwork experience—an experience that is "genuine" and cannot be challenged. This experience is both bodily lived and emotionally felt. I have made an earnest attempt to make it heard in this chapter.

Throughout the interviewing process, I tried to remain self-consciously aware of the power and privileges I held in relation to my informants. I came to realize that power is never unidirectional from the researcher to the researched, and it is not only the researcher who holds all power. Instead, power needs to be seen in relational terms, involving both the researcher and their informants. A number of fieldwork occurrences made me ponder this relational power dynamic. In many situations, I found myself powerless; I felt quite "othered" by my informants who critically interrogated my presence in the field. For example, some recruiting agency proprietors and state officials refused to give me an appointment or brushed off appointments they had made earlier; they responded hastily and cautiously if they did consent to talk to me. I was often interrogated about the actual purpose of my research and the particular organization (national or international) they suspected of funding my research. Even when I explained that the research project was my own doctoral work, it seemed impossible for them to believe that a young and unmarried woman could fly all the way from Canada to Bangladesh to carry out a challenging endeavour and claim it exclusively as her own. A striking example is the following: I was speaking to a recruiting agency proprietor about the purpose of my talk with him. He stopped me suddenly and said, "Before agreeing to sit with you for an interview, I had to carefully make sure from various sources that you are not coming from any intelligence body."

My gender clearly fuelled an ongoing power dynamic between me and my male informants. No matter whether my informant was a state official, recruiting agent, broker, or journalist, I invariably noticed curious and amused (and sometimes uneasy) looks at me during our meetings. I seemed to remain invisible to one recruiting agency proprietor throughout our entire conversation; he answered all my questions by looking at my male guide, who was sitting right beside me. In this situation, where did my privilege over my guide go? Obviously, I did not hold power over him based on my education, class, or transnational privilege. My power over my guide, to a considerable extent, was overruled by my inferior "second sex," a term coined by French philosopher and feminist Simone de Beauvoir in her groundbreaking work, *The Second Sex* (1957). While I tried to make sure that my guide did not see me just as his employer, I was not certain I could make him feel we were equal co-workers in the field. Ultimately, the unequal power relations remained, regardless of how well we interacted or got along in the research process. Consciously or unconsciously, both of us remained mindful of difference; nonetheless, we worked together and built our collaboration within boundaries of the difference.

At times, a potential male informant refused to co-operate. For example, the proprietor of a recruiting agency greeted me with tea and then simply asked me to leave his office, telling me that he would not respond to my questions. Beyond our obvious class and educational difference, gender difference hampered our connection. In another instance, when I was speaking to a journalist from a widely circulated national newspaper in Bangladesh about my project, he did not hesitate to tell me that he hates feminist academics.

Such events made me think: Would my male interviewees have behaved this way if I were a male? At the same time, I had no doubt that my gender exoticized my project. All my male informants seemed quite charmed by my apparent femininity and mannerisms, but it was difficult for them to accept my authority to ask them problematic questions. All these issues put me in an interesting but uneasy gendered power struggle. I acknowledged that no matter how powerful a female researcher may seem due to her social, economic, and other privileges, her female gender can still pose significant challenges to her in a fieldwork context.

Feminist scholars often talk about collaboration and strategies to build successful collaboration in their research. They say feminists need to take the lead to initiate collaboration in their research relationships with informants (for example, see Pratt 2002; Sultana 2007). Even when I was accepted cordially by my female informants, I could see the boundary they imposed on our interactions. The class difference may have hampered our initial connection. For example, they always addressed me as "Madam," thereby accepting and pointing to the obvious class and education division. Then, when I said I was trying to bring their experiences of migration into the limelight, I noted some wariness. Because of their fragile economic situation, they may have been looking for a material reward from the research; they may have thought I would provide them with a job as part of my research outcome. Some women even said this point blank. As I was unable to promise them a concrete material reward, they were not happy. Given our very different outlook on the research outcome, I did not think our collaboration was necessarily maintained to the extent I wanted, no matter how hard I tried; thus, I do not think commonality in gender can be regarded as either a necessary or a sufficient condition to sustain fruitful collaborative research when the researcher and informants measure the research outcome differently. In actual practice, differences in their expectations about the research outcome could reinforce the same hierarchy that the researcher pledges to challenge through her research.

Extraneous undesirable intrusions sometimes limited collaboration between me and my female informants in the interviewing scenario. One of my informants, Reshma,[1] was able to talk to me only in front of her husband. I noticed Reshma's guarded and cautious responses as we spoke; her husband often interrupted our conversation to give his own response. Another informant, Beauty,[2] often let her husband respond to my queries as well. A migrant woman to whom I was introduced by Reshma and who wanted to speak to me changed her mind because she failed to receive her husband's approval. These instances speak to the patriarchal and gendered milieu of my research and show how it jeopardized the possibility of (an even better) collaboration. My fieldwork experience taught me that the social and cultural context of fieldwork matters; it could obstruct or conduce the possibilities of a better research collaboration.

DEALING WITH DILEMMAS OF FEMINIST INTERVIEWING

How did I deal with the dilemmas I encountered as I interviewed my research informants? As I have indicated, my situation in the fieldwork context was more complex than simply setting up an insider/outsider binary. I was simultaneously an insider and an outsider to my informants; however, I do not think they saw me as more of an insider than an outsider or vice versa, nor do I think our collaboration would have profited if I had fit one category better than the other. The real significance is this: I lived through the entire research process and my lived experiences informed the data generated from the interviews. I used returned migrant women's perspectives and voices to produce knowledge about their migration experiences in their own terms, making a determined effort to transcend any generalized or taken-for-granted understanding of their situation.

Throughout my fieldwork and interviewing stages I was always embedded in unequal power relations with my informants. As a feminist researcher, I was aware of my control in the interview process. I had the power to randomly select research informants, decide the location and timing of interviews, and disseminate the research outcome. To balance the unequal power relations, I tried to develop rapport at the outset of every interview. I greeted my interviewees with *salam* (a word commonly used by Muslims as a greeting) and asked about their health and their family members. I told them about myself and explained the intent of my research. I tried to minimize my status as an outsider by relating my own experiences as an immigrant woman in Canada. When some of my female informants offered me a chair while they sat on the ground, I politely refused and said I would like to sit on the ground with them. The height of our sitting arrangement mattered to me, as a height difference could create a "vertical hierarchy" (Sultana 2007, 379).

Despite all my efforts, given our differences along lines of class, education, and social situations, and within the patriarchal and gendered contexts underpinning my research, I could not sustain a non-hierarchical collaboration with my informants as I interviewed them, at least not to the extent I wanted. The best I could do was to remain as faithful as possible to the information I gathered. As I analyzed the interview data, I remained aware that my presentation of their voices would be influenced by my class, education, and other privileges and opportunities, realms where I was significantly differentially situated.

Finally, the fact that I could not meet my female informants' expectations about the research outcome was quite troubling to me. I was not expecting it, and it represents an unresolved challenge for future research projects. I will work hard to build a bridge between my expectations of the outcome and those of my research informants.

CONCLUSION: MOVING FORWARD

This chapter has given me an opportunity to reflect on my experiences of interviewing in the context of international research. Because of my academic training, I was careful to pay attention to building a non-hierarchical and collaborative praxis as I interviewed my informants; however, in a "real world" research situation, I found such collaboration difficult to sustain, given my differential situation in relation to my informants. I held considerable power in the fieldwork because of my social status, class, and education. In addition, the power relations between me and my research informants took different twists and turns throughout my fieldwork. Finally, my informants and I seem to have valued the research outcome differently.

Such dilemmas in interviewing are likely a common component of international research. Critical researchers need to identify and work within their own particular dilemmas, negotiating with them to achieve their objective. Doing so enabled my critical engagement with Bangladeshi women's migration experiences.

CRAFTING QUALITATIVE RESEARCH EXERCISES

1. Imagine you are outside Canada to conduct interviews for an academic project. You and your interviewees are the same gender, but you have a higher class and education level. Your ethnic and cultural background is also quite different from your informants'; however, you speak and understand your informants' language and will conduct your interviews in their language. To what extent is your differential situation a problem? How will you address the situation?

2. In the scenario described in question 1, you could be perceived as an "outsider" to your informants because you are different along lines of class, education, ethnicity, and cultural background. If you were not an outsider, do you think you would collaborate better and generate better data? Explain your answer.

3. Given your very differential situation from your informants, the interview scenario is overshadowed by unequal power relations. What can you do to build a better collaboration within this relationship?

4. Is collaboration with informants a necessary condition for qualitative interviewing? Explain your answer. Why is it important to pay attention to collaboration in the research process?

NOTES

1. This is a pseudonym.
2. This is a pseudonym.

REFERENCES

Banerjee, Mita. 2002. "The Hipness of Mediation: A Hyphenated German Existence." In *This Bridge We Call Home*, edited by Gloria Anzaldula and AnaLouise Keating, 117–25. New York: Routledge.

de Beauvoir, Simone. 1957. *The Second Sex*. New York: Knopf.

Pratt, Geraldine. 2002. "Collaborating across Our Differences." *Gender, Place and Culture* 9 (2): 195–200.

Sultana, Farhana. 2007. "Reflexivity, Positionality and Participatory Ethics: Negotiating Fieldwork Dilemmas in International Research." *ACME: An International E-Journal for Critical Geographers* 6 (3): 374–85.

SECTION VII

COLLECTING OTHER FORMS OF DATA

There are almost infinite kinds of data one can collect from the social world. You are limited only by your senses, imagination, logistics, and the ethics of your proposed form of data. Remember that a big part of doing qualitative work consists of noticing patterns that emerge in your data. You can find patterns across photographs, maps, cartoons, graffiti, newspaper articles, stories, or just about anything else. Being open to noticing patterns and making connections between those patterns and your research is what we mean when we talk about things "emerging" from the data. What jumps out at you? What does your data teach you about what is relevant in that setting?

There are many surprising things that can become data. In a previous section, for example, you read about how rejection can actually also become data. You will see another instance of this in this section. Some other things people have collected as data may also surprise you. For example, GPS data can teach us about how we move through and talk about our social worlds. Data can even be the material things around us. Looking at patterns of wear in old maps, for example, can tell you something about how they were used (Griswold 2016). Do you notice any patterns in the books on your bookshelf? How about if you look in your fridge? What might the patterns you see if you looked into dozens of refrigerators tell you about the culture you are studying? Try to imagine a few other things that could be used as data.

One of the interesting things about collecting other forms of data, such as archival research, is that it can provide socio-historical context for other work. Sometimes innovative forms of data can stand alone, and sometimes they help us triangulate our observational or interview data. This will depend on the form of data you are collecting and how it relates to your research topic. Researchers have begun integrating more visual methods into their work, such as photographs taken by either the researcher or the participant, drawings, and even maps that researchers ask their participants to draw. The most important thing is to keep an open mind about what kinds of data you can collect.

In her chapter on collecting non-traditional and bold research, Deborah Landry covers several different forms of data and their usefulness. While interviews are important, Landry reassures us that stretching our sociological imaginations can also involve stretching our methodologies in new and exciting directions. She illustrates this with the successes she has had photographing grafitti and gaining new insights into the power dynamics at play. To demonstrate how a lack of access can be data in and of itself, she also describes a former student's work trying to gain access to the (officially available through the Freedom of Information Act) Canadian Citizenship Test. Landry argues that we must push the limits on forms of data as our intellectual project of social research moves forward.

Ariane Hanemaayer's chapter engages with the challenges and advantages of doing archival research. She stresses the importance of archival work as a "set of discourses" (Foucault [1969] 1996, 57) that become implicated in contemporary discourses. As you work with archives, you must become adept at *problematizing* the materials, seeking answers to absent questions of how things become problems, and analyzing the discourse with this problematization in mind. Hanemaayer guides you through identifying your object of analysis and constructing your archives, that is, gathering the materials relevant to your research and knowing when to stop gathering.

In chapter 29, Bree Akesson demonstrates the usefulness of neighbourhood walks and GPS data as an innovative form of research. She used neighbourhood walks to augment her interviews with families when working with children who lived in the West Bank and East Jerusalem. Akesson elaborates on how to go about conducting a neighbourhood walk, how to record this kind of data, and how to analyze it. This approach was particularly useful for children because it is well suited to their showing and telling, as well as evoking memories of place as they go on their walks.

In her chapter on researching inaccessible fields, Dawn Mannay discusses how photography helped her collect data on the private spaces of the home. It can be difficult to access such a private sphere. Mannay shares her decisions around using photo-elicitation and mapping to explore the everyday lives of her participants. As she relates here, she had participants take photographs and from these she was able to engage them in conversation about the resulting pictures. The mapping, which you will read about, allowed for children to share their perceptions about their environment more easily. These visual methods allowed her a certain kind of access to inaccessible realms of the social world.

Meghan Lynch and Catherine Mah share their experiences tackling the daunting task of collecting social media data. They stress that when engaging with social media as a source of data, one must first judge the appropriateness of the particular form of social media. This involves asking questions like, whom does the blog you are looking at represent? Once you have determined this, they emphasize the need to evaluate the ethical considerations involved. Included in their chapter are tips about the actual collection of social media data and how to engage with the credibility of the data you collect. Lynch and Mah's suggestions will help you cope appropriately and ethically with the nuances of the wealth of social media data available.

As you read the chapters in this section, let your imagination run wild. There are many forms of data you can collect and many ways to do it. Using innovative methods can make your project even more rewarding. The tips and tricks ahead will help you reconceptualize the limits of what constitutes data.

REFERENCES

Foucault, M. (1969) 1996. *Foucault Live*. Edited by Sylvere Lotringer. New York: Semiotext(e).

Griswold, Wendy. 2016. *American Guides: The Federal Writers' Project and the Casting of American Culture*. Chicago: University of Chicago Press.

27 Listening to Streets and Watching Paint Dry: Collecting Other Forms of Data

Deborah Landry

Nearly 20 years ago, my academic mentor assured me that sociologists would always bring keen observations to wider discussions about conflict and humanity, as long as we remained reflexive about the dynamic ways in which people create meaning about social order in any culture or community (Mangham and Overington 2005; Overington 1977). Changes in how we experience and recreate social order bring about changes in the kinds of evidence and methods social scientists can draw from; responding to these cultural shifts demands ongoing intellectual craftsmanship (Mills 1980). We must reflexively evaluate data and methods in relation to their usefulness in helping us find answers to emergent questions in the new world order (Ferrell 2009). This chapter highlights some of my experiences as a researcher of urban art regulation and as supervisor of original research projects taken up by criminology students over the past decade. This is not intended as an exhaustive survey of other kinds of data you may want to consider, although I do hope you find some inspiration. This is about locating meaning in meaningful locations. For me, this began by looking closely at the changing surfaces of a city in transition.

THE SECURITY AND BENEFITS OF LITERATURE/THE RISKS AND REWARDS OF LEAVING THE BEATEN PATH

Often guided by an enthusiasm and passion for a topic, each semester my research methods seminar is filled with students who—at least initially—believe that the only valid kind of qualitative evidence is the formal interview. While interviews are important, inexperienced researchers may overlook a key ethical consideration: If a research question can be answered any other way before talking to people, one should thoroughly chase down those avenues first (Canadian Institutes of Health Research 2010). On first blush, it does seem easier to simply ask someone for an explanation; in most instances, however, new researchers tend to seek answers to questions that have been answered in the literature (Torraco 2005; van den Hoonaard 2012). Therefore, a good engagement with the literature is an important resource to find out what is known and what is not. Ironically, students with creative approaches and unique ideas sometimes get dissuaded by what they do not see in the literature. I join others in inviting these students to take risks when choosing their data and demand that unique problems be looked at, particularly in mainstream criminology (Ferrell 2014; Hamm 2005). Kenneth Burke (1964, 1968) urges a sense of irony in exploring social problems, prompting scholars to ask about that which is not said. Questioning what narratives or evidence are missing from your literature is one way to locate the less travelled pathways to brave and reflexive research choices. Let us be reminded of what it means to have a sociological imagination (Mills 1959) and, for the challenges facing contemporary criminologists, a criminological imagination (Young 2011).

MORE THAN A FEELING: SENSING SOCIAL ORDER FROM THE BEGINNING

My own research has focused on how the City of Ottawa manages urban arts (such as graffiti and busking) and how performers and writers resist; it began with a hobby interest in photography. Instead of learning how to take the perfect shot, however, this sociologist became interested in what she was shooting: graffiti. I spent warmer seasons walking my city, developing a sense of where graffiti is hidden in plain sight and the vast ground graffiti writers cover. The importance of the placement and environment surrounding graffiti tags—what Ferrell and Weide (2010) call "spot theory"—only became apparent after months of walking and watching: walls, doors, sidewalks, blogs, Twitter feeds, Facebook pages, bylaws, civic meetings on graffiti policy, graffiti festivals, and similar gatherings were the many kinds of data collecting opportunities I used long before I knew what I really wanted to ask people involved in graffiti or its management. This initial groundwork helped me capture the tensions and anxieties about urban planning and aesthetics of security because I was open to thinking about evidence that others might have dismissed as meaningless scrawling on walls (Landry 2016).

Moreover, this slow approach foregrounds the embodiment of space, which is an oft overlooked valuable kind of data. I encourage students to question when they feel upset or uncomfortable in some places and not others. To these ends, students have completed clever projects about the social ordering of public space by examining graffiti-covered newspaper boxes and bus stops and the kinds of music played in public spaces, as well as the placement and changing texture of "do not" signs or the use of smell to manage how people move through public and private spaces (and all places in between). The "going without" autoethnography is a popular research strategy in my classes: one exceptional project involved giving up cellphones for a full week before doing observations of how others use cellphone technologies while navigating through public spaces. Others have attempted to go weeks without creating waste or making purchases. The conflict absence created in students' everyday relationships revealed how deeply invested our cultural identities are in consumption and communication, for better or worse. Streetscapes are not merely places to step, they are meaningfully created environments that affect our daily experiences.

LESSONS ALONG THE WAY: EMOTIONALITY, POWER, AND VOICE

As I walked the streets early in my career, it soon became clear that there was much to learn from being mindful of how I felt. You are a tool through which data is collected, and what a sensitive tool that is (van den Hoonaard 2012). When you feel agitated hearing something regarding your topic, for example, this is an opportunity to examine what is going on. Initially it was very difficult for me to hear personal attacks against graffiti writers by people in positions of power. I had developed deep empathy and respect for most of the graffiti writers I had met. They did not resemble the self-centred negative stereotypes circulating in police press releases, news reports, and municipal meetings. Nevertheless, that did not mean that the folks tweeting and writing angry letters to the editor were frustrated without reason. Academic defensiveness can be an appealing wall to build around your own knowledge, but a critical thinker wants to know when their findings or assumptions do not hold up; it is how inductive thinking brings us to broader understandings. A willingness to be wrong about something is a difficult but important characteristic of an intellectual traveller. My crime and media class participated in a flash mob rave and instant ethnography (Qualitative Analysis Conference 2007) as a final exam, and most participants expressed how initially they found security in assuming the project was about making "strangers" uncomfortable so that they could then write about how judgmental they presumed the public was. Initially, few recognized their own judgmental thinking about the Other; however, most ended up admitting that the excitement and fear of being vulnerable during this exercise brought them to a moment of reflexivity about their assumptions. Consequently, many made valuable insights into cultural identity and the collective emotional experience of collectively redefining public space—something few were expecting to find (Landry 2013).

Moreover, I urge new researchers to think about the priority we grant static text and visually observed data. Many tired content analyses continue to focus on song lyrics or text, as if popular culture were silent (Papenburg and Schulze 2016). My own research reveals that the surfaces of our cities are constantly in motion as graffiti and posters go up, are responded to, and are painted over again. The smells and sounds coming from some areas of town are manifestations of bylaw regulation and moral orders. Early in my teaching journey, I was fortunate to have a bright scholar in my senior research seminar who happened to be blind. It was on that first day of class that I realized how sight-centric qualitative research was; more importantly, I also realized how my pedagogy maintained this bias in the projects I assigned. I had not yet considered how important sounds, texture, emotion, and smell are to locating collective understandings of the world. Certainly, the aesthetic of the buildings and benches that mark our streets seems to take priority in urban planning meetings about the streets that are far more musical, pungent, and playful than policy seems to afford.

CONCLUDING THOUGHTS: EMBRACING WALLS AS DATA ABOUT STRATEGIES OF POWER

Some days, you have to turn away from the path that you planned to take. There is the research you plan to do, and then there is the research that you do. When time is a limitation, as with most master's and undergraduate level projects, access to your ideal data can be hampered for many reasons. These walls need not spell the end of your research, although you will probably change your research question for now. Graffiti writers see the beginning of a conversation about public space when they see a wall, whereas most people might see these walls as the end or a limit to their inquiry (Brighenti 2010). Walls can be opportunities to learn about the realities and art of research (Denzin and Lincoln 2008). Not being able to access some kinds of data says something about power, which you can analyze critically.

To illustrate, a former student, who was also a new Canadian, set out to understand the changes to the Canadian Citizenship Test (CCT). This student chose to pursue a Freedom of Information request to access all previous versions of the CCT. The response from the government was less than helpful; undeterred, and with the clock ticking, she insisted on her right to access the documents. What she finally received was disappointing: 12 pages of the same single question with some portions redacted! The student was devastated, feeling as though she had failed. As we reconsidered what she would use as data, she soon realized that all of the exchanges between her and the state were valuable data. The project turned out to be an excellent critical analysis of the institutional censure of public data in Canada under the Harper regime. While she did end up at a final destination that was consistent with her theoretical framework, the way that she got there was certainly not in her planned itinerary; however, her project was arguably better for it. She provided unique insights and contributions because of the detour.

I am now coming to the end of my journey crafting research, a career that has largely been spent in the classroom as a tour guide of sorts, informed by my experience reading the streets. As a supervisor and research methods teacher, one of the key travel tips I try to impress upon students to assure them is that it is okay to wander and slowly meander through curious streets before asking the locals for directions; new research need not replicate traditional research projects in order to be taken seriously. Researchers have an ethical obligation to understand the cultural artifacts produced by, with, and for the communities we are sociologically curious about. Let us come to terms with the many ways social life is experienced in these complex landscapes before or while we leap off into what can be a lifelong journey into critical ethnographic investigation. Certainly, we have unprecedented access to some information, which will only continue to change in unimaginable ways. As researchers who are curious about how social order is accomplished, maintained, or experienced, let us be brave enough to look up from the safety of the literature on occasion by recalling what it means to spark up our sociological (and criminological) imagination (Mills 1959; Young 2011).

CRAFTING QUALITATIVE RESEARCH EXERCISES

1. Smells Like Teen Spirit: Try your hand at capturing social order without your eyes. As you walk through a city shopping district or mall, pay attention to the smells and sounds coming from the stores. Do some stores or brands sound or smell like a kind of food or genre of music? What smells and sounds are missing? What story about life do these smells weave? The time leading up to Christmas or Valentine's Day is a great time to do this kind of project.

2. #MyNews: Find a news story that is presently trending on Facebook. Now, go to Twitter and search the top 20 tweets that emerge using that tag. Notice how the narratives about that story tend to use parody, memes, music, and images to tell the story. How do these elements work together to communicate the story beyond the text? What ideologies are paired together in telling this story? How do the people sharing stories connect the trending topics with their own biography using specific sounds and kinds of humour? Do you notice any regional trends?

3. Google Maps: Imagine if you could see how a street changes over time. Open Google Maps and locate three main streets or areas in diverse parts of your town, then "walk" down these streets using the Street View app. Now repeat this using the history function (in the top left-hand corner), which should take you back to 2007. What changes have occurred on these streets over the years? Do some areas change more than others? If so, how? Instead of thinking about changes in terms of improvements or decline, describe the changes using descriptive language. Now, take a walk with someone who has lived in this area and ask them to talk about these spaces. When you map these stories anew, what do you notice about the details that are missing from Google Maps?

4. Face the Wall: Do you notice any walls in town (or signs, or mailboxes) that seem to have graffiti tags or stickers on them? Pick one spot and monitor it over the course of a month or so. Each time you pass by it, take a photo with your cellphone. At the end of the month, look at your photos chronologically: What story do you see unfolding on that surface? Do you notice any patterns of style? Do you see a conversation happening? Whom is it between?

REFERENCES

Brighenti, Andrea Mubi. 2010. "At the Wall: Graffiti Writers, Urban Territoriality, and the Public Domain." *Space and Culture* 13 (3): 315–32.

Burke, Kenneth. 1964. *Perspectives by Incongruity*. Vol. 2. Bloomington: University of Indiana Press.

Burke, Kenneth. 1968. *Counter-Statement*. Berkeley: University of California Press.

Canadian Institutes of Health Research, Natural Sciences and Engineering Research Council of Canada, and Social Sciences and Humanities Research Council of Canada. 2010. *Tri-Council Policy Statement: Ethical Conduct for Research Involving Humans*. www.pre.ethics.gc.ca/pdf/eng/tcps2/TCPS_2_FINAL_Web.pdf.

Denzin, Norman K., and Yvonna S. Lincoln 2008. *Collecting and Interpreting Qualitative Materials*. Vol. 3. Thousand Oaks, CA: Sage.

Ferrell, Jeff. 2009. "Kill Method: A Provocation." *Journal of Theoretical and Philosophical Criminology* 1 (1): 1–22.

Ferrell, Jeff. 2014. "Manifesto for a Criminology Beyond Method." In *The Poetics of Crime: Understanding and Researching Crime and Deviance Through Creative Sources*, edited by Hviid Jacobsen, 285–302. New York: Routledge.

Ferrell, Jeff, and Robert D. Weide. 2010. "Spot Theory." *City* 14 (1/2): 48–62.

Hamm, Mark. 2005. "Doing Terrorism Research in the Dark Ages: Confessions of a Bottom Dog." In *Edgework: The Sociology of Risk-Taking*, edited by Stephen Lyng, 273–92. New York: Routledge.

Landry, Deborah. 2013. "Are We Human? Edgework in Defiance of the Mundane and Measurable." *Critical Criminology* 21 (1): 1–14.

Landry, Deborah. 2016. "Defensible Aesthetics: Creative Resistance to Urban Policies in Ottawa." In *Graffiti and Street Art: Reading, Writing and Representing the City*, edited by Konstantinos Avramidis and Myrtos Tsilimpounidi, 216–31. New York: Routledge.

Mangham, Iain L., and Michael A. Overington. 2005. "Dramatism and the Theatrical Metaphor." In *Life as Theater: A Dramaturgical Sourcebook*, 2nd ed., edited by Dennis Brissett and Charles Edgley, 333–46. New Brunswick, NJ: Transaction Publishers.

Mills, C. Wright. 1959. *The Sociological Imagination*. New York: Oxford University Press.

Mills, C. Wright. 1980. "On Intellectual Craftsmanship (1952)." *Society* 17 (2): 63–70. www.telegraph.co.uk/technology/google/5095241/Google-Street-View-Residents-block-street-to-prevent-filming-over-crime-fears.html.

Overington, Michael A. 1977. "Kenneth Burke and the Method of Dramatism." *Theory and Society* 4 (1): 131–56.

Papenburg, Jens Gerrit, and Holger Schulze. 2016. *Sound as Popular Culture: A Research Companion*. Cambridge, MA: MIT Press.

Qualitative Analysis Conference. 2007. *Instant Ethnography: A Panel*. Fredericton, NB: St. Thomas University and University of New Brunswick.

Torraco, Richard J. 2005. "Writing Integrative Literature Reviews: Guidelines and Examples." *Human Resource Development Review* 4 (3): 356–67.

van den Hoonaard, Deborah K. 2012. *Qualitative Research in Action: A Canadian Primer.* Don Mills, ON: Oxford University Press Canada.

Young, Jock. 2011. *The Criminological Imagination.* Cambridge, UK: Polity Press.

28 Doing Archival Research

Ariane Hanemaayer

If you are hoping to execute a project that requires historical and archival research, you will notice that there are few resources beyond the work of Denzin (1989), Hill (1993), and Hodder (2000) that provide strategic and practical advice about procedure, study design, and rationale. My chapter discusses the craft and value of first-hand investigation of social life through historical research and aims to update these resources and resolve this shortcoming by spelling out a methodological justification for *doing* archival research based in a Foucauldian sociology. Critical questions about the historical contexts in which social life emerges and transforms can be answered by collecting historical data from archival sources, used either as the primary or supporting material for sociological analysis. While the techniques and methods discussed in this chapter are used by a variety of approaches in historical sociology, my contribution focuses specifically on the operationalization of research questions through a critical engagement with the Foucauldian literature. I use examples from my research in the sociology of medicine to explain the following procedures: formulating research questions and the object of analysis, constructing an archive, developing sampling criteria and coding strategies, and overcoming obstacles.

FORMULATING RESEARCH QUESTIONS

Foucauldian genealogy begins in the archive. In order for you to get there, you will need to justify the role that your historical data will play in your analysis: What will you gather from the archive that you could not retrieve from, say, interviewing? Foucault is helpful here for understanding what an archive is: it is "the set of discourses actually pronounced … as a set that continues to function, to be transformed through history, and to provide the possibility of appearing in other discourses" (Foucault (1969) 1996, 57). An archive holds various collections of statements about social practices. Statements are "events" within a discourse (Foucault 1976, 4), and documents are "monuments" that have endured historical significance (Foucault 1976, 7). Documents in the archive allow you to observe the *veridical* and *juridical*[1] statements that various actors in institutions make about your topic, and to see how these relate to the organization of human activity.

Your research question will be formulated with this in mind: you are not analyzing how people interpret events, but, rather, how statements about a social practice changed over time. Your analysis of archival documents will show how complex institutional roles, routines, and practices are "actually a hodgepodge of bits and pieces, each of which has its own history" by moving outside of the point of view of those individuals in the institution (Walters 2012, 118). For example, my research examined evidence-based medicine (EBM),[2] the dominant science of clinical training and practice, and how it emerged from clinical epidemiology.

Craft a narrow and focused research question around definitional aspects about the nature of your topic. Starting your research question with the words "what is …?" will help you delimit which statements will be relevant. I started my research by asking, "What is evidence in EBM?" Formulating my research question in this way allowed me to investigate how evidence was defined in various clinical sciences and institutions, including educational and professional settings. Genealogy looks at the relationship between knowledge statements in the literature and institutional practices. Look for statements in the archive that answer these questions (e.g., what is evidence and how should it be used in practice?). The next step of your research will be to understand how the definitions of your topic came to justify the creation of institutional programs of conduct, a process that requires you to articulate the *object of your analysis.*

FROM RESEARCH QUESTION TO OBJECT OF ANALYSIS

Programs of conduct are installed in institutional settings to correct a problem or problems in human behaviour. In order to link statements about what must be known about a social practice to a program of conduct, you will need to examine the archive for statements that offer solutions to absent questions, which is referred to as *problematization.* This concept is defined as the investigation of "why certain things (behaviour, phenomena, processes) become articulated *as* problems, how they are linked up with or divided off from other phenomena, and the various ways (conditions and procedures) in which this actually happens" (Osborne and Rose 1997, 97). This means that you will be looking for statements that provide reasons for changing how people do things in particular institutions. For example, after crafting my research question, I began by reading medical journals to get a sense of the dominant concerns in medicine after the Second World War. I found evidence of a problematization of clinical uncertainties in the discourse of medicine; this included statements about the following: the relevance of laboratory science to bedside practice, practice variation, the effectiveness of clinical intervention, and measuring health outcomes, predominantly. In each instance, the documents contained questions about the authority of the doctor's decisions, which were problematic because they were not scientific, and were too "subjective" and unsystematic.

Deciding on your object of analysis before embarking on your archival research trip will give you focus and direction in the midst of an overwhelming number of documents. To make this step, ask what *thing* the knowledge in the archives is produced about (and what it is produced to change). Consider my example. Uncertainty was a problem in the medical discourse, and journal articles contained statements that offered solutions to those clinical uncertainties. I needed to understand what *thing* would have to change in order to resolve these problems? *What* required amelioration to eliminate clinical uncertainty? This shift of focus is difficult as there may be more than one target of intervention. Determining what the object of *your* analysis will be provides you with precision for directing your archival work, analytic consistency between your explanation and your evidence, and clarity with regards to your research contribution.

In my research, the object that needed to be improved through various programs of conduct was *clinical judgment*. This became my object of analysis, which was determined by making a sociological judgment about the quantity of statements that targeted how doctors make decisions. For example, there was a lot of debate about how to reform medical education so that physicians learned to apply evidence from the laboratory sciences; this would improve clinical practice. My research question directed my investigation to documents about evidence in medicine. My object of analysis, though, determined that I would include only those statements that problematized clinical judgments and offered solutions to those problems. I moved from examining how evidence was defined to how evidence ought to be used and why it should be used: Because clinical judgments were problematic if they did not rely on evidence, training programs needed to be installed to get doctors to use medical information in their clinical practices.

CONSTRUCTING THE ARCHIVE

In the archive, your object of analysis becomes your inclusion and exclusion criterion for assembling your data. I wanted to look at how problematized uncertainties served to found institutional programs of conduct, particularly ones that emphasized the use of evidence. I noticed that the first statements about EBM came from McMaster University. My research was carried out at the McMaster University Faculty of Medicine Archives (McMaster Archives). I wanted to explore how the McMaster medical school was created, and what problematizations shaped the program initiatives. This archive contained numerous documents about the history and creation of the clinical epidemiology program—the clinical science from which EBM emerged—and the medical school. I operationalized my object of analysis by setting the parameters for my archival research to focus on only those statements that sought to define and improve clinical judgments in the McMaster medical school and clinical epidemiology program and their curricula (programs of conduct).

I recommend that you consult the archivists and the database of files that are available, get a sense of how the series and fonds are ordered, and learn the process for ordering materials to review during your visit well in advance of your trip. Maximize the time you can dedicate to your research activities during your visit. I was interested in examining the rationale for the creation of each program. I only ordered documents from the date range within which the new medical program emerged (the mid-1960s).

The sample for your research is the collection of relevant documents that you find. The archive is full of statements that make up the workings of the institutions and organizations you are researching. It is up to you to let your object of analysis govern your judgments about what is included in your sample and what is not. For example, as I worked my way through meeting minutes and other curriculum documents at the McMaster Archives, I asked myself whether the statements in the document had anything to do with clinical judgments. I asked whether the reasons given for improving how doctors made judgments were justified in relation to their amelioration through educational reform. The following text box provides some questions to ask yourself while reading through archival materials.

Getting at the "Mentality" of an Organization: Questions to Ask Yourself

1. Roles and responsibilities: Looking at what different offices do gives you an idea about institutional strategies deployed at various levels of operation.
2. Reports—Sign posts of problematization: What questions does the report seek to answer? What solutions does it propose? Does the report get cited in other documents as a rationale for making institutional changes to roles and responsibilities?
3. Mission/policy/objectives statements: Compare earlier drafts and/or ratified versions to more recent versions: What were the changes? Were reasons provided for changing it?
4. Events—Getting to the material conditions: What was going on in the field or outside the field (e.g., government, society) to enable or constrain institutional changes? What events do the documents make reference to?

I refer to the sampling process as *constructing an archive* because you construct the sample of materials that you will use as "data" for your analysis by using your object of analysis as a yardstick for your research. You create a collection of statements that will answer your research question and explain the emergence of the object of your study. The archive is cross-sectioned; just as a geologist drills down into the earth to take a sample of the strata, you will dig down into the archive and order it through your criteria for the selection of documents that contain statements about the object of your study.

CODING STRATEGIES: ADVICE FOR GETTING YOUR HANDS DUSTY

You will code your materials in relation to the nature of your research project: What are you trying to explain? For example, to link the emergence of EBM to clinical epidemiology and the medical school program at McMaster, I organized my archival materials via the various interventions that shaped clinical judgments. I analyzed my materials in light of how themes from the order of discourse came, for example, to change the physical space of the Health Sciences Centre at McMaster. In this case, the statements from my archive were coded, first, for how "education reform" served to justify the development of a new medical school curriculum at McMaster. Second, I spelled out the role that the clinical epidemiology department played in designing the Health Sciences Centre. I explained how the design of the building aimed to ameliorate medical judgments by controlling how doctors interacted with patients and the clinical sciences by placing them side by side in physical space.

One of the most difficult judgments to make while doing archival research is that of saturation. While in the archive, a week can pass by pretty quickly, and it may seem that your work is incomplete. Keep detailed notes about the materials you review (even if you don't copy them) with bibliographic references. A Foucauldian sociology provides a methodological rationale for justifying the saturation point. Every statement you encounter in the archive is an "event" within the discourse, deployed by an institution to justify its objectives and programs of conduct. The quantity of repeated statements helps to signify which problematizations came to dominate the objectives of a program of conduct. Each utterance provides insights into relations that aimed to shape, intervene, and improve decision making in the clinic, for example, through education reform.

There were many practical obstacles that I encountered during my research. On my first day doing archival work, I had ordered so much material to review that I had no idea where I should start. I decided that I should keep records of which boxes and which files I had looked at. This decision was a pragmatic one, albeit uncoordinated, and it was unnecessarily time consuming to match my notes with the documents I had copied when I returned home. I suggest that you first choose a style guide and then keep very detailed notes about every document that you examine, noting the necessary bibliographic information so you can correctly source your materials in your final project.

Next, I suggest that you bring a device that can store digital copies of materials you consult. Many archives allow you to photograph the materials (with a few exceptions of extremely old or rare collections). I used my smartphone because of ease and accessibility. Although your note taking may be impeccable, it is extremely handy to be able to further engage in close reading with the documents later. I had a system of recording each box I looked in, then carefully listing the files, titles, and creators (see table 28.1 for an example of how to record information in an archive). I would take images of only the pages that were deemed relevant to my object of analysis. After each archive trip, I copied the image files to my hard drive and made a few backups.

Table 28.1: Note Keeping in the Archive

Fonds	Faculty of Health Sciences	
Series	Undergraduate Medical Education	
Subseries	Minutes	232.3
Subseries	Striking Committee 1967–1972	Box 011
File title	Faculty of Health Sciences Interim Council of the Division of Health Sciences, Minutes and Related Materials, September 1967–1970	
5 Photos	"Education Committee Minutes January 6, 1971"	
Notes	Building Health Sciences Centre; Library construction and organization; Library Committee Report	

To conclude, archival research strategies are excellent for those research questions that seek to understand the link between systems of knowledge and the institutional programs that aim to improve human conduct. Drawing on a Foucauldian genealogy helps to decentre the individual as the object of analysis, allowing sociologists to focus instead on how power operates in various institutional settings by justifying the organization of human activity through truth claims. The archive sheds light on the links between these two domains of knowledge and practice, and provides insight into the conditions that allowed various institutions to become what they are today. Institutions have their own "lines of descent," to borrow a phrase from William Walters, and their creation was a contingent, complex process that can be elucidated by analyzing statements in the archive.

ACKNOWLEDGEMENTS

Thanks to Kelly Struthers Montford, Tyler Brunet, and the Killam Trust at Dalhousie University for supporting this research.

CRAFTING QUALITATIVE RESEARCH EXERCISES

1. Choose a noteworthy news event. Next, search a scholarly database of articles for key words associated with that event. Read a handful of them—choose 5 to 10 however you like (e.g., randomly, every fifth one on your list, the most cited). Ask yourself what solutions are proposed to make sure that event does or does not happen again. Do different disciplines propose different solutions? What institutions would need to be changed for that to happen? Is there any evidence of new programs of conduct that seek to achieve that goal?

2. Choose an archive that you'd like to visit. If it has a website, familiarize your-self with its search engine. Read the instructions and watch any available videos on how to perform searches. Read the descriptions of the relevant fonds, series, and subseries, and make a list of which ones you would like to consult.

3. Choose a style guide and adapt table 28.1 to suit your research note-keeping needs.

4. Think of an activity that you would like to understand through some histori-cal research. Find a policy statement online from an institution related to that activity. Consider that statement as an "answer to an absent question." What problem does that policy seek to solve? What thing had/has to be changed in order to resolve that problem? The statement may or may not explicitly state what the target of the policy is. Use your Foucauldian sociological imagination.

NOTES

1. Veridical statements concern questions about knowledge (e.g., what must be known?), whereas ju-ridical statements concern the normative dimensions of intervention (e.g., what should be done?).

2. Evidence-based medicine is the conscientious and judicious use of medical research ("evidence") in clinical practice (Sackett el al. 2000, 1).

REFERENCES

Denzin, Norman. 1989. *Interpretive Biography.* Thousand Oaks, CA: Sage.

Foucault, Michel. (1969) 1996. *Foucault Live.* Edited by Sylvere Lotringer, New York: Semiotext(e).

Foucault, Michel. 1976. *The History of Sexuality.* New York: Vintage Books.

Hill, Michael R. 1993. *Archival Strategies and Techniques.* Thousand Oaks, CA: Sage.

Hodder, Ian. 2000. "The Interpretation of Documents and Material Culture." In *The Handbook of Qualitative Research*, edited by Norman K. Denzin and Yvonna S. Lincoln, 703–15. Thousand Oaks, CA: Sage.

Osborne, Thomas, and Nikolas Rose. 1997. "In the Name of Society, or Three Theses on the History of Social Thought." *History of the Human Sciences* 10 (3): 87–104.

Sackett, David L., Sharon E. Straus, W. Scott Richardson, and R. Brian Haynes. 2000. *Evidence-Based Medicine: How to Practice and Teach EBM.* Toronto: Churchill Livingstone.

Walters, William. 2012. *Governmentality: Critical Encounters.* New York: Routledge.

29   "Every Corner Tells a Story": Using Neighbourhood Walks and GPS to Understand Children's Sense of Place

Bree Akesson

In his book *The Practice of Everyday Life* (1984, 97), French scholar Michel de Certeau explained that a "story begins at ground level, with footsteps." This chapter describes a research methodology that you can use to better understand your participants' stories at the ground level, by walking through and talking about one's neighbourhood. This method is called a "neighbourhood walk."

A neighbourhood walk consists of the researcher accompanying a research participant as they walk through their neighbourhood and/or community in order to learn more about their relationship with their environment. This method is especially useful for gathering data from certain research participants—such as children—who may feel more comfortable communicating through physical movement than during a typical interview where the participant is sitting face-to-face with the researcher, answering questions. Therefore, over the past 20 years neighbourhood walks have been increasingly used as a research method with children (Christensen et al. 2011; Hart 1997; Langsted 1994). In one example, neighbourhood walks were used with children in projects related to environmental planning (Adams and Ingham 1998). In another study conducted to learn more about the daily lives of young children living in Nordic countries, five-year-old research participants took researchers on a "sightseeing trip of his/her daily life" (Langsted 1994, 34). Clark and Moss (2001) also used a walking methodology in their research with young children as a practical way to gain a deeper understanding of their lives. Neighbourhood walk methodologies have even been adapted from walking to cycling. For example, in an ethnographic study of Sri Lankan children, Trawick (2007) asked a child participant to lead her around his community via bicycle, narrating the relevance of different places.

FINDING MY WAY TO NEIGHBOURHOOD WALKS

I first used neighbourhood walks as a methodology in my research with Palestinian children living in the West Bank and East Jerusalem. There is literature that indicates that the physical environments where children live impact their lives, but there is less research on what happens when these places are compromised by violence and war (Akesson 2012). Therefore, I wanted to learn more about their sense of place and how they interact with an environment marked by political violence (Akesson 2014).

In order to learn more about their experience with place, I planned to conduct collaborative family interviews. The collaborative family interview includes all family members in a discussion of their experiences. During the course of the interview, I invited family members to draw maps of their journeys from place to place or of the important places in their communities. My idea to include map-making as an element of the research process came from Bridget De Lay's (2003) report on mobility mapping, which has been used as a tool for family tracing and social reintegration work with children separated from their families after the 1994 Rwandan genocide. Applied to my research, I have found that map-making illuminates research participants' observations, perceptions, and views related to place (Akesson 2015).

At first I had not planned to use a neighbourhood walk as a means of data collection. But because the research was focusing on the concept of place, I felt like I should try to include a methodology that would get at the physical environment in a tangible way. Because I had never used this method before, I piloted it in this study. In other words, I was trying the research method out, evaluating my successes and failures, and using these "lessons learned" to use the method again in the future.

CONDUCTING A NEIGHBOURHOOD WALK

Here is how the neighbourhood walk worked in my research, though you may uncover ways to adapt it to your particular research project. Before I started the neighbourhood walk, I had to get permission from the parents and the child. In most cases, the parents allowed their children to go on the walk. In several cases, they insisted that an older sibling or cousin accompany us to ensure our safety. And, in a few cases, the parents did not want us to leave the house because of environmental dangers such as bad weather or the potential for violence related to the conflict. Once I had permission, I asked the child(ren) to take me on a tour of their neighbourhood, for example, beyond the home, past the school, and through the playground. I asked them to show me places they are allowed to visit, places where their favourite activities occur, and places where their favourite people were. The walk lasted from a few minutes to about 45 minutes. Children were in charge of the walk and how it was recorded.

Conversation during the neighbourhood walk allowed for dialogue between me and the child(ren) to develop as the walk developed, prompted by the people and places encountered along the way. One of the most memorable moments for me was when I was walking with some children and I asked one of them to tell me about a place we were walking by that he had pointed out as important. He replied, "Every corner has a story," implying that his history and his family's history were tied to the places we were walking through, and therefore each location is a valuable piece of data to understanding his everyday experience living in the context of political violence.

RECORDING AND ANALYZING DATA

A challenge of using the neighbourhood walk as a research method is recording the data. I recorded the neighbourhood walk using multiple methods. First, during the walk I took notes of what the children said, the places the children identified, and any other observations. Because I took the notes quickly, I made sure to set aside some time after the neighbourhood walk to flesh out the notes with more details. (If you wait too long to add to your notes, you may forget details, so I would recommend that you fill in the details as soon as possible after the neighbourhood walk is completed.) Second, I took digital photos of the places and landmarks the children pointed out to me. I had originally wanted to give the children their own cameras to take photos; however, because of the political context, I determined that it was not safe for children to take photos of things that they might get in trouble for photographing. Therefore, I controlled the camera, but the children controlled what I took photos of. These photos became valuable data that I used in conjunction with the children's verbal explanations. Third, I recorded the neighbourhood walks using global positioning system (GPS) technology. I carried a small GPS wristwatch during the neighbourhood walk. The GPS technology recorded the length of the neighbourhood walk in terms of both distance and time. The aim of integrating GPS technology was to produce a visual record of the walk to correspond with any detailed and annotated commentary. Although the GPS data produced a factual record, this does not necessarily mean that the data material will produce an objective representation of the neighbourhood walk. All three means of data collection—notes, photos, and maps—were combined to form a sensory map of sights, sounds, and their corresponding feelings. By combining these three means of data collection, I was able to ensure that the children's experiences were not reduced to one aspect. This became another way to understand the multiple meanings of the environment through children's eyes.

During the analysis, I organized the data using concepts of time and space. In other words, I looked at the quantitative data such as the length of the walks and the distance we travelled, as well as the qualitative data represented in the conversations we had, the images we captured, and the notes I took. For the qualitative data, I found that it was important not to just interpret the data myself, but also to ensure that my understandings were rooted in the participants' understandings of their experience. This is best done by relying on what the participants said during the neighbourhood walk. In other words, it is important to give the children ample opportunity to explain their experiences in the neighbourhood walk using their words and physical movement.

FUTURE APPLICATIONS OF THE NEIGHBOURHOOD WALK

The neighbourhood walk methodology is best suited to children's natural ways of communicating, using a physical and mobile approach far more active than the traditional interview setting, as a means for gathering additional data. Overall, this methodological tool capitalizes on the relationship between physical movement, the rhythms of walking, and the telling of stories, which helps children to recount memories and trace a neighbourhood community's history (Spencer 2011).

Now that I have piloted this research methodology with Palestinian children, I am applying the lessons I have learned to another population. My current research project explores the social and spatial experiences of Syrian children and families who have been displaced from their homes due to the ongoing war. Using this methodology, I can explore these children's everyday mobilities—such as access to home, school, play spaces, and social networks—which have all been severely disrupted and compromised by displacement. The GPS-tracked neighbourhood walk is one component of a research process that also includes collaborative family interviews and map-making in order to better understand participants' relationship with the physical environment.

CRAFTING QUALITATIVE RESEARCH EXERCISES

1. Take a walk around your neighbourhood. Take written or audio notes about what you see and how you feel. If available, use a GPS tracking device on your phone to track the path you take. You can also use your phone to take pictures of things that interest you. What were the strengths and challenges of taking notes during the walk? How might you improve this method?

2. Think about a particular population with whom you could use the neighbourhood walk methodology. Why would a neighbourhood walk be particularly useful for learning about this population's relationship with the environment? How might you adapt the neighbourhood walk methodology for your chosen population? What obstacles might you encounter with this methodology when using it with this population?

3. The next time you read a story or watch a movie, try to determine what the sense of place is. Determine if sense of place is an important aspect of the story. What place is being represented and at what point in the story did you recognize this place? What methods does the author/director use to convey a sense of place? How is place described? Why is this place important to the development of the plot? How is this place relevant to the development of the characters?

REFERENCES

Adams, Eileen, and Sue Ingham. 1998. *Changing Places: Children's Participation in Environmental Planning*. London: Planning Aid for London and Children's Society.

Akesson, Bree. 2012. "The Concept and Meaning of Place for Young Children Affected by Political Violence in the Occupied Palestinian Territories." *Spaces and Flows* 2 (2): 245–56.

Akesson, Bree. 2014. "Contradictions in Place: Everyday Geographies of Palestinian Children and Families Living Under Occupation." PhD diss., McGill University, Montreal, Quebec.

Akesson, Bree. 2015. "Using Map-making to Study the Personal Geographies of Young Children Affected by Political Violence." In *Researching the Lifecourse: Critical Reflections from the Social Sciences*, edited by Nancy Worth and Irene Hardill, 123–41. Bristol, UK: Policy Press.

Christensen, Pia, Miguel M. Mikkelsen, Thomas A. S. Nielsen, and Henrik Harder. 2011. "Children, Mobility, and Space: Using GPS and Mobile Phone Technologies in Ethnographic Research." *Journal of Mixed Methods Research* 5 (3): 227–46.

Clark, Alison, and Peter Moss. 2001. *Listening to Young Children: The MOSAIC Approach*. London: National Children's Bureau and Joseph Rowntree Foundation.

de Certeau, Michel. 1984. *The Practice of Everyday Life*. Translated by Steven Rendall. Los Angeles: University of California Press.

De Lay, Bridget. 2003. *Mobility Mapping and Flow Diagrams: Tools for Family Tracing and Social Reintegration Work with Separated Children*. New York: International Rescue Committee.

Hart, Roger. 1997. *Children's Participation: The Theory and Practice of Involving Young Citizens in Community Development and Environmental Care*. London: Earthscan.

Langsted, Ole. 1994. "Looking at Quality from the Child's Perspective." In *Valuing Quality in Early Childhood Services: New Approaches to Defining Quality*, edited by Peter Moss and Alan R. Pence, 28–42. London: Paul Chapman.

Spencer, Stephen N. 2011. *Visual Research Methods in the Social Sciences: Awakening Visions*. London and New York: Routledge.

Trawick, Margaret. 2007. "Freedom to Move: A Bike Trip with Menan." In *Child Space: An Anthropological Exploration of Young People's Use of Space*, edited by Karen Malone, 21–40. New Delhi: Concept Publishing Company.

30 Ethnography in Inaccessible Fields: Drawing on Visual Approaches to Understand the Private Space of the Home

Dawn Mannay

INTRODUCTION

Hammersley and Atkinson (2007, 3) offer a parsimonious explanation of the craft of ethnography as involving fairly lengthy contact with people in everyday, rather than experimental, contexts. This involves participant observation and/or relatively open-ended interviews and the analysis of artifacts and documents associated with their lives; a process that, for Van Maanen (2009, 16), attempts to put into writing "what it is like to be somebody else."

Traditional forms of the ethnographic craft have explored multiple fields, such as opera, capoeira, and educational institutions (Atkinson 2013; Delamont 2006; Ward 2016); however, some sites remain inaccessible. As Lincoln (2012) argues, the home is a type of sanctuary, which is particularly impervious to forms of qualitative study. There is often a symbolic "No Entry" sign above the doorways to private spaces, which means that it is difficult for researchers to engage in forms of sustained observation. Interviews, rather than participant observation, become a necessary alternative.

Qualitative interviews have significant value and they can be enhanced with participant observation on the edges of public spaces of family life, such as parks and sports fields (Doucet 2006). Conducting interviews within the home can also be supplemented by appreciating the spaces in between, making field notes, and reflecting on the "waiting field" when we are with participants in their homes before and after interviews, and in "spaces of interruption/disruption" (Mannay and Morgan 2015).

However, the home has many spaces and routines that the researcher may not be physically present to witness, particularly those that are mundane and so imbued with familiarity that they become overlooked and invisible. Accordingly, this chapter will centralize the ways in which qualitative visual modes of data production can facilitate new insights into the impervious sanctuary of the home, its objects, practices, and mundanity. This chapter will discuss how I became involved with visual approaches, and highlight the advantages associated with their application.

CONTEXT

The reflections presented in this chapter draw on a four-year Economic and Social Research Council–funded study, conducted between 2008 and 2012, that explored the everyday lives of nine mothers and their daughters in a marginalized area of south Wales. The study was interested in the intergenerational experiences of living in a stigmatized locale and how locality, class, and gender impact identity, education, employment, and social networks; and how both the boundaries of the immediate culture and memories of the past mediated participants' life histories and their conceptions of the future. In addition to examining the wider geographical area, the study adopted qualitative methodologies to focus on the more differentiated aspects of participants' lives; this necessitated an understanding of their sense of "home" and the practices within particular residences.

VISUAL TECHNIQUES OF DATA PRODUCTION

I had previously lived in my field site, Hystryd (a pseudonym employed to preserve the anonymity of the research site), and this shared sense of geography positioned me as "experience near" (Anderson 2002, 23). Having conducted earlier research in the same locale, I was worried that my interview questions would be constrained by my perceptions of the area, and that my interactions would be characterized by a two-way, taken-for-granted cultural competence, as I entered the interview with preconceived knowledge and the participants communicated an assumption that I already understood their experiences.

To attempt to "fight familiarity" (Delamont and Atkinson 1995), rather than beginning with an individual schedule, I asked participants to engage in techniques of visual data production, including mapping, collage, and photo-elicitation to represent their interpretations of their everyday lives within the home and in spaces beyond the home. These visual productions were then discussed in elicitation interviews, where participants led the discussions around what they had created, which enabled them to present their reflections on their lives from their own world view, rather than being directed by questions that I had designed.

Employing these techniques gave me new insight into my participants' worlds, "making the familiar strange and interesting again" (Mannay 2010, 108). At the outset of the fieldwork, I centralized these visual techniques as tools to fight familiarity; however, on reflection, I also realized their importance in gaining a more nuanced understanding of the private spaces of the home. The following sections will explore the ways in which two different techniques, photo-elicitation and mapping, allowed me access to places and spaces that would otherwise have remained inaccessible.

PHOTO-ELICITATION

Photography has long been seen as advantageous in social science research (Becker 1974) and the techniques of self-directed photography and photo-elicitation, or "photo-voice," have been used successfully in a range of research studies (Dodman 2003; Mizen 2005). In this study, participants were issued a single-use camera and asked to take photographs to show their surroundings, to help explain what their lives were like and to illustrate the concept of "home." This was followed by participants discussing their photographs in interviews led by these images. These photographs not only provided graphical representations, which familiarity may have rendered inconsequential in a more traditional interview setting, but also allowed me to see, and gain an understanding of, spaces in the home that would not have otherwise been made available, as illustrated in figure 30.1.

The bedroom is often one of the first spaces over which young people have some sense of ownership. It is a space that, while still often regulated to some extent by adults in the family, is frequented by friends. It is not, however, a space that is always accessible to the social researcher, or one that is amenable to participant observation. Therefore, I never see 15-year-old Melanie's bedroom for myself, but her photographs, including

Figure 30.1: Melanie's Bedroom Drawer

Source: Photograph created by participant

clothing, shopping bags, music, films, magazines, technology, and overviews of the room, all provide insights into this space and its practices.

The presence of the researcher breaches traditional boundaries between the public and the private, but the images allowed Melanie to show and tell me about this space without me breaking this boundary. The image itself is simply a drawer containing Melanie's cosmetics; however, our discussion of her photograph provides me with an understanding of the process of getting ready and the daily practices involved in creating a face for the world beyond the home. The drawer speaks of the dual influence of the backyard and the wider world and how broader social norms and gendered power relations feature in the confines of this small container.

In this way, every commodity in the bedroom becomes imbued with self-referential meaning, and its materiality creates emblems of identity, which Melanie drew upon to explain her everyday life and sense of self. The drawer becomes a vehicle to discuss how Melanie creates an ideal femininity through these cosmetics, a femininity that is guided by the expectations of her family, local discourses of acceptable femininity, and the "technologies of sexy," which permeate the mediated forms and social networking that are represented in Melanie's other photographs (Ringrose 2013). Although ethnographers have been able to enter the space of the bedroom and confirm its significance in telling the story of participants' cultural interests and social lives (Lincoln 2012; McRobbie 1991), photo-elicitation can offer an alternative view when these spaces remain out of bounds for social researchers.

MAPPING

Another activity that participants took part in was the creation of hand-drawn maps representing activities, objects, and people inside and outside of the home. These maps were not accurate geographic representations but simple drawings that focused participants' responses so that they concentrated on the most salient features of their lives. Nossiter and Biberman (1990) argue that putting forward the unusual request for creativity can act as a tool to motivate respondents to analyze their everyday lives; the activity of drawing was novel for the majority of adults involved in the study.

Mapping exercises have proved valuable in previous studies of children's perceptions of their environment (Darbyshire, MacDougall, and Schiller 2005; Ross 2005), but they are less often incorporated with adult participants, who are often resistant to drawing activities (Richardson 2015). In this study, participants did initially find the idea of drawing incompatible with their general forms of communication, and in a participatory framework it is useful to offer a range of alternatives so that participants can select the techniques they feel are most appropriate (Mannay 2016). However, participants who produced drawings did find them useful to support their stories and to build their ideas, as they were left with the task for a few weeks before meeting for an elicitation interview.

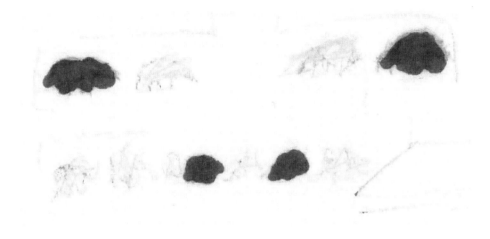

Figure 30.2: Elephants

Source: Extract from participant's hand-drawn map.

Figure 30.2 is an extract from a larger map created by Victoria, one of the mothers participating in the study. The image represents the ornaments and other household objects featuring elephants that Victoria has bought. Painting and sketching are always dependent on the artistic ability of the author (Damon 2000), and the elephants may not be instantly recognizable to the viewer. This emphasizes the importance of the elicitation interview, where the images are discussed and visual data explained, rather than the researcher, often incorrectly, assigning meaning (Mannay 2010). In this way, the interviews were not so much about an understanding *of* the data produced, as an understanding *with* the data produced about the lives of the participants (Radley 2011).

Similar to Melanie's cosmetics drawer discussed in the previous section, the elephant ornaments and trinkets are far more than decorative forms. "Narratives and objects inhabit the intersection of the personal and the social" (Hurdley 2006, 717), and Victoria collects these objects not simply because she "likes elephants," although this is her initial explanation. Victoria's affinity with the object is linked with her embodied form, and she discussed issues with her weight, and how the elephants provide a form of comforting familiarity: they are large and she feels large. Accordingly, their ornamental value is superseded by their emotional support, for although they are only inert objects, they are symbolically reassuring. The discussion of the elephants also leads to descriptions of family dynamics both in her current home and home of origin, and the ways in which the label of "fat" has been used to position her as lacking and outside of the realms of acceptable femininity, both at the level of the immediate locality and via wider mediated discourses.

Accordingly, display objects and collections of artifacts in the home are sites where individual stories are constructed, and the mapping activity allowed me to connect with these assemblages. I was unable to roam freely through Victoria's house and search out the objects and ornaments that featured elephants, but in making the map, Victoria brought a representation of her collection to the discussion table. Again, a visual and creative mode of data production helped to fill in some of the gaps that were created because of the lack of opportunity to engage in participant observation.

CONCLUDING REMARKS

In this study, I could not simply immerse myself within the territory of mothers' and daughters' homes. Therefore, the visual creations they produced became particularly significant, for they allowed me an opportunity to glimpse the private spaces of the home, and, importantly, to further discuss these spaces, objects, and related practices. Accordingly, visual data can offer researchers a foot in the door that reads "No Entry." For this reason, mapping and photo-elicitation could prove useful for researchers interested in the home; they can also add value for those wanting to conduct qualitative research in other, seemingly inaccessible, fields.

The visual has many potentialities but there are also ethical concerns and practical considerations around materials, artistic ability, and time involved that are beyond the scope of this chapter (see Kara 2015; Warr et al. 2016). Therefore, "before rushing to fight for the paint brushes we need to consider why we want to paint at all" (Mannay 2016, 107). Nevertheless, the data presented here offer some insight into the ways in which modes of visual data production can usefully be embedded into the craft of ethnography and other forms of qualitative inquiry, to gain a more nuanced understanding of participants' everyday lives, perspectives, and experiences.

CRAFTING QUALITATIVE RESEARCH EXERCISES

1. Consider the accessibility of a research site that you might study, and what you could observe and what may remain hidden. Are there aspects of this research site that you would not have physical access to? How could these limitations impact on your understanding of the site and participants' everyday interactions within this space?

2. Mapping and photo-elicitation are both forms of visual data production but they can elicit different forms of information and participants may prefer one method over the other. Try using photo-elicitation and mapping to record your own home and discuss your visual productions with a friend. What was different in the content produced using each method? What were your personal preferences in terms of the two methods? What do you feel are the advantages and drawbacks for each technique?

3. Photo-elicitation requires that participants have access to a camera, and mapping involves drawing, which participants may see as a barrier. What other techniques of visual data production could you adopt to overcome these difficulties and offer an alternative activity?

4. Reflecting on issues of confidentiality and anonymity, what ethical dilemmas could arise when employing forms of visual data?

REFERENCES

Anderson, Gary L. 2002. "Reflecting on Research for Doctoral Students in Education." *Education Researcher* 31 (7): 22–25.

Atkinson, Paul A. 2013. "The Mastersingers: Language and Practice in an Operatic Masterclass." *Ethnography and Education* 8 (3): 355–70.

Becker, Howard S. 1974. "Photography and Sociology." *Studies in the Anthropology of Visual Communication* 1 (1): 3–26.

Damon, Frederick H. 2000. "To Restore the Events? On the Ethnography of Malinowski's Photography." *Visual Anthropology Review* 16 (1): 71–77.

Darbyshire, Philip, Colin MacDougall, and Wendy Schiller. 2005. "Multiple Methods in Qualitative Research with Children: More Insight or Just More?" *Qualitative Research* 5 (4): 417–36.

Delamont, Sara. 2006. "The Smell of Sweat and Rum: Teacher Authority in Capoeira Classes." *Ethnography and Education* 1 (2): 161–75.

Delamont, Sara, and Paul A. Atkinson. 1995. *Fighting Familiarity: Essays on Education and Ethnography.* Cresskill, NJ: Hampton Press.

Dodman, David R. 2003. "Shooting in the City: An Autobiographical Exploration of the Urban Environment in Kingston, Jamaica." *Area* 35 (3): 293–304.

Doucet, Andrea. 2006. *Do Men Mother? Fatherhood, Care, and Domestic Responsibility.* Toronto: University of Toronto Press.

Hammersley, Martyn, and Paul A. Atkinson. 2007. *Ethnography: Principles in Practice.* 3rd ed. London: Taylor and Francis.

Hurdley, Rachel. 2006. "Dismantling Mantelpieces: Narrating Identities and Materializing Culture in the Home." *Sociology* 40 (4): 717–33.

Kara, Helen. 2015. *Creative Research Methods in the Social Sciences: A Practical Guide.* Bristol, UK: Policy Press.

Lincoln, Sian. 2012. *Youth Culture and Private Space.* Basingstoke, UK: Palgrave Macmillan.

Mannay, Dawn. 2010. "Making the Familiar Strange: Can Visual Research Methods Render the Familiar Setting More Perceptible?" *Qualitative Research* 10 (1): 91–111.

Mannay, Dawn. 2016. *Visual, Narrative and Creative Research Methods: Application, Reflection and Ethics.* Abingdon, UK: Routledge.

Mannay, Dawn, and Melanie Morgan. 2015. "Doing Ethnography or Applying a Qualitative Technique? Reflections from the 'Waiting Field.'" *Qualitative Research* 15 (2): 166–82.

McRobbie, Angela. 1991. *Feminism and Youth Culture: From Jackie to Just Seventeen.* Basingstoke, UK: Macmillan.

Mizen, Phil. 2005. "A Little 'Light Work'? Children's Images of Their Labour." *Visual Studies* 20 (2): 124–39.

Nossiter, Vivian, and Gerald Biberman. 1990. "Projective Drawings and Metaphor: Analysis of Organisational Culture." *Journal of Management Psychology* 5 (3): 13–16.

Radley, Alan. 2011. "Image and Imagination." In *Visual Methods in Psychology: Using and Interpreting Images in Qualitative Research*, edited by Paula Reavey, 17–28. London: Routledge.

Richardson, Michael. 2015. "Embodied Intergenerational: Family Position, Place and Masculinity." *Gender, Place and Culture* 22 (2): 157–71.

Ringrose, Jessica. 2013. *Postfeminist Education: Girls and the Sexual Politics of Schooling.* Abingdon, UK: Routledge.

Ross, Nicola J. 2005. "Children's Space." *International Research in Geographical and Environmental Education* 14 (4): 336–41.

Van Maanen, John. 2009. "Ethnography Then and Now: Qualitative Research." *Organizations and Management* 1 (1): 13–21.

Ward, Michael R. M. 2016. "'Placing Young Men': The Performance of Young Working-Class Masculinities in the South Wales Valleys." In *Our Changing Land: Revisiting Gender, Class and Identity in Contemporary Wales*, edited by D. Mannay, 88–197. Cardiff: University of Wales Press.

Warr, Deborah, Marilys Guillemin, Susan Cox, and Jenny Waycott, eds. 2016. *Ethics and Visual Research Methods: Theory, Methodology and Practice.* London: Palgrave Macmillan.

31 Collecting Social Media Data in Qualitative Research

Meghan Lynch and Catherine Mah

INTRODUCTION

It is easy to overlook social media when we rush out into the world, eager to do research, but it is important to consider social media in qualitative research. *Netnography*, *cyberethnography*, *webnography*, and *virtual ethnography* are terms used to describe adapting ethnography to the online world. Netnography, like ethnography, involves being immersed in the everyday life of a community and community members through participation, observation, and researcher engagement (Kozinets 2015). We will focus here on the practical process of collecting social media discussion data.

In this chapter, we will use examples from our study on kindergarten teachers' perspectives and experiences with play-based teaching to discuss social media data. We will cover practical skills and tips about the following: (1) appropriateness of social media analysis, (2) ethical considerations, (3) how to collect social media data, and (4) how to take steps to address data credibility and quality. The broad term *social media* refers to a number of forms and systems for online communication, such as blogs, chat rooms, and message boards. Our examples mainly involve message boards, though our tips can be applied to other social media forms.

DETERMINE THE APPROPRIATENESS OF SOCIAL MEDIA ANALYSIS

Social media discussions are intriguing data sources for researchers looking for alternative ways to learn about public opinions on a topic, but they are not always appropriate or advantageous. Before embarking on a social media discussion analysis study, it is useful to consider the fit between the research question you are asking, practical issues, and opportunities presented by social media data. Think about the following:

1. Who is represented online, and how does this compare with your study population or social group of interest? Remember, online discussions are often

limited to the perspectives of people who have Internet access and are literate (Wilkinson and Thelwall 2011).

2.   Do you want to learn about both current and past perspectives on a topic? Since social media discussions are generally archived and stored, you can access not only current, but also past discussions, increasing the historical scope of your study, within the time period of Internet communication (Nakki et al. 2011).

3.   Are you experiencing challenges with recruiting research participants through more "traditional" methods? How can social media complement other data collection? This is important because when people participate in online discussions they tend to focus on the negative aspects of the topic or situation. Social media discussion analyses can be combined with other "traditional" methods, such as interviews and focus groups, to understand social phenomena from multiple perspectives (Kozinets 2015).

Consider whether the group of people you are interested in studying has an online presence that has been previously researched. For our study, results of a literature review showed that teachers have described the convenience and support of message boards in enabling them to overcome barriers of time and isolation (Nicholson and Bond 2003; Stitzlein and Quinn 2012). This reasoning supported our use of social media to study teachers' perspectives.

What we did: For our study, we were interested in examining teachers' online discussions because we were having difficulty recruiting a large enough sample of teachers for in-person interviews. We knew from our literature review that teachers would not have issues with Internet access or literacy; however, we were still concerned that our findings from the social media discussions may not be applicable to the offline world. We decided to design our study so that first, we would conduct an analysis of teachers' social media discussions and then second, examine if similar findings could be found in a sample of offline, in-person interviews with kindergarten teachers.

ETHICAL CONSIDERATIONS

One of the most interesting aspects of social media research is the emerging research ethics issues around it. For example, whether or not researchers are required to seek the informed consent of social media discussion participants is a topic of debate amongst scholars in the field. One of the most appealing aspects of social media research is the potential for researchers to be "unobtrusive." This means that the researcher can collect data on the participants without disturbing their usual social interactions. Some researchers suggest, however, that this is different from observing people unobtrusively in places like a public park or café. So, is informed consent needed to observe people on a public discussion board? Are public spaces online the same as physical public places?

Another ethical consideration relates to the quoting of material from social media discussions. Even if identifying information is removed from the quotation, because the original information is stored in a publicly accessible place, quotations from social media sources could be typed into Internet search engines and lead the reader directly to the original source, such as a personal blog, "revealing" the participant.

Whether or not your research involves sensitive topics or vulnerable populations, it is important that you carefully consider research ethics before collecting online discussion data (Markham and Buchanan 2012). Since the ethics of social media research is a rapidly evolving field, be sure to critically examine current articles and position papers that discuss ethics in social media research (we highly recommend the up-to-date resources available through the Association of Internet Researchers website: www.ethics. aoir.org). We also recommend thinking through McDermott, Roen, and Piela's (2013) two questions for researchers interested in pursuing social media research:

1. What are the participants' likely expectations of privacy? To answer this question, you will need to examine message boards, chat rooms, and blogs to determine that they do not require membership, registration, or sign-in, and are publicly accessible through a popular search engine.
2. To what extent may observations potentially harm participants? In answering this question, consider the following: Are you researching a topic that would be considered sensitive? Are the participants vulnerable?

What we did: For our study, we used examples from similar studies to develop inclusion criteria that stated that we would only include message boards that were publicly available—defined specifically as those that did not require membership, registration, sign-in, or a password, and were publicly accessible through multiple search engines. We considered teachers' vulnerability, and concluded that they were not more vulnerable than the average person on a social media discussion board. We also did not feel that the topic of our research was sensitive. We did not report any of the names of the message boards or participants studied, to assist in de-identifying the information (Stitzlein and Quinn 2012).

DATA COLLECTION

Now for the fun part! Having worked through the previous two steps, you are set to begin collecting social media discussion data. A word of caution: collecting social media data might seem easy, since a simple Internet search can be returned in milliseconds.

Indeed, we had read in multiple articles that a main benefit of social media discussion analysis is how much faster you can collect data than with traditional methods (Kozinets 2015). We are hesitant to agree. In our study, we found systematically filtering the vast amount of data online to be *incredibly* time-consuming. So much so, in fact, that we found it beneficial to set time limits for collecting online data rather than setting a numerical goal of collecting a specific number of discussions.

Reading through my (ML) qualitative memo journal from my data collection days, I found the following quote: "I searched through the first 100 pages over the course of the day, taking breaks often, as my eyes would glaze over if I tried to go through too many in a row."

Below, we provide tips on the main steps in social media data collection: identifying message boards, identifying discussions, and keeping track of discussions.

Identifying Message Boards

A benefit of collecting social media discussion data is that no sophisticated equipment is needed to obtain data. We recommend putting yourself in the shoes of the people you are looking to obtain discussion data from. We thought to ourselves, How would the average teacher go about looking for a message board? We began by typing the phrases "teacher message boards" and "teacher forums" and "teacher chat" into the search engine Google. Try to be increasingly specific with your search terms. Also, one search engine is not enough. To ensure that the message boards represent a wide and diverse sample, you will want to repeat this search on multiple search engines.

What we did: We initially identified 10 message boards, but we rejected 3 because they did not meet the inclusion criteria: One board was password-protected. Two boards were daycare/child care/teacher boards which made it unclear when discussion participants were teachers. In total, 7 message boards were included in our final sample.

Searching for Discussions

Once you identify a message board, the next step in the search differs depending on the organization of the board itself. Smaller boards typically have simple set-ups, with only one discussion section amongst all participants, divided up into various different topics. These boards often do not have the option of an internal search engine, so you will be left to manually search through the discussions, which is a time-consuming process. Larger boards are typically much more complex, but may have the option of an internal search engine, which can greatly speed up the search! Remember to keep an open mind and to develop new and specific search terms based on words you see frequently reappearing in the discussions you initially identify.

What we did: We found smaller boards that had only one forum, but divided into broad categories, such as elementary, middle, and high school. Larger boards had separate forums for each grade level. On one large board, we were not getting many results returned through the internal search engine, and suspected something was wrong. Different search engines use different algorithms to return results, so this is where some detective work or trial and error can help. We stumbled across the option of searching for discussions depending on how they were "tagged" into sub-topics. Searching by tags, rather than keywords, returned dozens of pages of discussions. In total, we ended up with 78 discussions.

Keeping Track of Discussions

Create a table to keep track of the different discussions and ensure that you do not have duplicates, especially if you are using a variety of search methods. We found this crucial since we would often return to the message boards several times using different search terms.

What we did: For each discussion we found it useful to record the following:

1. The message board community it originated from
2. The topic of the discussion
3. The number of messages in the discussion
4. The number of participants in the discussion

CREDIBLE QUALITY DATA

Credibility and quality of data collected through social media requires special attention. A main concern with social media discussion data is the anonymity of the participants who create the data and the reliability of their reported behaviours and attitudes (Scanfeld, Scanfeld, and Larson 2010). Online communities are composed of people who might never meet outside the virtual community, who are largely unaccountable for the information they share, and who can remain anonymous. Social media communication doesn't contain body language, eye contact, tone of voice, posture, general mood, or movements that can help to provide social cues. Furthermore, online anonymity makes it possible for corporations such as manufacturers and retailers to pose as participants while promoting their products; thus, posts by participants that engage in promotion or linking to a particular product or company should be examined with suspicion (Kozinets 2015).

Still! Participant anonymity can also be viewed favourably; it can encourage shy people to participate and express aspects of themselves that they otherwise would not share in discussions.

Falsification of data is not only a social media issue. Ethnographic researchers use techniques such as prolonged length of engagement with participants, persistent observation, and researcher introspection to overcome the potential that the data they collect could be a false representation of people or social phenomena. Such safeguards can also be applied in online research (Kozinets 2015). You will need to be extra attentive to credibility and quality when using social media data. This is absolutely critical when defending your use of social media discussion data to other researchers and journal reviewers.

What we did: While it may be tempting to do so, collecting social media data is *not* about downloading a bunch of discussions that involve your search terms and immediately beginning your analysis. Careful and prolonged observation of the social media communities better enabled us to trust that the online discussions were between "real" kindergarten teachers and helped us to understand their challenges and experiences in their work.

Whenever possible, we read participant profiles and checked many posts by the same participant to look for consistency over time. We also used many social media sites (seven different discussion boards) to determine if the findings apply to more than one online setting. These kinds of techniques are sometimes called "triangulation" in other forms of qualitative data collection.

We also treated engaging with social media like other field research. We kept a detailed memo journal to have an account of what occurred that day, along with our personal reactions to discussions, similarities or discrepancies between participants' posts on different discussion topics, and unique insights.

ANALYSIS AND RESULTS

Full discussion of the data analysis and results of our research can be found elsewhere in articles by ML (Lynch 2014a, 2014b, 2015). Here we will talk about a few key findings as they relate to unique benefits of social media discussion data.

In message board discussions, we noticed how teachers seemed much more open to describing challenges they experience in class with play-based teaching. We also found novel results that were unreported in past research on the topic. We were then able to explore these insights in offline interviews conducted with kindergarten teachers in a later part of the research study.

We found the experience of analyzing the teachers' message board discussions beneficial and unique from reading published literature on the same topic. While there is a large amount of literature documenting kindergarten teachers' struggles with incorporating play in the classroom, reading "raw" discussions between teachers gave us a different experience than reading a polished article.

Why Might Participants Reveal More Online?

1. Clarity. Because they are writing on a public board, participants might try to write more clearly than usual (Nakki et al. 2011). Having the time to read others' writing on a discussion board at their own pace may help some people express themselves better.

2. Community. Message board discussions can create a strong sense of belonging to a message board community, a sentiment that often encourages participants to reveal more information than they might otherwise (Bullinger et al. 2012).

CONCLUSION

Examining social media discussions to explore public perspectives can allow for rich descriptions sourced from what was previously an overlooked area of publicly available information. In our study of kindergarten teachers' social media discussions, we found we were able to observe a wider range of teachers' perspectives than what was available in our immediate environment, and the findings introduced questions to explore in interviews with offline teachers. We hope to have excited readers about the possibilities of using social media in qualitative research, while also reinforcing the need to always be reflexive about the challenges and ethical issues that are part of this burgeoning type of qualitative data collection.

CRAFTING QUALITATIVE RESEARCH EXERCISES

1. Think about a few of the social groups you belong to. This could be a school group like a club or team, or a group that you identify with, related to your age, gender, sexual orientation, neighbourhood, or ethnicity. Do you interact with that group on social media? Have a conversation with some of the peers from your group about why they would or would not want their information on social media to be studied by a researcher.

2. Consider a social media study that aims to better understand how teenagers experience bullying by analyzing discussions on message boards. Write down some of the ethical issues you might encounter in designing this study and how you intend to resolve them.

3. Choose a discussion containing a number of participants on a social media site of your choice, for example, your Facebook page. Analyze the data, thinking about what language is used, the ideas that dominate the discussion, and the

opinions that people are trying to convey. What sorts of patterns do you see emerging?

4. Examine the comments from three different online news sites reporting on the same topic, for example, an environmental issue. Do you notice differences in the patterns or ideas being expressed? Why do you think that might be the case?

REFERENCES

Bullinger, Angelika C., Matthias Rass, Sabrina Adamczyk, Kathrin M. Moeslein, and Stefan Sohn. 2012. "Open Innovation in Health Care: An Analysis of an Open Health Platform." *Health Policy* 105 (2/3): 165–75.

Kozinets, Robert V. 2015. *Netnography: Redefined.* London: Sage.

Lynch, Meghan. 2014a. "Kindergarten Food Familiarization: An Exploratory Study of Teachers' Views on Food and Nutrition in Kindergartens." *Appetite* 87: 46–55.

Lynch, Meghan. 2014b. "Ontario Kindergarten Teachers' Social Media Discussions about Full Day Kindergarten." *McGill Journal of Education* 49 (2): 329–49.

Lynch, Meghan. 2015. "More Play, Please: Kindergarten Teachers' Perspectives on Play in the Classroom." *American Journal of Play* 7 (3): 347–70.

Markham, Annette, and Elizabeth Buchanan. 2012. *Ethical Decision-Making and Internet Research.* Chicago: Association of Internet Researchers. http://aoir.org/reports/ethics2.pdf.

McDermott, Elizabeth, Katrina Roen, and Anna Piela. 2013. "Hard-to-Reach Youth Online: Methodological Advances in Self-Harm Research." *Sexual Research Sociological Policy* 10 (2): 125–34.

Nakki, Pirjo, Asta Back, Teemu Ropponen, Juha Kronqvist, Kari A. Hintikka, Auli Harju, Reeta Poyhtari, and Petri Kola. 2011. *Social Media for Citizen Participation: Report on the Somus Project.* VTT Publications 755. VTT Technical Research Center of Finland.

Nicholson, Sheila A., and Nathan Bond. 2003. "Collaborative Reflection and Professional Community Building: An Analysis of Preservice Teachers' Use of an Electronic Discussion Board." *Journal of Technology and Teacher Education* 11 (2): 259–79.

Scanfeld, David, Vanessa Scanfeld, and Elaine L. Larson. 2010. "Dissemination of Health Information through Social Networks: Twitter and Antibiotics." *American Journal of Infectious Control* 38 (3): 182–28.

Stitzlein, Sarah M., and Sarah Quinn. 2012. "What Can We Learn from Teacher Dissent Online?" *Educational Forum* 76 (2): 190–200.

Wilkinson, David, and Mike Thelwall. 2011. "Researching Personal Information on the Public Web: Methods and Ethics." *Social Science Computer Review* 29 (4): 387–401.

SECTION VIII

ANALYZING YOUR DATA

Doing analysis is a highly creative process. Through our analyses we attempt to make sense of what our data mean and work towards generating original ideas. Sometimes, our research confirms what we already know. Other times, we arrive at entirely new insights. More often, however, our analyses result in a synthesis of previous findings and novel ideas. These analytical outcomes are the fruits of our research labour. Our creative analyses happen as we spend time mulling over our data, reading about others' findings, and writing down and revising our ideas. Instead of conceiving of analysis as something that happens after all our data are collected, qualitative researchers envision analysis as an ongoing feature of qualitative research. Your insights could arise serendipitously early in your data collection, or your "eureka moment" might not happen until you have collected all your data and are reflecting on what they tell you.

As early as the planning stage of a project, our preliminary analytical ideas are apparent. Perhaps we have a particular concept or theory we think will be central to our research. The research questions we develop and questions we plan to ask participants often have analytical ideas contained within them. The findings are unknown, but we still have a tentative framework in mind for making sense of our data. For example, the research question "How do female bodybuilders manage stigma?" makes an analytical assumption about the relationship between female bodybuilding and stigma. As we collect and reflect on our data, we revise early analytical thoughts, which give way to new insights arising out of our data. It is important we only use our early analytical ideas to sensitize us to possibilities, being fully prepared to discard them if they are inconsistent with what we are finding.

Our interim analysis begins more concertedly during data collection; as we gather our data, we are also spending time thinking about what our data mean. This is reflected in what qualitative researchers sometimes call memoing. Through memoing we consider things like how the data collection process is progressing and what substantive, conceptual, and theoretical findings are beginning to take shape. Our ongoing analysis allows us to formulate hunches and working hypotheses. It also allows us to see how our data connects with, diverges from, or extends other scholars' work in the field. This part of the analytical process is not rigid. While we might feel we are onto something, we are also wary about committing to an idea until we have collected more data. Based on what we are finding, we can introduce new questions to follow up on our hunches through additional data collection.

Once you reach the end of the data collection phase, you will engage in post-contact analysis. It is at this point that you will thoroughly analyze all of your data. Here you will be particularly thankful for the memos you made. Your memos offer some preliminary analytical insights about themes and patterns in your data, and your ongoing thoughts about what they mean and how they might connect back to concepts and theories. You can use your memos to generate some initial codes. As you review your data, though, you will formulate new codes. Codes are shorthand markers for themes and patterns in your data. They help you identify and summarize findings from your data, and begin formulating the analytical story you will eventually tell. As an inductive process, we focus on constructing stories grounded in what our data are telling us.

It is helpful to think of analysis as being akin to piecing together a puzzle; however, there is no set conclusion to the puzzle. Rather, analysis is about interpreting your data and developing connections between what different participants are doing, saying, or producing. Quite often there is a breakthrough moment when you notice something particularly interesting in your data. Do not, however, be put off by what, at first, might appear to be a mountain of seemingly meaningless information. There is no substitute for spending time with your data, reflecting on your codes, thinking about others' findings, and considering academic ideas you have encountered during your education. In doing so, your key findings will begin to emerge. The chapters in this section will help spur your analytical creativity and see you through the process.

In chapter 32, Amber Gazso and Katherine Bischoping compare standpoint theory and discursive positioning as reflexive strategies for analyzing an awkward moment during an interview. They end up concluding that while the two approaches complement one another, discursive positioning ends up offering greater insights for their analysis. Being reflexive about their methods permits them to consider different interpretations of their data. Their chapter also highlights how artifacts of the research process, like awkward moments, which sometimes catch us off guard, can serve as useful opportunities for practicing reflexivity as part of our analysis.

In chapter 33, Michael Adorjan takes us through the analytical phases of a qualitative research project. As his primary case study, he brings in examples from his and Rose Ricciardelli's research on adolescents' experiences with cyber-risk. Adorjan highlights the importance of recognizing that analysis happens throughout the research process, and he provides us with practical advice on how to proceed. He presents hands-on examples of using a literature review for analytical purposes. Anyone looking to use a computer program to assist with coding and analysis will find Adorjan's discussion of coding using NVivo particularly helpful.

In chapter 34, Jeffrey P. Aguinaldo confronts the quandary of how we manage the "dilemmas of voice" in our research projects. Whose voices we privilege is a common challenge experienced by researchers. Aguinaldo's chapter captures this dilemma well, presenting us with a possible theoretical solution in the form of social constructionism. The emphasis of the chapter is critical qualitative community-based health research, but his ideas and advice have broader reach. The question of whose version of reality we privilege in attempting to make sense of our data is one that qualitative researchers confront in their analyses regardless of topic.

In chapter 35, Carrie B. Sanders and Lisa-Jo K. van den Scott point out that material culture and human-object relations are insufficiently studied by social scientists. As such, they set out to delineate how we can go about better understanding these areas. Reflecting on Sanders's research on the use of emergency technology by police, fire, and paramedics and van den Scott's research on the Inuit's relationship to their houses, they take us step-by-step through their approach to coding and memoing. In doing so, they present ideas for how situational analysis can help us during our analyses in attending to materiality and human-object relations.

In chapter 36, Susan Diane discusses the value of using tree drawings as an analytical tool for conducting an arts-informed analysis. She describes how the use of tree drawings provided clarity and enabled her to develop representations for the life histories of her queer, activist, female participants. Tree drawings served as a heuristic device—an aid for organizing and making meaning out of her data. Through her personal reflections, she illustrates how adopting a creative approach, such as tree drawings, can provide analytic leverage and clarity.

32 Reframing an Awkward Moment: A Comparison of Two Analytic Strategies for Being Reflexive

Amber Gazso and Katherine Bischoping

Reflexivity, a central concern of qualitative researchers, is the asking of how one's self and methods are implicated in the knowledge one produces. Scholars are reflexive in limitless ways, pondering such questions as how their findings from a qualitative interview might have been different if they were the same ethnicity, age, or gender as their respondents (Soni-Sinha 2008), what it means for a divorced woman to interview divorced men (Arendell 1997), or how one's self-perceived "insider" status is not shared by others in the field (Oriola and Haggerty 2012). However, when it comes to understanding awkward moments in interviewing—those that are embarrassing, anxiety-inducing, horrifying, or downright thorny—a reflexive gaze is rarely employed. Being reflexive about awkward moments involves taking the risk of allowing others to witness the times that we, as researchers, speak or behave in ways that call into question our ethics, competence, and credibility.

We dare to take this risk. Indeed, our impetus was that the two of us could easily pinpoint the most discomfiting moments that had transpired in interviews that we conducted in qualitative projects done in Canada and the United States over our 30-odd combined years as researchers. This chapter is a case study of one such awkward moment, which we present in depth and analyze through two distinct strategies for the practice of reflexivity (see also Bischoping and Gazso 2016, 119–20). In this case study, we embrace the challenge of this edited volume, and illustrate how being crafty as a qualitative researcher can involve critically and reflexively revisiting and re-framing moments in interviews, even ones we would rather forget.

We begin by briefly discussing two strategies for reflexivity. The first—and the one perhaps better known to social scientists—is that of applying *standpoint theory*, which is often utilized by feminists, ethnographers, and narrative analysts (and any intersection thereof). The second strategy involves what linguists doing discourse analysis call *discursive positioning*. Following this discussion, we apply these two strategies to reframe an awkward moment in which one of co-author Amber Gazso's interview participants called her a "little squarehead." Our findings from this exercise coalesce in a pair of interrelated arguments: first, that the two strategies offer complementary ways to understand the origins of awkward moments; but, second, that on balance, it is the somewhat unsung discursive positioning strategy that bears more analytic fruit.

TWO STRATEGIES FOR REFLEXIVITY: STANDPOINT THEORY AND DISCURSIVE POSITIONING

In feminist standpoint theory, a *standpoint* refers to how a person's consciousness and interpretations develop according to the experience of being socially located in particular categories, performances, and intersections of race, class, gender, sexuality, citizenship, ability, and so forth (Collins 1989; Harding 1986; Intemann 2010; Weedon 1999). A standpoint is not given so much as achieved through reflection of how one's knowledge is shaped by prevailing power structures and cultural conditions (Intemann 2010). As we have discussed elsewhere, scholars can engage in reflexivity via standpoint theory when they consider how their social location vis-à-vis research participants is relevant to the stages of knowledge production, consider apparent tensions in standpoints (between researcher and participant, or among participants), or assess whether their research methods help multiple standpoints to be expressed (Bischoping and Gazso 2016, 47–50).

Discursive psychology, which linguists Derek Edwards and Jonathan Potter (1992) first developed, provides us with our second conceptual strategy for being reflexive. It is to consider discursive positioning, i.e., how individuals construct their experiences according to their positions in social settings that are themselves mediated by the discourses available (see also Adjei 2013; Davies and Harré 1990; De Fina 2013). Discourses, here, are webs of meanings, ideas, interactions, and practices that are expressed or represented in spoken, written, or image-based texts, within institutional and everyday settings (Bischoping and Gazso 2016, 129). To look at discursive positioning is to assume that talk is not simply a way to pour experiences into a tape recorder. It can also be rhetorical. Using this strategy for being reflexive about the interview therefore involves considering how interview respondents speak through and position themselves in relation to discourses. Scholars can also be reflexive about how the discursive positioning that interviewers and respondents participate in is influenced by the norms of the interview interaction (Bischoping and Gazso 2016, 179–80).

In contrast with standpoint theory's reflexivity, which asks, in part, "Who am I and how is my answer implicated in the knowledge I produce?" discursive positioning asks, "What is the 'I' that each speaker is constructing in a given moment? In relation to what discourse(s)? How is the 'I' produced or constrained by these or other discourses? How is all this implicated in knowledge production?"

AN AWKWARD MOMENT

We now turn to an example of an awkward moment, excerpted from an interview co-author Amber conducted with a woman we will call "Sam," as part of a project on how diverse families develop complex social support networks in order to manage low income. In the course of her interviewing, Amber discovered that participants' stories about managing low income in the present often were contextualized by "back-stories," i.e., stories of their pasts that they considered to have bearing on their present situation. In this excerpt, Sam is presenting the back-story of her addiction. As you will see, things go awry when Amber does not understand a street term that Sam uses.

Example: A Little Squarehead[1]

1   *Sam:* I started using hard-core illicit drugs. And you know one day my
2   mom showed up at my door, she goes, "I know you're using, I don't
3   want to hear it, get me a 50 piece." So, [I go], "You didn't tell my little
4   brothers [I'm using] did you?" No, she didn't tell my little brothers.
5   So I got her a 50 piece and she stayed.
6   *Amber:* What's a 50 piece? *You have to
7   *Sam:* *It's crack cocaine.
8   *Amber:* Got it, you've got to fill me in here.
9   *Sam:* We have a little squarehead.
10 *Amber:* I totally am. Believe me I think the most I ever did in my life was
11 marijuana and that was really fun. That was it. I fully admit it, that's why
12 you've got to fill me in.
13 *Sam:* Okay. Yeah.

Note: * means that the two speakers' talk overlapped, beginning at this point.

On the face of it, this excerpt might do little save evoke gulps of sympathy from the reader. But, let us see what we can learn when we first reflexively analyze how Amber and Sam's very different standpoints affect how the interaction unfolds. Importantly, in this analysis, as in many reflexive analyses of interviews via standpoint theory, the respondent was never asked to identify the social location from which she perceives and interacts in her environment. To be reflexive is to read Sam's standpoint in. Once Amber has asked, "What's a 50 piece?" (line 6), Sam and Amber are no longer sharing a standpoint as two women engaged in conversation with a research purpose, perhaps realizing a feminist aim of sisterly sharing. Instead, their differences become foregrounded. To Amber, it became salient that she had grown up in a nuclear family household in a rural area and had left home to attend university. She recalls feeling acutely ignorant and uncomfortable because she could not understand the language Sam had learned in living on the street and using drugs after leaving a disruptive childhood home. In asking, "What's a 50 piece?" Amber highlighted the relative privilege she had enjoyed from childhood onward.

In replying "we have a little squarehead" (line 9), Sam, in turn, further foregrounds her and Amber's differences. Other distinctions between the two women that Amber perceived in their interaction, or had learned of from Sam's answers to a demographic questionnaire, seemed to come to the fore: Amber is Caucasian; Sam is, in her own words, "Caucasian, Jamaican, and First Nations." Amber earns a wage as an academic; Sam's main source of income is social assistance or welfare. At the moment of being called "a little squarehead," Amber recalls feeling that Sam had locked her into a standpoint in which she could never experientially know Sam's world. From Sam's tone, it seemed to Amber that her question had angered Sam, that the gulf in privilege attached to the two women's social locations had become incredibly salient, that the interview itself risked being broken off. Amber felt dread and wondered, "How can I fix this??!!"

How can reflexivity about social location matter to moving past this stalemate? Reading on in the transcript, we see that Amber chose a certain fix to repair the awkward moment. (We invite you to consider what you would have done in her shoes.) As she remembers it, Amber wanted to re-establish rapport with Sam, essentially to re-establish the two of them as engaged in the interview as an exercise of joint meaning-making about Sam's experience of managing low income. Her fix was to simultaneously acknowledge her own social location and soften the differences that seemed to matter between Sam and her. In replying that she had used marijuana in the past and found it "fun" (lines 10–12), Amber remained an academic but revealed a prior social location: that of a young woman experimenting with drugs. In the moments following the awkward one, it seemed to Amber that her agreement with Sam's claim that she is a little squarehead, i.e., naive, and her honesty about having some knowledge about drug use appealed to Sam and smoothed over some tension. Sam could retain her role as teacher of her life and so could complete the interview from a position of some power (Hoffmann 2007), a woman expert in drug use and recovery from addiction.

Thinking through reflexivity via a discursive positioning strategy allows us to reframe this exchange in a way that goes beyond the microdynamics of comparing social locations and the power, privileges, and knowledges attached to them. The talk between Amber and Sam involved their positioning themselves in relation to a series of discourses, each laden with power-knowledge relations, and each having rhetorical effect.

- Line 1 is part of Sam's back-story of how she had become an addict. Her current recovery centres on her drawing on a discourse in which drug addiction is a disease, and in which addicts are responsible for coming to an understanding of their biography as addicts; thus, for Sam, doing the interview is part of positioning herself and performing the role of being in recovery.
- When Sam calls Amber "a little squarehead," this can be understood to be a belittling of Amber, which causes us to consider how Sam could have construed Amber's question as an attack. Here, standpoint theory and discursive positioning come to the same conclusion, that Amber's unfamiliarity with "50 piece" is a marker of painful differences. This makes Amber's reply to Sam, about how Amber had used soft drugs, especially interesting. To mitigate this painful difference, we see both Amber and Sam aligning with a discursive construction

of drug use as a sophisticated form of recreation and a process of self-discovery. All of a sudden, we see the tip of the iceberg of positioning around a discourse that utterly contradicts the interview's prevailing discourse of drug use as addiction. Finally, Amber's agreement that she is a squarehead positions her outside of a discourse that constructs academics as taking the moral high road.

- That Sam discusses how her mother came to her for a hit of crack cocaine is another act of implicit positioning, of placing her life experiences largely *outside* discourses of the family as nurturing. We can also notice that this discourse is in tension with one in which Sam *does* experience her family as nurturing. In line 4, both she and her mother are concerned about protecting the impressionable younger brothers from knowledge about Sam's crack use, and Sam is concerned about providing for her mother's needs—even if it is a need for crack. Here, Sam is speaking to being as moral as she can be given the constraint of her drug use.

Through being reflexive per discursive positioning, we see how Sam and Amber use discourses with rhetorical effect. Discourses of family as nurturing, drug use as addiction, drug use as sophisticated recreation, or academics as inhabiting an ivory tower variously denigrate or placate Sam and Amber, or position them as moral, immoral, naive, or sophisticated.

CLOSING

From our analysis of this case we gleaned important insights. The first that we can pass on to you is to never assume that a standpoint is fixed or coherent in an interview. Selves are multi-faceted, made up of several possibly contradictory identities, past and present, which different moments of the interview call forth. Several contradictory identities may be called forth at one and the same moment; thus, a research interview, however harmoniously it is proceeding, can near breakdown in moments when the rift between two standpoints gapes, such as when Amber's standpoint as a capable qualitative researcher, adept at probing, is met with Sam's assertion that she is a squarehead. Just as Amber's sense of self is threatened, so too is Sam's. Being reflexive using standpoint theory means attending to how power, privilege, and difference are negotiated in an interview, in this case, to whether Sam would feel comfortable telling her story and having knowledge produced from it. These are valuable considerations. If differences in standpoint seem to be why this awkward moment could burst forth, does that mean that standpoint theory is all you need to understand it?

We do not think so. Our second insight is that being reflexive, standpoint theory–style, can leave you stuck in the moment of awkwardness, in an analysis of microlevel interaction that is largely static. Only by applying discursive positioning did we come to understand how researchers and respondents may transcend an awkward moment, and to consider how our social locations are positioned in wider discourses that we can draw upon in dynamic ways. We observed, for example, that to keep the interview going, Amber invoked a drugs-as-sophisticated-fun discourse. (We suspect that, had she instead produced an academic-as-moral-authority discourse, the interview would quickly have come to a halt.) Being reflexive by using discursive positioning allows you to notice how different discourses, constituted by and within different social relations and assemblages of power-knowledge, are readily available to shape the interview. Further, discursive positioning lets you perceive which knowledge the interview largely privileged—which knowledge was given more power—in this case, in Sam's performance of being a "good addict" who confesses the badness of her drug use. In our view, examining discursive positioning alone, or in tandem with standpoint theory, is what can give qualitative researchers greater insight into how their methods affect the knowledge produced.

Our third, and most important, insight is that awkward moments in our transcripts need not be stuffed into our closets, lurking there and accusing us of being incompetent academics. Instead, we have learned that it is okay to be yourself during an interview, rather than trying to be the self a "true academic" should be—a self that possesses miraculous interview-saving skills. When awkward moments happen, you can embrace them, reframing them as golden opportunities for analytical practices of reflexivity.

CRAFTING QUALITATIVE RESEARCH EXERCISES

1. Watch Jesse Williams's speech from the 2016 Black Entertainment Television Awards. His speech was followed by a storm of petitions on Change.org. One petition called for Williams to be fired from *Grey's Anatomy*, while others supported him. Collect a sample of 15 petitions and assess the extent to which standpoint theory can be used to understand the differences among their authors' views.

2. Using the same sample of petitions, identify discourses that the authors use to position their views as valid.

3. Find on YouTube the interview that Chris Stark conducted with Mila Kunis. Assess the extent to which differences in their standpoints explain the awkward moments at the beginning of the interview. Then assess what discourses the two used to get past their awkwardness.

4. Think of an awkward moment that you experienced in an interaction with a friend or family member. Assess the extent to which differences in your standpoints explain the awkwardness. Then assess whether discursive positioning helps you to explain whether and how you overcame the awkwardness.

NOTE

1. The example analyzed in this chapter also appears in Bischoping and Gazso (2016, 119). Our interest here is in analyzing this example through two different perspectives on reflexivity.

REFERENCES

Adjei, Stephen B. 2013. "Discourse Analysis: Examining Language Use in Context." *Qualitative Report* 18 (50): 1–10.

Arendell, Terry. 1997. "Reflections on the Researcher-Researched Relationship: A Woman Interviewing Men." *Qualitative Sociology* 20 (3): 341–68.

Bischoping, Katherine, and Amber Gazso. 2016. *Analyzing Talk in the Social Sciences: Narrative, Conversation, and Discourse Strategies.* London: Sage.

Collins, Patricia H. 1989. "The Social Construction of Black Feminist Thought." *Signs: Journal of Women in Culture and Society* 14 (4): 745–73.

Davies, Bronwyn, and Rom Harré. 1990. "Positioning: The Social Construction of Selves." *Journal for the Theory of Social Behaviour* 20: 43–63.

De Fina, Anna. 2013. "Positioning Level 3: Connecting Local Identity Displays to Macro Social Processes." *Narrative Inquiry* 23 (1): 40–61.

Edwards, Derek, and Jonathan Potter. 1992. *Discursive Psychology.* London: Sage.

Harding, Sandra. 1986. *The Science Question in Feminism.* Ithaca, NY: Cornell University Press.

Hoffmann, Elizabeth A. 2007. "Open-Ended Interviews, Power, and Emotional Labor." *Journal of Contemporary Ethnography* 36 (3): 318–46.

Intemann, Kristen. 2010. "25 Years of Feminist Empiricism and Standpoint Theory: Where Are We Now?" *Hypatia* 25 (4): 778–96.

Oriola, Temitope, and Kevin D. Haggerty. 2012. "The Ambivalent Insider/Outsider Status of Academic 'Homecomers': Observations on Identity and Field Research in the Nigerian Delta." *Sociology* 46 (3): 540–48.

Soni-Sinha, Urvashi. 2008. "Dynamics of the 'Field': Multiple Standpoints, Narrative and Shifting Positionality in Multisited Research." *Qualitative Research* 8 (4): 515–37.

Weedon, Chris. 1999. *Feminism, Theory and the Politics of Difference.* Oxford, UK: Blackwell Publishers.

33

Making Sense of Your Data: From Paralysis to Theoretical Engagement

Michael Adorjan

Do not panic and stay calm! Qualitative research presents many challenges, including participant recruitment and access to populations, time constraints at every stage, and, above all, the steep learning curve regarding the *craft* of a wide array of methods such as ethnography, discourse analysis, and interviewing. Yet, perhaps lurking behind all these challenges lies the one often identified as most daunting to researchers both novice and expert alike: data analysis and theoretical development. I have been asked to write this chapter on analytical procedures by highlighting not only excellent existing literature (e.g., Coffey and Atkinson 1996; Miles, Huberman, and Saldana 2014), but also my own lived experiences conducting research. This contributes to a growing body of work that examines the "real politik" of research and lived experiences of researchers, capturing both pragmatic and empirically informed insights gleaned in the field (Adorjan and Ricciardelli 2016; Booth, Colomb, and Williams 2008; Pawluch, Shaffir, and Miall 2005). It happens that as I write this chapter I am settling into analysis of a series of focus groups conducted for research (with my colleague Rose Ricciardelli and funded by the Social Sciences and Humanities Research Council of Canada) on adolescents' experiences with cyber-risk. I will focus on this research here, though I also draw from experience conducting focus groups and one-to-one interviews in both Canada and Hong Kong on a range of topics, including fear of crime, perceptions of police, and youth crime. In the space provided I will highlight the "phases" (problematized below) of initial exploration, and developing "coding frames" and theoretical connections, and will discuss how to think through examining broader patterns versus interpretive details in the data.

INITIAL EXPLORATIONS

Although I speak of "phases" of research, research in practice often does not proceed in a smooth, chronological manner, where data analysis is a neatly encapsulated phase somewhere in between data collection and publication. Indeed, the early phases of initial research design, literature review, entering the field, and so on, *at all times* involve data analysis and theoretical thinking. As Strauss (1987) presciently stressed, a mindset of constant comparison and curiosity is not antagonistic nor agnostic towards theoretical development (he wrote "believe everything and believe nothing" [1987, 28]). Positionality is imperative to consider. This refers to active reflection of your position (e.g., standpoint, social identity) in relation to your research subjects and data; how may your particular lived experiences come to impact not only the research question framed, but also the sample and design of the project, the interpretation and analysis of the data, and so forth. Gender, race and ethnicity, sexual orientation, age, and class, among other factors, will likely bear strongly on your positionality (see, for example, Deutsch 2004). While conducting your research, and during *all phases*, reflect on your positionality and identity both in relation to your participants (or texts, etc.) and to the wider socio-political and cultural context within which you are embedded (Adorjan 2016). This is not at all abstract: you will arrive at your research questions with preconceived expectations, stereotypes, and convictions (e.g., towards notions of power and how power is experienced and exercised). The task becomes walking a tightrope between a reflexive stance towards existing theory and substantive findings and also understanding where your "tree" (i.e., individual research project and participants) falls within a broader forest of extant research and theoretical sedimentation.

So begin by reading widely. Google Scholar is more than apt for a general orientation, and a university library can offer more refined databases if needed. Scour references and snowball sources by mining the references of the books and articles you read. *Do not work in isolation* and do not be persuaded by the myth that success accrues by locking yourself in a broom closet (with WiFi) in order to concentrate on work. Ask around (a supervisor, fellow students, or departmental colleagues) for advice on early ideas or drafts. Drink coffee—two cups per day. Find out both what substantive findings have been revealed about a particular issue, group, social problem, etc., and then take note of the various theoretical perspectives in the literature framing understanding of the phenomena. Get sufficient sleep. Take memos all the time: from initial ideas to the development of coding frames and finalization of a manuscript for publication, memos embolden one's reflexivity and ability to proceed inductively and comparatively (Ruona 2005, 235).

Take my experience starting my current project on youth and cyber-risk. I have been teaching about cyberspace and "cyber deviations" for a few years and decided to pivot a bit in my research direction—which always involved a focus on youth—to examine adolescents' lived experiences with cyber-risk. I had some familiarity with literature on cyberbullying, hacktivism, and social networking sites, but before I submitted a proposal for research I conducted a thorough literature review on a number of additional areas, including sexting, the Internet and privacy, and cyber-surveillance. The literature review may take more time than you initially anticipate; do not underestimate this when conducting research under a limited timeframe (e.g., a one-term research project). I prefer to read electronic documents (e.g., PDF files of articles with optical character recognition) that I can highlight directly using software that allows me to edit PDFs. I can also embed comments at appropriate places. If I find a passage relevant and/or interesting, I put a small red arrow beside it. If I find a passage to be imperative and crucial to incorporate, and/or exceptionally insightful, I put a red box around it using the tools in the software I use (in my case Adobe Acrobat). These are saved with the PDF and if I leave the articles for a while, the markups remind me of my thought process when I return to them. There is no "right" number of articles to collect in this initial stage. Pragmatics usually apply related to time, energy, and deadlines (Ellingson 2011, 604).

Once a handful of informative articles and materials is acquired and reviewed, my method is to create a blank Microsoft Word document simply titled "the table." I think (reflecting as I am writing this) the title hearkens to the large (actual physical) tables qualitative researchers often employed to help arrange their research materials, though I apply this also to the literature review. I review the saved PDFs and copy highlighted text to the Word file. I use cyan highlighting for passages with an arrow beside them, red for those with a box around them, and include notes, in square brackets and highlighted in yellow, of my own memos made either during the initial reading of the file or of my current thoughts. I have used this system since grad school to highlight areas of readings relevant for particular projects. The file can be reused and resituated for follow-up projects with differently distributed highlights and analyses. Of course you may develop a different system, with different coloured highlights, or no highlighting at all, but some other method of identifying pertinent information. What matters is developing a consistent method of data analysis that can be applied to multiple research projects.

As you contemplate key ideas from the literature and your memos, you will notice concepts and theoretical frameworks relevant to your project begin to emerge. In my case I found several examinations of teens and social media sites that employed a social capital or Goffmanian dramaturgical perspective. Scholars who took up a qualitative design and examined "digital citizenship" online, and those who analyzed the various campaigns for online safety—often directed at female adolescents—were frequently informed by feminism (e.g., Bailey et al. 2013; Karaian 2013). A number of studies of cyber-risk and -surveillance also engaged with a governmentality framework (e.g., Koskela 2006). Again, bouncing ideas off of friends and colleagues at this point may help orient yourself to identifying important gaps in the literature and theory. Theory offers the paving stones to connect your data to wider social currents and processes; it goes a long way to answering the "so what" question related to your data. It is important not to select a theory based on its putative popularity and force data into its mould. Rather, theory at this point is itself a conceptual terrain to be analyzed and refined as you proceed with your analysis (Barbour 2008, 238; Strauss and Corbin 1990).

Be mindful of when you are procrastinating. It is all too easy to take a "short" break and catch up on trending social media, especially if you are working on a wired computer. Take breaks and recharge when needed. The difference between surfing for sources and spending time on irrelevant tangents is a fine line but one you should work to recognize. *Work to deadlines and self-imposed goals.* Over time, my literature review became pragmatically sufficient, enabling me to start drafting an application for research.

The advantage of applying for research funding (or drafting a research proposal for your supervisor) is that you are forced to advance some methodological and theoretical thinking. Despite notable exceptions (e.g., Bailey and Steeves 2015; boyd 2014; Livingstone 2008; Regan and Sweet 2015), I found a dearth of qualitative examinations of youth and cyber-risk, especially in Canada. Extant research often centred on quantitative assessments of cyberbullying, or lacked a sociological lens. My goal quickly became an exploration of how youth, expressed in their own words, experience cyber-risk and, moreover, their responses to the messages they receive about online safety and risk management (e.g., from schools, police, and parents).

ARRANGING THE PUZZLE PIECES

The next year was spent conducting focus groups with male and female adolescents aged 13 to 19 in both western and eastern Canada, and within both urban and rural regions (for more on focus groups, please see Madriz 2000; Morgan 1997; Stewart, Shamdasani, and Rook 2007). For the purposes of this chapter, I will jump ahead past the data collection and transcription period. Even before transcriptions were completed, I used the qualitative analysis software NVivo to create a file for the project and began to create some provisional codes. As with any qualitative analysis software, NVivo does no cogitation for you (certainly no sociological analysis) and its output is solely based on the conceptual and theoretical direction you give it (Barbour 2008, 195). Based on my literature review and teaching experience, I decided to set up some broad categories that I thought highly likely to be relevant. If they turned out not to be relevant I could simply delete or reorganize them at a later stage. I should note here that explicating the process of NVivo is beyond my scope, though I highly recommend using the software, or comparable packages, as they save *significant* time and offer excellent tools for analysis (see below). I turned first to "open coding," "the central purpose of which is to open inquiry widely" (Berg 2001, 251). I created NVivo "node folders" for themes such as "gender," "privacy," "school," "positive," and "negative." The latter two refer to positive and negative experiences of going online. I wanted to ensure that my early themes were inclusive: I was not out to confirm any presaged hypotheses about the morose conditions facing youth today (Barbour 2008, 238; Strauss and Corbin 1990). In short, these themes were geared to guide me as I began reading through interview transcripts, and were malleable with respect to emerging topics. After some initial pilot interviews were transcribed and received, several other overarching areas emerged, including "advice to students," "parental monitoring" (which quickly became a highly prescient topic), and "social media platforms" (capturing, often during the beginning of the discussion, a general exploration of what social media participants are using, how frequently, and for what purposes).

What sometimes challenges qualitative researchers at this point is determining the unit of analysis to code (see Berg 2001, 244), and how to get the ball rolling in terms of the creation of codes or, within NVivo, coding nodes. For focus groups I usually select as a unit of analysis a range of dialogue that began with a question posed by the interviewer and the various exchanges that follow, often involving multiple participants, up to the point of a change of topic by either the interviewer or participants themselves. For focus group discussions, this allows me to not only capture particular substantive themes, but also the dynamics of dialogue between participants themselves, which may be relevant in, for instance, an examination of conversation analysis. As for the coding itself, for the first couple of interviews I read the transcripts in full and then, after coffee, set things aside and foreground other tasks. Sometimes important connections are made while your thinking is focused elsewhere. When I get back to research after leaving it for a while, I often catch angles that I missed the first time I read a transcript.

When I am ready to code, I simply jump in, ignoring my trepidations about whether the codes I am creating will ultimately be useful. What is handy about NVivo is that the relevancy of codes emerges through *time and focus*. Take one example: I ran across a reference to "kids today" from the teens being interviewed. I found this interesting as it perhaps indicates a certain role distancing. I named the code something that would trigger my memory later on: "kids today referencing kids today." To date I only have this code referred to once during one group across the total currently coded (28). In the grand scheme of things, then, this does not seem to be very relevant to the "big picture" that is emerging; but if other groups reveal similar role distancing–type statements, I may create a new folder and move the coded material (in NVivo, coding nodes) to it. NVivo usefully displays both the number of groups (e.g., interviews, or, in this case, focus groups) where a code is applied as well as the coding references *across* all groups. Certain themes are already, for my dataset, clearly dominating above all others. These include "self-responsibilization" (i.e., references to self-control in response to cyber-risk and -surveillance), "front and back stage" (i.e., the dramaturgical presentation of cyber-self in everyday life), and "interviewing each other" (i.e., where participants begin interviewing each other, producing a fascinating knowledge exchange dynamic). When writing up findings, I will be able to easily refer to my NVivo summarized list of codes to report, say, that across 28 groups, 16 groups made 33 references to drama being specific to female teens, not males.

What is essential and, I argue, most exciting, about the analysis phase of research is linking codes with participant and/or group attributes. Using NVivo, the focus groups for my research were categorized by age (for my purposes, I created age ranges that help to identify trends among junior, middle, and senior adolescents), gender (male or female, though for other projects one could add other inclusive attributes), and location (in this case, eastern or western Canada). Although technical sounding, NVivo has a "query" feature called "matrix code" where I can enter particular nodes or themes and view patterns according to the attributes I have specified (e.g., whether more references are made to concerns over privacy by males or females, as participants age). One important thing to note here—regardless of whether software is used or not—is that a theme's dominance across various demographic attributes needs to be situated and properly contextualized. If I conduct 10 one-to-one interviews, 7 of them with women, and I run an analysis and find a significantly greater number of references to a particular theme or concept, that finding needs to be properly qualified given the greater proportion of women in the sample. This leads back to the point that data analysis and implications for future coding and analysis begin when planning research design (Ruona 2005, 237). Along with others (Barbour 2008, 215; Silverman 1993), I argue that some simple counting practices are very useful for indicating general trends in the data and enhancing others' confidence in your interpretation of the data. What matters, of course, are the interpretive insights gleaned from participant statements. Examining both quantitative trends to highlight overarching patterns and qualitative insights to mine lived experiences leads to thicker descriptions that simultaneously address breadth and depth. For example, my analysis reveals that a majority of statements expressing concern over how others, especially employers, perceive one's digital presence is concentrated with senior adolescents and undergraduate students. These are students who will soon be entering the work force. When examined in greater detail, a variety of angles emerge in these discussions related to privacy, surveillance, and self-responsibilization. Linkages to extant theoretical frameworks emerge as these connections are made. For instance, I found some resonance with examinations of youth and online privacy that take up a governmentality framework, though I will be using my own data to suggest ways that this approach may limit our understanding of the lived experiences of youth as they engage with various risks online. The important point is not to aim to reinvent the wheel, so to speak, but to find where your data opens spaces for a contribution that pivots from what we currently know.

To conclude, there is simply no substitute for data analysis; you must jump in and learn from the experience of conducting research itself, rather than reading what is written about conducting research (including this chapter!). Whether you are able to use computer software or not, I emphasize the importance of vacillating between the trees and the forest, appreciating that data analysis begins well before formal data is received, and, above all, remembering to include others in your journey in order to make sense of your data. Now put this away and get a coffee.

CRAFTING QUALITATIVE RESEARCH EXERCISES

1. Considering a qualitative project you have in mind, what theoretical frameworks do you think are likely to apply and help make sense of your data? Run a Google Scholar search on your topic and take note of the theories that researchers have drawn on to situate their findings. Are they different from the one(s) you had in mind? In what ways could you incorporate them? Do you identify any gaps in the theoretical literature on your topic?

2.   Once you have some data to work with, and some provisional codes and themes emerging, ask yourself if anything in your data does not fit with your hypotheses or ideas about the data, i.e., are there any "outliers" that deviate from your expectations? Do these warrant ignoring, or are they perhaps even more relevant given that they stand out? Discuss your findings with your professor, supervisor, or another student.

3.   If you have some data collected, have a go at creating some detailed memos as you review the data. Make notes on anything you find relevant—concepts, sociological insights, theoretical connections, methodological problems, and so on. Set the work aside for a week, and review again the data and your memos. Do you notice anything new? Are the notes still relevant or have you changed your mind about anything you've written? Try this exercise again as you get into the later stages of data analysis.

4.   If you already have data with some provisional codes applied, or even some unanalyzed data, take an excerpt and show it to someone else (e.g., your professor, a supervisor, another student, a friend) and see whether they identify the same themes and/or concepts as you do. For points of disagreement, discuss why you disagree and see if you can come to a resolution. Was the discussion useful regarding your confidence in interpreting the data? Consider why or why not.

REFERENCES

Adorjan, Michael. 2016. "The Ethical Imagination: Reflections on Conducting Research in Hong Kong." In *Engaging with Ethics in International Criminological Research*, edited by Michael Adorjan and Rose Ricciardelli, 36–51 New York: Routledge.

Adorjan, Michael, and Rose Ricciardelli. 2016. *Engaging with Ethics in International Criminological Research*. New York: Routledge.

Bailey, Jane, and Valerie Steeves. 2015. *eGirls, eCitizens*. Ottawa: University of Ottawa Press.

Bailey, Jane, Valerie Steeves, Jacquelyn Burkell, and Priscilla Regan. 2013. "Negotiating with Gender Stereotypes on Social Networking Sites: From 'Bicycle Face' to Facebook." *Journal of Communication Inquiry* 37 (2): 91–112.

Barbour, Rosaline. 2008. *Introducing Qualitative Research*. London: Sage.

Berg, Bruce. 2001. *Qualitative Research Methods for the Social Sciences*. 4th ed. Boston: Allyn and Bacon.

Booth, Wayne, Gregory Colomb, and Joseph Williams. 2008. *The Craft of Research*. 3rd ed. Chicago: University of Chicago Press.

boyd, danah. 2014. *It's Complicated: The Social Lives of Networked Teens*. London: Yale University Press.

Coffey, Amanda, and Paul Atkinson. 1996. *Making Sense of Qualitative Data*. Thousand Oaks, CA: Sage.

Deutsch, Nancy. 2004. "Positionality and the Pen: Reflections on the Process of Becoming a Feminist Writer and Researcher." *Qualitative Inquiry* 10 (6): 885–902.

Ellingson, Laura. 2011. "Analysis and Representation across the Continuum." In *The Sage Handbook of Qualitative Research*, 4th ed., edited by Norman Denzin and Yvonna Lincoln, 595–610. London: Sage.

Karaian, Lara. 2013. "Policing 'Sexting': Responsibilization, Respectability and Sexual Subjectivity in Child Protection/Crime Prevention Responses to Teenagers' Digital Sexual Expression." *Theoretical Criminology* 18 (3): 282–99. http://tcr.sagepub.com/content/early/2013/09/26/1362480613504331.

Koskela, Hille. 2006. "'The Other Side of Surveillance': Webcams, Power and Agency." In *Theorizing Surveillance: The Panopticon and Beyond*, edited by David Lyon, 163–81. Cullompton, Devon, UK: Willan Publishing.

Livingstone, Sonia. 2008. "Taking Risky Opportunities in Youthful Content Creation: Teenagers' Use of Social Networking Sites for Intimacy, Privacy and Self-Expression." *New Media and Society* 10 (3): 393–411.

Madriz, Esther. 2000. "Focus Groups in Feminist Research." In *Handbook of Qualitative Research*, 2nd ed., edited by Norman Denzin and Yvonna Lincoln, 835–50. Thousand Oaks, CA: Sage.

Miles, Matthew, A. Michael Huberman, and Johnny Saldana. 2014. *Qualitative Data Analysis: A Methods Sourcebook*. 3rd ed. Los Angeles: Sage.

Morgan, David. 1997. *Focus Groups as Qualitative Research*. 2nd ed. Thousand Oaks, CA: Sage.

Pawluch, Dorothy, William Shaffir, and Charlene Miall. 2005. *Doing Ethnography: Studying Everyday Life*. Toronto: Canadian Scholars' Press.

Regan, Priscilla, and Diana Sweet. 2015. "Girls and Online Drama: Aggression, Surveillance, or Entertainment?" In *eGirls, eCitizens*, edited by Jane Bailey and Valerie Steeves, 175–97. Ottawa: University of Ottawa Press.

Ruona, Wendy. 2005. "Analyzing Qualitative Data." In *Research in Organizations: Foundations and Methods of Inquiry*, edited by Richard A. Swanson and Elwood F. Holton III, 233–63. San Francisco: Berrett-Koehler Publishers.

Silverman, David. 1993. *Interpreting Qualitative Data: Methods of Analyzing Talk, Text and Interaction*. London: Sage.

Stewart, David, Prem Shamdasani, and Dennis Rook. 2007. *Focus Groups, Theory and Practice*. 2nd ed. London: Sage.

Strauss, Anselm. 1987. *Qualitative Analysis for Social Scientists*. New York: Cambridge.

Strauss, Anselm, and Juliet Corbin. 1990. *Basics of Qualitative Research: Grounded Theory Procedures and Techniques*. Newbury Park, CA: Sage.

34 "Dilemmas of Voice" in Community-Based HIV Research

Jeffrey P. Aguinaldo

Community-based research (CBR) has gained popularity in Canadian social science research. Grounded in the principles of community participation and local knowledge, CBR is an approach that attempts to engage community members as experts in their own lives and on their own terms (Flicker 2008). Many HIV researchers in Canada have taken up CBR as a critical enterprise to resist the supremacy of psycho-behavioural methods in social research on HIV. Community-based HIV research (CBHR), as a form of resistance, has been accomplished in two ways. The first involves the active participation throughout the research process of those affected by HIV. This principle is enshrined in key policies such as the *Greater Involvement of People Living With HIV/AIDS* (UNAIDS 1999) that I have committed to in my own CBHR. The second, which is the focus of this chapter, is the use of in-depth interviews and qualitative analysis to privilege the perspectives of research participants.

In this chapter, I engage in a discussion of the qualitative analytic assumptions upon which CBHR is based. My central concern is with the tensions that arise from CBHR's core commitment to privilege the perspectives of research participants while promoting the aims of critical HIV research. By "critical HIV research," I am referring to the explicit rejection of individualizing and victim-blaming notions inherent in mainstream public health HIV research and the adoption of a social determinants of health approach that advocates for social change to address the needs of people affected by HIV. While I focus my discussion within the context of CBHR, clearly there is broader applicability to the breadth of (critical) qualitative research that has as its goal the "privileging," "prioritizing," or "validating" of participants' perspectives. Nevertheless, the issues I raise in this chapter are rather acute for community-based researchers who rely primarily on what participants share during a qualitative research interview to inform community health initiatives and policy reform.

In what follows, I first articulate the assumptions that guide qualitative analysis in CBR and their adoption in CBHR. I then present data that would pose dilemmas for the community-based HIV researcher who commits to these assumptions and I problematize the ways community-based HIV researchers have dealt with these dilemmas. Finally, I offer an alternative qualitative analytic framework, characterizable as social constructionism, as a possible way forward. I conclude the chapter with the broader implications for novice qualitative researchers both within and beyond CBHR.

QUALITATIVE ANALYSIS AND CBHR

To privilege the perspectives of research participants, CBR relies on a set of analytic assumptions about what qualitative data represents and what constitutes analysis. Harper, Jamil, and Wilson presume data collected through qualitative interviews provide direct access to "the voices and life experiences" (2007, 112) of their participants. Doing qualitative analysis typically involves summarizing data into categories or themes and, in the case of Trans PULSE Project—a CBR project examining the health consequences of discrimination and social exclusion on transgender people—direct quotes from participants are used "to give priority to the voices and lived experiences of" (Bauer et al. 2009, 350) participants and their constituencies. Some community-based researchers advocate that qualitative analyses be commensurable with the interpretations of the research participants (Ristock and Pennell 1996). In treating qualitative data in this way, qualitative analysts function simply as conduits for participants' perspectives to guide and direct social action. Such an analytic approach positions research participants as best suited to describe the conditions of their lives and to represent community needs. For some researchers, then, qualitative analyses that privilege participants' perspectives are seen to be a form of activism that can give voice to previously ignored members of society; however, this approach to qualitative analysis is not without its challenges.

DILEMMAS OF VOICE

Of the participants I have interviewed for a range of qualitative studies on HIV, many do not conceive of their health or their communities in social or political terms. Some do not believe that their social contexts impede or facilitate well-being. Most overtly reject their gender, race, class, or sexuality as determinants of their health. In fact, most participants I interview do not engage in a radical analysis at all. On occasion, participants offer narratives such as these (quoted from Aguinaldo 2012, 771):

> There's also a good percentage of the gay population, and I don't know if this would be like my age, but I know from like older people, like, a lot of guys in their 30s and 40s and things like that … just, really don't care anymore. They have no desire to have safe sex. First or last or never. They just don't care. And I mean a lot of them probably are already HIV positive anyway. (Ryan, gay, HIV negative)

> If you're healthy, you won't get sick. The people that get sick from it [unsafe sex]
> are already sick. And if you let somebody cum up your ass, you deserve to die.
> (Timothy, gay, HIV positive)

These represent just some of the data I constantly face. Data of this type pose what I
call "dilemmas of voice" and represent, in these cases, participants' perspectives that a
research analyst might consider problematic and that one should not simply privilege.

Such dilemmas are not specific to the data I have collected. Indeed, such accounts
abound from those who purport to speak on behalf of their (marginalized) communities.
For example, in an autobiography, Terri Webb, a self-identified male-to-female transsexual, writes,

> We pretend to be other than we are. Many transsexuals claim to be women when
> we are in fact men. Whereas a couple of years ago I could only speak for myself
> when stating this view, now I feel able to speak for all male-to-female transsexuals
> when I say that without any doubt we are men, albeit men with a desperate need to
> be women. (1996, 190)

In a study on lesbian identities, Jane states,

> I suspect we [lesbians] are in a slightly retarded state. Well "retarded" is perhaps not
> quite right. It's a fear, an inability to relate to the opposite sex. There's nothing you
> can do about it. (Kitzinger 1987, 119)

To be perfectly honest, I would find it positively disastrous to prioritize these participants' perspectives in my research and I am no longer willing to privilege uncritically
what participants say during a qualitative research interview.

Feminist scholars (e.g., Kitzinger 2004) have theorized the relationship between
what is said during a qualitative research interview and what it is assumed to represent,
but these discussions have not significantly informed CBHR methodological discussions in Canada. Only a few Canadian researchers have been diligent in documenting
the problems of dilemmas of voice in CBHR. In a reflexive discussion on the Positive
Youth Project, Flicker reports not believing one of her research participants. She "knew"
intuitively that "something did not make sense" and that "something was amiss" (2004,
531). She evaluated the participant's account as "highly unlikely" (2004, 531) because it
did not correspond with the existing medical literature on the experience of HIV. Upon
weighing the methodological choices available to her, she decided during the analysis
to be "very attentive to which 'pieces of data' came from his interview" (2004, 534). I
take her "attentiveness" to mean she was selective about which of this participant's data
to include in the analysis. Of course, this is one pragmatic decision that a community-
based HIV researcher might make and one that Flicker chose to do with approval from

the advisory committee of the project. From a CBHR perspective, I might have done the same. There are nevertheless a number of problems in treating the data in this way.

First, if CBHR assumes what participants say as providing direct access to the perspectives of participants, then selective attention to the data is simply the silencing of particular perspectives. Second, in judging the truthfulness of participants' claims, community-based HIV researchers, as Flicker herself rightly points out, assert themselves as the "arbitrator of truth" (2004, 534) and no longer as conduits for participants' perspectives. Third, by omitting data because that data do not fit the established accounts in the medical literature, she affirms the epistemological authority of medical science as offering "the truth about HIV." In short, community-based HIV researchers violate core commitments of CBR to manage dilemmas of voice.

It is important to note that if Flicker's work features prominently in my discussion, it is only because she is committed to principles of transparency. She has been fully reflexive in her role in numerous CBHR projects and is diligent in redressing the challenges she faces as a researcher. Elsewhere, she has documented the barriers to community members' full participation in CBHR (Flicker 2008). Meanwhile, others have not been so forthcoming with their CBHR practices, thereby preventing interrogation of their work. To single out Flicker or her scholarship as somehow exceptional in these regards serves only to obscure what I take to be a more pervasive problem in CBHR.

THE WAY FORWARD

The problem, as I see it, is not what research participants might share during a qualitative interview; rather, it is that community-based HIV researchers commit to analytic assumptions that are untenable given the realities of what research participants may say. CBHR rests upon an essentialist or realist approach to qualitative data. It treats what participants say as transparently reflecting their perspectives, or, in some cases, their community's perspectives. Researchers who take up this assumption share a positivist commitment with traditional public health research that there is a "correct" or objective standpoint from which the truth (about community, health, HIV, etc.) can be told; however, CBHR shifts epistemological authority from the (often academic) researcher to the research participants. For this to work within a CBHR context, researchers must rely on romanticized notions of "the community" and idealize research participants to "say the right thing." This places researchers in a bind when participants do not "say the right thing." And when this happens, community-based HIV researchers seemingly abandon their own principled commitments in order to deal with the realities of the data.

Following others (see Kitzinger and Wilkinson 1997), I recommend that community-based HIV researchers consider a social constructionist approach to data analysis. In this approach, one should not treat what participants say as reflective of an unassailable truth, but rather as one of many interpretations. There is no single truth that can be told, only multiple ways of constructing lives, communities, and HIV. Contradictory and even patently "false" accounts can be useful for understanding their social and political significance; thus, "analysis" is not the unveiling of objective facts about the world proffered by all-knowing research participants. Rather, it is the interrogation of the different ways people construct their reality. This places the onus on the researcher to articulate the value judgments upon which particular accounts are evaluated and, by extension, the broader politics the research project seeks to promote. This approach to analysis in which all knowledge claims are held suspect and open to critical interrogation is perhaps the hallmark of good rigorous scholarship and it is an approach from which I think CBHR would likely benefit. If anything, this approach offers CBHR concrete tools to deal with the types of data I have presented here.

Taking a social constructionist approach to qualitative analysis would look something like this: An analyst would present the range of accounts of their participants, even those a critical observer may find problematic. Under the assumption that all truth claims are suspect and open to interrogation, analysts would evaluate all accounts and, in some cases, disagree (respectfully) with those with which they are at odds. The analyst must then provide a radical alternative to those perspectives they deem problematic. The role of analysis is not to validate only those perspectives that analysts believe to be "true." Instead, analysis articulates the social and political implications of each perspective and advances those that the analyst believes to be aligned with the broader vision of the research politics.

Simply privileging the perspectives of Ryan and Timothy is not a critical approach to HIV. And yet, ignoring their perspectives is not analysis. So what, then, can be gleaned through an analysis of Ryan and Timothy's talk? Both Ryan and Timothy construct HIV in strictly behavioural terms. At least some members of the community to which Ryan's and Timothy claim membership individualize their own and their community's sexual health. In doing so, community members reproduce through their talk a social world where HIV transmission is conceived not as interactional phenomena, influenced by the myriad contexts that shape people's lives, but as personal fault and failure. The discursive effect of these types of accounting practices privatize the transmission of HIV and foreclose interventions aimed outward toward the social realm.

The findings from such an analysis are not the bald claims that gay men in fact "don't want to use condoms" or that people "deserve to die" if they choose not to use condoms. Rather, it is that community members capitulate to the social and political forces that oppress them. The action potential from such findings is to challenge these widely held taken-for-granted assumptions about the causes of health. In their place, researchers should advance what they see as an explicit critical perspective on HIV; one that, for example, promotes a social determinants approach, which recognizes the role that the social context plays in people's sexual health. It is my recommendation, then, that social constructionism be one concrete analytic practice that community-based HIV researchers use to address dilemmas of voice.

CONCLUSION

Through this chapter, I hope to compel novice researchers to consider the foundational assumptions upon which their own qualitative analyses are based. For community-based qualitative researchers, qualitative analysis should do more than merely privilege the perspectives of their participants. Critical scholarship actively challenges taken-for-granted assumptions about the social world. By extension, critical HIV research should challenge taken-for-granted assumptions about HIV. It should promote the need for HIV prevention campaigns irrespective of Ryan's claim that gay men have no desire to use condoms. It should advocate for accessible treatments for HIV-positive people irrespective of Timothy's claim that people who do not use condoms deserve to die. Put simply, I argue that CBHR (if it is indeed a critical enterprise) should advance the need for HIV prevention and treatment, not because research participants necessarily say so, but because these embody the values and politics of the society in which we should live. In doing so, CBHR is reframed to prioritize, not participants' perspectives per se, but critical politics and health equity despite what participants may share during a qualitative research interview.

CRAFTING QUALITATIVE RESEARCH EXERCISES

1. This chapter offers social constructionism as a panacea for the dilemmas that arise from an essentialist approach to data analysis. Nevertheless, there are costs of a social constructionist approach for critical inquiry. Identify the costs and benefits of an essentialist approach and a social constructionist approach to qualitative analysis for critical inquiry.

2. Apply an essentialist and then a social constructionist analytic approach to the account provided by Terri Webb (1996) in this chapter. Identify the concrete steps for each approach. How are these approaches procedurally similar and distinct from one another?

3. Many researchers conduct qualitative research as a form of critical inquiry on and for marginalized communities. Analyze the data provided by Jane (Kitzinger 1987) in this chapter. How might what Jane shared be used to promote a critical perspective on lesbian identities and LGBT identities more generally? In answering this question, develop your own understanding of what you mean by "critical" and how your analysis of Jane's data realizes that understanding.

4. The issue of "whose perspective" we privilege through our research is a long-standing quandary among expert and novice qualitative researchers. Think

through your own social and political principles and values that you hope to achieve through your (qualitative) research. How might an essentialist *and* a social constructionist approach to qualitative analysis achieve those commitments?

REFERENCES

Aguinaldo, Jeffrey, P. 2012. "Qualitative Analysis in Gay Men's Health Research: Comparing Thematic, Critical Discourse, and Conversation Analysis." *Journal of Homosexuality* 59 (6): 765–87. https://doi.org/10.1080/00918369.2012.694753.

Bauer, Greta R., Rebecca Hammond, Robb Travers, Matthias Kaay, Karin M. Hahenadel, and Michelle Boyce. 2009. "'I Don't Think This Is Theoretical; This Is Our Lives': How Erasure Impacts Health Care for Transgender People." *Journal of the Association of Nurses in AIDS Care* 20 (5): 348–61.

Flicker, Sarah. 2004. "'Ask Me No Secrets, I'll Tell You No Lies': What Happens When a Respondent's Story Makes No Sense." *Qualitative Report* 9 (3): 528–37. http://www.nova.edu/ssss/QR/QR9-3/flicker.pdf.

Flicker, Sarah. 2008. "Who Benefits from Community-Based Participatory Research? A Case Study of the Positive Youth Project." *Health Education and Behavior* 35 (1): 70–86.

Harper, Gary W., Omar Bashir Jamil, and Bianca D. M. Wilson. 2007. "Collaborative Community-Based Research as Activism: Giving Voice and Hope to Lesbian, Gay, and Bisexual Youth." *Journal of Gay and Lesbian Psychotherapy* 11 (3/4): 99–119.

Kitzinger, Celia. 1987. *The Social Construction of Lesbianism*. London: Sage.

Kitzinger, Celia. 2004. "Feminist Approaches." In *Qualitative Research Practice*, edited by Clive Seal, Giampietro Gobo, Jaber F. Gubrium, and David Silverman, 125–40. London: Sage.

Kitzinger, Celia, and Sue Wilkinson. 1997. "Validating Women's Experience? Dilemmas in Feminist Research." *Feminism and Psychology* 7 (4): 566–74.

Ristock, Janice L., and Joan Pennell. 1996. *Community Research as Empowerment: Feminist Links, Postmodern Interruptions*. New York: Oxford University Press.

UNAIDS. 1999. *From Principle to Practice: Greater Involvement of People Living With or Affected By HIV/AIDS (GIPA)*. Geneva: UNAIDS.

Webb, Terri. 1996. "Autobiographical Fragments from a Transsexual Activist." In *Blending Genders: Social Aspects of Cross-Dressing and Sex-Changing*, edited by Richard Ekins and Dave King, 190–95. London: Routledge.

35 Analyzing Materiality

Carrie B. Sanders and Lisa-Jo K. van den Scott

INTRODUCTION

Everyday life involves myriad interactions with material objects. The social and the material are not independent, but instead they make up each other. In fact, material artifacts incorporate the various political subjectivities, norms, and values of their designers and users (Amicelle, Aradau, and Jeandesboz 2015). We can see the political ideas in the social shaping of technologies everywhere around us. For example, park benches that have dividers in them or are circular in shape allow people to sit in the park, but prohibit people from being able to sleep in the park. This is just one example of how the values, norms, and political ideas of designers can become embedded in objects.

While designers influence the shape, use, and functionality of materiality, so too do the actions of users. Material objects, such as park benches, do not have objective meanings, but instead their *meaning*, *value*, and *purpose* arise through their very adoption and use. What can be designed for one purpose, through its use, can come to serve a completely different function. A drinking glass, for example, might be turned upside down and used to cut biscuits from dough. Understanding and making sense of social life requires researchers to be attentive not only to human actions and meaning-making processes, but also their interactions with objects and material culture.

We believe that ethnography provides "analytic leverage" (van den Scott, Sanders, and Puddephatt 2016) for analyzing and theorizing human-object relations, as it enables researchers to capture the messy complexities of social life. This social life includes human actors, objects, and materiality, as well as the discourses embedded within the situation of interest, all of which need to be identified and theorized (Clarke 2005, xxxv). An ethnographic inductive approach is attentive to the interactions and processes involved in human-object relations.

While there are numerous works dedicated to describing the methodological process of data collection and materiality, there are fewer resources available for understanding how to analyze *human-object relations and material culture*. How does one stay analytically attentive to the dynamic relation between humans and objects? How do we analyze and theorize about the ways in which (1) humans get inside of and shape objects and materiality, and (2) the ways in which objects and materiality, through their use, shape human actions and social structures? Our chapter addresses these questions by drawing on our respective ethnographic research studies on human-object interactions.

We begin by describing our approach to coding and memoing. We then introduce a technique called situational analysis, which we found helpful in theorizing materiality in human-object relations. Next, we look at the way in which Sanders employed situational analysis to understand how the on-the-ground use of emergency technologies shaped and affected the collaborative work practices of police, fire, and emergency medical services. We then look at the way van den Scott connected interactions with how people relate to the material in an Inuit village. Despite vast differences in setting, memos and situational analysis were integral for assisting each researcher to attend to the human-object relations too often omitted or overlooked, despite their relevance to the social experience.

CODING

As Sanders and van den Scott each collected field notes and interview transcripts, they began the process of coding their data by looking for themes and noting, or coding, chunks of data accordingly (van den Hoonaard 2014, 159–62). We engaged in three processes of coding: open, focused, and analytic. Open coding involved coding the transcripts and texts in manageable chunks (e.g., line-by-line or incident-to-incident) for key themes, concepts, and discourses. These codes were given descriptive names that portrayed the activities or meanings the participants brought to them. For example, when van den Scott (2009) was coding her interviews about airplane travel in the Arctic, she found the theme of North versus South frequently emerged. As patterns gradually emerged and relevant themes were identified, she shifted to "focused coding," which primarily entailed fleshing out the broader themes. Focused coding was a process of "continual refinement" (Glaser and Strauss 1967) that drew links to other theoretical findings and orientations within the social sciences. When van den Scott read through her data again, she found that participants understood one difference to be centred on language and applied more focused codes. For example, "street language" was her code for when they talked about what language was predominantly used in street interactions. Once these two phases of coding were completed, she began to analyze her data by engaging in "analytic coding" (Glaser and Strauss 1967). Analytic coding involved comparing codes to see where similarities and differences lay, and incorporated intense interpretation and reflection on the meaning of coded text. Van den Scott was able to flesh out how airplane travel isolated different groups in the Arctic such that her participants viewed a town further north than theirs as being more "Southern" due to the prevalence of English as the language of the streets. They understood the higher airplane traffic as influencing the use of English in everyday interactions.

MEMO WRITING

Memo writing was integral throughout the process and enabled Sanders and van den Scott each to think through her own data and to identify relationships among her data. Throughout the research, they kept small notebooks with them at all times so they could write any thoughts, questions, insights, and concerns that might arise. While coding, memoing became more detailed. For example, while they read and coded the transcripts they would write about the connection among codes, and also links between each of their own codes and other theories or readings they had done previously. Memos also addressed areas of similarities or differences. This process of data analysis was how each author advanced her abstract coding to a more theoretical level (Charmaz 2014). It also identified areas where each needed further clarification and follow-up data collection.

SITUATIONAL ANALYSIS

The coding process, in many ways, treated the social and material as distinct, unrelated entities that did not adequately account for the complexity of the situation. Sanders and van den Scott wanted to be more analytically attentive to the role materiality played in the situation because material objects "structurally condition the interactions within the situation through their specific properties and requirements" (Clarke 1991, 139). They adopted Adele Clarke's situational analysis in order to identify and take into account all components of the situation, including human actors, objects, discourses, and silent actors (2005). One accomplishes situational analysis by creating maps that explicitly and intentionally include materiality. These situational maps lay out all the relevant parts of the scene so one can visualize what is going on overall, and are attentive to humans, objects, discourses, and cultural elements and analyze the relations among them (Clarke 2005). In what follows, two illustrations of Sanders's and van den Scott's individual experiences using situational analysis are provided.

(A) Emergency Technologies and the Work of Police, Fire, and Paramedics

The terrorist attacks on the World Trade Center in 2001 sparked Sanders's research interests in emergency response. Reports surfacing after the attacks claimed that police did not tell the fire department the second tower was going to collapse, and, as a result, hundreds of front-line emergency responders lost their lives in the line of duty. The *9/11 Commission Report* framed these deaths as resulting from "inadequate emergency communication interoperability" and made a number of recommendations—with information and communication sharing being at the forefront (National Commission on Terrorist Attacks 2004). Sanders's research sought to understand how emergency technologies, such as interoperable radios and records management systems, enable or constrain collaborative action among police, fire, and paramedics during multi-agency incidents (where more than one service responds).

Figure 35.1 is an example of an *abstract situational map* of a multi-agency incident in rural Canada. This map developed and continually changed throughout the research process as Sanders considered and added the following: Who and what things matter in the broad situation of emergency response? Who and what things matter in producing "response"? Eventually, her map identified rural police, volunteer firefighters, information technology designers, Bell Canada, records management systems, interoperable radio systems, computer-aided dispatch systems, and more as key actors and material objects.

After drawing the map, Sanders then sat down with her map and asked herself questions, such as what discourses, ideas, and concepts shape how different emergency

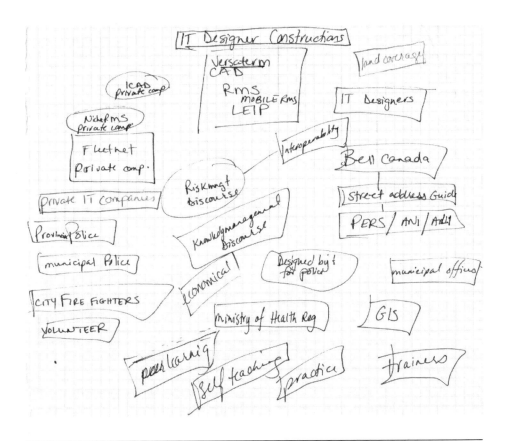

Figure 35.1: Messy Abstract Situational Map

workers and information technology designers think about, conceive of, and define emergency technologies, information sharing, and collaborative action? Figure 35.1 also identifies various discourses around risk management, knowledge management, and technologies as shaping discourses throughout rural multi-agency incidents.

This situational map is an abstract map that provided the opportunity for Sanders to see all of the discourses, objects, and actors involved in multi-agency incidents, as well as the relations and negotiations among them. Continually asking relational questions—how things relate to each other—helped to produce her maps. After she created these abstract maps, she then created ordered versions of the map for each case-study setting (see figure 35.2). She made several copies of the ordered maps so that she could think about her data in various ways. She drew lines from each position to each of the others to examine their relations. Meanwhile, she continued with her memo writing.

These maps proved most useful for two reasons. First, they provided a means for analyzing police, fire, and paramedics and their collective action within a multi-agency incident response. Second, because she had two case-study settings (rural and urban), producing multiple maps for both case study locations enabled a comparative analysis between the two organizational contexts.

Situational analysis enabled Sanders to uncover how the structural, cultural, and operational contexts of police, fire, and emergency medical services meant members of different organizations came to give meaning to emergency technologies differently. By finding a way to conceptualize the socio-material relations, her analysis illustrated how the hierarchical relations and organizational conflicts among police, fire, and paramedics were both played out and reinforced through the use of emergency technologies (Sanders 2014).

(B) Engaging with Technologies: Passive and Active Engagements

Van den Scott focused on the material culture of the house, and has since developed a sociology of walls. Her field site is a remote Inuit hamlet where housing has only been introduced in the last 50 years—before that the Inuit there had lived in igloos and tents. She wondered how they were developing meaning for the walls in this new context: How did living within walls affect them? How did they work to bring their culture "indoors" and define their space and themselves in that space? She employed situational analysis to help her attend to human-object interactions.

For example, van den Scott wrote each focused code, question, and emergent concept from her data on an index card (see figure 35.3). She was then able to position and reposition these cards in different orders and groupings over and over again. This way she could continually reorient her thinking around different sets of themes and relational questions.

Next, van den Scott organized her thinking into a more structured map. The index cards were grouped and regrouped until she felt she could develop a more formal argument about the patterns in her field site. She noticed that there were two

Rural Case Study

Individual Human Elements/Actors
Emergency call(er)

Nonhuman Elements/Actants
ICAD
ARISSII
Niche RMS
Niche MDT
Fleetnet and Municipal Radio
FirePro
ANI/ALI
CACC

Collective Human Elements/Actors
Communication workers
9-1-1 communication workers
Police communication workers
Fire communication workers

Discursive Constructions of Collective Actors
Authenticity/legitimation
Professionalism
Economics/many users
Police officers
Firefighters
Paramedics
IT designers

Temporal Elements
Tiered response
Major accident/critical situation
Natural disaster

Political/Economic Elements
Provincial Information Act
Volunteer
Provincial government
Regional government
Municipal government

Major Contested Issues/Debates
Hierarchical information sharing/information needs → police different info needs than EMS/fire
Varying importance/professionalism → varied information needs/perceived needs
Policies and procedures
Insiders/outsiders
What is critical/important information → understanding of work/needs to complete work

Implicated/Silent Actors
General public

Discursive Constructions of Nonhuman Actants
Risk management → emergency worker safety
Information sharing
Inter- and intra-operability

Symbolic Elements
Professionalism → pay/volunteer
Organizational control—i.e., provincial vs. volunteer
Public accountability
Emergency uniforms/civilian clothing
Independent and joint training

Spatial Elements
Geographical boundaries/coverage areas by the various emergency workers
Distance between emergency communication centres and corresponding workers

Related Discourses
Fast response
Protection

Figure 35.2: Abstract Organization Disconnect Map

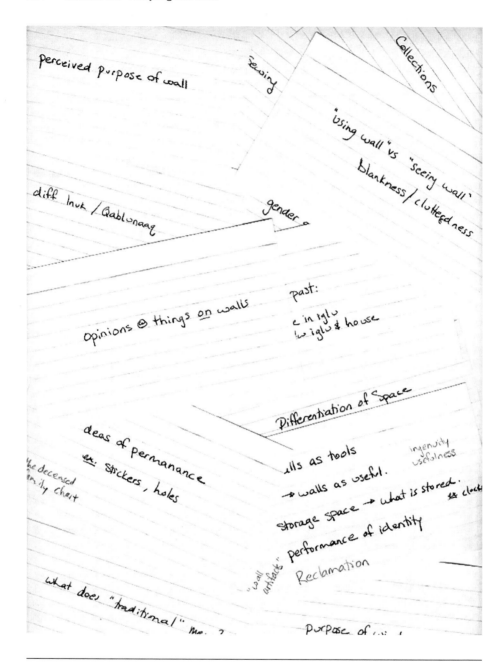

Figure 35.3: Themes and Emergent Concepts on Index Cards

main ways in which people related to their walls: passively and actively. Through mapping and memoing, she came to define passive engagements as "instances where technology itself brings consequences to bear on society, often resulting in human

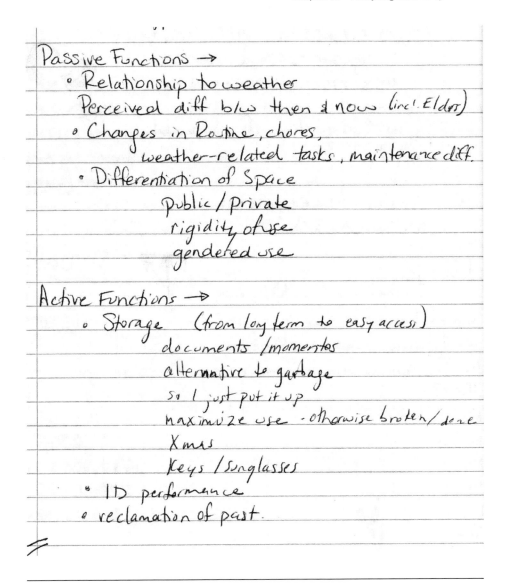

Figure 35.4: Passive and Active Engagements Being Fleshed Out

adjustments. Active engagements refer to interactions that are human-guided and that result in technological adjustments, either in form, function, or meaning" (2016, 33). While these are not dichotomous, she realizes that her participants often act as if they were. She drew a diagram to help progress her thinking (see figure 35.4).

She was later able to structure a book chapter around these concepts (van den Scott 2016), so, not only did this help her to understand her data better, but it also organized her presentation of the data in an approachable way.

CONCLUSION

As you begin to analyze your own social worlds, you will find it helpful to think beyond those who are actively present in the scene to include those who may be influenced and those who have influence over meanings and interactions in the scene. For example, designers of technologies imbue those technologies with their own understandings of the world that, in turn, affect their users. Sanders found that IT designers assumed that organizations, such as police and fire, would be eager to share emergency information; however, organizational cultures and policies impeded the sharing of information. Van den Scott found that the architects of the housing shipped up to the Inuit had inscribed their notions of public and private in how they divide the internal spaces. The Inuit living within the walls, however, adapted some of their behaviours to these internal room divisions, but also treated some rooms differently than the architects had anticipated.

Objects and material culture, as shown here, embody the subjectivities, norms, and values of their designers, which, in turn, shape and influence the social environment. Yet, as evidenced by our research, materiality, such as emergency response technologies and walls, holds no one inherent meaning or objective, but instead, "it is the use made of [them] that brings [them] into the life of the society" (Wagner-Pacifici and Schwartz 1991, 416). By employing situational analysis and engaging in ongoing memoing, we were able to deeply theorize the co-constituted nature of the social and the material.

CRAFTING QUALITATIVE RESEARCH EXERCISES

1.   Look around the room and pick one object. Think about who designed it and what some of their social, cultural, economic, or political assumptions may have been in the design process.

2.   Sitting in your classroom, look at the way space is organized and used. How does this reflect or reinforce the roles each person has in the classroom? How is power implicated in the design and use of classroom space?

3.   Watch the movie *The Gods Must Be Crazy* and be attentive to the way in which different social groups came to relate to the Coke bottle. How did their interactions produce meanings for the bottle?

4.   As you walk around campus, take note of how the doors are decorated (or not). Can you see any patterns? How may door decorations provide insight into the status, norms, and hierarchies associated with various positions?

5.   Look at your cellphone. Cellphones have changed a lot in the few years since their inception. How have they changed in shape and use? What social, economic, or cultural influences may have led to some of these changes?

REFERENCES

Amicelle, Anthony, Claudia Aradau, and Julien Jeandesboz. 2015. "Questioning Security Devices: Performativity, Resistance, Politics." *Security Dialogue* 46 (4): 293–306.

Charmaz, Kathy. 2014. *Constructing Grounded Theory*. Thousand Oaks, CA: Sage.

Clarke, A. 1991. "Social Worlds/Arenas Theory as Organizational Theory." In *Social Organization and Social Process: Essays in Honor of Anselm Strauss*, edited by David Maines, 119–58. New York: Aldine de Gruyter.

Clarke, Adele. 2005. *Situational Analysis: Grounded Theory after the Postmodern Turn*. Thousand Oaks, CA: Sage.

Glaser, Barney, and Anselm Strauss. 1967. *The Discovery of Grounded Theory: Strategies for Qualitative Research*. New York: Aldine de Gruyter.

National Commission on Terrorist Attacks upon the United States. 2004. *The 9/11 Commission Report: Final Report of the National Commission on Terrorist Attacks upon the United States*. New York: W. W. Norton.

Richards, Lyn. 2005. *Handling Qualitative Data: A Practical Guide*. London: Sage.

Sanders, Carrie B. 2014. "Need to Know vs. Need to Share: The Intersecting Work of Police, Fire and Paramedics." *Information, Communication and Society* 17 (4): 463–75.

van den Hoonaard, Deborah K. 2014. *Qualitative Research in Action*. 2nd ed. Don Mills, ON: Oxford University Press Canada.

van den Scott, Lisa-Jo K. 2009. "Cancelled, Aborted, Late, Mechanical: The Vagaries of Air Travel in Arviat, Nunavut, Canada." In *The Cultures of Alternative Mobilities: Routes Less Travelled*, edited by Phillip Vannini, 211–26. Surrey, UK: Ashgate.

van den Scott, Lisa-Jo K. 2016. "Mundane Technology in Non-Western Contexts: Wall-as-Tool." In *Sociology of Home: Belonging, Community and Place in the Canadian Context*, edited by Gillian Anderson, Joseph Moore, and Laura Suski, 33–54. Toronto: Canadian Scholars' Press.

van den Scott, Lisa-Jo, Carrie B. Sanders, and Antony Puddephatt. 2016. "Reconceptualizing Users through Rich Ethnographic Accounts." In *Handbook of Science and Technology Studies*, 4th ed., edited by Clark Miller, Ulrike Felt, Laurel Smith-Doerr, and Rayvon Fouché, 501–28. Cambridge, MA: MIT Press.

Wagner-Pacifici, Robin, and Barry Schwartz. 1991. "The Vietnam Veterans Memorial: Commemorating a Difficult Past." *American Journal of Sociology* 97 (2): 376–420.

36 Tree Drawings: Visual Analysis and Representation of Queer Activist Life History Research

Susan Diane

INTRODUCTION

An example of an arts-informed analysis (Cole and Knowles 2008), this chapter describes the intuitive drawing of trees as a heuristic analytical device in a qualitative research doctoral thesis. These freehand tree drawings were beneficial to the analysis, but then became integral to the representation of this life history research with queer women activists. The messiness and chaos of data collection and analysis became streamlined into roots, trunks, and branches that were labeled with each participant's interview data. A specific species of tree became a metaphor in the interpretive writing and representation of each unique life history. These life stories moved from their ethnocultural roots, through oppression(s) on trunks of childhoods, to the leafy branching out into queer/feminist, world-making activism (Berlant and Warner 1998; Zerilli 2005). My autoethnographic writing style led to my own activist/researcher life history becoming a drawing following this organic and chronological tree structure. By outlining my creative process in this chapter, I hope to encourage students and other researchers to consider ways that an arts-informed approach might be helpful in their own qualitative projects.

TREE DRAWING AS A HEURISTIC

Data analysis, to me, is the ultimate crunch time in the research process. Is there anything of importance or even of interest in the enormous collection of hard-won data? Has all the work of reading literature, proposal and ethics review writing, participant finding, interviewing, and transcribing been worth it? What is the research saying or not saying? This stage can become stressful as meaning-making is paramount in the research process.

In my doctoral life-history research data, there were pages of transcripts from interviews plus many photographs and artifacts from the personal and professional lives of my queer women activist participants. Cole and Knowles (2001, 98) comment on "the importance of developing a system or scheme that will make manageable the potentially overwhelming amount of material a life history researcher is likely to accumulate." I attempted to utilize a more traditional technique of interview data analysis by preparing hard copies of my transcribed interviews with an empty column on the right-hand side. Here I made notes of important phrases and recurring topics. I used sticky notes in different colours for different recurring themes. This led to knowing my data well, yet I felt frustrated as I did not see an obvious path to meaning-making.

I had discerned a pattern in the way each participant's heritage, the historical roots of their ethnocultural and socio-economic backgrounds, were often reflected in the directions that their adult activist endeavours took. An example would be that someone who had experienced racism and whose relatives had historically been subjected to racism with severe socio-economic and life-damaging consequences became an activist in the fight against racism in Canada. As I contemplated this idea of roots and how these later branched out to activist projects, the image of a winter deciduous tree came to mind.

I doodled this in pencil on a scrap piece of paper. As I looked at the drawing, it dawned on me that both their heritage and life experiences in their respective childhood stories had been very influential in their later careers of activism. I drew a knot on the penciled tree as I thought of the pain in some of the childhood stories I had witnessed. I mentioned to my office mate that I wanted to draw a tree and label it with information from my participant's data. She pulled a piece of bristol board from a corner of the office and told me to go for it; thus, a drawing from the roots of heritage, moving up the trunk of childhood, into the multiple branches of education/work/activism came into being. Figure 36.1 is the first tree drawing.

A dialectical process developed between my first participant's life stories in the transcripts, and my drawing of the tree structure with notations on it. At the time it seemed very experimental, a trial-and-error method. I did not know what I was doing exactly, yet I kept going as the data was finally becoming ordered and making meaningful connections for me. Besides noting life events on the tree in chronological order, I began including the dates and geographical locations along the right margin. In the left margin I then labelled themes and literature that resonated with the events on the tree. For example, the feminist world-building (Zerilli 2005) and queer world-making (Berlant and Warner 1998) literatures were significant when considering my participants' activities in the branches of their adult careers/activism.

Once I was finished this first tree drawing, I had no idea what to do next. With trepidation I decided to take the drawing to my co-supervisor. She pointed out that I had made interpretative decisions about what was important in my data as I placed notations on the tree. The next step, she concluded, was to write about the participant's life history guided by this drawing. She used the word *heuristic* in discussing my tree drawing. *Heuristic* is defined as "of or relating to a usually speculative formulation serving as a guide in the investigation or solution of a problem" (American Heritage Dictionary of the English Language 2016); thus, the tree drawing was a heuristic device that helped to solve my problem of organizing and making meaning from my research data.

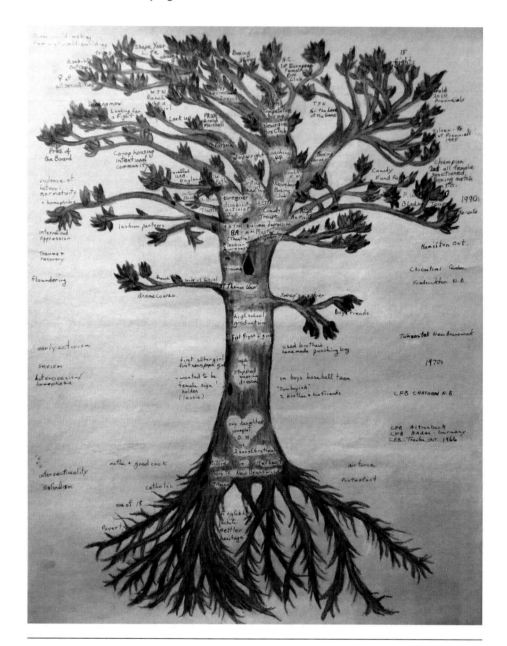

Figure 36.1: Tree Drawing #1

Although the tree seemed an epiphany out of nowhere, upon reflection I saw a mix of influences that came together in an intuitive fashion. Why would a tree heuristic occur to me as opposed to any other tool or visual and representational metaphor?

INFLUENCES OF CHRONOLOGY, ORGANICITY, AND THERAPY

The life history of an individual does have a chronological and longitudinal journey. Life begins at birth and continues through the years of lived experience. In the case of my life history work, the stories started before my participants' births with descriptions about their parents' lives and their geographical, socio-cultural, and historical environments. I started my research interviews cognizant of this chronological order and I attempted to use Brotman and Kraniou's (1999) "life lines" as a method, where "each woman was asked to identify significant events, memories, and relationships in her life starting from her birth and moving through her life chronologically on a sheet of paper on which a straight line was drawn" (424). I had asked my participants to start the "life line" before birth, knowing the vital importance of their contextual environments, such as their heritage, geographical locations, and the social, political, and historical events individuals are born into and surrounded by.

Having the participant or myself construct a life line drawing during the interview became difficult. Participants' stories did not necessarily follow a chronological order. After the first couple of interviews, I let go of the life line as a method as it was disruptive to the flow of conversation. My agenda needed to be more open to follow the threads of a particular participant's narrative: "skilled in-depth interviewers may deviate from the research protocol, to go where the informant seems to want to go or perhaps to follow what appears to be more interesting leads" (Johnson 2001, 113). Later in the research process, as I labelled the tree drawings, I was bringing back the "life line" but in the form of an organic tree structure. As one of my co-supervisors pointed out, both life histories and tree drawings have an organic flow as opposed to the rigidity of a straight line.

My background as a clinical counsellor also meant I was familiar with the art therapy use of tree drawings. As a therapeutic tool, I had asked clients in clinical settings to talk about the tree they had drawn: What kind of tree was it? What did the tree need? What would it say if it could talk? This was a projective tool to help gain insight into clients' feelings and beliefs about themselves. I also used a book, *Assessing Personality through Tree Drawings* (Bolander 1977), which states, "the drawn tree seems to represent the history of the life process of the individual, encompassing his[/her] origins, his[/her] experience to date, and his[/her] hopes or plans for the future" (31).

The chronology of life histories, the organic nature of trees and human lives, and my familiarity with tree drawings as representative of the human psyche and life processes, may all have been underpinnings to my intuited tree drawings in my research. I have, of course, had many other connections with trees, such as climbing them during my childhood in small-town Ontario, and identifying subspecies in science classes and on walks with family. They are of spiritual importance in my Wiccan, earth-based religion. Yet my course in arts-informed research was by far the most influential in terms of my being open to this alternative, intuitive, and artistic way of conceptualizing research.

INTUITION AND ARTS-INFORMED RESEARCH

Arts-informed research principles and "scholartistry," with the latter describing arts-informed involvement in scholarly work, were influential to my thinking during my doctoral studies (Knowles, Promislow, and Cole 2008; Neilsen 2002). Cole and Knowles (2008, 61) state, "the creative inquiry process of arts-informed research is defined by an openness to the expansive possibilities of the human imagination." Words like "intuition" and "serendipity" are used to describe this non-linear or non-rational process (61). Neilsen (2002, 212) also discusses liminality as integral to the scholar's use of the arts in research and representation.

> Brink. Threshold. Edge. Waystation. You are leaving the country, walking on shifting ground, you are breathing in, or is it out? You are here, not here. There, not there. You are in a place of transition, a place of possibility, open-ness, ambiguity, heightened awareness, imagination. A place of unsteadiness, a place to let go. (Neilsen 2002, 207)

I had perused many arts-informed theses, created an artful course project, and read about scholartistry; thus, I was open to jumping off the proverbial cliff and utilizing an intuitive and unconventional method to solve my messy, confusing data analysis problem. The frustration I was feeling with the traditional data analysis method was my place of liminality, the place where an intuitive idea took me into uncharted territory. I then followed this path as these tree drawings developed into a writing and representational metaphor. Although not discussed in this chapter in detail, I eventually disseminated part of this research knowledge with a community art gallery exhibit, which, not surprisingly, included some real tree branches nailed to the walls. This step is discussed in my thesis and illustrates how arts-informed research can be brought out of academia into a public forum (Diane 2015). I will turn now to pictures of the other participants' trees to show the progression of my drawing/writing process.

MOVING FROM HEURISTIC TO METAPHOR

As you can see when comparing the tree drawings, each tree is unique. When I came to draw the tree for and write about my second participant I had another eureka moment. This participant's tree needed to be an evergreen, not a deciduous tree. With this awareness, my trees started to become a metaphor for how I intuited my interpretation and representation of my participants' life history narratives. I looked on the Internet for information about evergreen trees and this confirmed my intuition.

> Evergreen trees … conserve energy and nutrients by slowly growing new foliage year-round, which can be an advantage in regions where nutrients are tight, as

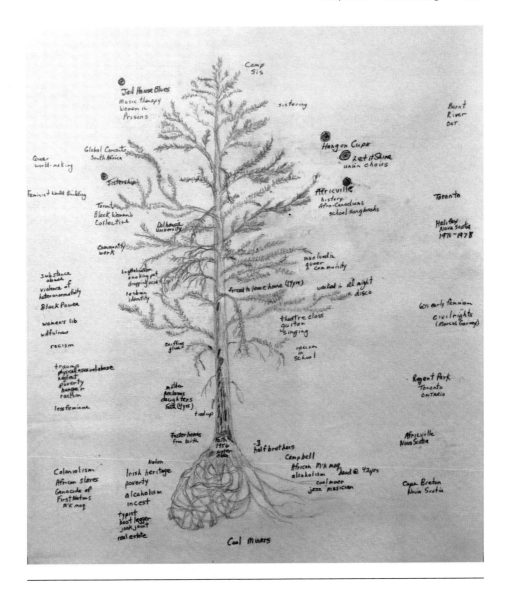

Figure 36.2: Tree Drawing #2

an evergreen can endure a rough season, while a deciduous tree might fail. The leaves also provide insulation for the tree, preventing sun and frost damage on the branches and trunk. Evergreen trees also fertilize themselves, thanks to their nutrient-rich leaf litter, which also acts as mulch to protect the roots. (McMahon 2003, 1)

In this participant's discussion of her life, I intuitively connected the poverty in her childhood and other factors to the evergreen tree. She grew up "where nutrients were tight." She survived through many a "rough season" and needed "insulation" as

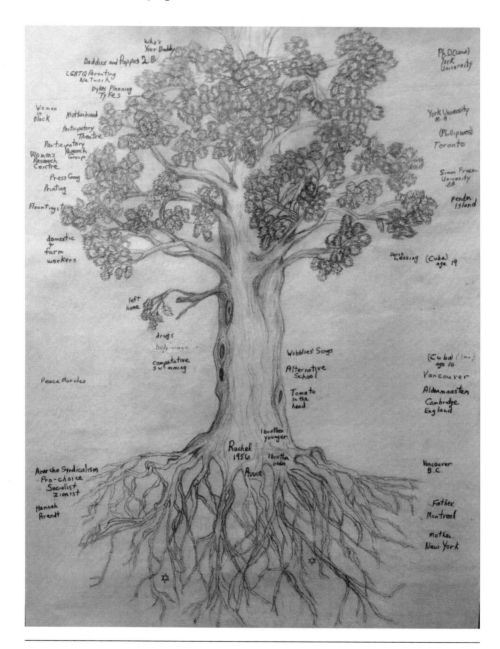

Figure 36.3: Tree Drawing #3

she endured the violence of poverty, childhood abuse, and the oppressions of sexism, racism, and heterosexism. She had to nurture herself, and journey to find her roots as a mixed-race person in a racist Canada. She has survived and thrived to enrich lives and help others through her music and her activism (Diane 2015).

The trees took on this poetic metaphorical quality through the interpretation of a species subtype. I intuitively knew that an oak tree was what I needed to draw for my third participant (see figure 36.3). She had an activist heritage, with both her parents deeply involved first with Jewish activist communities and then numerous social justice causes. She remembers marching in an anti-nuclear demonstration in England at age five (Diane 2015); thus, to me, she was an oak tree with an enormous network of activist roots from her heritage and the solid strong trunk of her childhood life: "The oak represents courage and endurance and the protective power of faith.… The oak reminds us all that the strength to prevail, come what may, lies in an open mind and a generous spirit" (Gifford 2000, 70).

Along my analysis and writing journey, I came to realize that my first participant's tree had been a ubiquitous deciduous tree and so I had to think more about my first participant. I decided she would be an elm tree. I subsequently found that elm trees have been described as "majestic" and "stately" and this seemed to fit well with my participant's life, which included being a champion boxer.

SELF-REFLEXIVITY, AUTOETHNOGRAPHY, AND THE FOURTH TREE

In a thesis committee meeting, it was pointed out to me that the writing I had seen as self-reflexive was actually more autoethnographic. By writing about the social, cultural, and historical circumstances of my personal life events and the literature that is relevant to these, I had moved beyond reflexivity: "Autoethnography is an approach to research and writing that seeks to describe and systematically analyze (*graphy*) personal experience in order to understand cultural experience (*ethno*)" (Ellis, Adams, and Bochner 2011, para. 1). An example of this combination of the personal and theoretical is the stories of my small-town Ontario, white childhood that I combined with literature on white privilege (Ahmed 2007; Dyer 1997).

My committee suggested that I draw a tree as representative of myself as I was another queer woman activist whose life stories were part of the research (see figure 36.4). I would then be integrating my autoethnographic approach more consciously and claiming my own activist life history. A deciduous tree in the winter came to mind. The maple tree was familiar due to its consistent presence in my Ontario childhood: "Maple tree meanings include balance, promise and practicality. The maple is seen as a happy tree, alluring, mystically bringing together all who gather under it's [*sic*] sheltering branches" (Spirit Walk Ministry 2015). This reference to gathering people together seemed significant in relation to my role as eldest and big sister, in a sibling line of seven, and also in my nurse/counsellor/teacher professional careers.

As I wrote up the data analysis, I followed this metaphor by writing about the roots of each woman's heritage; the trunks of childhood stories, including oppressions/

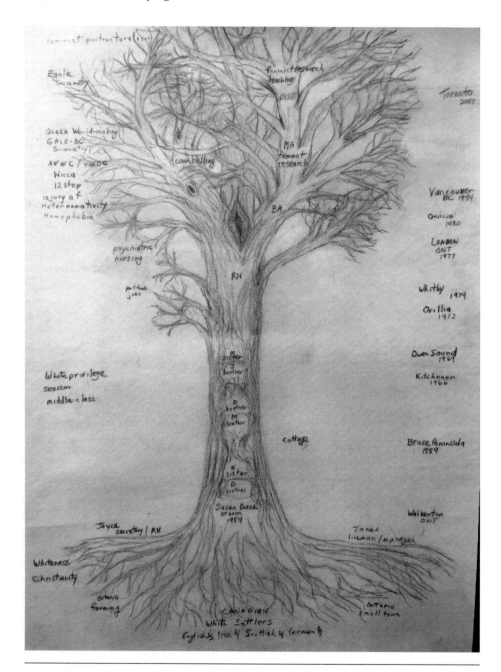

Figure 36.4: Tree Drawing #4

privileges; and the branches of career and activism in adulthood. I have outlined the process that culminated in four tree drawings entwined with four queer women activists' life stories as analyzed and represented in my doctoral research. My hope is that other qualitative researchers and students will find helpful this description of my intuitive process that found a creative, visual way out of the chaos of data analysis. Following through with this data analysis heuristic into a metaphorical representation also gave a structure and an artful poetic to the writing. Although not outlined in this short chapter, I did represent one participant's story in an installation in a community art gallery. I would encourage other researchers and students to consider an arts-informed approach as they follow their own creative paths through the complexities of a research project.

CRAFTING QUALITATIVE RESEARCH EXERCISES

1. If you were drawing a tree of your own life history, what species of tree would it be? Make a quick sketch of this tree. How is this tree significant to you as you consider the environment and geographical location(s) of your life journey?

2. Autoethnography considers the larger social/historical and cultural influences as reflected in one individual researcher's life. Can you think of any historical and cultural events that have been influences in your heritage and your life? Form a small group (this could also be done with a partner) and listen to what each person wishes to share about their experience regarding tree choices and various historical/cultural influences.

3. Expanding on your tree choice, consider your own life experiences and draw a more substantial tree in the centre of a large piece of bristol board, making sure there are margins on both sides of the tree.
   a) As you consider the dates and geographic locations of your parents'/caregivers' lives, place these in one margin beside the root system of your tree. Consider the historical, social, and political context of their lives and place these in the other margin. Do you know much about these influences that you were born into and that surrounded you as you grew up? Would you need to talk with your parents further or research what was happening in their particular culture and historical time? What oppressions and privileges did your parents have?
   b) What oppressions and privileges surrounded the trunk of your childhood? What historical and cultural events were important to your generation and nationality? Place these in notations in the margin beside the trunk of your tree. Are there any traumatic experiences that you have been through? Note any special positive experiences that influenced you as a child.
   c) As you became an adult (the leaves and branches of your tree) were you influenced by any of these childhood or historical familial experiences? For example, was your interest in a particular program or courses at university

or the career direction for which you are preparing initiated by your social/ cultural environment or from your heritage?

4.   Why is self-reflexivity important in qualitative research? What are the similarities and differences between autoethnography and self-reflexivity? Did your tree drawing increase your self-awareness? Would this help in your process of becoming more self-reflexive as a researcher? What topics would you need to research in the literature if you were to write about your tree as an example of autoethnography?

REFERENCES

Ahmed, Sara. 2007. "A Phenomenology of Whiteness." *Feminist Theory* 8 (2): 149–68.

American Heritage Dictionary of the English Language. 2016. *American Heritage Dictionary of the English Language.* 5th ed. Houghton Mifflin Harcourt. http://www.thefreedictionary. com/heuristic.

Berlant, Lauren, and Michael Warner. 1998. "Sex in Public." *Critical Inquiry* 24 (2): 547–66.

Bolander, Karen. 1977. *Assessing Personality through Tree Drawings.* New York: Basic Books.

Brotman, Shari, and Kraniou, Stavroula. 1999. "Ethnic and Lesbian: Understanding Identity through the Life-History Approach." *Affilia* 14 (4): 417–38.

Cole, Ardra, and J. Gary Knowles. 2001. *Lives in Context: The Art of Life History Research.* Lanham, MD: Altamira Press.

Cole, Ardra, and J. Gary Knowles. 2008. "Arts-Informed Research." In *Handbook of the Arts in Qualitative Research: Perspectives, Methods, Examples and Issues*, edited by J. Gary Knowles and Ardra L. Cole, 55–72. Thousand Oaks, CA: Sage.

Diane, Susan. 2015. "Willful Women Creating the World: Life Stories of Feminist and Queer Activists." PhD diss., University of Toronto. https://tspace.library.utoronto.ca/ handle/1807/69319.

Dyer, Richard. 1997. *White.* London and New York: Routledge.

Ellis, Carolyn, Tony Adams, and Arthur Bochner. 2011. "Autoethnography: An Overview." *Forum Qualitative Sozialforschung/Forum: Qualitative Social Research* 12 (1). http:// nbn-resolving.de/urn:nbn:de:0114-fqs1101108.

Gifford, Jane. 2000. *The Wisdom of Trees.* New York: Sterling.

Johnson, John M. 2001. "In-Depth Interviewing." In *Handbook of Interview Research*, 2nd ed., edited by Jaber F. Gubrium and James A. Holstein, 103–20. Thousand Oaks, CA: Sage.

Knowles, J. Gary, Sara Promislow, and Ardra Cole, eds. 2008. *Creating Scholartistry.* Big Tancook Island, NS: Backalong Books.

McMahon, Mary. 2003. "What Are Evergreen Trees?" *WiseGeek.com.* http://www.wisegeek. com/what-are-evergreen-trees.htm.

Neilsen, Lorri. 2002. "Learning from the Liminal: Fiction as Knowlege." *Alberta Journal of Educational Research* 48 (3): 206–14.

Spirit Walk Ministry. 2015. "Nature Spirits." *Naturewalkministry.com*. http://www. spiritwalkministry.com/nature_spirits.

Zerilli, Linda M. G. 2005. *Feminism and the Abyss of Freedom*. Chicago: University of Chicago Press.

SECTION IX

LEAVING THE FIELD

How do we know when it is time to conclude our data collection, bid farewell to participants, and exit from our field sites? There are a variety of factors that influence when we leave the field. If you can choose when to do so, the main question to ask yourself is whether you feel you have enough data to answer your research questions. In his reflection on leaving the field, Steven Taylor (1991, 242) writes, "A study is close to being finished when one can begin to recognize the puzzle and how all the pieces fit together." He continues by recommending that we stay in the field until our data become repetitious—i.e., we are noticing the same themes over and over. We often face other constraints, though, that dictate when and even how we will leave the field.

The amount of time you have to carry out your research can determine when you leave the field. If you are conducting research as part of a course, the end of your course will place a hard stop to your data collection. Some course instructors will also stipulate how much data to collect, such as the number of interviews or observations you are to include in your research. Even when we do not have such obvious structural constraints, the amount of time we can devote to any one project has its limits. Running out of research funding can bring a project to a conclusion. Sometimes, when working collaboratively on a project, researchers might have varying amounts of time to devote and even different ideas of what constitutes "enough data." Your research time is also limited by how much time participants are willing to give.

It is likely clear by now that qualitative research can be demanding. A commitment to "being there when the action is happening" can mean forgoing other areas of our personal, academic, and work lives. Not only do our research struggles place demands on us, but, as illustrated by Tony Christensen in chapter 3, they can also impact those to whom we are close. Recognizing this aspect of qualitative research reminds us to be conscious of the social and emotional tolls that our research can take. It is important to acknowledge this aspect of leaving the field, as we often commit a great deal of ourselves to our projects. Some of the stories we hear from our participants will be pleasant, while others can be harrowing. Participants may have opened up to you about aspects of their lives that they have never shared with anyone else. While it is rewarding when people place such trust in us, it is also important to recognize how these types of experiences can linger, staying with us long after our research is done. It is helpful to surround ourselves with colleagues we can lean on so that we can discuss both the tribulations and triumphs of our efforts.

It is important to consider future research relationships with those you have been researching. Try to avoid burning any bridges for yourself and future researchers. Respect your participants by treating them as you would want to be treated. Sometimes this might simply mean a friendly goodbye and thanks, while other times it can entail honouring bargains you made and your ethical commitments.

Some questions you might consider at this stage to help reflect on what your research journey has meant to you include the following: How has the project changed for you? Where did you begin? Where did you go? Where did you end up? What would you do differently if you could start over? What is left to do? What aspects of your research do you think will stick with you? What have you learned about the craft of qualitative research? The chapters in this section will help you work through these and other aspects of leaving the field.

In chapter 37, Jeffrey van den Scott emphasizes paying respect to our field communities and honouring our commitments to them when we leave. As he notes, our "fields" are constituted by any number of places, such as physical, social, cultural, virtual, and mental spaces. Van den Scott points out that our fields share some of the responsibility for our success, so we should give this our consideration. He draws on his field research on the musical life of the community in Arviat, Nunavut, to discuss some of the theoretical and practical factors involved in concluding our data collection. Van den Scott offers advice on balancing the needs of the researcher and the needs of the community as considerations in leaving the field. He also relates his experience of adjustment as he entered back into the academic community in a very different cultural context.

Critical qualitative researchers are often drawn towards tackling some of the most challenging research topics. Such research can be particularly exhausting, both emotionally and physically. In chapter 38, Sarah Benbow and Jodi Hall share their experiences of concluding emotionally difficult fieldwork as novice health researchers. They share advice on navigating the tensions and muddy waters of leaving the field when researchers and participants have put so much of themselves into their projects. They speak of the emotional toll of their research, how they coped by reaching out to colleagues, and how they came to embody the stories of their participants. They also highlight the need for inaction—a time when researchers can recharge and rejuvenate, focusing on caring for their own well-being.

In chapter 39, William Shaffir begins by discussing his research on medical students, and, although academically and professionally rewarding, his desire to move on to different research. In his career-long study of Hasidic Jews, he found an area of research that was both academically and personally rewarding. Recounting his experiences in gaining entry and subsequently exiting different Hasidic communities, he offers insights into the value of chance opportunities, the utility of taking on membership roles in the communities we research, and the tentative nature of our presence in the field. He takes us through his gradual and voluntary departure from one sect, and then reflects on his abrupt involuntary departure from another.

In chapter 40, Nichole Edwards reflects on the emotional connections she established during her study of feminism and heterosexuality. She considers what this meant for data collection, ethics, and her ability to truly leave the field. Being an insider—i.e., being a heterosexual feminist herself—deepened her emotional connection to the research. As an insider, reflecting her ideals as a feminist researcher, she was open to sharing her own experiences with participants, building trust and rapport and gaining intimacy through reciprocity. Edwards discusses how, after leaving the field, she continues to reflect back on her research experiences. In doing so, she discusses how we symbolically and emotionally re-enter the field, recalling events and thinking about how our participants are doing.

REFERENCE

Taylor, Steven J. 1991. "Leaving the Field: Research, Relationships, and Responsibilities." In *Experiencing Fieldwork: An Inside View of Qualitative Research*, edited by William B. Shaffir and Robert A. Stebbins, 238–47. Newbury Park, CA: Sage.

37 Leaving the Field/Can You Leave the Field?

Jeffrey van den Scott

When challenged with the task of writing a chapter on "leaving the field," my initial thoughts centred around a single question: Did I ever leave the field? On the one hand, this question is due to the recent completion of my own PhD. On the other hand, it begs attention in considering the role the field (and, in particular, that first foray into the field) plays throughout your career. The field, as you have likely discovered through reading and through experience, can be any number of places; it can be physical, social, cultural, virtual, mental, or any combination of these features. Your field, particularly as an early career scholar, will define your work. To some degree, your field shares some of the responsibility for your success. Your relationship with the field, therefore, deserves more consideration than simply taking your leave and moving on to other endeavours.

A decade ago, finding helpful sources about leaving the field proved challenging. Since then, several sources have emerged, highlighting theoretical questions (e.g., when do I have enough data?) alongside ethical concerns and best practices. Two brief articles (Fox 2008; Gobo 2011) provide concise overviews of these concerns and draw heavily on two earlier seminal publications: Snow's "The Disengagement Process" (1980) and Glaser and Strauss's *The Discovery of Grounded Theory* (1967), which introduce theoretical concepts for when to leave the field. While I draw on these works for context, in the spirit of this volume, I will focus on more practical examples from my own experience.

For me, the field was a community in Nunavut, the Canadian territory formed through a land claims agreement between the Indigenous Inuit population and the Canadian government. All of Nunavut's communities are remote, with air links being the primary mode of transportation. While there are no roads among communities (or between Nunavut and the rest of Canada), hardy travellers can and do use snowmobiles (in winter) or boats (in summer) to get around. Located on the western shores of Hudson Bay, Arviat boasted a population of approximately 2,500 people during my fieldwork, with approximately 95 percent of that population being Inuit. The remainder consisted largely of Canadians from the South working in government positions, such as teachers, nurses, and mid- to high-level government administration, or retail store management. I spent five years living in Arviat as a music teacher. My researcher hat came later, as I returned to the community periodically to conduct research on the musical life of the community over a five-year period. My study, therefore, finished a full decade after my introduction to this community, witnessing changes in how traditional music is practiced and how popular music increasingly plays a role in continuing the oral history of the community as did traditional music before. Leaving the field, for me, includes the shift from being a regular visitor to someone unsure of when he will next see friends and participants who played such a vital role in my early career and life.

While we are generally prepared to enter the field—with guidance from supervisors, colleagues, and others—knowing when the time has come to leave, and how to achieve this gracefully, can be a greater challenge. Answers to this question can come from different directions, and include theoretical and practical concerns. Leaving the field requires reflexivity just as urgently as all other aspects of your fieldwork; this reflexivity must attend not only to your needs as a researcher, but also the needs of the community and its members as your relationship with them changes.

THEORETICAL FACTORS

Unlike a statistical survey, which may try to optimize itself through the gathering of as much data as possible, "in ethnographic research everything is vaguer, more rarefied, subjective. This is why the question 'how do I know when it is time to leave' is anything but banal" (Gobo 2011, 308). For qualitative researchers, one of the best-known and oft-cited models for knowing when to leave the field is Glaser and Strauss's "theoretical saturation" (1967, 61). At its simplest, theoretical saturation suggests that you know when you have gathered enough data because you have stopped learning new or significant trends. Mark Mason engaged in a study of doctoral candidates in 2010 to determine what sample size leads to saturation in qualitative studies. What might be overlooked here is that qualitative research is not limited to interviews, but entails a broader range of ethnographic methodologies supporting a study. Arguing, for example, that "30 interviews provides sufficient data for the majority of doctoral studies" fails to acknowledge the benefits of and learning available through participant observation and other ethnographic techniques that may not result in interview transcripts.

David A. Snow discusses "taken-for-grantedness" in his 1980 article on the subject of "disengagement" from the field (102). Similar to theoretical saturation (which Snow also discusses with reference to Glaser and Strauss), he describes the condition of taken-for-grantedness as being when "the cultural and behavioral patterns associated with the group or situation under study are perceived as 'matter of course' rather than as a 'questionable topic of investigation'" (1980, 103). Along with taken-for-grantedness, Snow describes a partnered condition of "informational sufficiency" (1980, 101), whereby the researcher has gathered enough data to "sufficiently answer pre-existing or emergent questions, to shed empirical light on pre-existing or emergent propositions, or to render an accurate description of the world under study" (1980, 102). The ideal result of achieving taken-for-grantedness and informational sufficiency is that the researcher achieves a sense of "high confidence" in their work (Glaser and Strauss 1967, 226).

Reflecting on my own fieldwork, one of the key indicators I found of my readiness to leave is a dramatic reduction in the quantity and quality of my field notes. Toward the end of my final month-long fieldwork session in Arviat, I find my entries more filled with descriptions of how I spent my days, and less occupied with excitement at new discoveries or concerns with how to extend both my empirical study and its theoretical implications. My interview transcripts also contain phrases suggesting my familiarity with the field and topic were becoming commonplace. Research participants would begin answers by saying, "as you know" or "like you've done before." These, combined with general observations that "things are the same," and a lack of surprises coming from my participants or from the life of the community where I conducted research, signalled the time to stop looking for new data, and to take leave from the field.

PRACTICAL FACTORS

While having high confidence in reaching theoretical saturation through your fieldwork is the theoretical goal of much qualitative research, there are also many practical concerns that will determine when to leave the field. Gobo suggests such factors can be considered in three areas: institutional factors, interpersonal factors, and intrapersonal factors (2011, 307).

For many researchers, particularly those early in their careers, institutional factors may dominate in determining when to leave the field. The goals of theoretical saturation and taken-for-grantedness attach themselves to bracketed timelines, such as the number of years of funding you have for graduate school, or the length of a grant for a post-doctoral fellowship, particularly when these funding agencies (e.g., universities, government councils) demand results at the end of a grant. As a graduate student, these grants can be very short—the length of a semester or quarter. Undergraduates, too, face intense time restrictions on their work, often being asked to design and/or complete a project, with ethics approval, in a four- to eight-month period as part of a course or thesis.

Researchers—particularly those like me whose fields are some distance from a home base—are tied to family and can find travel between home and field, or extended periods away to be a strain on personal life. Such strains introduce interpersonal factors that have little to do with your research goals, which contribute to the end of fieldwork. This can be a factor even when fieldwork is close to home; consider being away from family every weekend or evening while conducting research (Gobo 2011, 307).

Likewise, intrapersonal conflict, such as mental exhaustion, contributes to the decision to leave the field. As mentioned above, I found my later field notes to lack the energy and vigour of earlier entries. In the middle of my last visit (from December 2013 to January 2014), I found myself writing, "slow morning today—whether it is the cold, solitude, or whatever else, after only a few days, I'm finding the mornings difficult" (field notes). This was my third dedicated research trip to my field site, and the end of ten years' experience in Arviat. The town itself did not contribute to this exhaustion; instead it was the result of the joint pressures of continually seeking something new and worrying whether what I found was "good enough."

Before you leave the field, take time to consider and to plan for the "ethical dimensions of leaving the field" (Fox 2008, 484). Just as you do when entering the field, you must consider the effects of your leaving on yourself and on your participants and their community—taking into account how power might change between yourself and your community. You might find it useful to consider the following areas beyond the obvious benefits you gain as a researcher: the commitments you have made to your research community, and concerns that might arise for you, as a researcher and someone who might seek to return to the field in the future. In the reflection below, you will get a taste of how these questions emerged in my experience.

REFLECTION: COMMITMENT TO FIELD COMMUNITY

The Nunavut Research Institute reviews all projects being conducted in the territory of Nunavut, with a goal of ensuring that research benefits are not one-sided and that the community will also gain from these studies. One of the questions they ask, which marks good practice for any research community, is how you will return knowledge to the field you have studied. At the most basic level, this might include sending a copy of your resulting publication to the community alongside a granting agency or review board. Deeper levels might differ in varying contexts. In my case, I hoped that my research might result in my participants feeling proud about the music being made in the community. I have some evidence that I was successful in this regard. At the end of one of my interviews, Kent (a pseudonym) said, "thanks for the interviewing, and it's our appreciation that after long years there was never been any interview or music interview or trying to find out how the Inuit people can sing, too, and it's our pleasure, too." In leaving the field, I try to remember statements like Kent's, leaving me with a sense of duty to my participants and field community.

A second sense of duty reminds me to keep in touch with my participants. In this age, this is easier than ever. My field is thousands of kilometres from my home, and accessible only by airplane. Yet, through social media—particularly Facebook—I am able to stay in contact with research participants, and the community as a whole, keeping tabs on the ins and outs of the town and continuing to monitor the musical life of Arviat from afar.

Keeping in touch with my participants and field community further allows me the opportunity to revisit the site, either socially or in a research capacity. Gobo writes, "keeping in touch is the best strategy to enable a return to the 'scene of the crime'" (2011, 312). Not staying in touch has the potential to close both doors. Arviat, when I visited in 2013, was the site of over 20 research projects—a possibly overwhelming number for a community of under 3,000 people. Many of these projects are fly-in studies, where the researchers come to town for short stints of only days or a couple of weeks. The community has become familiar with this type of research, and often either "tells them [researchers] what they want to hear," (my wife and I would hear *Arviammiut*[1] speak this way about researchers) or fails to engage with the researchers. My foray into the field was unconventional, having already lived in the community for five years, but my exit (or lack thereof) also requires a commitment to stay in touch. The single project I undertook opens many more opportunities for research. The friends made in the field will lose faith in my friendship if I do not stay in touch and then magically reappear, looking to take more from the community for my own gain as a scholar.

An additional concern for your community, which may double as a concern for you, is a potential sense of betrayal when you leave the field. Gobo reminds us that this is particularly true in a place of significant "social deprivation or hardship" (2011, 311). My situation was very fortunate, with participants like Kent (quoted above) sharing his wish for his experience to be shared. If you have been in a field for an extended period, you will also seek ways to prepare your field community for your departure (Gobo 2011, 311), which will also help you to prepare yourself. The most poignant moment in my departure came not when I was done my research, but as it was beginning. As mentioned above, my entry into research was unconventional, having lived in the community for five years. Leaving after those five years, my wife and I decided to systematically tell the community about our decision to leave Arviat and return to graduate school. Our first stop was to visit an Elder with whom we had formed a friendship. On hearing our news, this Elder first shed a quick tear before demonstrating the Inuit value of moving forward. She said that we must do what is best for us, then finished her own analysis of our situation with the plea, "tell them about us." With that mandate, we were able to not only plan research for the future, but also think about issues moving forward, including the promise to keep in touch and communicate with the community.

My willingness to communicate with my field community and to follow through on my commitments to them has led to a great honour for me in community life. At Inuit drum dances, men dance to their own songs. If they do not have a song of their own, they will generally dance to a song by a relative. In the case of *qablunaaq*[2] visitors, there is a special song for them. The last time I danced in Arviat, the Elders chose a new song for me: the song about the person who does what they say they will do. To me, this suggests that I have been able to "do right" by my community and participants, and follow through on the appeal to "tell them [i.e., the rest of the world] about us."

MOVING FORWARD: RETURNING TO THE RESEARCH COMMUNITY

The often unspoken aspect of leaving the field is that you might also be re-entering the academy after an absence. In my case, this meant the shift from a relatively isolated field, in a small community, back to the hustle and bustle of Chicagoland; from being surrounded by Inuktitut to the analytic and philosophically bent English of the university; and, given the time of year, literally from the darkness of the Arctic into the bright lights of the city. This step will look different for every researcher in every setting. For me, a great part of this adjustment was to talk to people, be they from the university community, or friends outside. Being able to share my experiences in the field with others through stories made the experience more real, and continued a process of analyzing information.

CONCLUSION

Leaving the field—if we ever truly do—is a process more complex than simply physically moving from one location to another. It involves a series of integrated reflections and planning. The most obvious of these, or at least that which runs the risk of most preoccupying our minds, is the question of whether you have gathered enough data. More important, perhaps, are issues of respecting your field community and the commitments you might have made to them in the process of conducting your research. Finally, there is the oft-forgotten aspect of returning to the rhythm of life of the university and how that rhythm could be filled with a culture shock when contrasted with your experiences in the field. When I look back and consider these factors in respect to my own fieldwork, though the physical departure is complete, I continue asking to what degree the field has left me.

CRAFTING QUALITATIVE RESEARCH EXERCISES

1. Consider a time in your life that you have moved: to a new town (or a new part of town), from middle school to high school, or from high school to university. In the course of these moves, you left one situation for another. Reflect on how these changes affected you: Did you stay in touch with the same friends? Can you think of someone you have lost touch with? What feelings emerge in yourself when you think of these occasions?

2. Imagine a qualitative research project you could design that would take you to a field away from your home. We often consider strategies for getting to know

people and for beginning our research. Instead, write down some of the ways
that you can stay in touch with members of this field site. Do you think these
ways are equally effective? Which would be best if you were to decide to return
to the field at a later date?

3. Sometimes, after spending a long time in the field, saying goodbye is a real
    goodbye. Consider times you have had to say goodbye to someone who has
    been part of your life. How did you feel? What did you do to cope with this
    change? Write down some ideas for ways that you can help to prepare your
    participants for this change.

4. Consider knowledge that you take for granted, for example, which social
    groups existed in your high school experience. How did you learn this knowl-
    edge? Make a list of questions that would help you to identify such knowledge.
    Now, imagine a new research project. How could you adapt these questions to
    a new situation?

NOTES

1. *Arviammiut* is the demonym for residents of Arviat, Nunavut. The *-miut* suffix is translated as "peo-
    ple of."
2. *Qablunaaq* is the Inuktitut word for non-Inuit, particularly Caucasians.

REFERENCES

Fox, Nick J. 2008. "Leaving the Field." In *the SAGE Encyclopedia of Qualitative Research
    Methods*, edited by Lisa M. Given, 484. Thousand Oaks, CA: Sage.
Glaser, Barney, and Anselm Strauss. 1967. *The Discovery of Grounded Theory: Strategies for
    Qualitative Research*. Chicago: Aldine.
Gobo, Giampietro. 2011. "Leaving the Field." In *Doing Ethnography*, 306–13. Thousand Oaks,
    CA: Sage.
Mason, Mark. 2010. "Sample Size and Saturation in PhD Studies Using Qualitative
    Interviews." *Forum: Qualitative Social Research* 11 (3). http://www.qualitative-research.net/
    index.php/fqs/article/view/1428/3027.
Snow, David A. 1980. "The Disengagement Process: A Neglected Problem in Participant
    Observation Research." *Qualitative Sociology* 3 (2): 100–22.

38 Negotiating Tensions in Exiting the Field of Critical Qualitative Research

Sarah Benbow and Jodi Hall

> Once that journey into the other's experience has been taken, we cannot return "home." We can only create a new home, one furnished with the understandings of them and of ourselves that we have developed in the course of our research. Research of this type not only changes the audience, moving them from stillness to action, it also alters where we dwell as scholars and as beings-in-the-world.
>
> —Lesa Lockford, *"Breaking Habits and Cultivating Home"*

This chapter is based on our experiences as novice health researchers employing critical qualitative methodologies with marginalized groups. Included in this chapter are questions that arose for us when leaving the field during our own PhD dissertation research and as graduate research assistants over the span of seven years. We have drawn on our experiences conducting research with criminalized women, women and mothers experiencing homelessness, standardized patients teaching pelvic examinations, mothers who have experienced trauma, and street-level sex workers. In the course of answering a variety of research questions related to these topics, we utilized a multitude of qualitative methodologies such as critical narrative methodology, autoethnography, case study design, and grounded theory, and methods such as body mapping, photo-elicitation, participant observation, and in-depth individual and group interviews.

Common to our research objectives was the desire to co-construct meaningful research relationships with participants, and generate findings that would problematize existing societal practices and policies that perpetuate social exclusion and marginality in the lives of women. We strove to engender research relationships between participants and ourselves built on trust, transparency, authenticity, and reciprocity. For example, as participants shared intimate aspects of themselves and their lives, sometimes disclosing very painful experiences for the first time, we would in turn share aspects of ourselves to highlight common or shared experiences. Such intentional positioning as a researcher reflected our feminist theoretical lenses and our commitment to critical work that aims to lessen power differentials and prioritize relationships.

Within the spaces of field research, we held in tension several personal and professional identities. Our identities as health promoters (Benbow, a mental health nurse, and Hall, a trauma counsellor/doula) shaped our desire to pursue the research topics we did, calling attention to "wicked problems"—social issues so complex that resolution through policy is difficult to achieve (Head 2008); however, the very aspects of ourselves that compelled us to focus on these issues and guided our way of being with research participants muddied the water for us in transitioning out of the field at the conclusion of data collection. Furthermore, there were times when our own identities felt contradictory in nature—i.e., having the identity of being helping professional and the identity of researcher. For many researchers, "the primary purpose of promoting rapport is to get at data. The human interaction is secondary to the primary purpose of seeking data" (Nunkoosing 2005, 701). Such a perspective on research relationships challenged how we envisioned our role, purpose, and identities as helping professionals. For us, the human interaction was paramount, something to be nurtured, as we believed that the quality of the data we collected would be a representation of how well we fostered this connection.

The depth of connection, the stories shared within the field by research participants, and our commitment to social change mean the work continues to linger for us. Reflecting on conversations we have had between us over these years, negotiating if and how to leave the work behind or exit the field continues to be a recurrent theme. In this chapter, we explore the nuances of leaving the field when difficult topics are investigated, and when the stories of participants become embodied by the researchers. In doing so, our hope is to create awareness among student researchers and supervisors about the tensions and lingering "haunting" that can persist at the formal conclusion of fieldwork, and to offer our suggestions in working through similar realities.

"THE WORK CONSUMED ME": THE EMOTIONAL IMPACT OF OUR WORK

Our identities as "helpers" created tensions for us in understanding how we could ever possibly leave the field behind. While we could physically remove ourselves from the spaces of data collection, we were left holding on to the voices, images, sights, and sounds we witnessed while in the field. We were literally immersed in participants' stories of extreme injustices, their lived realities of unspeakable violence, trauma, and victimization. We were humbled to hear such stories of oppression, punctuated with examples of resilience and resistance people enacted in surviving their circumstances.

Our professional backgrounds and training prepared us for the relational practice of qualitative work, such as in responding to issues of safety, negotiating emotional triggers, and making referrals for counselling or other community services when necessary. Despite our prior experience and professional training, we still found ourselves overwhelmed at times with lingering emotions, such as confusion and rage, and questioning how to cope with the psychological weight of participants' stories.

The question of how to negotiate leaving the field was particularly foregrounded in our doctoral work where we were the sole contact: interviewer, transcriber, coder, report writer, and presenter of findings. Our centrality to the research meant we were constantly immersed in the talk and text of participants' lives. Beyond holding the heaviness of the interview itself, the incredible injustices participants faced reverberated into our personal lives (Connolly and Reilly 2007; Matthiesen and Binder 2009). We were haunted and emotionally distressed by what we had witnessed, what we had heard, and the responsibility we felt we held as "critical" researchers, as helping professionals, trying to make a difference. The emotional impact was not a new phenomenon for us given our prior careers and research experiences (Benbow et al. 2013); however, conducting doctoral work is often more isolating than other work (Matthiesen and Binder 2009), such as being a nurse within a health care team, or a research assistant collecting data alongside others.

After each point of data collection, the stories and experiences of the participants were carried with us. As we were stirring in the emotions of what to do with what we had witnessed and embodied, we often distanced ourselves from social gatherings, family, and places of employment (opting to work at home). Reconnecting with everyday mundane aspects of life was difficult, as these tasks seemed so inconsequential in comparison to the bigger issues our participants faced. We were not struggling to secure housing, to leave abusive relationships, or to face what participants often felt were hostile case managers who acted in judgment toward them about their decisions. One area we struggled with in particular was the broader implications of negative societal views and political discourses held toward people like our participants, juxtaposed with the very material needs and experiences of the participants. As we worked through these emotions, the data analysis and self-reflection process was never-ending as our lives were framed through our research lens.

Simultaneously, we inherently felt guilt and shame admitting the emotional distress we faced to our colleagues and superiors/supervisors. We felt that we did not deserve to *feel* our own pain because we would return to our privileged lives—i.e., lives free from violence and poverty—after data collection. We felt unsure if these feelings were "normal" and "allowed" as part of the research process, which further contributed to feelings of isolation. There did not seem to be anyone within the academic environment addressing these issues, which contributed to concern that maybe there was something wrong with how we were approaching and responding to the research process.

Jung used the term *wounded healer* in reference to psychotherapists and their own vulnerability in the therapeutic relationship (Wheeler 2007). We believe that qualitative researchers, like good therapists, are fundamentally motivated to create meaningful relationships with participants as a means of exploring questions "about the experiences and meaning people give to dimensions of their lives and social worlds" (Hewitt 2007, 1149). Furthermore, the skill required to encourage such exploration in others is strengthened by the researcher's capacity to empathize with the experiences of others, recognizing, however, that this also makes *researchers* along with participants potentially vulnerable in the research relationship (Hewitt 2007). While the counselling psychology and nursing literature addresses issues such as compassion fatigue, vicarious trauma, and "burnout," less has been written about the *researcher's* subjective experience and their emotional and psychological well-being (Coles et al. 2014).

"I FINALLY REACHED OUT": HOW WE COPED

Out of necessity, we eventually found ways to mitigate the overwhelming emotions we were wrestling with. For example, we connected with an informal network of doctoral students employing critical qualitative methodologies who were also working with marginalized groups. We created time and space to exchange and normalize our feelings. We also engaged in intentional acts of self-care. For instance, on days that Benbow was working as a mental health nurse, she would not book research interviews before or after her shift. Hall used a combination of movement practices, such as dance, alongside stillness practices, such as journalling and meditation. These approaches reduced the potential for overwhelming emotional exhaustion and allowed for recovery time between such emotionally intense work. The emotional impact of the research was important, and we believe it was required in carrying out empathetic fieldwork in critical research; however, managing the impacts and acknowledging the toll in staying present with these stories cannot be minimized. Families and friends can play an important role in normalizing the impetus to retract from social encounters, and can look toward fostering connection by acknowledging the toll of the research process. Creating opportunities for the emotional support of researchers, normalizing the tensions and periods of identity dissonance is an important component of the research process that is often overlooked (Coles et al. 2014).

"WE HAVE A RESPONSIBILITY": EMBODIMENT AND (IN)ACTION

We have carried the stories of our participants in our everyday lives: in our politics, in our activism, and in our life's purpose. Our research influences our way of being in the world, how we approach situations with others, and where we dedicate our resources. While we were already involved in activism, our research further propelled us. We both attend numerous rallies, protests, and marches related to our work and the issues that impact so negatively on the lives of our participants. For example, we participate in Take Back the Night marches, Pride parades, and events recognizing murdered and missing Aboriginal women. We participate in letter-writing campaigns, such as through petitions pertaining to the need for a national housing strategy and a national poverty reduction strategy. These examples of activism are closely related to and have resulted from our research and the lives of those research participants with whom we have worked.

We also enact our activism in our roles as professors by encouraging our students to think critically through a social justice–informed lens, and by providing spaces where assumptions about what contributes to "poor life choices" can be unpacked and critiqued. We make deliberate choices about the resources we include as readings, which raise these issues for consideration. Within our institutions of work and social circles we are able to share research experiences and findings to begin to influence change at a microlevel. We continue to document the process of research and the impact the relationships with our participants have on us. We note areas where we have learned to disengage more thoroughly, and discuss openly what has aided this—e.g., sleep patterns, supportive relationships, institutional support. We have also learned to embrace the tensions as part of a health process, and shrug off the self-judgments we once held for the difficult emotions that lingered. We honour these feelings as "simply" part of the process. The inevitability of being impacted by our research is a key indicator of our wellness—not a deficit.

Additionally, we have recognized inaction as a form of self-preservation and care. Inaction involves time spent to rejuvenate and restore our reserves. This has involved learning to say "no" and learning to pace our research projects and the work that happens within them. Within an academic environment it can feel fatal to turn down invitations to participate in upcoming grants; however, we have learned that compiling too much emotionally charged research leads to burnout, feelings of resentment, and extreme fatigue. Alongside inaction, we have also intentionally nurtured collegial relationships built on trust, reciprocity, and care. Caretaking for one another means we pay attention to the well-being of our fellow researchers, ensuring we share the responsibility for the workload that has the potential to carry emotional weight, checking in with one another, and debriefing however and whenever necessary. With so many ways to communicate today, we take advantage of these technologies to stay in touch, whether through text or email.

SUGGESTIONS BASED ON OUR LESSONS LEARNED

We view the embodiment of what we experienced when interacting with participants as not only a necessary and an anticipated part of the work, but also an aspect of research that is not openly embraced and honoured in many academic and research-intensive settings. As mentioned, our experience of leaving the field behind is a recurring theme in our work, influenced by the embodiment of our research and our way of being as critical researchers. In anticipation of similar realities experienced by novice researchers, we have constructed the following table of our suggestions for preparing for and coping with challenges and tensions in leaving the work behind.

Table 38.1: Preparing for and Coping with the Difficulties of Exiting the Field

Suggestions	Possible topics to explore
Explore vigilant subjectivity Arts-based methods Autoethnography Journalling/reflection	• What experiences shape who I am? • What values do I bring into this research? • What are my privileges and personal vulnerabilities?
Foster relational interviewing skills Practice process using a combination of narrative, role plays, and vignettes	• Interviewing techniques—e.g., probing questions, building rapport, working with resistance • Responding to disclosures, immediate support strategies • Making referrals • Vicarious trauma • Establish(ing) healthy boundaries
Create a self-care plan	• Do you have a peer support group? • What has helped you cope with challenging situations in the past? • What destressing exercises will you incorporate into your routine?
Look for continuing education opportunities	• Seek out opportunities to observe interviewing with experienced researchers • Identify skill-development opportunities—e.g., critical incident stress management, crisis intervention training, mental health 101

CONCLUDING THOUGHTS

In this chapter, we have outlined the nuances and tensions of concluding emotionally difficult fieldwork. We shared our experiences of negotiating how to best deal with the hauntingness of participants' lived realities and we problematized the notion that we can ever truly leave the field behind. The significance of embodiment cannot be overstated; embodiment was an essential and significant component of our research, but without the proper resources and support, the impact can be overwhelming and potentially disabling to the novice researcher. Through our own lived experiences and suggested strategies, it is our hope that we have begun to normalize the emotional toll of our work as qualitative researchers.

CRAFTING QUALITATIVE RESEARCH EXERCISES

1. Practice qualitative interview techniques with a classmate or colleague using your research focus/interview questions as a semi-structured guide. Ask your "participant" to throw you "curveballs" in their emotional reactions to your questions or resistance to your questions. Afterward, reflect on how you can best prepare for these situations in your actual research fieldwork. Are there additional educational opportunities that might help to better prepare you? How do you think a research participant's responses might emotionally impact you?

2. Develop a self-care plan in anticipation of the potential emotional toll of your research (e.g., consider who you can debrief with). Share and discuss your plans with classmates/supervisor/partners, and have them do the same. How do your plans differ? Why might this be? What obstacles do you anticipate in carrying out your self-care plan?

3. Reflect on your relationship with your thesis supervisor. Are debriefing experiences prioritized in your research meetings? Would you feel comfortable disclosing and debriefing personal coping with your supervisor? What might increase that comfort?

4. Reflecting on your past or present lived experiences and values, can you identify topics you would struggle with hearing about in a research context? How will you manage?

5. Research and list the signs and symptoms of vicarious trauma. How can you best prepare for the potential of vicarious trauma during your fieldwork?

REFERENCES

Benbow, Sarah, Jodi Hall, Kristin Heard, and Lorie Donelle. 2013. "Conducting Research with Criminalized Women in an Incarcerated Setting: The Researcher's Perspective." *Canadian Journal of Nursing Research* 45 (3): 80–91.

Coles, Jan, Jill Astbury, Elizabeth Dartnall, and Shazeen Limjerwala. 2014. "A Qualitative Exploration of Researcher Trauma and Researchers' Responses to Investigating Sexual Violence." *Violence Against Women* 20 (1): 95–117.

Connolly, Kate, and Rosemary C. Reilly. 2007. "Emergent Issues when Researching Trauma." *Qualitative Inquiry* 13 (4): 522–40.

Head, Brian W. 2008. "Wicked Problems in Public Policy." *Public Policy* 3 (2): 101–18.

Hewitt, Jeanette. 2007. "Ethical Components of Researcher-Researched Relationships in Qualitative Interviewing." *Qualitative Health Research* 17 (8): 1149–59.

Lockford, Lesa. 2002. "Breaking Habits and Cultivating Home." In *Ethnographically Speaking: Autoethnography, Literature, and Aesthetics*, edited by Arthur Bochner and Carolyn Ellis, 76–87. Walnut Creek, CA: Altamira Press.

Matthiesen, Jane, and Mario Binder. 2009. *How to Survive Your Doctorate Education: What Others Don't Tell You*. New York: Open University Press.

Nunkoosing, Karl. 2005. "The Problems with Interviews." *Qualitative Health Research* 15 (5): 698–706.

Wheeler, Sue. 2007. "What Shall We Do with the Wounded Healer? The Supervisor's Dilemma." *Psychodynamic Practice* 13 (3): 245–56.

39 Leaving the Field Trajectories: Researching Hasidic Jews

William Shaffir

INTRODUCTION

My first encounter with field research following the completion of my doctorate was a study of the socialization and professionalization of medical students. The study was conceived by three newly minted PhD sociologists recently employed at McMaster University—Jack Haas, Victor Marshall, and myself—where a new and "innovative" medical school had recently opened. A proposal to study an incoming cohort of students was submitted to the school and the proposed granting agency, the Canada Council. After one year's delay, permission for the study was granted, though not without the begrudging co-operation of some of the school's representatives. In effect, the research ended when the student cohort graduated. The research generated several journal articles and a monograph and was well received by several of the students that had read ongoing drafts of the research. Leaving the field was unproblematic and even expected: Following graduation the class was dispersed and the research was never intended to track the students as they embarked upon their medical practice. Although such research might have contributed to a deeper understanding of medical professionalization, I had had enough. Although rewarding, the research proved terribly demanding from a time management standpoint. I felt it was time to move on. While academically and professionally rewarding, I was glad when the research ended.

By contrast, my studies of Hasidic Jews fascinated me both academically and personally. As a Jew, I was struck by their customs and traditions and fascinated by how they, individually and collectively, met the challenges of preserving their distinctive lifestyle. I thoroughly enjoyed visiting their neighbourhoods and engaging them in conversation. While gaining access to the Hasidim occasionally proved challenging, especially to the Tasher Hasidic sect, I slowly learned how to prepare for the challenge. I was unprepared when I was invited to leave. In this chapter, I recount some of my experiences around leaving the field following the completion of my doctoral dissertation. I discuss how the problem manifested itself with the Lubavitch Hasidic community, the subject of my doctoral dissertation; however, I mainly concentrate on an experience with the Tasher sect, which underscored the tenuous nature of field relations as it pertains to leaving the field. It should be noted that, from the beginning, I conducted field research among these groups simultaneously. I never attempted to pass as one of them. I believe that such efforts are not only inadvisable but also bound for failure.

THE HASIDIM

The Hasidim are ultra-religious Jews who live within the framework of their centuries-old beliefs and traditions and who observe Orthodox law so meticulously that they are set apart from most other Orthodox Jews. Even their appearance is distinctive: the men bearded in black suits or long black coats with black hats over side curls and the women in high-necked dresses of considerable length with kerchiefs or traditional wigs covering their hair. They are dedicated to living uncontaminated by contact with modern society. They do not own television sets, nor do they frequent movie theatres. They pursue religious studies zealously, but shun the universities. They carefully co-ordinate and control the secular subjects that are taught in their school to ensure that there will be no conflict with the pupils' religious upbringing. Boys and girls do not date and marriages are arranged. They dress and pray as their forefathers did in the 18th century, and they reject Western secular society in order to preserve a distinctive way of life. While seemingly a homogeneous collective to uninitiated outsiders, the Hasidim are divided into a number of distinctive sects. While commonly committed to the observance of Orthodox Jewish law, the sects differ in details of customs and traditions, and, most importantly, in commitment to the teachings of their charismatic religious leader, or Grand Rabbi.

GETTING STARTED, STAYING CONNECTED, AND MOVING ON

I happened to study the Hasidic community by chance. Actually, in my final year as an undergraduate I decided to do an ethnographic study of a pool hall that I planned to continue for my master's thesis. But a casual conversation with my thesis advisor, Malcolm Spector, led me to change topics. I knew very little about the Hasidim and what little I knew about them was laden with popular stereotypes: They kept to their own, and were fanatical and entirely disinterested in engaging in conversations with outsiders. Malcolm knew even less. So I plunged ahead, and this proved to be one of the more significant decisions I have ever made. It shaped my academic career and impacted my Jewish identity. Time flies, as they say; by now, I have been a student of Hasidic life for over 40 years. During this period, the "field" of the research has shifted. My presence in it has been more intense at certain periods than at others, owing in large measure to other research commitments and personal circumstances. More to the point, though the field has shifted, and even changed, I have never left entirely.

My doctoral dissertation examined the Lubavitch Hasidic community in Montreal. While visiting the community, I initially downplayed my research intentions, while emphasizing my interest in Judaism and Jewish life. Before long, however, my research intentions were known to all that were interested. Though collecting data by way of participant observation and interviewing was my primary objective, I was equally challenged by the Lubavitch teachings concerning Jewish identity and assimilation. I was also enormously impressed by the practical efforts taken by the Lubavitcher to reach out to Jews in the wider Jewish community to experience Jewish life Lubavitch-style. Lubavitcher proselytized among Jews and I was the beneficiary. I was welcomed into the community: I received invitations for Sabbath meals, and was invited and encouraged to travel to Lubavitch headquarters in Brooklyn, New York, commonly known as "770," to experience first-hand the teachings of the Lubavitcher Rebbe. I was always treated warmly when I joined the Lubavitcher in prayer services at the yeshiva. I would have maintained my intense connections to Lubavitch upon the completion of the dissertation save for two events that altered my life: First, I moved to Hamilton, Ontario, to accept a position at McMaster University; and second, I was introduced to the Tasher Hasidim and their enclave in Boisbriand.

My move to Hamilton, some 600 kilometres from Montreal, limited my visits to the Lubavitcher yeshiva, the place for me to be if I wished to be seen. So, at best, my visits became sporadic. No matter. When I did drop by the yeshiva, I was gently quizzed about my whereabouts and prolonged absences. My response was entirely satisfactory: I was no longer living in Montreal. But this response only partially addressed the fuller picture. After three years of intensive field research, I was tired. And initially fascinated by how the community developed and sustained itself, continued visits to the yeshiva failed to reveal new data. Still, I felt I owed the community a huge debt: It had allowed me to conduct research in the hope that I would become a more observant Jew. My exit was both gradual and voluntary.

In the course of familiarizing myself with the Hasidic community in Montreal, I heard about an enclave situated some 25 kilometres north of the city, populated by Tasher Hasidim. I was intrigued. Unlike the other Hasidic sects that resided in the Mile End and Outremont areas of Montreal, the Tasher, led by their Grand Rabbi, established a community in what is currently the municipality of Boisbriand. Purchasing a plot of land from a local farmer, the Grand Rabbi believed that the nascent community would be better able than its Hasidic counterparts in the city to stave off assimilative influences of secular culture. Most importantly, its boundaries would be more clearly defined. It was painfully clear that any outsider would be noticed immediately and their presence questioned. I had every reason to believe that I would not be welcomed to "hang around." I was right. But luck intervened.

My biggest challenge was to devise some means whereby I could be present in the enclave on a regular basis without arousing suspicions as to my actual intentions, that is, to conduct research. The community's distance from Montreal limited the kinds of explanations I might offer to account for my presence. For example, I could claim that their community aroused my curiosity as a Jew, or even as an aspiring sociologist, but such excuses would wear thin after a few visits. And if I were interested in Hasidim, there were plenty of places in Montreal where my curiosity would be satisfied. Though such justifications might be proffered occasionally, I did not expect they would be accepted to sustain my regular presence.

I believed this difficulty might be overcome when, while visiting the community, one of the rabbis informed me that he would soon be searching for a part-time instructor for secular studies. My hopes were raised when I was invited to interview for the position, but dashed when I was informed that I would probably be bored teaching students whose interest in secular studies was minimal. When I assured the rabbi to the contrary, I was told, "Actually you wouldn't be suitable because of your dress and appearance. It just wouldn't work out." Based on my appearance, my lifestyle might, and probably would, disqualify me. Very simply, the person sought to fill the position was one whose lifestyle would not adversely affect the student body. Thus, an Orthodox Jew or a Gentile would be preferable to someone like myself, a Jewish male whose affiliation with Orthodox Judaism was judged far too minimal. This experience underscored my impression that the community would not knowingly co-operate with an outsider like me whose interest in the community was to conduct research.

A chance encounter, some months later, with an ex-employee of the community helped me to secure a clerical position: I was hired to compose letters to prominent individuals that would include some background information about the Tash enclave and its new yeshiva, and request a monetary contribution. When asked during the interview why I was interested in the position, I explained that I was searching for part-time work and that, as a Jew, I was intrigued by the Hasidic lifestyle. I was offered the position by one of the individuals who believed I was unsuitable for the teaching post.

Based on my suspicion that the leadership of the community would not sanction an academic investigation of it, I chose not to inform my employers that I was collecting data. I did share with those that were interested, however, that I was a student at a local university and was studying sociology. I successfully used my interest in sociology to add legitimacy to the kinds of questions I asked about the community. When anyone expressed surprise as to my interest in certain community affairs—for example, the population of the community, the organization of secular education for the boys and girls—I would claim that my inquisitiveness was linked to my academic background. This explanation not only sufficed, but even provided some with reason to volunteer information that was assumed to be of interest to someone studying social organization.

Though my status as a university student was common knowledge, it was one that few people in the community could comprehend. Owing to this Hasidic group's insulation from the larger society, only a handful of its members were familiar with the academic world. Instead, and not surprisingly, these Hasidim conferred upon me a status that they could comprehend: that I aspired to become a more committed Jew, and wished to begin observing many of its commandments. I neither discouraged nor objected to this status and probably, both actively and passively, contributed to its rein-forcement. Thus, I listened attentively to the explanations provided for the observance of various Jewish laws, participated in prayer services when called upon, and expressed appreciation when anyone took the time to explain the rationale for the commandments that surround Orthodox Jewish life.

While working in this Hasidic community during the day, my evenings were spent conducting interviews and participant observation research among members of a different Hasidic group—Lubavitch. I soon realized that the time spent in my position at the Tasher Hasidim would have to be reduced if I were to meet my deadline for completing my master's thesis. Accordingly, I met with the two Tasher with whom I worked most closely, explained that I was required to write a master's thesis for my graduate degree, and requested that I be permitted to work only half-days. When asked, I explained that the thesis would deal with a pool hall in downtown Montreal. At this point, one of the persons described to the other his image and impression of a pool hall, and both quickly agreed that I ought to be dissuaded from pursuing this research. They suggested that, instead, I consider writing a thesis about the Tash community. One said, "Look, you know us. Why don't you write about us and we can help you?" Stunned, I agreed to meet them the next day to discuss the suggestion.

By the following day, both individuals no longer considered their suggestion viable. One maintained that he did not want his name in print, while the other claimed that non-Jews would read about the Hasidim and conclude that "the Jews are funny." Both agreed that since my knowledge of Orthodox Judaism was severely limited, I would not know the significant questions worth asking. At least two or three years of study in a yeshiva would be required to ameliorate this deficiency. One of them suggested that, instead, an excellent thesis topic would deal with "good government in Canada" and promised to provide me with his ideas on the matter. At the same time, I was informed that the yeshiva was strapped for funds and was unable to continue paying my salary.

Attempts at persuading them to reconsider their decision were unsuccessful. My departure from the field, though immediate, was amicable. I was assured that I would be a welcome guest whenever I visited and that the community and they would attempt to secure part-time employment for me elsewhere. While an offer of other employment was never forthcoming—I did not think it would be—I was always favourably received during visits to the community. My contact with the community continues to this day. I have never disclosed to anyone in the community that I once conducted research among them surreptitiously.

CONCLUDING THOUGHTS ON STUDYING HASIDIC LIFE

My tenure as an office employee proved disappointing for collecting data on facets of community life that interested me. I attribute this mainly to the covert nature of the research: Restrictions were placed on the kinds of conversations I might have with members of the community, but especially adolescents and young married males; however, my tenure as an office clerk served as a springboard for chatting with Tasher, especially when they entered the office for help or advice. And it was these very contacts that enabled me to remain in the field, that is, in Tash, even though I was no longer on the payroll. I was occasionally invited to community celebrations, such as weddings and holidays. And when I established a favourable relationship with a Hasid whose role in the community was central—in effect, he came to serve as my "Doc," a key informant—my connections to Tasher increased exponentially. I could and would visit the enclave at will, meandering in the synagogues and shopping centre, and engaging Hasidim in friendly conversations. I had gained a measure of trust and was invited to establish a website featuring the community that included several of my publications about the community.

Based on my experiences doing ethnographic research, I am hard-pressed to identify a magical formula attending to how, when, and why to leave the field. There are, of course, some obvious considerations: funding for a project ends thereby bringing the research to a close; sufficient data have been gathered so that "nothing new" is being discovered; and, perhaps most importantly, the initial excitement that characterized the research has worn off and fatigue has set in.

In point of fact, however, I would make the case that even while diminishing one's ties with informants, or severing one's connections completely, the researcher never leaves the field entirely. To be sure, there are degrees of leaving. But some parts of one's experiences from the field remain—be these recollections or reminiscences—that, in some form or manner, impact upon the researcher.

I continue visiting the Tash enclave, though the purposes of my visits have changed. I am no longer as committed to writing about them as I was earlier in my career; however, the underlying question that shaped my research about them remains: How has the community organized itself to ensure that secular influences do not impact negatively on the distinctive identity it has fashioned? Or, more simply, how does the community deal with change?

Occasionally, I find myself thinking about why the Tasher have not asked me to leave permanently. After all, I am an outsider. But I am more than tolerated: I seem to enjoy an honorific status. One key reason, perhaps, is that I am not perceived as a threat, and I display a warm appreciation for the lifestyle they have chosen. More fundamentally, perhaps, I have managed to earn a deep measure of trust.

CRAFTING QUALITATIVE RESEARCH EXERCISES

Write down your responses to the following questions. If you are involved in a research project now, consider the implications for your study. You can also consider any past research you or others have conducted. Discuss your ideas with a classmate, your professor, or your supervisor.

1. How might our departure from the field impact upon subsequent researchers interested in studying the same setting? Do we have an obligation to the discipline to ensure that the research setting will not be closed off prematurely owing to the "damages" left behind by the field researcher? Is there an ethical obligation that we should consider? Is it possible to lay out/outline considerations that, essentially, prepare our informants for our departure?

2. Do we have an ethical obligation to leave the field if individuals in it object to our presence?

3. All research has a beginning and an end. How do we know when it is time to leave the field? Are there certain signals that we can identify that indicate that our departure is/might be imminent?

4. How does one plan for leaving the field? Do we announce our departure to all informants with whom we have connected during the course of the research? Can we consider distributing a flyer announcing that our presence in the field has come to an end?

40 On (Still) Being Emotionally Attached to the Field

Nichole Edwards

When initially collecting my thoughts for how I would approach this chapter, I kept circling back to one question: Do you ever really leave the field? The simple answer, for me, is no. Almost four years have gone by since I spent the second year of my PhD conducting fieldwork, and I truly do not believe that I have left the field emotionally. My research explored the relationship between feminism and heterosexuality; in particular, it considered how one's feminist values shape or inform one's heterosexual practices, identities, and relationships, and, in turn, how one's practices, identities, and relationships shape or inform one's feminist beliefs. This was the primary, two-pronged question at the heart of my research, where 17 feminist-identified women explored this complex relationship through solicited diaries and follow-up interviews. It is my contention that had I not employed these methods, and were I not positioned as an insider (I, too, am a feminist-identified woman who engages in sexual and romantic relationships with men), I may not have become so emotionally invested in the research—and my participants. Most importantly, though, the rich and fruitful findings that became a part of my thesis may never have emerged as a result. Even if you do not identify as an insider within your field, I still think there is something to be learned here about the role that participants continue to play in our lives once we pack up our literal and figurative bags, and the difficulty we may have in doing so.

DOING FEMINIST RESEARCH

My research, in all facets, was feminist-informed. Like a lot of feminist research (and politics), my motivation to unpack the relationship between feminism and heterosexuality stemmed from personal experience. It often feels like one of the most clichéd feminist things to say, but the personal truly is, or has the potential to be, political. As noted, I am a feminist-identified woman who engages in relationships with men. This is not only a relationship I have grappled with throughout my adult life, but it singlehandedly led me to wonder if and how other feminist-identified women were navigating this seemingly incongruous relationship, or rather, what we may have thought was seemingly incongruous based on radical feminist critiques of heterosexuality. You can immediately start to see how I became emotionally attached to the women and experiences I was so interested in learning more about.

There is a consistent and undoubtedly rich body of literature—most prominently beginning in the 1960s, but also present in today's feminist debates—about the often tenuous relationship between heterosexuality and feminism. While these debates ultimately lie outside the scope of this chapter, the bottom line is this: it's complicated. For instance, is choosing to be submissive within acts of heterosex misaligned with the ideals of feminism? What about fantasies of rape? Or the silencing of one's own sexual desires in lieu of constant consideration for one's male partner? These are just a few of the tensions that emerged from my participants, some of which I also recognized in my personal navigation of heterosexuality and feminism. If these are among some of the issues I was reflecting on in my own experiences, you may be asking yourself, how could I not be setting myself up, so to speak, for the difficult task of eventually leaving the research field, particularly as I focused on an area in which I had invested years of my own personal thought and reflection? In hindsight, I realize that my position as an insider was inherently going to leave me vulnerable to emotional attachment; thus, leaving the field was always going to be a difficult task. This does not mean I would have changed any part of how I conducted my research, as I firmly believe that without employing the methodological and ethical considerations outlined below, my PhD may have become something entirely different.

ETHICS OF BEING AN INSIDER

Inspired by Oakley's (1981) seminal publication on research methodologies, "Interviewing Women: A Contradiction in Terms?" in which she argues that a feminist who researches women (and other feminists) is "by definition both 'inside' the culture and participating in that which she is observing" (57). I made no effort to conceal my positionality as an insider from my participants—they were fully aware that I had been attempting to navigate the same relationship that I was now asking them about. It is important to note here that this was not an attempt to dissolve power imbalances, as I understand this can never be possible; however, it was part of a concerted effort to present myself in a non-hierarchical way, and I believe it served to reduce social distance, where possible (Oakley 2016, 198). This was confirmed by a number of participants. Danielle, a 29-year-old woman, described having a peer perception of me, enabling a sense of comfort and trust in sharing her stories. Likewise, 25-year-old Vanessa admitted that there was no way she would have shared this kind of information with a non-feminist—or a man! Furthermore, 36-year-old Wendy appreciated that I shared information about myself in the weekly reminder emails I sent during the diary phase; it let her know that I was invested in the research in more ways than she had expected.

Specifically within the interview phase of my research (half of which were conducted in person and half online, due to geographical distance), I did not want to be viewed as a collector of data, and so the interviews entered a conversational mode where I became one half of a discussion surrounding life's intimate experiences (Oakley 1981, 41). It was my contention that establishing this type of relationship would promote and encourage a high quality of information. Like Oakley (1981), I answered questions when asked, but it was imperative that I let participants know I was using my own experiences to form the opinion I made. The motivation behind this sense of active involvement stems from the notion that in order to get the most from participants, I must be willing to disclose my own experiences when appropriate. As Oakley (1981, 49) states, feminist researchers cannot "gain intimacy without reciprocity," and so it became my duty to ensure this occurred. It is not coincidental to me that Oakley's (2016) participants had similar responses to mine when asked to reflect on their experiences of taking part in fieldwork. Although her research involved only interviews, the fact that I implemented a similar ethical approach (and that both sets of responses revolved around feelings of positivity), speaks to the way in which a researcher's commitment to active, emotional involvement has the ability to cut across different methods and topics. I often wonder if Oakley similarly struggled to leave the field, as she spent 30 years conducting research on the same topic, with the same participants. If my single year of fieldwork tells me anything, leaving the field may be a more difficult task than we collectively acknowledge, particularly as we often exit knowing that we have other people's experiences to unpack, not necessarily our own.

You might be asking yourself if this goes against some of the methodological and ethical considerations that social science researchers have historically been taught to maintain. That is, if objectivity is the goal of "good" research, you must only ever be a collector of data and, as such, detach yourself from the research process. I hope you can see why I wholeheartedly argue against these myths. Not only do I believe that emotional investment is oftentimes a simple and practical reality of doing social research, but I also think it would be naive to assume we can turn off our human emotions for the purpose, and apparent benefit, of conducting "good" research. However, in the conventional, masculinist approach to qualitative research, particularly when considering interviews, the person asking the questions is meant to dictate the framework of dialogue, while the person answering questions is said to be relatively powerless; in other words, the information passes one way (Oakley 2016). As outlined above, I worked hard to ensure that did not, in fact, happen. It is important to reiterate that I was not willingly sharing my own experiences; however, if and when asked, I responded in a conversational manner. The result of this approach meant becoming emotionally invested in the stories of my participants, which, in my case, contributed to the difficult task of emotionally leaving the field; however, I, alongside Oakley, firmly believe that this is the way research should be conducted. As Oakley (1981, 58) states, "a feminist methodology requires that … the mythology of 'hygienic research' with its accompanying mystification of the researcher and the researched as objective instruments of data production be replaced by the recognition that personal involvement is more than dangerous bias—it is the condition under which people come to know each other and to admit others into their lives."

Again, I am not saying I reciprocated in such a way that I became a part of the research findings, swayed my participants' opinions, or showcased my own unless asked—I believe that would have walked a fine line, ethically speaking. What I am saying is that because I promoted a non-hierarchical view of myself and positioned myself as an insider, I did not have to labour at establishing rapport. Furthermore, I did not make any effort to close off my own emotional responses to the lives, experiences, and identities of the women who invested their time and energy into my research. I believe *that* would have been dangerous and unethical.

THE USE OF DIARIES

My strategy behind asking participants to keep diaries before the interview phase was a means through which to encourage the sharing of intimate information. I needed to employ a well-known means of expression that matched the level of intimacy I was interested in unpacking, and the diary is regarded as a form of "intimate confessional[;]... the space to say what cannot be said out loud" (Harvey 2011, 675). The diaries also allowed participants to take control over what kind of information was disseminated so that when it came to the interview phase, not only did I already know a lot of intimate personal information about each woman, but I also had an indication of what they were and were not going to be comfortable discussing during their interviews.

Because the diary method is relatively underused in feminist sex research, I was interested in finding out how my participants felt about keeping the diary. In other words, what did they want to share about their experiences in the field before we parted ways? When asked if the contents of their diary would be affected by the knowledge that I would read them, the majority of my 17 participants said no. The importance of honesty, the ease with which they discuss sex in their personal lives, the importance of research that is beneficial to women, and the anonymity they had been guaranteed were all cited as reasons for non-censorship. Moreover, all but one found the diary stage personally beneficial. It allowed them to explore their relationship to feminism in ways not previously considered, encouraged them to think critically about their sexualities, and was regarded as therapeutic and cathartic. Before you leave the field, you may find asking your participants about their experiences a worthwhile activity, particularly if you employ methods that are not consistently found within your field. While I turned my participants' responses into a short report, I only briefly discussed them in my thesis and have not published them elsewhere; however, it proved to be a great exercise in reflexivity, reconfirmed my choice of methods, and continued to highlight how important my participants' voices were during all aspects of the research process.

EMOTIONALLY ATTACHED TO THE FIELD

As highlighted throughout this chapter, there was a series of carefully calculated ethical and methodological approaches that I employed throughout my research, and I believe that these choices impacted my ability to leave the field emotionally; however, as also noted, in Western philosophy, emotions are typically considered as impediments to knowledge, and the latter is seen as best achieved through rational, distanced, unemotional means (Jagger 1996). Yet, becoming emotionally attached to your research, and invested in the lives of your participants, is oftentimes just a practical reality of conducting research. Once you leave the field, you are still going to spend years of your life coding and analyzing your participants' experiences, writing and rewriting their stories into sociological existence. Moreover, if you see your own lived realities reflected back through those of your participants, it is of little wonder that leaving the field may prove to be a difficult task.

In writing this chapter, I am once again connected to these women, wondering how they are doing, and still very much emotionally bound to my fieldwork. So much happened in their lives during the time I knew them—one became pregnant, one had an abortion, one attended a sex party with her partner, another purchased her first sex toy. Some began new relationships, others ended. Some grappled with their sexual practices and identities, others with their commitment to monogamy. Did Danielle marry the partner she was engaged to but with whom she lacked sexual chemistry? Did Ruby tell anyone (other than me) about her experience of rape? Is Cleo now exclusively dating women? Is Ashley, simply, okay? To say that I have left the field would be naive as these women have played, and continue to play, an important role in my life as an academic, a feminist researcher, and a feminist-identified woman who engages in relationships with men. They are also inherently the reason I have a PhD—a simple fact of reality. So I ask you, how could I not be emotionally attached to the field? How could I truly ever leave? It is my contention that if we purposefully incorporate certain ethics and methodological approaches that promote a level of active, emotional involvement, we have the potential to become invested in more ways than perhaps envisioned, and while this may mean that we find ourselves thinking about our participants years down the road, I do not think we need to shy away from this potentiality, or the benefits that may emerge as a result.

Finally, I also ask you to consider that emotional attachment is a pillar of human connection and, as such, why should social science research not include these aspects of ourselves? If we, as researchers, are interested in unpacking the complexities and realities of various populations in order to produce the most nuanced understandings of their lived experiences, is it not our duty to ensure that we do *not* become disengaged, detached, and disembodied? While this may be easier to achieve as an insider, even if you do not position yourself as such, you are still a social science researcher and, by default, that means you care about the human condition. Becoming engaged, attached, and embodied in your own work has the capacity to produce knowledge that is passionate and exciting. Why not consider incorporating that sense of emotion into your methodological and ethical practices?

CRAFTING QUALITATIVE RESEARCH EXERCISES

1. Consider asking your participants about their time in the field. You may want to format this as an open-ended questionnaire so that they can take the time to put their reflections in writing. Include five or six questions, and be sure to make this optional as your participants have already invested a significant amount of time and energy in your research. Allow yourself to be open and honest about the information you receive back as this can prove to be a great exercise in practicing reflexivity.

2. Ask yourself: What are the costs and benefits to my research if I become emotionally attached to the people I am studying? Some researchers do not want to feel emotionally attached to their research and/or participants, and so it is important to find what works best for you. If you think you need to create a set of boundaries, write down a number of strategies that you can employ to ensure this does not happen, and contemplate the ways in which you will continue to ensure that these boundaries remain intact once you leave the field.

3. Even if you are not a feminist researcher, and do not position yourself as an insider within your field, take the time to read Ann Oakley's 1981 publication on social research methodologies. Consider why it was such a seminal piece, and how it may be beneficial for all qualitative researchers, regardless of your own particular area of study.

4. In which areas of your life, professional or personal, do you allow and encourage yourself to connect emotionally to people and/or ideas? Consider if there are any similarities between those identities and your identity as a researcher. In what ways do you think you could, should, and/or would harness those emotions within the context of your research practices?

REFERENCES

Harvey, Laura. 2011. "Intimate Reflections: Private Diaries in Qualitative Research." *Qualitative Research* 11 (6): 664–82.

Jagger, Alison. 1996. "Love and Knowledge: Emotion in Feminist Epistemology." In *Women, Knowledge and Reality: Explorations in Feminist Epistemology*, edited by Ann Garry and Marilyn Pearsall, 166–90. New York: Routledge.

Oakley, Ann. 1981. "Interviewing Women: A Contradiction in Terms?" In *Doing Feminist Research*, edited by Helen Roberts, 30–61. Boston: Routledge.

Oakley, Ann. 2016. "Interviewing Women Again: Power, Time and the Gift." *Sociology* 50 (1): 195–213.

SECTION X

DISSEMINATING YOUR FINDINGS TO SCHOLARS AND OTHER AUDIENCES

Professor Michael Burawoy, during his 2004 presidential address to the American Sociological Association, implored sociologists to engage "publics beyond the academy in dialogue about matters of political and moral concern" (5) and to "promote dialogue about issues that affect the fate of society, placing the values to which we adhere under a microscope" (Burawoy et al. 2004, 104). In response to his call, there has been growing interest and pressure for academics to "go public" with their research findings (Cain et al. forthcoming). This push for academics to go public and to engage with people outside of the academy coincides with larger discussions concerning the role of publicly funded universities and the impact of their research (Cain et al. forthcoming). In fact, universities across Canada are making pledges to better the lives of the communities and publics within which they operate (Walker 2008). As a result, researchers are looking for creative ways to engage the public, such as through public lectures, media releases, art, performances, documentaries, and publications. But should one go public and, if so, how should one do so? How does one present their research to public audiences and others who are maybe not familiar with, or even interested in, academic theories and concepts? How do we communicate complex ideas in ways that are easily accessible to those both informed and uninformed on the topic? Whom should we be responsible to when disseminating our findings—our research participants, other scholars, our colleagues, or taxpayers? These are all important and difficult questions that researchers must think about.

As demonstrated in the section on leaving the field, many qualitative researchers do not wish to simply engage in "research tourism" or "hit-and-run" research, wherein they collect data without giving back to the community they conducted research on or with. Instead, they want to give the research findings back to the participants in a way that is meaningful to them. Yet, how we present and communicate our research findings to our participants is often quite different from how we would present our research findings to other scholars. As such, research dissemination requires us to really think about who the audience is and to allow the audience to shape the type of dissemination used. For example, let's think about conducting research with police services. Most police services are not interested in receiving academic journal articles, but instead, would find it more valuable to receive research summaries or reports (often referred to as "grey papers") that are devoid of academic jargon, and in-person presentations that highlight the findings in a way that are meaningful and/or applicable to their service.

In this section of the book, authors reflect on the importance of, and experiences with, disseminating their research findings to both academic and non-academic audiences. The chapters discuss, and provide advice for using, different approaches to knowledge dissemination, such as art projects, documentaries, media, social media, and academic manuscripts. The chapters also provide advice on such things as communicating complex ideas effectively and managing public reactions to one's research.

We begin with a chapter by J. I. (Hans) Bakker entitled "Communicating Your Ideas and Publishing Readable Texts." In this chapter, Bakker discusses the difficulties academics face when attempting to communicate research findings clearly to uninformed audiences. Using his research on Bali, Bakker illustrates the importance of defining key terms and contextualizing research findings for the audience. He also emphasizes the importance of closely reading key texts when citing them. Using the concept of "definition of a situation" as an example, he demonstrates how students and scholars alike can often cite concepts without having read the original work and thereby inaccurately apply them to their own research settings. He concludes by providing advice on how to write publishable texts.

We then move away from traditional dissemination activities, such as publishing articles and books, to consider other ways to "go public." Snežana Ratković and Bharati Sethi's contribution discusses the importance of going public—to both academics and non-academics—for promoting social justice. In their chapter, they reflect on their use of conference presentations, community reports, calendars, and photovoice for translating and mobilizing the knowledge generated from their research on the experiences of immigrant and refugee women. Not only do the authors provide invaluable insight into different and unique ways to engage in art-based knowledge dissemination, but they also demonstrate the potential academics have to improve the lives of the marginalized.

Next, we move beyond discussions of how to "go public," and direct our attention to what happens after you do go public. In chapter 43, Chad Walker discusses the activism that can surround disseminating qualitative research. Reflecting on his own personal experiences with conducting qualitative research on wind turbines, Walker explores the backlash that he received from both his interview participants and the general public on his research findings. In this chapter, Walker discusses some of the risks associated with going public and concludes the chapter by giving advice on how to navigate public response to one's research.

Our final two chapters look at the use of media for disseminating research findings. In "After the Fine Cut: Disseminating Video-Based Research," Sarah Abbott and Phillip Vannini discuss the use of film as an effective tool to create and share ethnographic knowledge. Film, they argue, more than any other medium, has the ability to broadly disseminate a visual representation of participants' lived experiences. Drawing on their experiences of using film and documentaries, they outline useful tips and tricks for producing high quality video products, and share valuable advice for where to distribute video-based research (film festivals, Internet distribution, theatrical distribution, television broadcasts, and educational venues).

In this section's final chapter, Christopher J. Schneider discusses the difficulties academics can face when attempting to find and connect with news media. Drawing on his own personal experiences working with media and social media outlets, Schneider provides suggestions for connecting with *reputable* media outlets, such as getting involved with university public affairs offices, reaching out to journalists, and making use of social media platforms. He concludes by providing important tips on how to connect and interact with journalists.

REFERENCES

Burawoy, Michael. 2004. "For Public Sociology." *American Sociological Review* 70 (1): 4–28.

Burawoy, Michael, William Gamson, Charlotte Ryan, Stephen Pfohl, Diane Vaughan, Charles Derber, and Juliet Schor. 2004. "Public Sociologies: A Symposium from Boston College." *Social Problems* 51 (1): 103–30.

Cain, Katy, Krystle Shore, Crystal Weston, and Carrie B. Sanders. (forthcoming). "Knowledge Mobilization as a Tool of Institutional Governance: Exploring Academics' Perceptions of 'Going Public.'" *Canadian Journal of Higher Education*.

Walker, Judith. 2008. "Social/Corporate Accountability: A University's 'Trek' towards Excellence." *Canadian Journal of Higher Education* 38 (2): 45–71.

41 Communicating Your Ideas and Publishing Readable Texts

J. I. (Hans) Bakker

How can you get published? If what you write is a blog or popular article in a magazine, it is less difficult. But if you tackle a complex issue, it becomes more difficult. John Abromeit (2011, 1) begins his discussion of the life and thought of a famous thinker by quoting another famous social theorist—the essence of the quotation is that it is very difficult to comprehend a phenomenon and it is even harder to form an adequate representation of it. This discussion concerns the difficulty we face after we have done our research and want to disseminate the results. Getting published is difficult, but getting the results widely read and understood is even harder. Many academic articles are only read by a small group of people who are already very knowledgeable about the topic. It is rare for solid academic research to reach a wider audience. Erving Goffman managed to do that, as did C. Wright Mills, but they published primarily in books. Other researchers publish primarily in articles (e.g., Bakker and Bakker 2006). How can you publish your findings in such a way that you communicate your ideas clearly? In this chapter, I will discuss how to get your point across to people who have had little experience in the study of the topic.

USING AND DEFINING KEY CONCEPTS

One aspect of communication to a non-scholarly audience is use of key terms. The academic terminology well known to a small group of researchers may not be widely understood. For example, in the research paradigm called symbolic interactionism, the phrase "definition of the situation" (Bakker 2007) is well known, but the meaning of that phrase is not widely understood. Even well-educated people often question its meaning. Indeed, there is also considerable controversy as to its precise meaning. It could simply refer to the importance of an actor's specific understanding of a situation in real life, but it might also be interpreted to mean a broader set of rules or applicable cultural norms and values. If you use a term like "definition of the situation" in your writing, you need to present it in such a way that the average reader will not stumble on it. At the same time, leaving out all technical terms tends to weaken an argument and may make your findings much less valuable. Moving beyond common sense statements often requires the use of some words or phrases that are not a part of everyone's everyday vocabulary.

The Example of Writing about Bali

Moving beyond common sense phrases and introducing new terms becomes particularly problematic if your research is in a significantly different subculture or national culture. An example from my own research will illustrate this point. I have done interviews and observations in Bali, an island province in Indonesia. The project began with casual visits to the island as a tourist. After many encounters, some patterns seemed to emerge. The heart of the findings concerned the ways in which Balinese people engage in community activities. Somewhat like academics, Balinese people have their own terminology. Moreover, they use certain key phrases to distinguish a Balinese from someone who is a citizen of Indonesia but not Balinese. A research article or book explaining the words that the Balinese use requires a bit of general cultural knowledge on the part of the reader. Ironically, those readers who have spent time travelling abroad are much more likely to understand key terms than those who have never been to another country. The more the reader already knows, the easier it is for them to also comprehend some of the more subtle points that emerged from the ethnographic fieldwork.

Hence, when I write about Bali, it is often difficult to communicate the subtle aspects of the findings. I cannot expect the average reader to know anything about Indonesia. Those readers who may have a little bit of knowledge may have been misled by the mass media. While there are many Muslims in Indonesia, there are also four other world religions that are respected, including what we call Hinduism, and Buddhism (Faure 2009). Bali is neither Hindu nor Buddhist, as those religions are understood by most people in the Global North today. Instead, it has its own very specific blend of the two religions, a synthesis that dates back to the sixth and seventh centuries. It is therefore useful to use the term *agama Bali*. The term *agama Bali* refers to the specific Buddhist-Hindu belief system that the majority of people born in Bali still adhere to today. Despite the influx of millions of tourists from all over the world, the inhabitants of Bali remain Balinese in part because they focus many of their activities on agama Bali.

In various publications, I have written about the ways in which agama Bali influences the daily life of the average Balinese person. It constitutes part of the "definition of the situation" of the Balinese. Outside of Bali there are relatively few places where the same beliefs still have such a strong impact today. A key to Balinese social action is the way in which they follow a very elaborate calendar; however, when I write about Bali I cannot assume that the average reader will know anything whatsoever about the Balinese calendar. But it is often useful to introduce the term that the Balinese use for their own calendar. It is called the *wuku* calendar. The wuku calendar is quite different from the Common Era calendar based on the Roman Catholic Gregorian calendar, the one we all use to get to an airport anywhere in the world, even the airport in Bali.

Balinese people have no difficulty using the world calendar, with 12 months and 365 1/4 days. But when it comes to agama Bali they have to rely on their wuku calendar.

Naturally, the more those Balinese terms are introduced, the more difficult it starts to become to fully get it. In seminars I often have to repeat key terms. Inevitably, some of the students will miss questions on the final exam because they have still not learned the key new words. If I were to simply say or write that the Balinese have a calendar and it influences the "Hindu" practices, then the discussion would go no further than a superficial guidebook presentation. Some people visit Bali for a week and stay at a five-star hotel. They never learn about agama Bali and the crucial importance of the wuku calendar. Qualitative research findings that do not go beyond common misperceptions found in guidebooks are not really valid findings. But it is difficult to make real findings based on extensive participant observation clear to anyone who knows very little or may even have acquired false stereotypes. I have sometimes spoken to tourists who insist that the guidebooks are right and that my findings could not possibly be valid. When I presented at various conferences I found that only a few students and faculty members had patience with the subtle nuances.

Part of the problem also has to do with generations. Older readers will understand some terms and not others. Many older people know the phrase "Gregorian calendar" but I have found that most of my students do not know about the idea of a Common Era calendar derived from a Roman Catholic pope's reforms of an earlier calendar (i.e., the Julian calendar). So if you want to reach a very broad audience keep in mind that if you yourself are relatively young it might at times be important to explain background information that members of Generation X, Y, or Z know but that baby boomers will not know.

In general, to disseminate research findings requires writing clearly and keeping in mind that the terms that we may have been socialized to use in our graduate education may not be generally understood by the reading public. There is currently less interest in the use of footnotes or endnotes to explain terms, so you have to incorporate the explanation into the body of the text. Since that can become cumbersome it is often wise to not use key terms at all. In most social science disciplines and paradigms the clear statement of key findings is preferable; yet there is always a balancing act involved. You want to be understood but you also do not want to throw out the baby with the bathwater. That is, you probably will feel that you have discovered something. Your findings are probably not widely known. So you have to try to present the findings in such a way that the creative and original part of your work does not become so diluted that the research is written off as simply a set of common sense observations. There is a notion that "everyone" is already a psychologist and a sociologist. But after years of training and education you most likely know things that people who did not study those disciplines do not know. Indeed, psychologists know things that sociologists do not always know, and vice versa. Moreover, even within a discipline, the different research paradigms often have their own specific technical terms. So when you submit your work to a journal try to choose a journal that will have some open-mindedness about the terms that are common to people doing similar research.

Complex Thoughts Require a Somewhat Complex Text

There is no simple way to express complex thoughts in a straightforward manner. But one clear rule is to avoid introducing terms that you know your reader will likely have to look up in a dictionary. At the same time, it is sometimes delightful to read authors who indulge in very complex pyrotechnics, but that is usually at a more advanced level of scholarship. For example, the quotation referred to at the beginning of this chapter is a quotation from the work of Georg Wilhelm Friedrich Hegel. For most philosophers and many social scientists, the work of Hegel is relatively well understood, at least at an introductory level. Here is the full quotation: "To judge something that has substance and solid worth is quite easy; to comprehend it is much harder; producing an adequate representation of it, which unifies judgement and comprehension, is the most difficult of all" (Hegel 1996). The author citing that quotation (Abromeit 2011) is writing about a very well-known thinker named Max Horkheimer. The work of a major theorist like Horkheimer requires that we think carefully. Ultimately, really valuable social science ideas require more than superficial study. We disseminate our findings in such a way as to allow everyone access, but, at the same time, we also often realize that there are levels of learning. We cannot expect the second year ("sophomore") student to fully grasp ideas that a PhD student struggles with understanding. But we can open the door very wide.

Finally, it is also true that many articles are cited but not necessarily read in depth. For example, academic work is represented in scholarly journals. Relatively few under-graduate students read academic journal articles; in term papers, they often cite articles they have not read carefully, in part due to the rush of an academic quarter or semester. Yet, ultimately, there is no substitute for careful, slow reading of texts. In a paper that I presented at a conference, I focused on a ritual in Bali, but I made some incidental comments about the way in which a very well-known anthropologist had used the term *thick description*. Many of the members of the audience were far more interested in my remarks about that term than they were in my ethnographic findings about the ritual. When I eventually modified the paper for publication I put more emphasis on that term and its meaning. For me, the foreground was the ritual and the background was a well-known methodological term. But for many people in my audience the methodological term was the foreground and the Bali material was of less concern. It became clear to me that many people who claimed to have read the famous article to which I referred had probably only skimmed that article. They then cited it to be able to indicate that they were familiar with the famous term: *thick description*. My essential criticism was that the anthropologist had not actually demonstrated the use of thick description.

After many years I have sometimes returned to key texts and discovered that I had missed a lot. I thought I understood what a specific author was saying, but certain nu-ances became clearer only after much more experience. Ironically, sometimes the easiest way to access the thinking of complex philosophically included social theorists is to read their lectures rather than just stick to their published works (e.g., Foucault 1997).

Similarly, it is sometimes an English translation of a work that makes that complex study more accessible (Hegel 1996). Sociological theory is often difficult to read, but when we use social theories of all kinds in our research publications, it is wise to obtain the absolute best translations and to read those translations thoroughly to get the overall intent of the original author, be that a Hegel or a Foucault.

CONCLUDING THOUGHTS

There is no hard and fast rule about the dissemination of findings. Some articles and books that are relatively less easy to read catch on, while other publications written in a very straightforward manner are quickly forgotten. There is a big difference, for example, between textbooks written for undergraduate students and books that are written for a wider audience. Popular books are sometimes cited for a very long time, while many textbooks are forgotten soon after they have been published. Do introduce technical terms somewhat slowly so that you do not make it hard for a reader to start to get involved in reading your text. Do not use your published work to try to demonstrate knowledge of complex ideas you yourself do not fully understand. If you cite someone, try to actually read the whole article or book as carefully as time allows. When submitting work do not write off the comments of referees and yet, at the same time, do not take each and every word a reviewer states as the whole truth. It is the overall criticism that is most important. Incidental comments may simply be spur of the moment ideas the reviewer themself has not thought about carefully. Keep in mind that getting published in academic books and journals is exciting but it requires hard work.

CRAFTING QUALITATIVE RESEARCH EXERCISES

1. Go to the university library and find a *printed journal*. Look at recent issues and find one refereed, scholarly journal article on a subject that seems very unfamiliar. Read the article three times, carefully. Take notes the second time. After reading and rereading the article, ask yourself what you have learned. Are there still questions that need to be answered? Then, and only then, look up key terms and perhaps turn to online sources to get better acquainted with background issues.

2. Find an *online research article* from a refereed, scholarly journal. Go through the same exercise as in question 1; however, while reading the article the first time look up anything you want online or in printed books (e.g., dictionaries, encyclopedias). Was it easier for you to then read it the second time? Were your

notes longer or shorter? You now have a basis for thinking about why today's students read or do not read classical versus contemporary research articles.

3. Find a *book* by C. Wright Mills and read it. Sit down and read the whole book from cover to cover. Do not read anything else until you have finished the book. Ask yourself the following questions and write down your answers in a notebook. (Write them out; do not just type or text them.) Is the book a good read? Did it flow from one chapter to the next? Are all the chapters interconnected? Did you learn anything you did not know before? Why do you think many people have been drawn to Mills's books?

4. Find an *article* by C. Wright Mills or Erving Goffman. Compare reading one of their articles to steps 1, 2, and 3 above; that is, do Mills and Goffman write more clearly than the scholarly research articles you have read? Are they easier to understand? How does an article by Mills or Goffman compare to a book by Mills? Was it necessary to look up new words?

REFERENCES

Abromeit, John. 2011. *Max Horkheimer and the Foundations of the Frankfurt School*. Cambridge, UK: Cambridge University Press.

Bakker, J. I. (Hans). 2007. "Definition of the Situation." In *Blackwell Encyclopedia of Sociology*, Vol. 3, edited by George Ritzer, 991–92. Oxford and Malden, MA: Blackwell. Blackwell Reference Online. http://www.blackwellreference.com.

Bakker, J. I. (Hans), and Thoreau Bakker. 2006. "The Club DJ: A Semiotic and Interactionist Approach." *Symbolic Interaction* 29 (1): 71–82.

Faure, Bernard. 2009. *Unmasking Buddhism*. Malden, MA: Wiley-Blackwell.

Foucault, Michel. 1997. *"Society Must Be Defended": Lectures at the College de France, 1975–1976*. Translated by David Mackey. New York: Picador.

Hegel, Georg Wilhelm Friedrich. 1996. *Phenomenology of Spirit*. Translated by Terry Pinkard and Michael Baur. Cambridge, UK: Cambridge University Press.

42   Dissemination and Social Justice

Snežana Ratković and Bharati Sethi

> If you promise that you will try very hard so that your work does not gather dust in a cupboard.... If you promise to bring my voice, thoughts, and suggestions to the larger audience, especially those who make policies then you can interview me. I will give you my time and undivided attention. (Rudo)

This honest and emotionally laden statement is from Rudo (pseudonym), one of the 20 participants in Sethi's (2014) doctoral study. This participant's statement and expectation that knowledge created through research should be made accessible to academics and non-academics, including stakeholders, immigrants, refugees, practitioners, policy-makers, and the general public, is critical to researchers committed to social justice work. While other participants may not articulate their desire for research dissemination as frankly and eloquently as Rudo did, we found that at every interview the participants quietly enquired: "What are you going to do with the interview data?" This question was not surprising to us; telling a migrant story to Canada, and the world, was the main reason we pursued our doctoral studies. Fulfilling the contract with Rudo means making sure that participants' messages, imparted through photographs, interviews, and/or other forms of data collection strategies, reach academics and non-academics.

Disseminating the findings in a manner that would be accessible not just to scholars, but also to the general public is important to us on a personal and an academic level. We are both immigrant women. We have often been marginalized due to our immigrant status, geography, nationality, and/or gender. Although we are now citizens of Canada, we are often perceived as newcomers, the Other. The stories of our research participants often haunt our sleeping hours. As transnational feminist researchers, we are committed to developing "reciprocal relationships from which both researchers and participants benefit" (Tilley 1998, 325). Social justice goals cannot be achieved unless academic knowledge produced through a rigorous research process is accessible to *both* scholars and other "people in the field" (e.g., health care practitioners, employers, social workers, policy-makers, educators, and newcomers). It is important that all people in the field are included in conversations about racialization, citizenship, and other important issues related to immigrants and refugees. Further, research dissemination that can occur while the research project is in progress (e.g., publishing an article on literature review or methodology) or immediately after completing the project, is important to building new research knowledge (Pellecchia 1999). Moreover, practitioners and stakeholders can use the research findings to improve their practice and policy.

In recent years, there have been increasing calls for academics to build community-university alliances and find ways of translating research findings into public policy and community reports that can be understood by lay people. To accomplish this critical goal of respectful research and social justice work, we engaged in knowledge translation and knowledge dissemination. Knowledge translation (KT) is defined as "a dynamic and itera-tive process that includes synthesis, dissemination, exchange and ethically-sound applica-tion of knowledge" to improve the lives of marginalized populations (Canadian Institutes of Health Research 2016). Knowledge dissemination (KD) is an "active process to com-municate results to potential users by targeting, tailoring and packaging the message for a particular target audience" (Canadian Institutes of Health Research 2010, 2016).

We translated our findings through photographs, transcript poems, metaphors, bi-lingual texts, research summaries, and a calendar. We disseminated our findings through national and international peer-reviewed conferences, national and international peer-reviewed journals, edited books, the Centre for Excellence in Research in Immigration and Settlement (CERIS) website, art exhibits, and/or YouTube. The following are some of the questions that guided our diverse dissemination strategies:

1. How does the dissemination method accomplish the research goal(s)?
2. Who are the audiences that would benefit from the research dissemination strategies?
3. Is the chosen dissemination strategy suitable for the research project? For ex-ample, if photos are not part of the data collection strategies but they do include creation of other art forms, how can such data be displayed?
4. Have the participants given informed consent for dissemination of the find-ings at every stage of the project, including creation of art pieces, planning the exhibit, and creation of the community calendar?
5. Is confidentiality of the participants maintained through dissemination?

In this chapter, we combine the research strategies we used in our research projects to discuss the five KD strategies we used to reach academics and non-academics:

1. Arts-based knowledge dissemination using photovoice
2. Community report
3. Calendar
4. Dissemination of preliminary findings
5. Conference presentations and speaking engagements

ARTS-BASED KNOWLEDGE DISSEMINATION USING PHOTOVOICE

As the goal of the first study (Sethi's study) was to foster economic integration of immigrant/refugee women, it was established at the beginning of the project that once knowledge was created through data collection and analysis, it must be translated into a language that was accessible not just to academics, but also to practitioners and policymakers. The KD strategies were included in the research process even prior to data collection. For example, it was agreed that participants and researchers would convert participants' photographs collected during the study into art pieces and display them in various art exhibits throughout Canada. Efforts would also be made to have the exhibits available online to enhance accessibility. The following steps were involved in the creation of the art exhibit:

1. A local photographer/graphic artist was recruited and paid an honorarium to work individually with each participant from the beginning of the project. The task of the photographer was to teach women how to use digital cameras and take care of the cameras throughout the research, provide tips for taking professional photographs, and show them how to download and save the photos to the USB stick that was provided to them.

2. Sethi worked with the participants to select the photos that they were comfortable sharing at local and national art exhibits. The participants gave consent to use the photograph for one-on-one and focus group interviews and to display the photograph at art exhibits. It is important to revisit the process of informed consent throughout the research process, especially during the development of KD strategies. See figure 42.1 for an example of a photograph. This photo included the following quote: "Represents desire for freedom. Because I am an immigrant I am not free to do what I like to do as far as employment is considered."

3. After the participants selected the photographs they were willing to share with the public, the photos were arranged thematically. The themes included the following: Pre-migration Expectations Do Not Meet Post-migration Reality; Barriers to Integration, Work, Health and Family; and Adaptation. For details on the themes, see Sethi 2014.

4. Sethi worked with the graphic artist to convert the photographs into art pieces. Participants chose the layout, colour, and design. Each art piece represented a particular theme.

5. Sethi launched her research as an art exhibit at the Yellow Brick Wall Gallery, Wilfrid Laurier University, in Grand Erie. The research launch was attended by over 150 people, including the local member of parliament, the mayor's office, the local member of provincial parliament, employers, health care practitioners,

Figure 42.1: Bird Cage by Ding

      academics, social workers, immigrants, refugees, religious leaders, and community members. The local media also wrote about the exhibit (see Marion 2014; Toms 2014). Following that exhibit, Sethi presented photovoice research at several academic and community conferences. She also held exhibits in Toronto, Hamilton, Kitchener, Waterloo, and London. An evaluation form was given out at the first exhibit and provided evidence that the art exhibit was a powerful method to disseminate research findings.

6.   Sethi is in the process of exploring ways to develop a virtual art exhibit that can be available online to a wider audience, including international audiences.

Art exhibits are demanding in terms of time and finances, but exciting and innovative in terms of dissemination and social change. They have the potential to reveal the power structures hidden in the discourses of citizenship and the Other. The exhibits created safe spaces for discussions about uncomfortable topics, such as racism. The relationship between "visible minority immigrant/refugee women" and "Canadian state" has been complex and elusive for hundreds of years. Reaching practitioners, policy-makers, and community members can lead to new understandings of citizenship and new alliances between visible minority immigrant women and the Canadian state.

COMMUNITY REPORT

Community reports written in non-academic language are important sources of information for community practitioners. Such reports provide concise information about the research project and findings of the study. Local service providers can use this information to apply for government funding and enhance their services for newcomers. Sethi developed a 41-page community report from her doctoral photovoice project. She wrote this report in plain language and provided the study's background, an overview of the photovoice project, and recommendations. The hard copy of the report was distributed to community partners and other local service providers if they chose to use it in training their staff to provide culturally sensitive services to immigrants and refugees. The report also outlined the needs of local immigrants and refugees.

CALENDAR

In addition to the community report, Sethi wanted to develop a tool that could be useful in translating the findings to employers in a simple, accessible format. She created a 24-month desk calendar from her photovoice project to reach employers and create an awareness of employment issues that visible minority women experience in Grand Erie, and in Canada. Each month of the calendar featured a particular photo from the project with the participant quote. For example, the calendar featured a photo of a rock (figure 42.2) by Sherman with the following quote: "The Rock—The rock represents how hard employers' hearts can be. My message to employers is to have empathy put yourself in their shoes."

DISSEMINATION OF PRELIMINARY FINDINGS

During her PhD studies, Ratković was studying part time, working full time, and taking care of her family. In such a complex situation, Ratković's doctoral supervisor advised her to focus on completing her dissertation, rather than on publishing. Ratković, however, yearned to achieve some tangible results while navigating the challenging landscape of dissertation writing. She published her preliminary findings (Ratković 2011, 2013) in Canadian and international peer-reviewed journals before completing her PhD. She was aware that writing these two journal articles hindered her PhD completion and postponed her graduation. At the same time, these two publications motivated her to continue writing during some desperate times of exhaustion, confusion, and identity crisis. During these challenging times, Ratković would remind herself that transnational feminist researchers work for reciprocity and social change; she was on a quest to make her participants' voices accessible to policy-makers, service providers, and education authorities locally, nationally, and internationally.

Figure 42.2: Rock by Sherman

Seeing her work published in peer-reviewed journals strengthened Ratković's commitment to her dissertation; "somebody out there" cared about refugee women's stories, realities, and opportunities. Her research findings reached Canadian and international audiences before her dissertation was even completed. Moreover, her work (Ratković 2014) informed transdisciplinary scholars, including scholars of education, forced migration, gender studies, and research methodology. She was exhausted and happy.

CONFERENCE PRESENTATIONS AND SPEAKING ENGAGEMENTS

Since completing her dissertation in 2014, Sethi has presented her photovoice project at several local and national conferences and conducted workshops for students and practitioners. She has been invited by community organizations to present the research to staff and management. She has also held six photovoice exhibits at various venues in Ontario.

Since 2008, Ratković has been an invited guest speaker across educational settings, including universities, high schools, and CERIS. Identifying, reaching, and convincing her audience(s) remains an imperative in her scholarly work. She presented her doctoral research to high school students, teachers, principals, teacher candidates, graduate students, faculty members, deans of education, refugees, and immigrants. Ratković has taught these diverse audiences about refugee women's professional integration in Canada, migrant students' and teachers' lives, transnational education, and transnational feminist methodology. Additionally, a scholar from Glasgow, Scotland, invited Ratković to co-author a book chapter (Ratković and Pietka-Nykaza 2016) about refugee women teachers' professional integration in Canada and the United Kingdom. Currently, Ratković is in the process of devising an ethnodrama based on her doctoral work.

CONCLUSIONS

As academics, we have strived to follow through on our promise of making sure that the participants' data do not gather dust in academic cupboards. We sought and embraced opportunities to disseminate research findings in a variety of ways. We have made every effort to bring participants' voices to policy-makers to inform them that refugee and immigrant women's full participation in economic, social, and political life in Canada entails much more than shelter. It requires a "deliberate collaboration" between service providers, all levels of government, researchers, and refugee and immigrant women. In an era of globalization and migration, Canada must go beyond tolerating diversity to celebrating diversity. As responsible and respectful citizens of Canada and the world, we must acknowledge that immigrant and refugee women enhance Canada's cultural, racial, and intellectual diversity. While today we are proud to be Canadians, we look forward to a day when refugee and immigrant women will not be racialized and marginalized in this country—that, to us, would be true freedom. Dissemination of research can open pathways where the truth can be seen, heard, and honoured. Until the truth, however ugly, is openly dealt with, true freedom and social justice are not possible.

CRAFTING QUALITATIVE RESEARCH EXERCISES

1. Pick a target audience that would benefit from your research. Design a knowledge translation and dissemination activity suitable to reach this target audience. Explain why your proposed activity is beneficial and what challenges may arise when implementing this activity.

2. Discuss the strengths and challenges of social media as a dissemination strategy.

3. How do you feel about publishing other people's voices? What strategies would you use to present your participants' voices in a respectful and credible manner? What challenges do you anticipate? How would you address those challenges?

4. Discuss the importance of using multiple data sources and multiple modes of data representation in a research study. What might be the benefits for research participants? What might be the challenges for the researcher? Create a sample project that contains a minimum of three data sources and three modes of data representation.

REFERENCES

Canadian Institutes of Health Research. 2010. "Knowledge Dissemination and Exchange of Knowledge." http://www.cihr-irsc.gc.ca/e/41953.html.

Canadian Institutes of Health Research. 2016. "Knowledge Translation at CIHR." http://www.cihr-irsc.gc.ca/e/29418.html.

Marion, Michael-Allan. 2014. "Photovoice Exhibit Features Work of Immigrant Women." *Brantford Expositor*, April 5, 2014. http://www.brantfordexpositor.ca/2014/04/04/photovoice-exhibit-features-work-of-immigrant-women.

Pellecchia, Geraldine. 1999. "Dissemination of Research Findings: Conference Presentations and Journal Publications." *Topics in Geriatric Rehabilitation* 14 (3): 67–79.

Ratković, Snežana. 2011. "Transitions from Exile to Academia: Experiences and Identities of Refugee Women Teachers from the Former Yugoslavia." *Power and Education* 3 (3): 196–209.

Ratković, Snežana. 2013. "The Location of Refugee Female Teachers in the Canadian Context: 'Not Just a Refugee Woman!'" *Canada's Journal on Refugees* 29 (1): 103–14.

Ratković, Snežana. 2014. "Teachers Without Borders: Exploring Experiences, Transitions, and Identities of Refugee Women Teachers from Yugoslavia." PhD diss., Brock University, St. Catharines, Ontario. https://dr.library.brocku.ca/handle/10464/5243.

Ratković, Snežana, and Emilia Pietka-Nykaza. 2016. "Forced Migration and Education: Refugee Women Teachers' Trajectories in Canada and the UK." In *Diversifying the Teaching Force in Transnational Contexts: Critical Perspectives*, edited by Clea Schmidt and Jens Schneider, 179–200. Rotterdam, Netherlands: Sense Publishers.

Sethi, Bharati. 2014. "Intersectional Exposures: Exploring the Health Effect of Employment with KAAJAL Immigrant/Refugee Women in Grand Erie through Photovoice." PhD diss. (Comprehensive), Faculty of Social Work, Wilfrid Laurier University, Waterloo, Ontario. http://scholars.wlu.ca/cgi/viewcontent.cgi?article=2737&context=etd.

Tilley, Susan A. 1998. Conducting Respectful Research: A Critique of Practice. *Canadian Journal of Education* 23 (3): 316–28. http://dx.doi.org/10.2307/1585942.

Toms, Colleen. 2014. "Innovative Research Project Gives Immigrant Women a Voice." *Cambridge Times*, April 15, 2014. http://www.cambridgetimes.ca/news-story/4466145-innovative-research-project-gives-immigrant-women-a-voice.

43 Promoting Qualitative Research in the Public Sphere: Lessons Learned from Online Criticisms

Chad Walker

INTRODUCTION

What will you do when research participants and others threaten to terminate your study? Though public disapproval of research is nothing new, there has been little discussion surrounding activism against academics. More often, discussions relate to the role of the academic *as* activist (see Castree 2000). In this short chapter, I take the reader through my story of taking qualitative research into the public sphere. To do so, I first outline my graduate research and explain why I chose to engage with participants and the public more broadly. Next, in order to illustrate the potential negative feedback qualitative researchers in particular may face, I highlight the comments received as a result of my work. Finally, the chapter closes with some first-hand advice—providing the reader with an opportunity to learn how I was able to get through these difficult moments and continue on with an academic career.

BACKGROUND

Under the encouragement of two academic mentors during my undergraduate program, I decided to begin a research-based master's degree (MA) in geography at Western University in 2010. The MA research employed in-depth qualitative interviews (n = 21) to examine social responses to wind energy development in Ontario. I chose interviews because I was interested in understanding the in-depth, daily life impacts—including health problems—of those living near wind turbines. While credible research has since been done showing a lack of direct health effects (i.e., mediated through noise annoyance and planning processes; see Chapman 2014; Michaud et al. 2016; Walker, Baxter, and Ouellette 2015), during the time of my studies there was some media and grey literature that suggested otherwise. This uncertainty in rural communities helped breed degrees of resentment and conflict amongst local residents (Walker, Baxter, and Ouellette 2014) and between residents and the provincial government (McRobert, Tennent-Riddell, and Walker 2017; Songsore and Buzzelli

2014); thus, the issue of wind energy had become politically charged and I was ready for the possibility of interviews becoming emotional or contentious in nature. Further, due to recent calls for broadly defined environmental research to be more applied (Clark and Dickson 2003; Garb, Pulver, and VanDeveer 2008) and presented as "usable knowledge" (Owens 2005, 287), I decided to make a conscious effort to make my findings visible and accessible. To do so, I made sure my thesis was posted to a publicly available online forum, and for select publications that followed, I helped write media releases and made myself available for the interview requests. This resulted in meetings with several local and regional media organizations who eventually shared my research findings across their respective outlets. While I enjoyed these experiences and still think it was the right thing to do, at the time I could not have imagined what was to come as a result of "going public."

CRITICISMS FROM PARTICIPANTS

In the pages to follow, I share the criticisms faced in the months after my research was published and promoted. First through participant feedback and then online forums, criticisms of my work began somewhat constructively and then evolved into personal assaults on my integrity, intelligence, and abilities as an academic.

The first set of comments that were directed at me personally was received as a result of a member checking exercise used to increase qualitative rigour (see Baxter and Eyles 1997). Member checking, which has been called "the most crucial technique for establishing credibility" (Lincoln and Guba 1985, 314), occurs when researchers take interpretations back to participants. In order to member check, I created a 10-page summary document of preliminary findings and sent it to all 21 participants, asking them if I "got it right" or fairly represented conversations with them. Though most of the feedback I received (n = 12) showed appreciation for the research conducted in the community, there were a few instances in which this was not the case. Most of these comments made were on the grounds that the *qualitative* analysis provided was not seen as credible research. This critique was not entirely surprising, as qualitative researchers have long faced criticisms from the public and other academics including the perceived lack of validity and secrecy behind qualitative analysis (Anfara, Brown, and Mangione 2002; Sale, Lohfeld, and Brazil 2002). As a result, there is a tendency for the general public to hold quantitative research to a higher standard (Labuschagne 2003). In one response following the member checking exercise, a participant clearly disagreed with the methodological basis for the research:

> There is so little data in your interpretation that anyone doing a peer review would be at a loss to say there is any validity to the comments you compiled.... There are just too many incommensable [*sic*], anecdodal [*sic*] stories. ("Barbara")

"Barbara's" comment showcases a common criticism of qualitative research. Her need for more data and fewer anecdotal stories suggests she values the breadth of quantitative data over the depth provided by qualitative research. In the weeks following sharing of the member checking document, I received an email that was several thousand words long from another participant opposed to wind turbines. In the email, he explained that I did not fairly represent his views and that because he saw my research as unethical, he would be taking up his complaints with the university administration—including the president. The idea of my research—something I was passionate about and spent so much of my life preparing for—being terminated because it was perceived as unethical was a scary proposition. In an attempt to best address the situation, I immediately met with my supervisor who suggested I contact the administration, including the research ethics board at my university, and set up a meeting. After the board reviewed my case, I was assured that because the research I had conducted was approved and no wrongdoing was evident from their perspective, I should not be worried about threats to shut down the project.

CRITICISMS FROM THE PUBLIC

I also faced backlash from a range of online anti–wind energy activists. Following the publication of my thesis and later journal articles, I took part in interviews with media organizations. This led to several newspaper articles and radio broadcasts related to my research. Public remarks were enabled through discussion boards posted below these online media reports. One of the first comments seen relating to my work was posted beneath a media article that outlined a paper written by my supervisor. Despite the fact that the paper referred to a separate research project from my own, the majority of the conversation turned to my work during and following my MA.

> This young fellow is not a science or engineering major. So what does he really know about IWT (Industrial Wind Turbine) scientific issues?... Since when does a geography department have students write "research" papers on subject matter outside of there [*sic*] knowlede [*sic*] sphere?... This is an opinion piece of work. ("Barbaron")

This type of criticism may sound familiar to social scientists. Though academia is increasingly aware of the merit of social scientific inquiry (see Weber 2015), there are still some factions of the general public who see researchers outside of the natural sciences to be inferior. Other online commenters continued the assault on my research by explicitly attacking the reputation of Western University. I believe such comments—including those from "Sarahon," below—are meant to discredit *both* the research conducted and the graduate degree acquired.

For many years Western has been known as the "party" university. Learning to drink beer is more important than academics. (Each university has their own calling among the kids.) Anyway it seems like nothing has changed re Western and a secondary degree from here is worth about as much as your first degree. Diddly squat!! ("Sarahon")

Within the same comment board another person, "WillRon," found the link to my thesis[1] and asked people to "please download and save a copy. I have." They went on to suggest that the paper was undeserving of being deemed academic research when they said, "Are the standards really this low for a Master?" Together these comments illustrate a personal attack that simultaneously questions the academic standards of the university and my successful thesis defence.

Another theme found throughout the comment boards among those who disagreed with the findings from my thesis was criticism for being biased and/or funded by the green energy industry. Through these discussions, there emerged the perception that any research that suggested the expansion of renewable energy—however indirectly—was not to be trusted.

This student has swallowed the [Liberal] green aid totally, even footnotes Liberal talking points on the benefits to air quality.... A failure for sure!! Poor student. (Martin)

Someone should ask this "student of green madness" if he received or is still now receiving any monetary return for his biased Master's thesis.... Students are very burdened with money worries as they continue with their pursuit of "higher/lower learning." ("Thebiggreenlie")

As these comments show, when people disagreed with the findings they would reframe the findings to be biased and unethical. Interestingly, when a 2014 publication in *AIMS Energy* was promoted on the website of an anti-wind organization, people seemed to be more accepting of (some of) the findings when they agreed with their own ideas. While there were still some negative comments—such as "Highly disrespectful!" from a person named "Free Thinker"—most were encouraged by the fact that some findings agreed with their opinions. For example, a major conclusion from the publication was that turbines may negatively impact the value of some homes. "Barbara" and others tended to agree with this assertion and in doing so, avoided making any serious accusations of problems with the research or myself.

When you change the character of any neighbourhood/area this affects property values. This [research] is nothing new. ("Barbara")

DISCUSSION: TIPS FOR NEW RESEARCHERS

Though disapproval of academic research by the public is not new, writing about the difficulties faced by researchers is still rare. In using real examples of the backlash I faced, the goal of this chapter is to help novice qualitative researchers in particular begin to understand problems that can arise when research goes public. As was shown throughout the preceding pages, there can be tremendous risk when taking research findings into the public sphere—especially when studying controversial issues.

In my own example, a group of people became exposed to my research, disagreed with the results, and became very critical of it (and, in turn, me). My experiences in publishing and promoting qualitative research also suggest that people are much more likely to be critical of research findings when the findings disagree with their ideas about reality. This should be a point that researchers keep in mind when making their research public. That is certainly not to say that academics should conform their findings to fit what will be accepted by the public; rather, researchers should expect that research that challenges the status quo—a goal of many in the profession—will inevitably lead to critical examination from the public. Anticipating that activists and others will read your work should also make you more aware of any of its possible shortcomings. For example, based on the types of response I received during and after my MA, I am now more careful not to overstate any conclusion—even those that are supported by empirical evidence. Preparing for this kind of "public defence" may also help with thesis defences and journal article publication processes.

In the aftermath of a wave of criticisms and threats, there were a few things I did that enabled me to continue on toward my MA, and, later, a career in academia. It is my hope that the reader can learn from these in order to avoid any possible setbacks in similar cases. First, I was fortunate to have an experienced supervisor whom I felt comfortable talking with about the path forward in the face of some serious resistance. He was especially instrumental in reviewing my research and later assuring me that my practices were ethically sound. It is important for novice researchers in particular to meet with these types of people whose experience and mentorship abilities will bring some degree of calm.

Another suggestion I have also relates to the first steps that should be taken when researchers are faced with ethical or other accusations. As I did, I encourage people to reach out to their research ethics boards or offices for guidance. To this point, novice researchers in particular should not underestimate the ethics approval process at their own university. If I had left out even a minor detail from my ethics application (e.g., estimated sample size), the public may have had the means to shut down my research. Attention to these details and being truthful with ethics boards can assist in this way.

Third, upon the advice of my research supervisor, I also set up meetings with other members of the university administration—including the three who were named as potential contacts for concerned citizens to get in touch with. These meetings were helpful in establishing a strong support system within the university—while I also sought comfort from people outside the academy. I was again fortunate to have a group of family and friends who assured me that I was not the type of person who would conduct unethical research. These assurances also allowed me to retain my mental well-being through some turbulent times.

CRAFTING QUALITATIVE RESEARCH EXERCISES

1. In order to understand the public response you may receive as a result of your research, find a recent online news article that summarizes a paper in or related to your field of study. How was the research summarized and what kind of questions would you expect to come from the public? If there is a comment board, what kind of responses do you find? Do they match your expectations?

2. If you are collecting data through interviewing or focus groups, write down 5 to 10 questions or topics that may be contentious in nature. Make sure these issues are made clear in your ethics application. How could you best ask these types of questions without creating too much conflict or tension between yourself and your research participants? Practice asking them with other students who are playing the role of activists to see how you would respond to resistance and hostility.

3. Do your best to predict all probable major outcomes (at least three to five) from your study. For example, if you are studying access to abortion clinics, a major finding could be: "There is a general lack of abortion clinics in low-income neighbourhoods" or "Women often avoid clinics because of a social stigma." What types of public responses do you think you would receive based on these findings? Are you ready for the possible backlash? Discuss with your academic supervisor.

4. In recent years, academics have turned to Twitter and other social media platforms to promote their research. Using #ScholarSunday and other discipline-specific hashtags, search Twitter for examples of researchers in your field who effectively shared their research. Using what you learned in question 1, what are the advantages of using social media over traditional news media outlets? Based on your new insights, what do you think is the best way to make your research public?

NOTE

1. Western University makes all graduates theses publicly available through its Electronic Thesis and Dissertation Repository (http://ir.lib.uwo.ca/etd/). It will be helpful to know if your university has the same type of system in place.

REFERENCES

Anfara, Vincent, Kathleen Brown, and Terri Mangione. 2002. "Qualitative Analysis on Stage: Making the Research Process More Public." *Educational Researcher* 31 (7): 28–38.

Baxter, Jamie, and John Eyles. 1997. "Evaluating Qualitative Research in Social Geography: Establishing 'Rigour' in Interview Analysis." *Transactions of the Institute of British Geographers* 22 (4): 505–25.

Castree, Noel. 2000. "Professionalisation, Activism, and the University: Whither 'Critical Geography'?" *Environment and Planning A* 32 (6): 955–70.

Chapman, Simon. 2014. "Factoid Forensics: Have 'More Than 40' Australian Families Abandoned Their Homes Because of Wind Farm Noise?" *Noise and Health* 16 (71): 208.

Clark, William, and Nancy Dickson. 2003. "Sustainability Science: The Emerging Research Program." *Proceedings of the National Academy of Sciences* 100 (14): 8059–61.

Garb, Yaakov, Simone Pulver, and Stacy VanDeveer. 2008. "Scenarios in Society, Society in Scenarios: Toward a Social Scientific Analysis of Storyline-driven Environmental Modeling." *Environmental Research Letters* 3 (4): 045015.

Labuschagne, Adri. 2003. "Qualitative Research—Airy Fairy or Fundamental?" *Qualitative Report* 8 (1): 100–3.

Lincoln, Yvonna, and Egon Guba. 1985. *Naturalistic Inquiry.* Vol. 75. Newbury Park, CA: Sage.

McRobert, David, Julian Tennent-Riddell, and Chad Walker. 2017. "Ontario's Green Energy and Green Economy Act: Why a Well-Intentioned Law is Mired in Controversy and Opposed by Rural Communities." *Renewable Energy Law and Policy Review* 7 (2): 91–112.

Michaud, David, Katya Feder, Stephen Keith, Sonia Voicescu, Leonora Marro, John Than, Mireille Guay, Allison Denning, D'Arcy McGuire, Tara Bower, Eric Lavigne, Brian Murray, Shelly Weiss, and Frits van den Berg. 2016. "Exposure to Wind Turbine Noise: Perceptual Responses and Reported Health Effects." *Journal of the Acoustical Society of America* 139 (3): 1443–54.

Owens, Susan. 2005. "Making a Difference? Some Perspectives on Environmental Research and Policy." *Transactions of the Institute of British Geographers* 30 (3): 287–92.

Sale, Joanna, Lynne Lohfeld, and Kevin Brazil. 2002. "Revisiting the Quantitative-Qualitative Debate: Implications for Mixed-Methods Research." *Quality and Quantity* 36 (1): 43–53.

Songsore, Emmanuel, and Michael Buzzelli. 2014. "Social Responses to Wind Energy Development in Ontario: The Influence of Health Risk Perceptions and Associated Concerns." *Energy Policy* 69: 285–96.

Walker, Chad, Jamie Baxter, and Danielle Ouellette. 2014. "Beyond Rhetoric to Understanding Determinants of Wind Turbine Support and Conflict in Two Ontario, Canada Communities." *Environment and Planning A* 46 (3): 730–45.

Walker, Chad, Jamie Baxter, and Danielle Ouellette. 2015. "Adding Insult to Injury: The Development of Psychosocial Stress in Ontario Wind Turbine Communities." *Social Science and Medicine* 133: 358–65.

Weber, Max. 2015. *On the Methodology of the Social Sciences*. Morrisville, NC: Lulu Press.

44 After the Fine Cut: Disseminating Video-Based Research

Sarah Abbott and Phillip Vannini

Film can be a very effective tool for the creation and sharing of ethnographic knowledge. Film and video bring representations of people and cultures to life through the impression of movement created by successive film/video frames, evoking a sensation of living presence and action that extends beyond the capacities of writing and photography. More than any other medium, film "uses experience to express experience" (Barbash and Taylor 1997, 1). We, the authors of this chapter, have been working in film and video respectively for over 5 (Vannini) and 20 years (Abbott), and are continually inspired by film's potential to activate audiences' imaginations, senses, and emotions, and stimulate discussion among a wide range of viewers. Abbott is a filmmaker and associate professor of film production. Her work covers a range of social concerns and film genres, including documentary and narrative filmmaking. Along with national and international festival selections and television broadcasts, Abbott has screened her work online, in educational settings, and in association with public panel discussions she organized on the social issues her films deal with. Vannini, a Canada Research Chair and professor of culture and communication, is engaged in making ethnography enjoyable for wide audiences beyond academia. His ethnographic film work has screened at domestic and international festivals, on television, and online via video on demand.

The potential for dissemination of ethnographic knowledge via film to broad public audiences is enormous; however, all too often, the creation of an ethnographic film is viewed as the end point of a project and not enough attention is given during production and post-production to the broadcast quality of the picture and sound—a shortcoming that, in the end, can deeply affect the extent to which a film can be disseminated and appreciated. In light of this, the focus of our chapter is twofold. First, we share some useful tips to help boost project production value. Second, we discuss various film distribution avenues and their pros and cons. In our writing, we use "film" and "filmmaking" interchangeably with "video" and "video-making" to refer mainly to digital recording and editing technology.

AIMING FOR HIGH QUALITY PRODUCTION

We can't stress enough the importance of producing high quality video and sound from the moment a project is conceived. Viewers nowadays want crisp technical elements that relay a sense of professionalism, are appropriate to the film's subject matter, and create a feeling of "being there." Preparations to tackle projects with high production value in mind must begin at the budgeting and pre-production stages so that all of the equipment and know-how is in place before filming begins.

High quality video refers to a number of elements, including good resolution, which is the level of detail on a screen resulting from the amount of pixels in a digital image. The more pixels, the sharper and more detailed the image. We recommend familiarizing yourself with the various video camera formats: standard definition (SD), the different types of high definition (HD), 2K and 4K resolutions. Keeping with current standard broadcast requirements means recording at least full HD (1920 x 1080), but increasingly projects are being shot on 4K, especially as the price of 4K cameras comes down; however, filming in 4K requires significant storage capacity for large video files. Editing can be done with lower res files, but extremely powerful computers and/or assistance from a professional film post-production company are necessary for finishing the film.

High quality video also consists of well-captured images using clean, reliable equipment: camera on a tripod or steadily hand-held; smooth and/or dynamic, well-paced camera movements; appropriate and unique camera angles; dynamic and appropriate framing, composition, aesthetics, and interview backgrounds; and proper and effective exposure and lighting. How a film is edited also speaks to its production value: smooth cuts, effective shot and sequence lengths, and editing rhythm and style that align with the subject. Lastly, after the film is locked and no more editing will occur, the colour of the shots should be corrected to give the film a visually unifying polish.

It is important to pay equal attention to both sound and picture during all stages of the project. High quality audio should be properly recorded during production: microphones and recorders need to capture clean sound and must be well-positioned in relation to participants and audio sources, levels should be adjusted to minimize peaking in the audio, minimal to no background sounds should be present during interviews, and ambient recordings ought to be made in all locations. The common expression "we'll fix it in post" may save time, but cutting sound corners while filming most often proves time-consuming and expensive during post-production. Strong sound work during editing includes layering voice-over and interview dialogue with other sound, such as ambience; smooth edits without abrupt sound changes or drop-outs; appropriate use of ambient location sound and sound effects; and suitable music used strategically to intended effect rather than profusely—music tracks laid out throughout an entire film become annoying, distracting, and manipulative. After the film is locked, a sound mix should be done to balance levels of the various tracks.

AIMING FOR WIDE DISTRIBUTION

Where precisely a film is shown is largely determined by its production value. The higher the quality, the greater the chances a film will be selected for film festival screenings or television broadcast, and the greater your chances of making future films. From the get-go, it is important to anticipate your audience and aim high while balancing these ambitions with the realities of your budget, funding, and project parameters.

Publicity

During production and post-production, collect dynamic, eye-catching still images that reflect the heart of your project. These stills can be photographed during production or taken from the video footage if necessary. Filming at high resolution makes it easier to reproduce high quality video stills. Create a strong poster, postcard, and/or website for the project. If you anticipate festival screenings, a postcard is good way to inform potential audiences at the festival itself. Write a succinct one-line synopsis (logline) and a 25- to 50-word synopsis. Edit a trailer. Spread word of your film through social media and media releases sent to all media outlets that may potentially be interested in talking to you and/or your participants about your film.

Film Festivals

Thousands of cities and towns the world over organize film festivals that attract dozens of filmmakers and industry professionals, and hundreds of spectators. Film festivals vary in size, from showcasing a handful of films to well over 100; these films range in length from short to feature, in genre from experimental to documentary to narrative, and in theme from none to specific, such as LGBTQ, race, environment, outdoors, and so on. Film festivals also differ from one another in terms of prestige and status. Sundance and the Toronto International Film Festival generally attract large-budget films produced by well-established production companies. Though these festivals are always on the lookout for dynamic independent films, the competition among thousands of submissions is steep. Other, less internationally prominent, festivals tend to be more open to small productions and even student films. Ethnographic films are documentaries so they should be submitted to festivals specializing in both ethnographic and documentary film. Ethnographic film festivals for makers and researchers of ethnographic films and topics are uniquely meaningful venues to learn about colleagues' work, share one's research, and develop valuable friendships and collaborations.

The process of submitting films to festivals can be resource-intensive with regard to money and time. Submission fees range from a few to over 100 dollars, while travel to one's own film screening is usually the responsibility of the filmmaker. The efficiency of online festival submission websites, such as Withoutabox, FilmFreeway, and FilmFestivalLife can save significant time. Filmmakers can input extensive information about their film and upload it on a secure private screener to these sites, choose from hundreds of listed film festivals to submit their film to, and pay festival fees by credit card. We suggest prudence when selecting from these festival lists: it is exciting to find so many potential festivals for one's film, but the cost of submitting to all of them quickly adds up. Some festivals request film screeners be sent on DVD rather than uploaded to these websites; this means costs for creating and mailing the DVDs. Festival projection format requirements are generally digital files nowadays: Apple ProRes and DCP (Digital Cinema Package). The latter format requires technical knowledge to properly produce and may require hiring the (expensive) expertise of a professional film finishing house.

Unlike submitting to most academic conferences, submitting to film festivals is very competitive. Selection committees may consider the credentials of a filmmaker, and perhaps their associated production and distribution companies. This is not because film festivals are exclusive in principle, but because not all films submitted can be programmed over the short duration of the festival. Films may also be selected for the degree to which they fit a festival's mission, and their length. Longer films require more time in a festival's schedule, so acceptance of shorter films can be easier to secure. The production value of a film is considered as well: no matter how terrific the content, festival programmers will not consider a film if it looks or sounds bad.

There are many positive and not-so-positive aspects associated with film festival submission and participation. Significant time on the film festival circuit can delay a film's broader release, making it less timely and relevant when it reaches the public through other venues. It takes research and effort to connect with industry professionals, and lesser-ranked festivals may offer limited opportunities for networking. And the submission process can become discouraging when rejection letters pile up. There will be acceptances and non-acceptances—to play the game of festival submissions means being prepared to lose some battles. On the positive end, it is exciting and important for a film to be selected into and, ideally, awarded at film festivals. Festival laurels improve the odds that a film will be selected by other film festivals, picked up for theatrical distribution and/or television broadcast, and garner funding for future projects. Professional connections made at film festivals can lead to future production collaborations and distribution agreements.

Internet Distribution

Online distribution may occur in conjunction with or after screenings on the festival circuit, or if a filmmaker bypasses film festivals altogether. There are several ways to distribute a film on the web and related digital platforms, and these are constantly evolving. The simplest approach is to make a film available for free via YouTube or Vimeo. After uploading, a filmmaker would be wise to generate web traffic through social media and create publicity through newspaper, television, and radio interviews, blogs, magazine and newspaper articles, and so on. The pros of this option are obvious: it is relatively easy and fast. The cons become evident after some time: limited views and quickly declining interest. Additionally, after a film is made freely available, it is virtually impossible to find a distributor or broadcaster who will be interested in it. Many academics working with video do little beyond making their productions "accessible" by uploading them to the Internet. In so doing, they may fail to actualize the potential impact of their research.

If a film has good production value, the first move to increase its online audience impact is to release a trailer on the Internet, and direct people to a project-dedicated website via social media. The next task is to seek distribution through video on demand (VOD) platforms that allow viewers to rent or purchase films for small fees. Among the simplest such platforms is Vimeo On Demand. Its contract allows filmmakers to retain most sales revenue after paying an annual subscription fee to the website. Though an ethnographic filmmaker may never become rich from VOD sales (and, arguably, that is not the point anyway), having a video protected from fully open public view makes it possible to find theatrical distribution and broadcast licensing deals. It also lends the film value and generates interest, as most viewers feel that paying for something makes it more desirable than something that is free.

VOD platforms like iTunes, Amazon, and Google Play do not allow self-distribution like Vimeo on Demand does. To have a film featured on those platforms, a filmmaker must be represented by a content aggregator, which is essentially a distribution company specializing in doing business with those platforms. Securing a distribution agreement with an aggregator requires good networking, but companies like Distribber are making it easier for the average DIY filmmaker to reach out to large-scale VOD platforms. It should be noted that digital distribution on VOD platforms is now infinitely more sensible than selling DVDs—an onerous task requiring significant investment by a distribution company and, therefore, something that is beyond the financial and time capacities of most ethnographic filmmakers. Subscription video on demand (SVOD) platforms like Netflix operate similarly in terms of doing business only with aggregators, yet much less profitably (there is very little money in Netflix for independent producers). Rather unique among SVODs is Kanopy: a sort of Netflix for universities, specializing in educational and intelligent content.

Theatrical Distribution

Ethnographic filmmakers interested in screening their films before live audiences for theatrical release have essentially three options. The first entails securing a distribution deal with a well-established company. The company will recoup its initial costs then take a percentage of the revenue, while doing all the marketing and accounting work. Sadly, few ethnographic films receive this kind of theatrical distribution. The second option entails filmmakers organizing movie theatre screenings themselves. Most cities and university campuses have one or more independently owned cinemas that specialize in independent and alternative (non-Hollywood) productions. Many theatre managers will happily rent their venue for single or multiple screenings of a film. Others may offer to split ticket-sale revenues instead of charging a rental fee. The third option for theatrical screenings is through web-based networks like Tugg, a company that has established hundreds of agreements with movie theatres in select countries. The agreement consists of a film playing in any movie theatre if a minimum number of tickets are pre-sold by a certain date before the scheduled screening. If the minimum threshold is not met in pre-sales, ticket purchases are refunded. If pre-sales are successful, Tugg, the movie theatre, the screening promoter and the filmmaker (the latter two may be the same) split the revenues in varying percentages.

Television Broadcast

Television broadcast, another distribution avenue, ensures large audiences for a film through initial broadcast, re-broadcasts, and availability online through cable company VOD platforms. Television broadcast deals can be difficult to secure without a distribution company and a product that appeals to wide viewership. Filmmakers without distributors can contact television broadcasters to pitch their completed films, works-in-progress, or production ideas to sell their films or find project funding. The most likely television venues for ethnographic films remain, at the time of writing, public broadcasters with an educational mandate and public access community channels. We recommend consulting broadcasters' requirements before beginning to edit your work, as broadcasters have strict specifications when it comes to content, length, and breaks for advertising.

Educational Venues

Community organizations and events, school boards, classrooms, university departments, libraries, and even prisons are excellent educational venues to pursue for screenings and sales. For short films, you don't have to wait to hold educational screenings until after a film has run the festival circuit and received television broadcast. Filmmakers themselves, or knowledgeable teachers, students, or community members, can host educational screenings at community centres and movie theatres. These screenings can be paired with panel discussions or activities for the public related to the issues dealt with in the film.

CONCLUSION

A lot of work is involved in making a film with high production value for distribution to wide audiences. It requires forethought, effort, rigour, and commitment. It involves knowing your audience, aiming big, and doing what it takes within your budget to make the film come together. As a final gesture to maintain quality before releasing your film to the public, have a few pre-screenings and invite feedback from trusted, critically minded friends who aren't afraid to point out your mistakes. Project the film as large as possible to magnify the picture, and listen for sound inconsistencies. Be ready to continue to work hard after the film is completed in order to find broad distribution for your film. Many filmmakers don't anticipate this stage and let their energy drop when the film is finished. Ultimately, through all this hard work, have fun and enjoy the process. Film is an amazing way to connect people, knowledge, culture, and issues.

CRAFTING QUALITATIVE RESEARCH EXERCISES

1. Spend time analyzing short films. Study video projects to better understand how the technical elements are successful (or not successful) in creating high production value according to our list of elements presented in the chapter.

2. Make a three-year distribution plan for a film you intend to make. Decide who your audience is and what themes your film resonates with. Research and list screening venues that pertain to your film's topic, including festivals, television broadcasters, and educational venues. Make a one- to two-year strategically planned schedule for film festivals that puts the more prestigious festivals in the first year. Decide which festivals you would like to premiere your film at, internationally, nationally, and locally.

3. Learn more about producing and distributing high quality video projects. Research the aspects of video and sound production, post-production, and distribution described above to understand them in depth and detail. Practice production skills and watch for these elements when viewing films. Look into the roles of people involved in production, distribution, and broadcasting of films.

4. Prepare a film project in its development stage. Make a budget for the pre-production, production, post-production, and distribution stages of a project. Look online or in books and follow templates that contain details for the many expenses associated with making a film; decide which expenses are relevant to your production.

REFERENCE

Barbash, Ilisa, and Lucien Taylor. 1997. *Cross-Cultural Filmmaking: A Handbook for Making Documentary and Ethnographic Films and Videos*. Berkeley, CA: University of California Press.

45 Disseminating Qualitative Research in Media

Christopher J. Schneider

Since acquiring my PhD in 2008, my research and commentary have appeared in more than 450 radio and television broadcasts and print publications across the world. I have written elsewhere about some of my experiences with news media in a short essay entitled "Interacting with News Media Journalists" (Schneider 2012). In this chapter, written for qualitative student researchers, I develop a few points from my previous piece (which was written over 200 interviews ago) and provide some additional tips and advice on how to draw attention to your research in media.

For a variety of reasons, getting qualitative research into the media can be a difficult endeavour. A basic explanation for this is that qualitative research findings can be difficult to concisely parse down to neatly fit the format of various media platforms, both traditional and new media. Consider the latter: for instance, a 280-character tweet on Twitter is not likely to convey the intricacies expressed by your interview participants. While this almost goes without saying, the first and most important piece of beginner advice in my view is as follows: identify and learn the parameters of your chosen dissemination platform. This includes how materials are organized to fit within the logic of each particular medium: Instagram is an image medium, YouTube a video-based medium, etc. Since the dissemination of our work is largely text based, i.e., written (with exceptions), I first suggest starting with print news media to begin to craft and fine-tune your research dissemination skills.

START WRITING LETTERS TO THE EDITOR

As a graduate student, I subscribed at any given time to at least three different newspapers (old-fashioned, I know): one local daily, one large metropolitan daily, and one national "agenda-setting" newspaper.[1] I enjoyed reading the papers, and in doing so, made it a habit a few times a week to find stories that related in one way or another to my research. In my downtime, usually during breaks from my academic work, I would write a letter to the editor of one of the three newspapers. (Depending on the publication, most letters are usually 150 words or less.)

This exercise will be more difficult for some than for others, depending on research focus. If I could not find a story or topic related to my work, I would look for one that I found of general interest. A letter to the editor is usually only accepted within a week of the publication of a story. Several of my letters were published in the local daily paper and one letter was even published in the *New York Times*. This simple exercise, turned into a weekly habit, will teach you to get creative in relating your work to contemporary news topics.[2] You will also learn how to be very concise, an important and useful skill in your academic writing. Lastly, this exercise will give you a good sense about the format (i.e., print medium), and time constraints that govern the news media cycle.

UNIVERSITY PUBLIC AFFAIRS NEEDS YOU!

After completing my graduate studies, I started my first gig as an assistant professor at the University of British Columbia (UBC). As a new faculty member, it wasn't long before the UBC public affairs office contacted me. Most universities have an office of this sort (sometimes these offices are listed under different names, such as media relations). Its primary task—no matter what the name—is to connect members of the university with media in order to help generate news stories. The generation of news stories in media serves a few purposes. Each time your name appears in news media, it appears alongside the name of your university. This is free advertising and, depending on the outlet (e.g., national or local news media), this free advertising can sometimes be worth tens of thousands of dollars in ad value.[3] Of course, the promotion of research in media is also meant to spotlight the important work being done at your university, research conducted often at the expense of the taxpayer.

The point to stress here is that your university wants to promote your ideas even when you are a student. Don't let your student status (undergraduate or graduate) prohibit you from reaching out to your public affairs office on campus. One email can go a long way, more than you might think. You may even consider sending the public affairs manager one of your letters to the editor.[4] This will give the people at public affairs a sense of your developing work and research. Think that you are doing something innovative? Chances are the staff at the public affairs office might agree! In my experience, contacting public affairs about an idea or recent publication has, on occasion, led to the generation of news media releases about my work. This may not produce a news story for you right away, but it will get you on their radar, and you may perhaps find an email from public affairs in your inbox.

Before I continue, you may be justifiably thinking to yourself, Why would I need a public affairs office to help me spotlight my research when I have social media accounts already to do this? This is a good point and I will briefly address social media below. The late qualitative researcher Professor Bud Goodall once remarked to me in a conversation sometime in 2008 that "the cultural space is crowded." He was, of course, correct in his observation and, since then, the cultural space has grown and become more crowded. If you can get your research profiled by public affairs at your university, it can provide an institutional legitimacy that will help spotlight your research in these crowded spaces. But if this proves to be difficult, you can reach out to the journalists themselves, sometimes with the help of public affairs and your faculty advisor.

WANT TO SEE THE MAN BEHIND THE CURTAIN? JUST ASK.

I have made many friends in the media industry over the years. Public affairs are the keepers of the contact information of media journalists and other industry insiders. This is, of course, no mystery. While much of this information is freely available on the Internet, you can save yourself a lot of time and energy searching for it by simply getting to know the university public affairs people. Once you have established a good relationship, you may just consider politely asking for this information. As an example, I recently switched institutions and had not yet become acquainted with media relations at my current institution. I was looking to promote my new book so I reached out to a former public affairs colleague and asked for a list of contacts. This person emailed me an Excel spreadsheet containing the names and contact information of nearly every mainstream book and literature journalist across Canada. These contacts proved to be quite useful and generated a few book reviews, including one in *Maclean's* magazine.

ONLINE SLEUTHING

If asking for the contact information of journalists fails, you can resort to searching the old-fashioned way online. Journalists are people like you and me. They are often looking for ideas for stories to pitch to their editors and producers. A good place to start is on social media. Many journalists have Twitter accounts. Just tweet your pitch at them. This is where a short edit and a little reworking of a letter to the editor may come in handy. You will also sometimes find emails and other relevant contact information in Twitter biographies. If that fails, you can usually locate people by entering into Google versions of what you think their email may be. Start with the end of the email of the news organization (this is usually quite easy to find). As an example, consider my institutional email, @brandonu.ca and possible versions of my email, Christopher.Schneider@brandonu.ca or C.Schneider@brandonu.ca, etc. These email addresses are incorrect, but Google searches return the correct email.

INCREASED MILEAGE ON YOUR RESEARCH IN THE "POSTJOURNALISM" ERA

"Postjournalism" is an idea coined by Altheide and Snow (1991). The basic premise is that stories and issues that journalists write about are often themselves products of media

(Altheide and Snow 1991). In other words, journalists write about stories prepared else-where, such as reporting on the details of a government press release. This logic applies in much the same way to media stories themselves. Interviews generate other interviews. Typically, the more high profile the media outlet (i.e., agenda setting), the more subsequent attention by way of additional interviews such coverage will generate. As an example, I was asked to comment on guidelines issued by the privacy commissioner regarding police body-worn cameras.[5] These remarks were featured in a front-page article of the *Toronto Star*, Canada's most circulated newspaper. Nine live radio interviews followed its publica-tion as a direct result of the article. If possible, you will want to get your research profiled in some sort of print media, as these articles are readily searchable online. Journalists often resort to Google (or known contacts) when seeking comment on an issue. The trick is to get your name and research associated with a particular issue.[6] Print media are quickly accessible online and can lead to future interviews. A few months after the publication of the *Toronto Star* report, I was contacted by various print, radio, and television news orga-nizations about the issue of police body-worn cameras. Subsequent television interviews included one with CTV's *Canada AM* and another with CBC's *The National*.

It can take years to build this kind of momentum so do not be discouraged. Start with your local newspaper or your student paper. Send a version of your letter to the edi-tor to a local/student reporter about your research. Your letter will situate your work in a contemporary topic of interest and will hopefully generate an article (hooray for post-journalism!). Once published, send a link of the article to the media contacts that you have located online or that public affairs has provided to you. You will then also want to post the link of the news story featuring your research to your social media accounts. For instance, you might tweet the link to media journalists and producers, as well as to your university social media accounts.

SOCIAL MEDIA

Thus far, I have mostly steered clear of discussing social media; my doing so is certainly not meant to minimize the importance of social media. But social media are just one piece of the much larger research dissemination puzzle. Anyone can say anything about themself online. When media outlets cite you as an expert in your field, this often carries more credibility than if you say so yourself. That said, establishing an online presence is, of course, still important. You should also build a webpage. This can be quite easy and free (see www.webs.com as one example).

Numerous academics post blogs and record podcasts and video lectures. A quick online search will produce many good "how-to" tutorials. Many scholars also tweet and post links to their blogs, podcasts, and videos, and this can help build your online presence and disseminate your research. You may also consider discussing your ongoing research with scholars on social media. Better yet, if possible, tweet any peer-reviewed publications to those in the field and/or those scholars whom you are citing. In some circumstances, this can quickly spread your work across the vast social media landscape. Consider a recent paper that Deana Simonetto (her work is included in this volume) and I co-authored on sociologists and Twitter (see Schneider and Simonetto 2016). We tweeted our basic research findings, including a link to our article, at the American Sociological Association and the Canadian Sociological Association; each retweeted our work. This attracted attention from other scholars doing work in this area (e.g., public sociology online). A few tweeted critical comments back at us regarding our paper, leading to some dialogue with a few suggestions for future research. This also gave us a chance to contextualize our qualitative work, e.g., our dialogue ended with a tweet that I sent to five colleagues in response to some warranted criticisms that read, "The data are not intended as a representative sample."

INTERACTING WITH MEDIA JOURNALISTS[7]

There are a few things to keep in mind when interacting with journalists when the opportunity comes for you. First, you are never in control of how journalists will use your research. If this bothers you then I suggest, if possible, that you stick with live media interviews like radio. This will allow you to be in control of what you say and how you say it. If you choose to do radio or live television, ask the producers before you go to air how long you will have to speak (usually a producer will contact you with an interview request a day, or at least a few hours, in advance). The time constraint is good information to have so you do not ramble on too long trying to make a single point (most radio interviews are usually six to seven minutes). You should practice speaking about your work with a colleague for the allotted time that you are given before the interview. Fun fact: Sometimes the producers will even share with you the questions in advance, so it does not hurt to ask.

Second, if contacted, inquire with the journalist what their angle to the story is, that is, what they are looking for you to say or support. Sometimes they will have a concise answer for you. This will save you time and energy by not doing the interview if the journalist is simply interested in getting you to affirm a position or statement that you would rather not. Third, and I cannot stress this point enough, be very careful discussing the work of others (i.e., the research literature) with journalists. On a few occasions, I was astonished to see the ideas of other scholars attributed to me in news media articles in spite of the fact that I was very clear during the interview that these ideas were not mine!

CONCLUSION

Of the many things my father imparted to me, the following question has stayed rolling around my head from an early age: What is the point of becoming a learned person if such knowledge is not shared in a way that it is also beneficial to others? The media can be a valuable tool for the dissemination of research. The presentation of your work can be a fun and rewarding experience, but, more importantly, it can be an excellent way to promote your work in a way that can be beneficial to others.

CRAFTING QUALITATIVE RESEARCH EXERCISES

1. Search online for a few news stories that relate to your research. Select two or three. Explain briefly how your research connects to the issues discussed in the stories. Now go to your favourite news site (or newspaper if you are old-fashioned) and select one or two stories from today's news. Identify why you selected these stories and how your research connects to issues in these articles. Was limiting yourself to a single news source and time frame more difficult? Why or why not?

2. Choose one of the above stories and write a 150-word letter to the editor that draws from your ongoing research and/or findings.

3. Familiarize yourself with the formats of social media platforms Twitter, YouTube, and Instagram. How would you disseminate your research on each platform and why? Does the format of each accurately translate your work? Why or why not?

4. Locate and identify the staff at your university public affairs office. Edit the letter that you wrote for question 2 into an email that you would send to the public affairs manager. If you received your email would you be convinced that your research was relevant? Why or why not?

5. Write four or five questions that you would like to be asked about your research and then engage in a mock "live" six-minute radio interview with a colleague.

NOTES

1. Print and digital subscriptions can often be secured for little or no charge through your university.
2. Published letters might be listed under the heading "other publications" in your curriculum vitae and, while these letters are not peer reviewed, these publications will demonstrate your interest in various forms of public engagement.

3. As an example, an interview I gave with the *New York Times* following the June 2011 Vancouver riot was worth an ad value of $500,760 whereas an interview with the *Globe and Mail* on the same topic (also in June 2011) was worth an ad value of $17,145 (UBC University Relations 2011).

4. I recommend discussing this possibility with your faculty advisor.

5. Some of my work has addressed the issue of police body-worn cameras (Schneider 2016).

6. As I am writing this chapter, I received the following email from a reporter with Agence France-Presse that, in part, read: "I'm working on an article on how social media and online video have changed the nature of policing ... and came across your name as a researcher and author in this field." When speaking with the reporter, he told me he had read my university press release about my book online.

7. For an expanded discussion, see Schneider 2012.

REFERENCES

Altheide, David L., and Robert Snow. 1991. *Media Worlds in the Postjournalism Era.* Hawthorne, NY: Aldine de Gruyter.

Schneider, Christopher J. 2012. "Interacting with News Media Journalists: Reflections of a Sociologist." In *Popularizing Research: Engaging New Genres, Media, and Audiences,* edited by Phillip Vannini, 216–20. New York: Peter Lang.

Schneider, Christopher J. 2016. *Policing and Social Media: Social Control in an Era of New Media.* Lanham, MD: Lexington Books/Rowman and Littlefield.

Schneider, Christopher J., and Deana Simonetto. 2016. "Public Sociology on Twitter: A Space for Public Pedagogy?" *American Sociologist.* https://doi.org/10.1007/s12108-016-9304-2.

University of British Columbia University Relations. 2011. "Media 360 Report: June." http://universityrelations.ok.ubc.ca/publicaffairs/media360/201106/2011_June_UBCO_Peeks.pdf.

CONTRIBUTORS

Sarah Abbott is a Vanier scholar, Canadian filmmaker, an associate professor in the Department of Film at the University of Regina, and a doctor of social sciences candidate at Royal Roads University. For over 20 years, her independent films have received national and international attention through film festivals, television broadcasts, awards, and grants.

Michael Adorjan is an associate professor in the Department of Sociology at the University of Calgary, and fellow with the Centre for Criminology, University of Hong Kong. His research and teaching focus on youth crime and cyber-risk, fear of crime, and perceptions of police. His research appears in *British Journal of Criminology*, *Theoretical Criminology*, *Sociological Quarterly*, *Journal of Contemporary Ethnography*, and *The Prison Journal*.

Jeffrey P. Aguinaldo is an associate professor in the Department of Sociology at Wilfrid Laurier University. He trained in social and behavioural health sciences at the Dalla Lana School of Public Health, University of Toronto, and his research is situated at the intersections of gay men's health, critical public health, and qualitative methods. He is currently pursuing research in conversation analysis.

Kritee Ahmed is a PhD candidate in sociology at York University. His research centres on the everyday operation of customer service discourse within public transit organizations in Toronto, Canada, and London, United Kingdom, and its effect on perceptions of public transit workers specifically, and public servants broadly. Kritee's research interests focus on the sociology of work and labour, race and racialization, and the thought of Michel Foucault.

Bree Akesson is an assistant professor in Wilfrid Laurier University's Faculty of Social Work. Her research program ranges from micro-level understandings of the experiences of children and families to macro-level projects to strengthen social welfare and mental health systems in crisis-affected countries. She has used the neighbourhood walk methodology with Palestinian families living in the West Bank and East Jerusalem and Syrian families living in Lebanon.

J. I. (Hans) Bakker taught at the University of Guelph between 1980 and 2012. Since retirement he has taught at Brandon University, edited two books, and published three chapters. His main focus lately has been patriarchalism/patrimonialism and the use of Max Weber's and Charles Sanders Peirce's epistemologies. The subject matter of his research has ranged widely, from fieldwork among the Bajo in Indonesia to reflections on 20 years spent teaching yoga.

Sarah Benbow, RN MScN PhD, is a professor in the School of Nursing at Fanshawe College, and an adjunct professor in the Arthur Labatt Family School of Nursing, Western University. Her practice and research areas of expertise include mental health nursing; housing, health, and homelessness; marginalized mothering; social justice and health; and poverty and public policy. She employs qualitative research methods, primarily focusing on critical and narrative research methodologies.

Lesley J. Bikos, a former police officer, is a PhD candidate in sociology at Western University. Her research interests are primarily in the intersection of gender and workplace culture, with a current focus on policing and reform. Currently, she is working on a nationwide study of Canadian police officers and the impact of police culture on their on- and off-duty lives. In addition to her research, Lesley is a professor, public speaker, expert witness, workplace investigator, and a consultant for workplaces looking to improve their diversity and gender equity policies.

Katherine Bischoping, an associate professor of sociology at York University, studies the behind-the-scenes work of methodologists, gendered cultural narratives, and the role of narration in oral history and memory studies. Recently, she co-authored (with Amber Gazso) *Analyzing Talk in the Social Sciences: Narrative, Conversation, and Discourse Strategies*, and co-edited (with Yumi Ishii) a special issue of *Oral History Forum d'histoire orale* entitled "Generations and Memory: Continuity and Change."

Gül Çalışkan is an associate professor of sociology at St. Thomas University. She studies the following three areas: diasporic citizenship (experiences of being and belonging), social resistance and activism, and neo-racisms and critical whiteness studies. Her methods are qualitative, with narrative analysis playing a central role. Gül is currently finalizing a monograph entitled "Forging Diasporic Citizenship: Berlin's German-Born Turkish Ausländer" and an edited volume entitled *Gendering Globalization, Globalizing Gender: A Postcolonial Approach.*

Tony Christensen is an associate professor in the Department of Criminology at Wilfrid Laurier University. His teaching focuses on both qualitative and quantitative methods, while his research explores the social construction of crime and social problems. More than 10 years after leaving his field research on the "seduction community," he and his partner are still together, married with two children.

Susan Diane is a queer feminist activist of white-settler heritage with post-graduate degrees from the University of British Columbia and the University of Toronto. Through life history research, she has explored marginalized women's identities, careers, and activism in an oppressive society. Arts-informed research in her doctoral work added an intuitive, accessible heuristic for data analysis and representation. Susan teaches at Centennial College.

Mark S. Dolson earned a PhD in anthropology in 2012 from Western University; an MA in the anthropology of medicine from McGill University; and an honours BA in anthropology from Western University. Following a SSHRC-funded post-doctoral fellowship at the University of Cambridge, Mark's recent research centres on the relationship between globalization, tourism, and social exclusion in Reykjavik, Iceland.

Nichole Edwards obtained her PhD from University of Leeds in 2015. She is currently a sessional instructor (primarily) at Brescia University College and Western University, and has also taught courses at University of Guelph, Trent University, and Wilfrid Laurier University. Nichole teaches courses on gender and sexuality, particularly as they relate to pop culture, the family, youth, and stigma. Beyond this publication, she has written about sexual embodiment, and sex education.

Michael A. Fleming earned a PhD in sociology from Memorial University of Newfoundland. He is currently an assistant professor in the departments of sociology and criminology at St. Thomas University. Mike has travelled extensively throughout eastern North America with long-haul truck drivers as part of his ongoing interest in the cultural and socio-economic dimensions of the trucking industry.

Amber Gazso, PhD, is an associate professor of sociology at York University. Her main areas of research include citizenship, family and gender relations, research methods, poverty, and the welfare state. She specializes in research that explores family members' relationships with social policies of the neoliberal welfare state. Her current research explores how people living with addiction experience social assistance receipt. A passion of hers is the study and practice of qualitative methods.

Scott Grills is a professor of sociology at Brandon University. He is the editor of *Doing Ethnographic Research* (1998), co-author (with Robert Prus) of *The Deviant Mystique* (2003), co-editor of *Kleine Geheimnisse: Alltagssoziologische Einsichten* (*Little Secrets: Everyday Sociological Insights*) (2015), and co-editor of the forthcoming *Die Welt als Drama: Schlüsselwerke Symbolischen Interaktion* (*The World as Drama: Key Works in Symbolic Interaction*). His current research attends to the development of an interactionist research agenda for the study of management processes.

Jodi Hall is a professor and research consultant in the School of Nursing and Centre for Research and Innovation (Fanshawe College), and an adjunct professor in the Arthur Labatt Family School of Nursing (Western University). Her research and teaching interests include the critical appraisal of information and communication technologies in the lives of marginalized populations, social justice, trauma-informed practice, and health equity.

Ariane Hanemaayer is an assistant professor of sociology at Brandon University. She has published in the areas of the sociology of sport, classical sociological theory, public sociology, and the sociology of health and medicine. Her current research examines the role of evidence-based medicine in professional regulation.

Cathlene Hillier is a PhD candidate in the Department of Sociology and Legal Studies at the University of Waterloo. Her earlier research examined teachers' responses to policies on religious inclusion and religious accommodation. Cathlene's doctoral research explores how lower socio-economic status parents and children engage teachers and schooling processes in developing children's early literacy skills. She recently published a co-authored article in *Qualitative Research Journal.*

Abhar Rukh Husain is a research associate with York Centre for Asian Research, York University. She holds a PhD (2016) in gender, feminist, and women's studies from York University, and a master's degree in economics from the University of Connecticut, under the J. William Fulbright Scholar Exchange Programme (2000–01). Previously, she worked as an assistant professor in the Department of Economics, University of Rajshahi, Bangladesh (2002–04).

Katherine Irwin, PhD, is a professor of sociology at the University of Hawaii, Manoa. Her research areas include youth culture, women and drug use, youth violence, girls in the juvenile justice system, and delinquency prevention programming. She is the co-author (with Meda Chesney-Lind) of *Beyond Bad Girls: Gender, Violence, and Hype.* Her most recent book (with Karen Umemoto) is titled *Jacked Up and Unjust: Pacific Islander Teens Confront Violent Legacies.*

Matthew S. Johnston is a PhD candidate in the Department of Sociology and Anthropology at Carleton University. He has published journal articles on the topics of gender and mental health, most notably in *Qualitative Research*; *Men and Masculinities*; *Crime Media Culture*; *Gender, Work and Organization*; *Social Movement Studies*; and *Punishment and Society.* His doctoral research examines how persons labelled as mentally ill navigate their involvement with the psychiatric apparatus.

Krystal Kehoe MacLeod, PhD, teaches in the departments of Health Sciences, Public Policy and Administration, and Social Work at Carleton University in Ottawa. She is a contributor to *Creative Teamwork: Developing Rapid, Site-Switching Ethnography* (2018). Krystal is an Ontario Women's Health Scholar. She writes on issues related to home care, integrated care, gender, aging, and public policy. Krystal has worked as a policy-maker in Ontario and in New South Wales, Australia.

Steven W. Kleinknecht is an associate professor of sociology at Brescia University College. He is also an approvals editor for the *Qualitative Sociology Review*. His qualitative research has focused on the computer hacker and Old Order Mennonite subcultures. With Antony Puddephatt and William Shaffir, he co-edited *Ethnographies Revisited* (2009). He has been involved in the Qualitative Analysis Conference as a participant, session chair, and organizer for the past 18 years.

Deborah Landry: After 12 years as an adjunct professor and independent researcher, this is my last academic publication. I am walking away. Writing about the joys of teaching is a good note to end this career on. The sexist, classist, racist walls of the academy I failed to scale are left for others to smash down. For more information on academic precarity in Canada, see https://ocufa.on.ca/.

Meghan Lynch, PhD, is a post-doctoral fellow at the Dalla Lana School of Public Health at the University of Toronto. In her emerging research program, she has focused on exploring new methodologies and data sources, particularly through her research using netnography. Her work has additionally focused on analyzing policies and programs focused on improving children's health; for instance, critically examining Ontario's full-day kindergarten policy, nutrition policies in kindergartens, sport-for-development, and social pediatrics policies.

Catherine Mah, MD FRCPC PhD, is an associate professor in the Faculty of Health at Dalhousie University. She also holds an appointment at the Dalla Lana School of Public Health at the University of Toronto. Catherine directs the Food Policy Lab, a multidisciplinary program of research on the determinants of healthier consumption, with a focus on health-promoting innovations in the food system. Her food and nutrition research draws from several areas of interpretive policy analysis, particularly frame analysis and practice approaches.

Dawn Mannay is a senior lecturer in social sciences at Cardiff University. Her research interests include class, education, gender, and inequality, and she employs visual and creative methods in her work with communities. Dawn edited the collection *Our Changing Land: Revisiting Gender, Class, and Identity in Contemporary Wales* (2016), and was the sole author of *Visual, Narrative, and Creative Research Methods: Application, Reflection, and Ethics* (2016).

Chris McCormick teaches in the Criminology Department at St. Thomas University. He has authored books on crime and media, corporate crime, deviancy theory, and the history of criminal justice in Canada. His main teaching areas are cultural and visual criminology, discourse and crime, and wrongful convictions. His theories are critical and his method is inductive.

Colleen McMillan is a qualitative health researcher and practicing therapist who believes that therapy and research are reciprocal, relational, and constructed processes that hold the potential to inform the other. She is an associate professor and director at the School of Social Work, Renison University College, University of Waterloo.

Javier Mignone is an associate professor in the Department of Community Health Sciences, Faculty of Health Sciences, University of Manitoba. He conducts collaborative and community-based research on intercultural health, HIV, and health information with Indigenous partners in Guatemala, Colombia, Argentina, Dominica, and Canada. Javier is the author of approximately 50 peer-reviewed publications, aside from reports to government and other organizations.

Emily Milne is an assistant professor of sociology at MacEwan University. Her research focuses on education, Indigenous peoples, social inequality, and policy. She is currently researching the implementation of educational initiatives to foster reconciliation between Indigenous and non-Indigenous Canadians. Her research has been published in academic journals including the *Canadian Review of Sociology* and has been featured on news outlets including Global News, CTV News, CBC News, and the *Globe and Mail*.

Thaddeus Müller is a senior lecturer at the Law School of Lancaster University (criminology). He is an active member of the Society for the Study of Symbolic Interaction and its European counterpart. He has researched a range of topics, such as the regulation of cannabis, hooligans, the marginalization of "ethnic" youth, the social construction of safety, transgression in the rock/pop world, academic fraud, and defaulting homeowners "fighting Wall Street." Within these themes, he is especially interested in the effects of stigma/labelling, and resisting stigma/labelling (and its effects) through the construction of empowering (counter)narratives.

Taylor Price is a PhD student in sociology at the University of Toronto. He specializes in sociological theory and the sociology of culture. He is currently designing a dissertation project that considers how prestige influences ideals of authenticity within various communities of cultural production.

Antony Puddephatt is an associate professor of sociology at Lakehead University. He is interested in the social pragmatism of George Herbert Mead, symbolic interactionism and ethnographic research, and the sociology of knowledge, science, and technology. Most recently he has been interested in studying the possibilities of microsociological theory for environmental sociology, as well as open access publishing in Canada.

Snežana Ratković is a research officer and an instructor in the Faculty of Education at Brock University. She arrived in Canada in 1998 as a refugee woman teacher from the former Yugoslavia. Her research interest lies in migration and indigeneity, transnational and transdisciplinary teacher education, social justice leadership, decolonizing methodologies, research education, and knowledge mobilization.

Kerstin Roger is an associate professor in the Department of Community Health Sciences, Rady Faculty of Health Sciences, University of Manitoba. She is director of the undergraduate program and facilitates the qualitative research group. Her research questions focus on aging and the family; wellness, caregiving, and community; and how these interface with health care and chronic illness. She has worked on multi-site national research, international collaborations, and local not-for-profit community initiatives, and continues to co-author with and engage students in her research.

Ellen Rose is a professor at the University of New Brunswick, where she teaches courses in educational technology and instructional design. Her research focuses on the social, cultural, ethical, and phenomenological dimensions of educational computing. Her most recent book is *On Reflection: An Essay on Technology, Education, and the Status of Thought in the Twenty-First Century* (2013).

Carrie B. Sanders is an associate professor of criminology at Wilfrid Laurier University. She is an interpretive theorist and qualitative researcher with an interest in studying policing, technology, police cultures, and surveillance. Her research has received funding from the Social Sciences and Humanities Research Council of Canada and has been published in high impact journals, such as *British Journal of Criminology*, *Policing and Society*, and *Gender and Society*.

Christopher J. Schneider is an associate professor of sociology at Brandon University in Manitoba. His current research and publications focus on information technologies and related changes to police work. His most recent book is *Policing and Social Media: Social Control in an Era of New Media* (2016).

Bharati Sethi is an assistant professor at King's University College, University of Western Ontario. Her research interests are immigration, arts-based research, and intersectionality. She is currently a co-investigator in two SSHRC-funded multi-site research projects impacting immigrant/refugee integration in Canada. Her research has earned her several prestigious awards, including the Ontario Women's Health Scholarship, Tutor-Primary Health Care Fellowship, the Vanier Canada Graduate Scholarship, and the Hilary M. Weston Scholarship.

William Shaffir is a professor of sociology at McMaster University. He is the author of books and articles on Hasidic Jews, professional socialization, and field research methods. He has published on a Depression-era ethnic riot in Toronto, the dynamics of becoming religious and of leaving religious life, and the sustained efforts of Hasidic Jews to preserve their traditional lifestyle while addressing the challenges of modernity. He has also studied how politicians cope with electoral defeat. His most recent work examines the social organization of police work, particularly among recent immigrants and racialized minorities, and racial profiling.

Deana Simonetto is an assistant professor in the Department of Criminology at Wilfrid Laurier University. Her research interests include symbolic interactionism, qualitative methods, deviance, sports, and family. She recently published the articles "I Was with Him Before He Was Anything: The Identity Talk of Football Wives" (forthcoming 2018, *Studies in Symbolic Interaction*) and "Expanding our Methodological Tool Box: The Place of Twitter in the Ethnographic Endeavour" (2016, *Qualitative Sociology Review*).

Kathleen Steeves is a sessional lecturer in social psychology at McMaster University, and is also the campus's graduate student writing consultant. Her interests include qualitative methods, symbolic interactionism, gender, religion, and identity work. Her current research centres around identity dilemmas faced by female pastors in the Christian church, and graduate students' "scholarly identity" development. Her recent publications include "Experiencing a Call to Ministry: Changing Trajectories, Re-structuring Life Stories" (2017, *Qualitative Sociology Review*).

Kalyani Thurairajah is an assistant professor in the Sociology Department at MacEwan University. Her research focuses on the political identities and national loyalties of second-generation immigrants. She is currently working on a cross-national comparison of Canada, the United Kingdom, and Germany. She is also currently examining the role of education in perpetuating racial and ethnic inequalities in Canada.

Deborah K. van den Hoonaard is professor emerita (St. Thomas University) and social science editor of the *Canadian Journal on Aging*. She was Canada Research Chair in Qualitative Research (2006–15) and wrote *Qualitative Research in Action: A Canadian Primer* (2012), *By Himself: The Older Man's Experience of Widowhood* (2010), and *The Widowed Self: The Older Woman's Journey through Widowhood* (2001), as well as several books with Will C. van den Hoonaard.

Will van den Hoonaard is professor emeritus, University of New Brunswick. He has published in the field of research ethics, sociology, cartography, religious studies, resource management in Iceland, history, immigration, Bahá'í studies, ethnography, and Scandinavian studies. His *Map Worlds: A History of Women in Cartography* (2014) covers 700 years of women in map-making. He is founding member of Canada's Inter-Agency Advisory Panel on Research Ethics.

Jeffrey van den Scott is an adjunct professor of musicologies at Memorial University of Newfoundland. He earned his PhD in musicology at Northwestern University in 2016 with a research program that examines the intersection of composed Canadian music and the culture of the nation's Inuit population.

Lisa-Jo K. van den Scott is an assistant professor of sociology at Memorial University of Newfoundland. Her work centres around space, place, and time, and argues for a sociology of walls. Her empirical focus has been the introduction of housing in Arviat, Nunavut. She has published in such journals as the *Journal of Contemporary Ethnography* and *American Behavioral Scientist*. She is currently an associate editor for the *Journal of Empirical Research on Human Research Ethics*.

Phillip Vannini is a professor in the School of Communication and Culture and Canada Research Chair in Public Ethnography at Royal Roads University. He is author/editor of over a dozen books, including the most recent, *Non-representational Methodologies: Re-envisioning Research* (2015), *Wilderness* (2016), and *Off the Grid: Re-assembling Domestic Life* (2014).

Chad Walker is a white settler-scholar and currently a post-doctoral fellow in geography and planning at Queen's University. He earned a BA in environmental policy and analysis in 2010 (Bowling Green State University), as well as MA (2012) and PhD (2017) degrees in geography at Western University. His general research interests lie at the intersection of climate/environmental policy and communities experiencing low-carbon development, such as energy and transportation projects.

Crystal Weston is a PhD candidate at the University of Guelph in the Department of Sociology and Anthropology, specializing in sociological criminology. Her research areas include policing, intelligence-led policing, patrol policing strategies, and police technology.

Magdalena Wojciechowska is a PhD candidate in sociology (Sociology of Organization and Management Department, Faculty of Economics and Sociology, University of Lodz, Poland). Her research interests lie in studies of members of marginalized social groups. She is the author of *The Escort Agency: An (Extra)Ordinary Workplace* (2012) and is executive editor of *Qualitative Sociology Review*.

Justin Wright completed his MA in sociology at the University of New Brunswick. He has been a defence scientist in the Department of National Defence since 2006, working in applied military personnel research. His areas of study include diversity and inclusion, employment equity, human rights, military socialization, and identity.

INDEX